POSITIVE ATTITUDE

POSITIVE ATTITUDE

A DILBERT™ BOOK
BY SCOTT ADAMS

07 08 09 10 11 RR2 10 9 8 7 6 5 4 3 2 1

ISBN-13: 978-0-7407-6379-3
ISBN-10: 0-7407-6379-2

Library of Congress Control Number: 2006936968

www.andrewsmcmeel.com

www.dilbert.com

ATTENTION: SCHOOLS AND BUSINESSES

Andrews McMeel books are available at quantity discounts with bulk purchase for educational, business, or sales promotional use. For information, please write to: Special Sales Department, Andrews McMeel Publishing, LLC, 4520 Main Street, Kansas City, Missouri 64111.

Other DILBERT® books from Andrews McMeel Publishing

Try Rebooting Yourself
ISBN: 0-7407-6190-0

What Would Wally Do?
ISBN: 0-7407-5769-5

Thriving on Vague Objectives
ISBN: 0-7407-5533-1

The Fluorescent Light Glistens Off Your Head
ISBN: 0-7407-5113-1

It's Not Funny If I Have to Explain It
ISBN: 0-7407-4658-8

Don't Stand Where the Comet Is Assumed to Strike Oil
ISBN: 0-7407-4539-5

Words You Don't Want to Hear During Your Annual Performance Review
ISBN: 0-7407-3805-4

When Body Language Goes Bad
ISBN: 0-7407-3298-6

What Do You Call a Sociopath in a Cubicle? Answer: A Coworker
ISBN: 0-7407-2663-3

Another Day in Cubicle Paradise
ISBN: 0-7407-2194-1

When Did Ignorance Become a Point of View?
ISBN: 0-7407-1839-8

Excuse Me While I Wag
ISBN: 0-7407-1390-6

Dilbert—A Treasury of Sunday Strips: Version 00
ISBN: 0-7407-0531-8

Random Acts of Management
ISBN: 0-7407-0453-2

Dilbert Gives You the Business
ISBN: 0-7407-0338-2 hardcover
ISBN: 0-7407-0003-0 paperback

Don't Step in the Leadership
ISBN: 0-8362-7844-5

Journey to Cubeville
ISBN: 0-8362-7175-0 hardcover
ISBN: 0-8362-6745-1 paperback

I'm Not Anti-Business, I'm Anti-Idiot
ISBN: 0-8362-5182-2

Seven Years of Highly Defective People
ISBN: 0-8362-5129-6 hardcover
ISBN: 0-8362-3668-8 paperback

Casual Day Has Gone Too Far
ISBN: 0-8362-2899-5

Fugitive from the Cubicle Police
ISBN: 0-8362-2119-2

It's Obvious You Won't Survive by Your Wits Alone
ISBN: 0-8362-0415-8

Still Pumped from Using the Mouse
ISBN: 0-8362-1026-3

Bring Me the Head of Willy the Mailboy!
ISBN: 0-8362-1779-9

Shave the Whales
ISBN: 0-8362-1740-3

Dogbert's Clues for the Clueless
ISBN: 0-8362-1737-3

Always Postpone Meetings with Time-Wasting Morons
ISBN: 0-8362-1758-6

Build a Better Life by Stealing Office Supplies
ISBN: 0-8362-1757-8

For ordering information, call 1-800-223-2336.

Introduction

There's a big difference between optimism and insanity. An insane person keeps doing the same thing over and over again expecting a different result. An optimist does that, too, but he doesn't know he's doing the same thing over and over. For example, an optimist might go to work every day and imagine that today's series of meetings will be the ones that fix all of the problems caused by yesterday's series of meetings. Optimists believe that's totally different from insanity, because the meetings are not in the same room every time.

I understand optimists because I am one. When I began my corporate career, I expected that my hard work and talent would be rewarded, despite all evidence to the contrary. I came to work every day, sat in my fabric-covered box, and expected something terrific to happen at any minute. I had a positive attitude that was, again, totally different from insanity.

Every time my corporate employer announced a new round of downsizing, my first thought was that it would soon be easier to find parking. When I worked on a project for a year only to have it canceled for budget reasons, I was happy because it freed my schedule so I could—if I were lucky—go fail at something more interesting.

Eventually I became a cartoonist. But I imbued Dilbert with my irrationally positive workplace attitude. He carries on in my tradition, showing up for work every day and expecting some good to come of it.

Speaking of good things, there's still time to join Dogbert's New Ruling Class. Just sign up for the free *Dilbert Newsletter* that is published approximately whenever I feel like it. To sign up, go to www.dilbert.com and follow the subscription instructions. If that doesn't work for some reason, send an e-mail to newsletter@unitedmedia.com.

S. Adams

Scott Adams

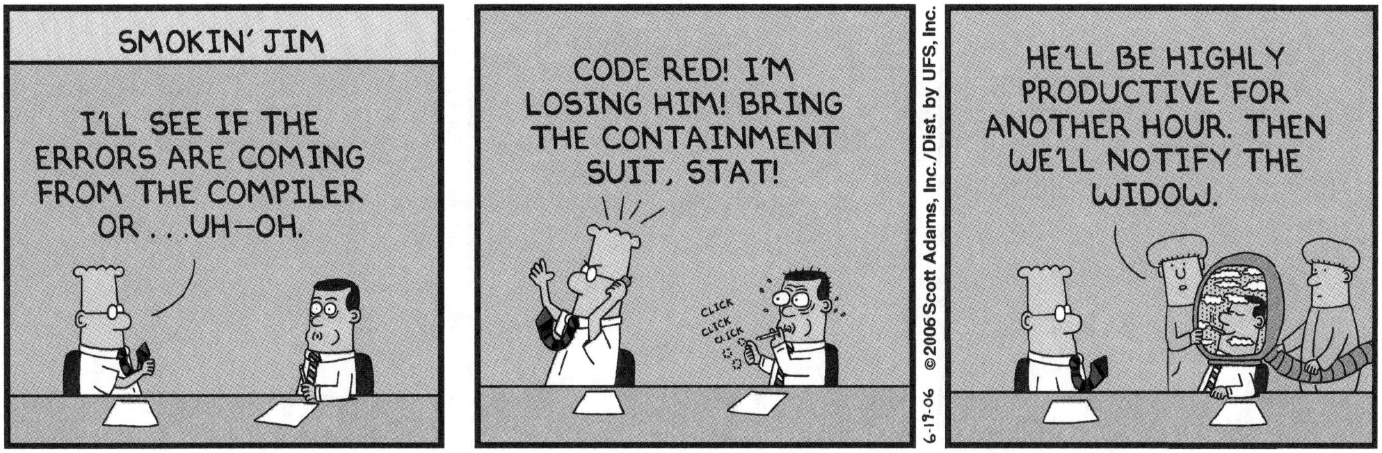
SMOKIN' JIM
I'LL SEE IF THE ERRORS ARE COMING FROM THE COMPILER OR . . .UH–OH.
CODE RED! I'M LOSING HIM! BRING THE CONTAINMENT SUIT, STAT!
CLICK CLICK CLICK
HE'LL BE HIGHLY PRODUCTIVE FOR ANOTHER HOUR. THEN WE'LL NOTIFY THE WIDOW.
6-19-06 ©2006 Scott Adams, Inc./Dist. by UFS, Inc.

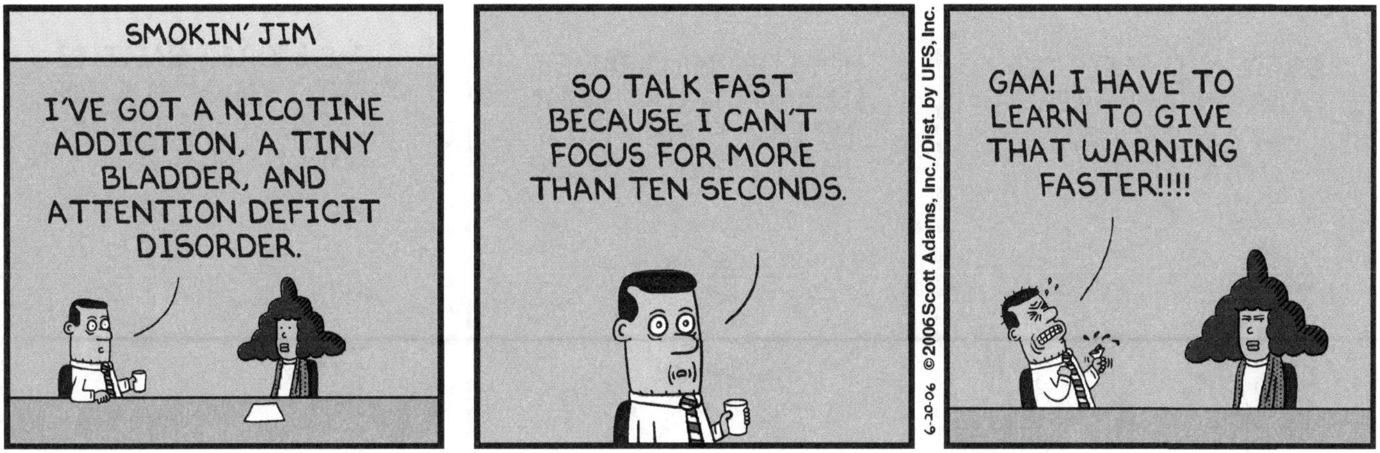
SMOKIN' JIM
I'VE GOT A NICOTINE ADDICTION, A TINY BLADDER, AND ATTENTION DEFICIT DISORDER.
SO TALK FAST BECAUSE I CAN'T FOCUS FOR MORE THAN TEN SECONDS.
GAA! I HAVE TO LEARN TO GIVE THAT WARNING FASTER!!!!
6-20-06 ©2006 Scott Adams, Inc./Dist. by UFS, Inc.

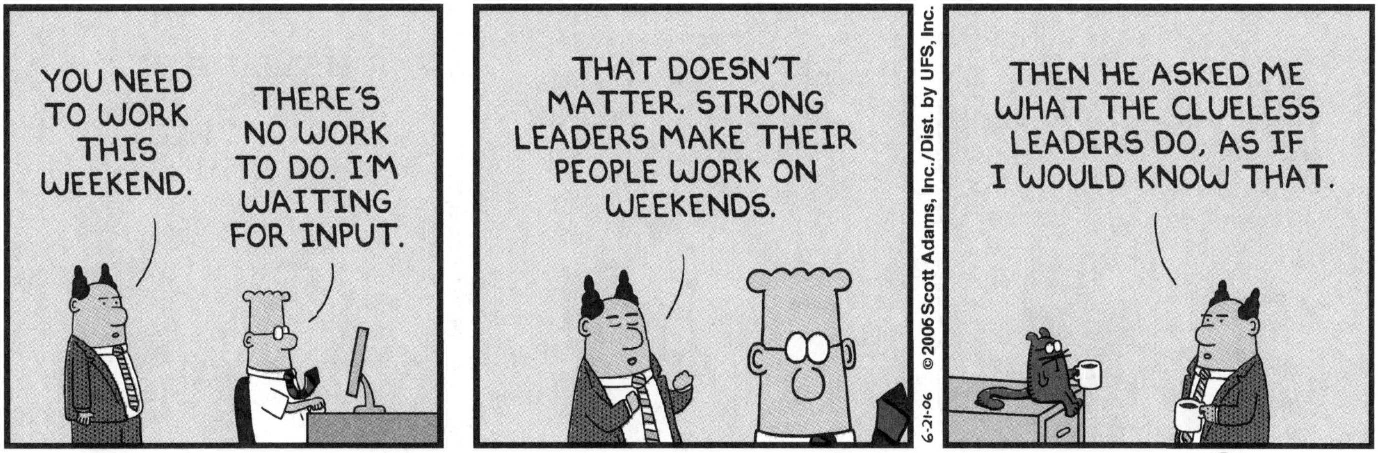
YOU NEED TO WORK THIS WEEKEND.
THERE'S NO WORK TO DO. I'M WAITING FOR INPUT.
THAT DOESN'T MATTER. STRONG LEADERS MAKE THEIR PEOPLE WORK ON WEEKENDS.
THEN HE ASKED ME WHAT THE CLUELESS LEADERS DO, AS IF I WOULD KNOW THAT.
6-21-06 ©2006 Scott Adams, Inc./Dist. by UFS, Inc.

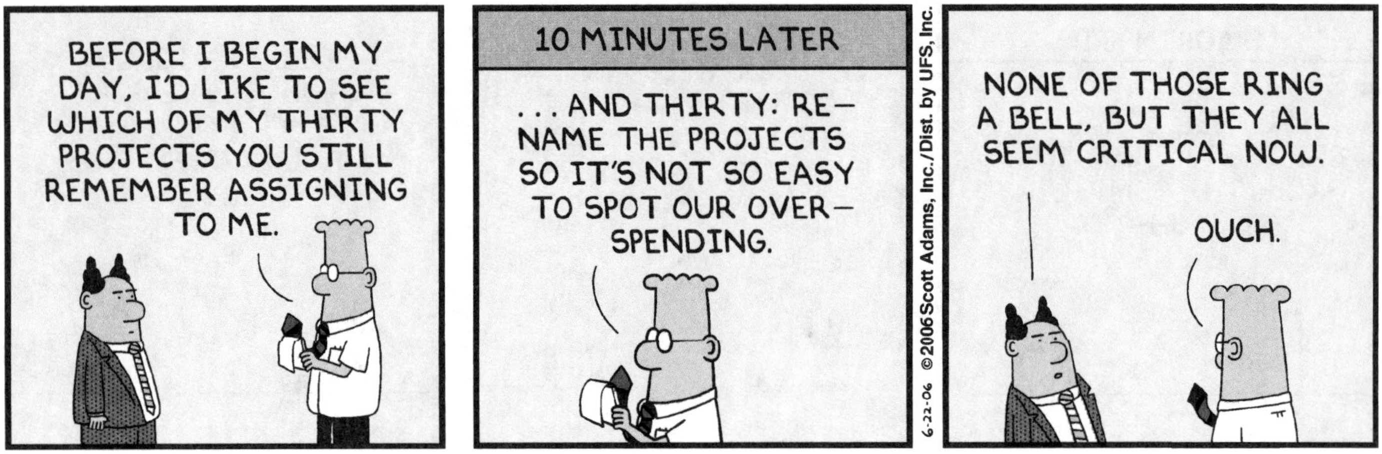
BEFORE I BEGIN MY DAY, I'D LIKE TO SEE WHICH OF MY THIRTY PROJECTS YOU STILL REMEMBER ASSIGNING TO ME.
10 MINUTES LATER
. . . AND THIRTY: RE- NAME THE PROJECTS SO IT'S NOT SO EASY TO SPOT OUR OVER- SPENDING.
6-22-06 © 2006 Scott Adams, Inc./Dist. by UFS, Inc.
NONE OF THOSE RING A BELL, BUT THEY ALL SEEM CRITICAL NOW.
OUCH.

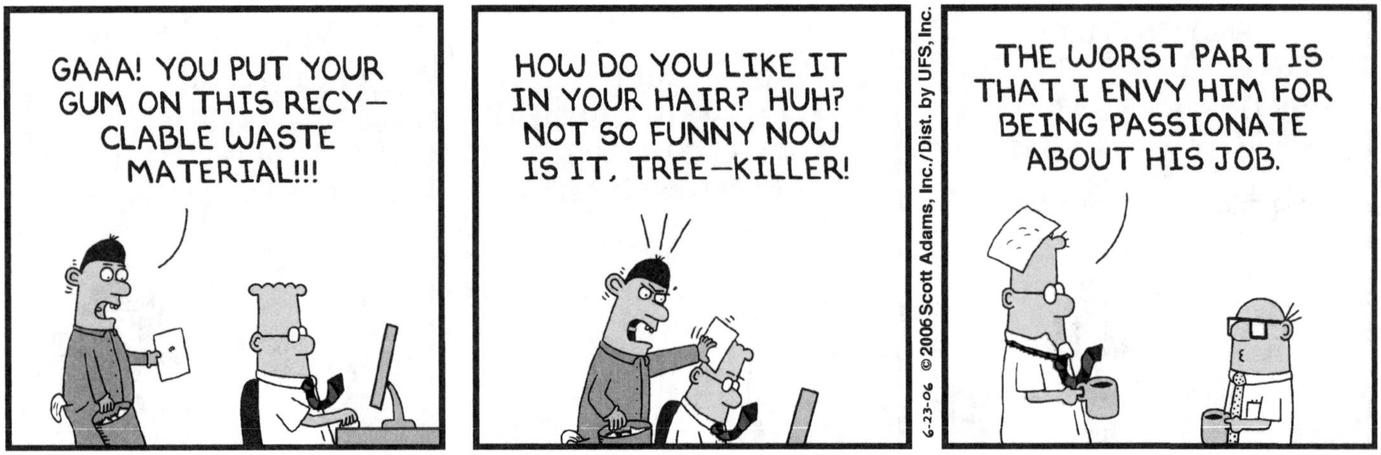
GAAA! YOU PUT YOUR GUM ON THIS RECY- CLABLE WASTE MATERIAL!!!
HOW DO YOU LIKE IT IN YOUR HAIR? HUH? NOT SO FUNNY NOW IS IT, TREE-KILLER!
6-23-06 © 2006 Scott Adams, Inc./Dist. by UFS, Inc.
THE WORST PART IS THAT I ENVY HIM FOR BEING PASSIONATE ABOUT HIS JOB.

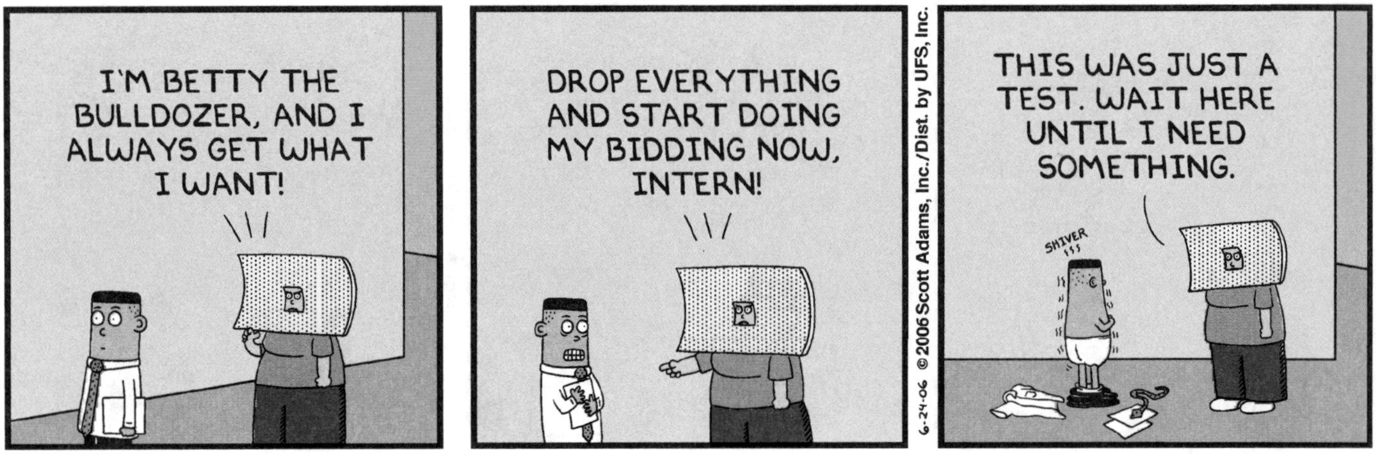
I'M BETTY THE BULLDOZER, AND I ALWAYS GET WHAT I WANT!
DROP EVERYTHING AND START DOING MY BIDDING NOW, INTERN!
6-24-06 © 2006 Scott Adams, Inc./Dist. by UFS, Inc.
THIS WAS JUST A TEST. WAIT HERE UNTIL I NEED SOMETHING.
SHIVER

WELCOME TO DOGBERT'S ACCELERATED SALES TRAINING COURSE.
TODAY YOU WILL LEARN HOW A PERSON CAN SIMULTANEOUSLY DRINK AND GOLF.
WHAT WILL WE LEARN TOMORROW?
TOMORROW? WHAT PART OF "ACCELERATED" IS CONFUSING YOU?
© 2006 Scott Adams, Inc. /Dist. by UFS, Inc.
AS YOU KNOW, THE HARD PART ABOUT DRINKING AND GOLF-ING IS THAT THEY BOTH REQUIRE YOUR HANDS.
THAT'S WHY I INVENTED THE SPORTSMAN'S BEER MUZZLE.
GIVE THIS TO YOUR CLIENT AND THE SALE WILL PRACTICALLY MAKE ITSELF.
OOH!
OOH!
OOH!
6-25-06
THIS ISH THE BESHT DAY OF MY LIFE!
I'LL PUT YOU DOWN FOR TEN PALLETS OF MOUSE PADS.

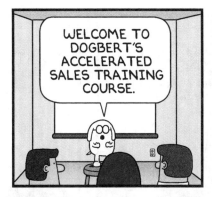

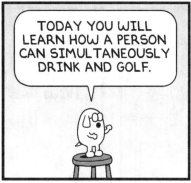

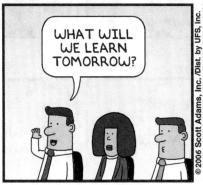

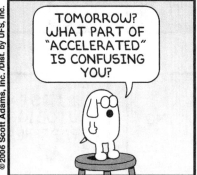

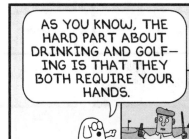

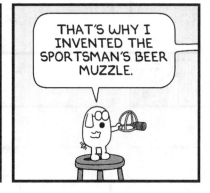

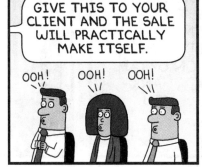

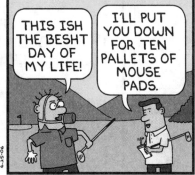

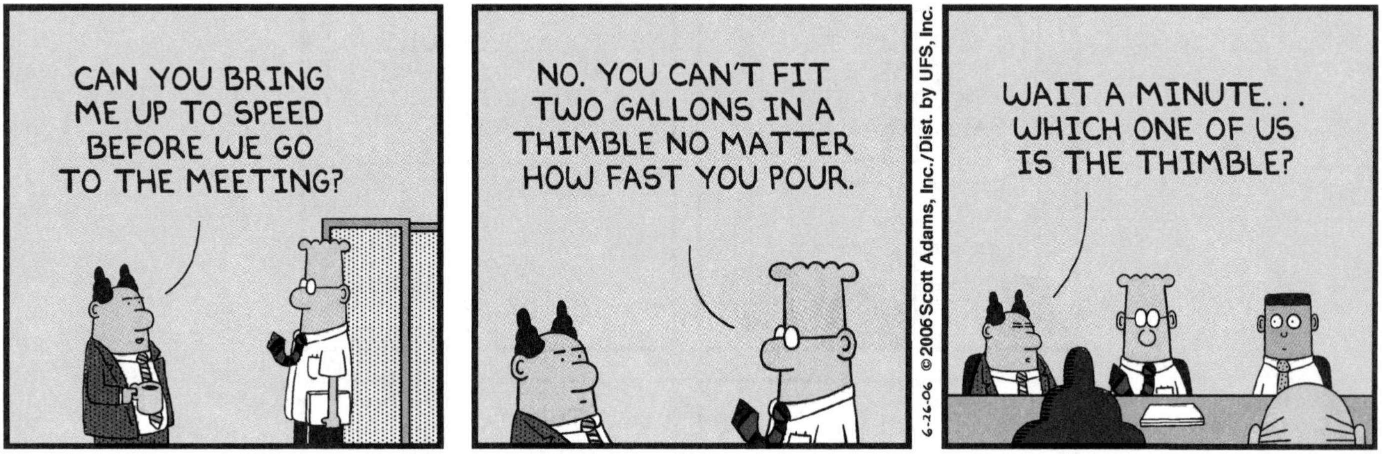
CAN YOU BRING ME UP TO SPEED BEFORE WE GO TO THE MEETING?
NO. YOU CAN'T FIT TWO GALLONS IN A THIMBLE NO MATTER HOW FAST YOU POUR.
WAIT A MINUTE. . . WHICH ONE OF US IS THE THIMBLE?
6-26-06 © 2006 Scott Adams, Inc./Dist. by UFS, Inc.

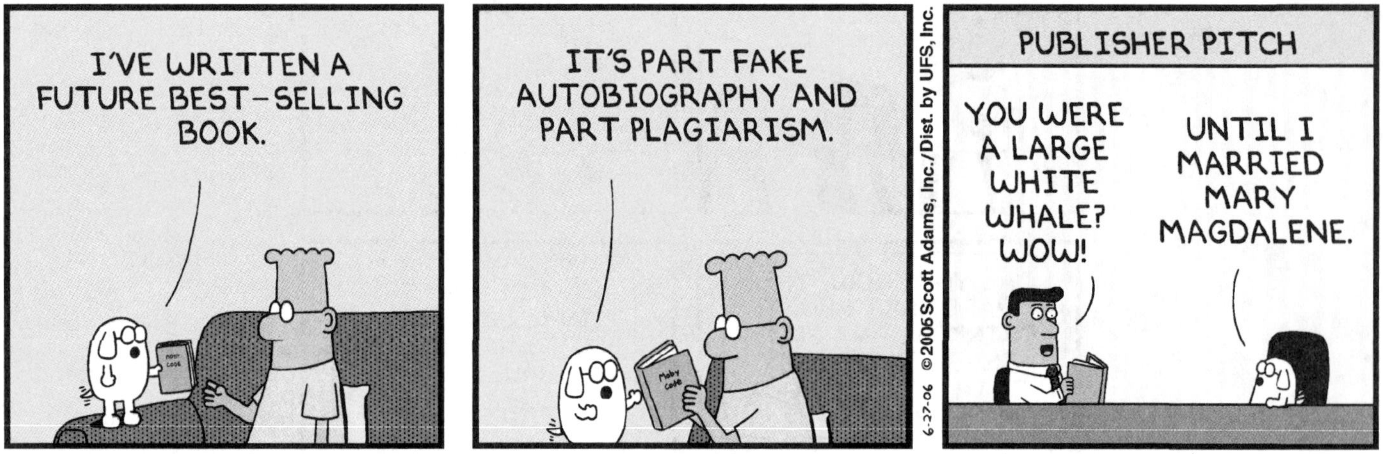
I'VE WRITTEN A FUTURE BEST-SELLING BOOK.
IT'S PART FAKE AUTOBIOGRAPHY AND PART PLAGIARISM.
PUBLISHER PITCH
YOU WERE A LARGE WHITE WHALE? WOW!
UNTIL I MARRIED MARY MAGDALENE.
6-27-06 © 2006 Scott Adams, Inc./Dist. by UFS, Inc.

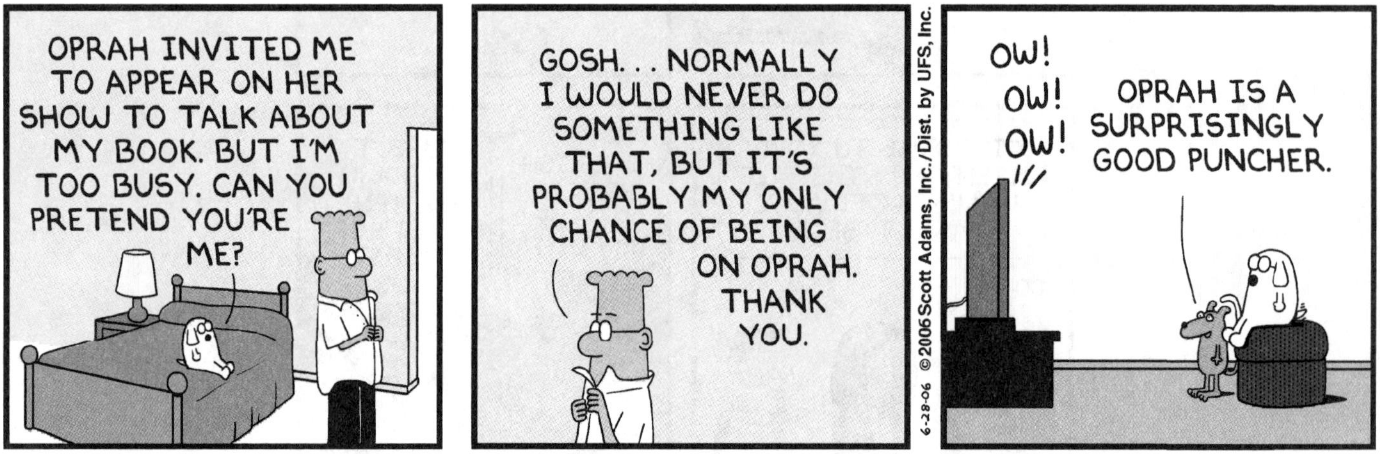
OPRAH INVITED ME TO APPEAR ON HER SHOW TO TALK ABOUT MY BOOK. BUT I'M TOO BUSY. CAN YOU PRETEND YOU'RE ME?
GOSH. . . NORMALLY I WOULD NEVER DO SOMETHING LIKE THAT, BUT IT'S PROBABLY MY ONLY CHANCE OF BEING ON OPRAH. THANK YOU.
OW! OW! OW!
OPRAH IS A SURPRISINGLY GOOD PUNCHER.
6-28-06 © 2006 Scott Adams, Inc./Dist. by UFS, Inc.

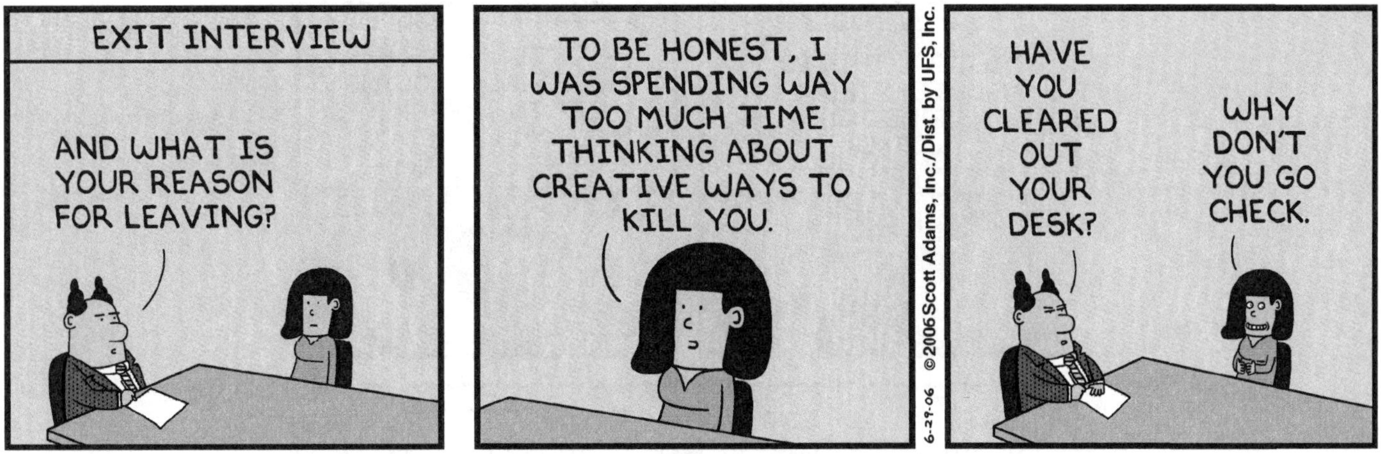
EXIT INTERVIEW
AND WHAT IS YOUR REASON FOR LEAVING?
TO BE HONEST, I WAS SPENDING WAY TOO MUCH TIME THINKING ABOUT CREATIVE WAYS TO KILL YOU.
6-29-06 ©2006 Scott Adams, Inc./Dist. by UFS, Inc.
HAVE YOU CLEARED OUT YOUR DESK?
WHY DON'T YOU GO CHECK.

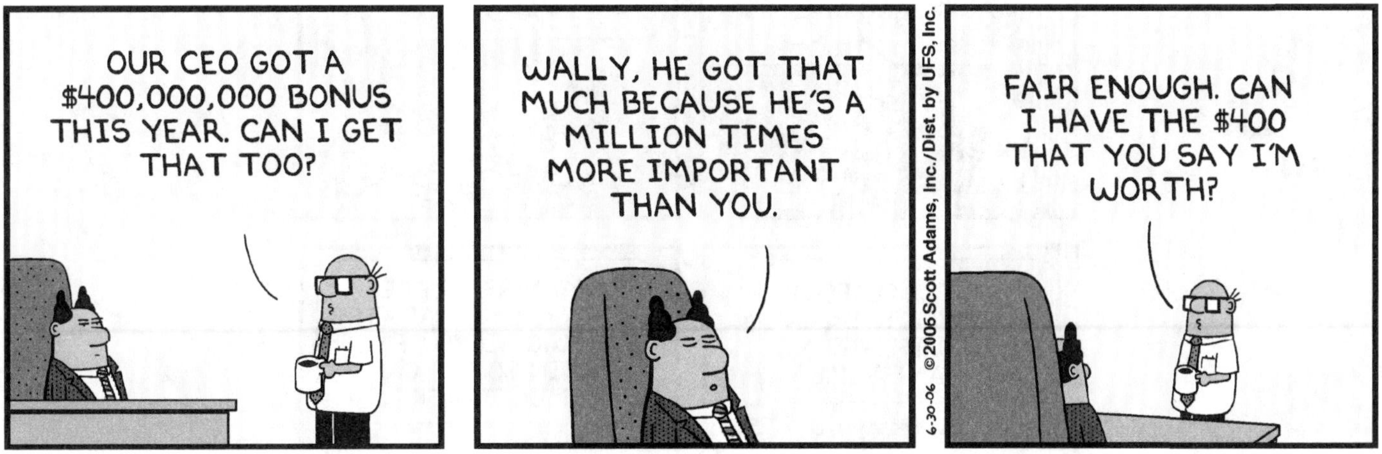
OUR CEO GOT A $400,000,000 BONUS THIS YEAR. CAN I GET THAT TOO?
WALLY, HE GOT THAT MUCH BECAUSE HE'S A MILLION TIMES MORE IMPORTANT THAN YOU.
6-30-06 ©2006 Scott Adams, Inc./Dist. by UFS, Inc.
FAIR ENOUGH. CAN I HAVE THE $400 THAT YOU SAY I'M WORTH?

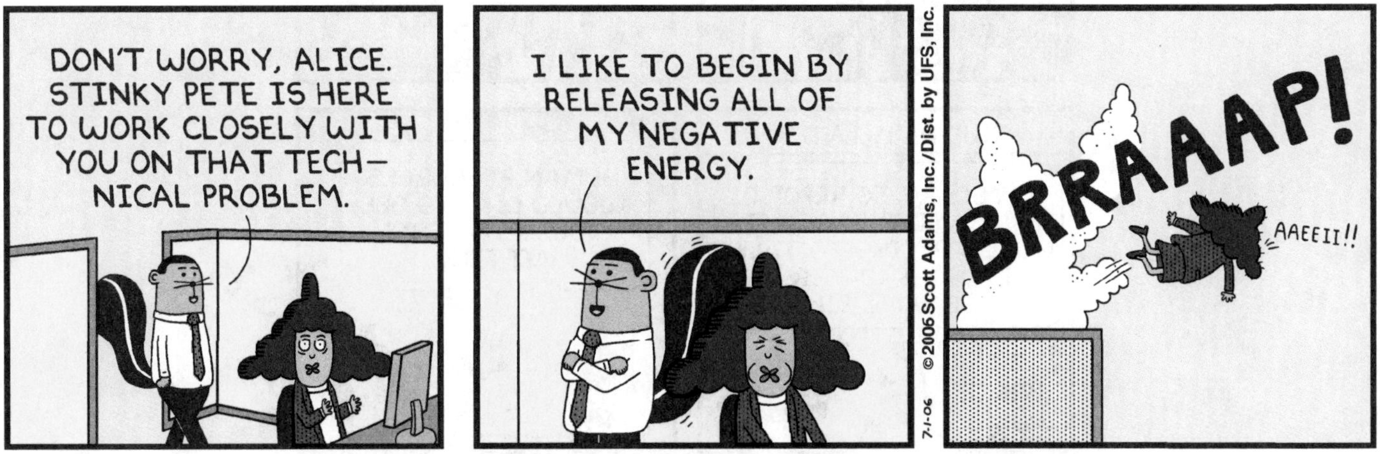
DON'T WORRY, ALICE. STINKY PETE IS HERE TO WORK CLOSELY WITH YOU ON THAT TECH–NICAL PROBLEM.
I LIKE TO BEGIN BY RELEASING ALL OF MY NEGATIVE ENERGY.
7-1-06 ©2006 Scott Adams, Inc./Dist. by UFS, Inc.
BRRAAAP!
AAEEII!!

DILBERT, THIS IS AMBER DEXTROUS, YOUR NEW CO-WORKER
NICE TO MEET YOU. NICE TO MEET YOU.
SHE'S GOING FOR THE HUG.
OH HECK, I'LL JUST GO WITH THE FLOW AND FOR ONCE NOT BE THE SOCIALLY AWKWARD ONE.
©2006 Scott Adams, Inc./Dist. by UFS, Inc.
SHE WASN'T GOING FOR THE HUG. SHE SHAKES WITH BOTH HANDS.
SHE'S THE PERFECT EMPLOYEE. SHE CAN DO TWO THINGS AT THE SAME TIME!
HUMAN RESOURCES SURGICALLY SEPARATED THE TWO SIDES OF HER BRAIN SO SHE CAN MULTITASK.
TWO DAYS LATER
I'M SORRY TO REPORT THAT AMBER DROWNED WHILE TRYING TO TALK AND DRINK WATER AT THE SAME TIME.
7-2-06
HUMAN RESOURCES WOULD LIKE TO SEE YOU AFTER THIS MEETING.

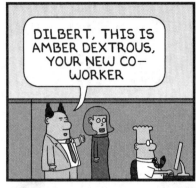

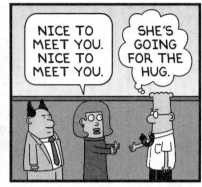

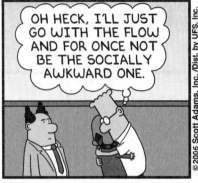

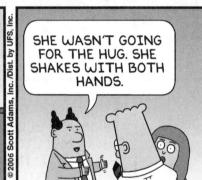

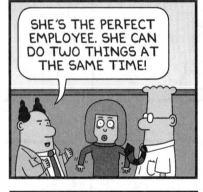

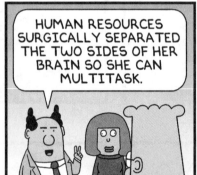

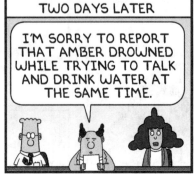

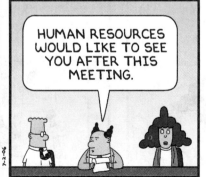

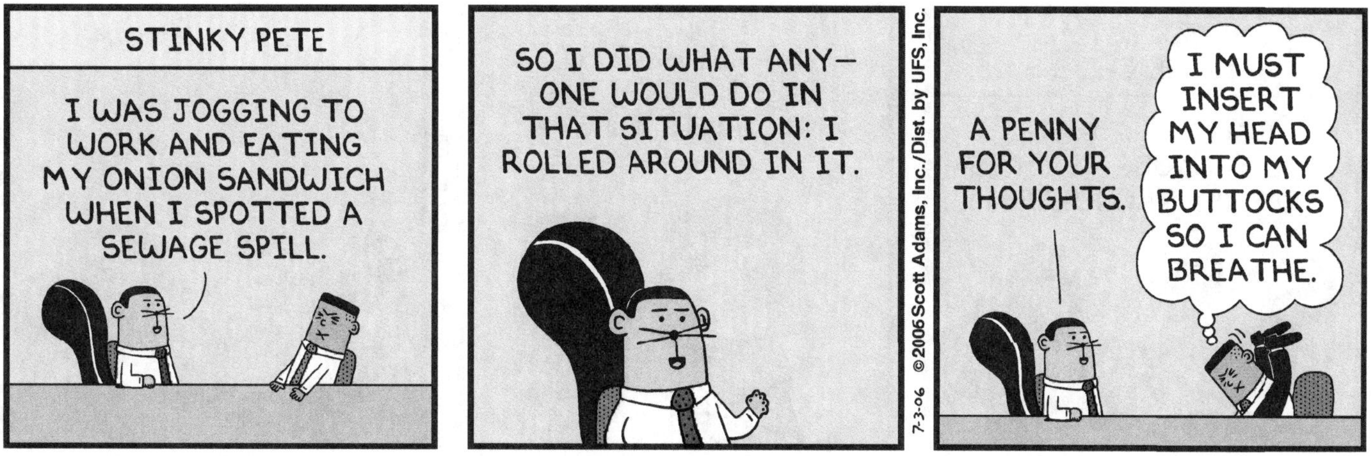
STINKY PETE
I WAS JOGGING TO WORK AND EATING MY ONION SANDWICH WHEN I SPOTTED A SEWAGE SPILL.
SO I DID WHAT ANY-ONE WOULD DO IN THAT SITUATION: I ROLLED AROUND IN IT.
7-3-06 ©2006 Scott Adams, Inc./Dist. by UFS, Inc.
A PENNY FOR YOUR THOUGHTS.
I MUST INSERT MY HEAD INTO MY BUTTOCKS SO I CAN BREATHE.

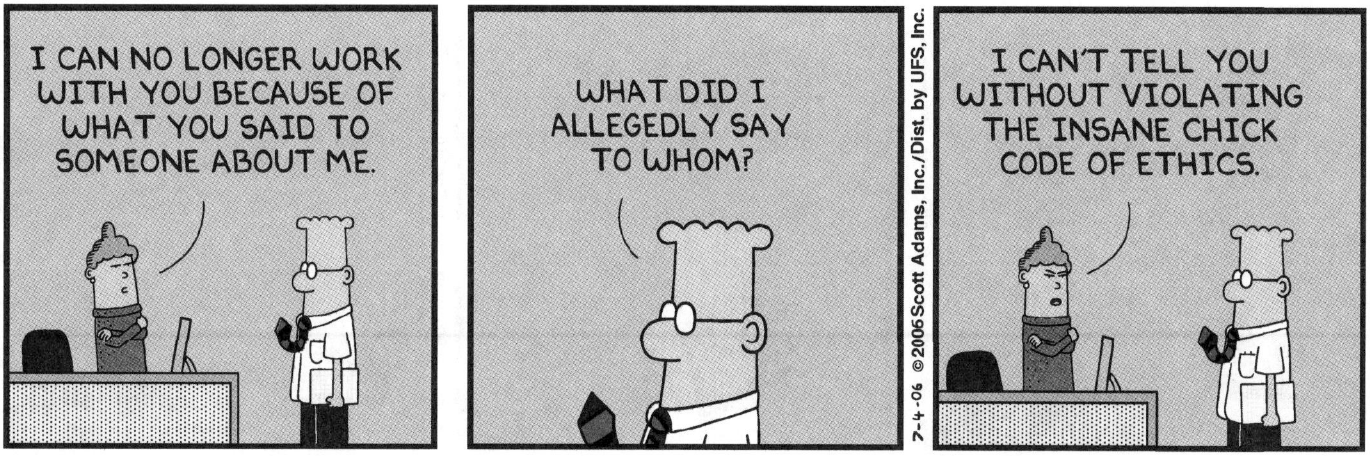
I CAN NO LONGER WORK WITH YOU BECAUSE OF WHAT YOU SAID TO SOMEONE ABOUT ME.
WHAT DID I ALLEGEDLY SAY TO WHOM?
7-4-06 ©2006 Scott Adams, Inc./Dist. by UFS, Inc.
I CAN'T TELL YOU WITHOUT VIOLATING THE INSANE CHICK CODE OF ETHICS.

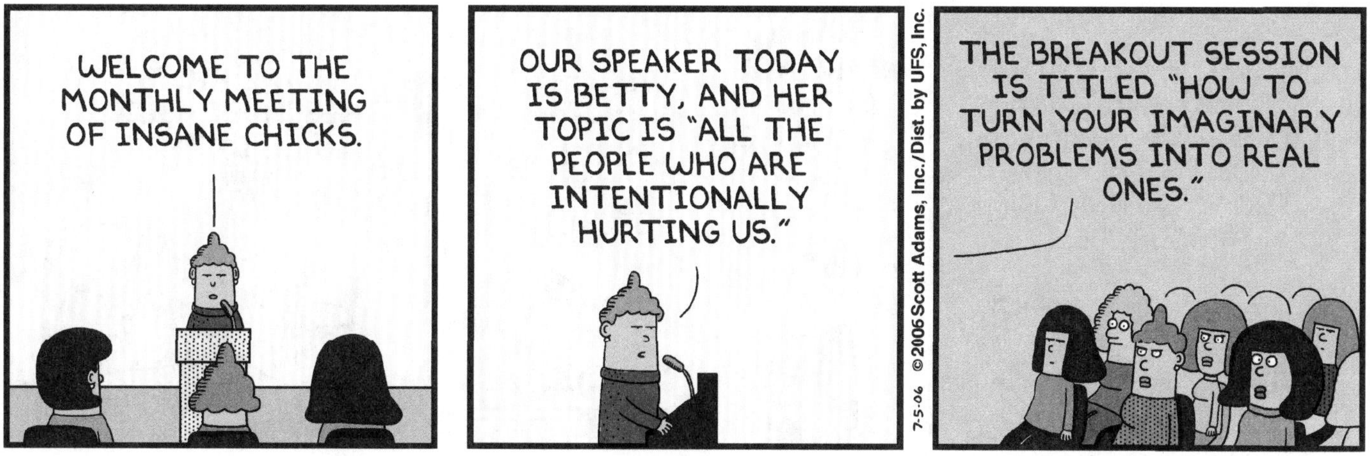
WELCOME TO THE MONTHLY MEETING OF INSANE CHICKS.
OUR SPEAKER TODAY IS BETTY, AND HER TOPIC IS "ALL THE PEOPLE WHO ARE INTENTIONALLY HURTING US."
7-5-06 ©2006 Scott Adams, Inc./Dist. by UFS, Inc.
THE BREAKOUT SESSION IS TITLED "HOW TO TURN YOUR IMAGINARY PROBLEMS INTO REAL ONES."

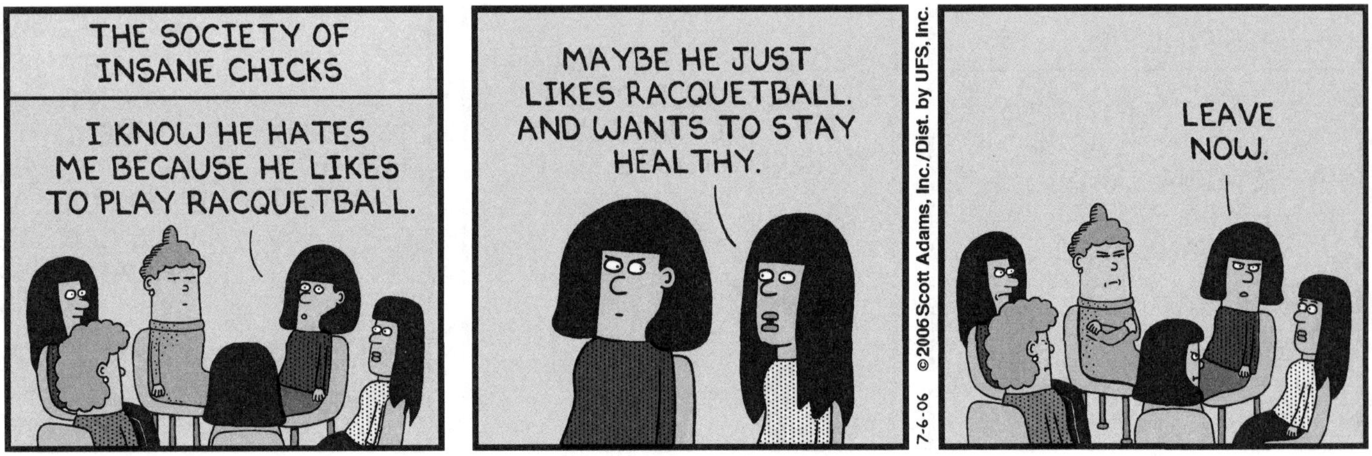
THE SOCIETY OF INSANE CHICKS
I KNOW HE HATES ME BECAUSE HE LIKES TO PLAY RACQUETBALL.
MAYBE HE JUST LIKES RACQUETBALL. AND WANTS TO STAY HEALTHY.
7-6-06 ©2006 Scott Adams, Inc./Dist. by UFS, Inc.
LEAVE NOW.

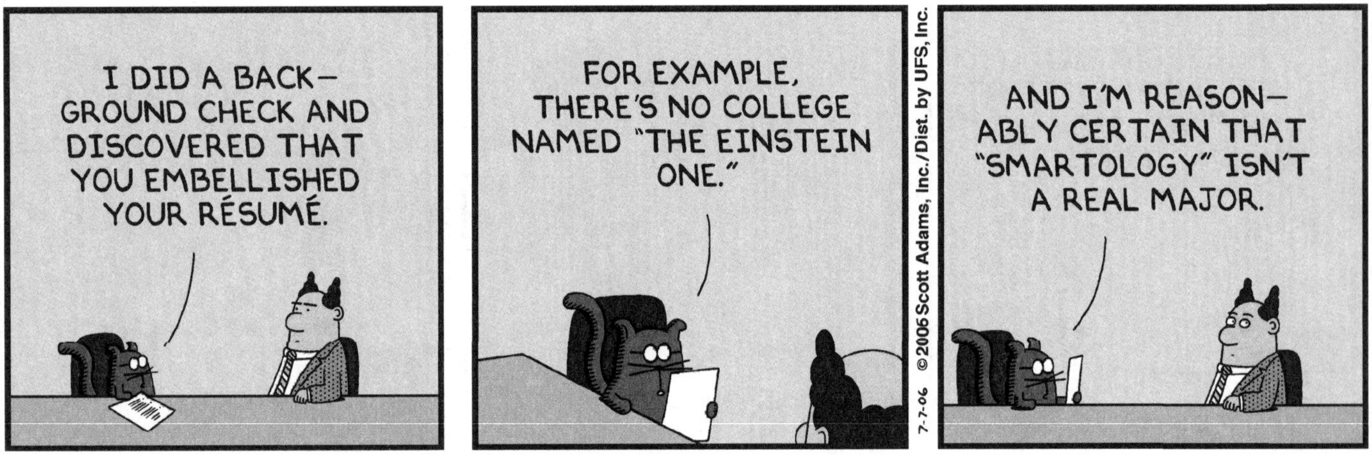
I DID A BACK-GROUND CHECK AND DISCOVERED THAT YOU EMBELLISHED YOUR RÉSUMÉ.
FOR EXAMPLE, THERE'S NO COLLEGE NAMED "THE EINSTEIN ONE."
7-7-06 ©2006 Scott Adams, Inc./Dist. by UFS, Inc.
AND I'M REASON-ABLY CERTAIN THAT "SMARTOLOGY" ISN'T A REAL MAJOR.

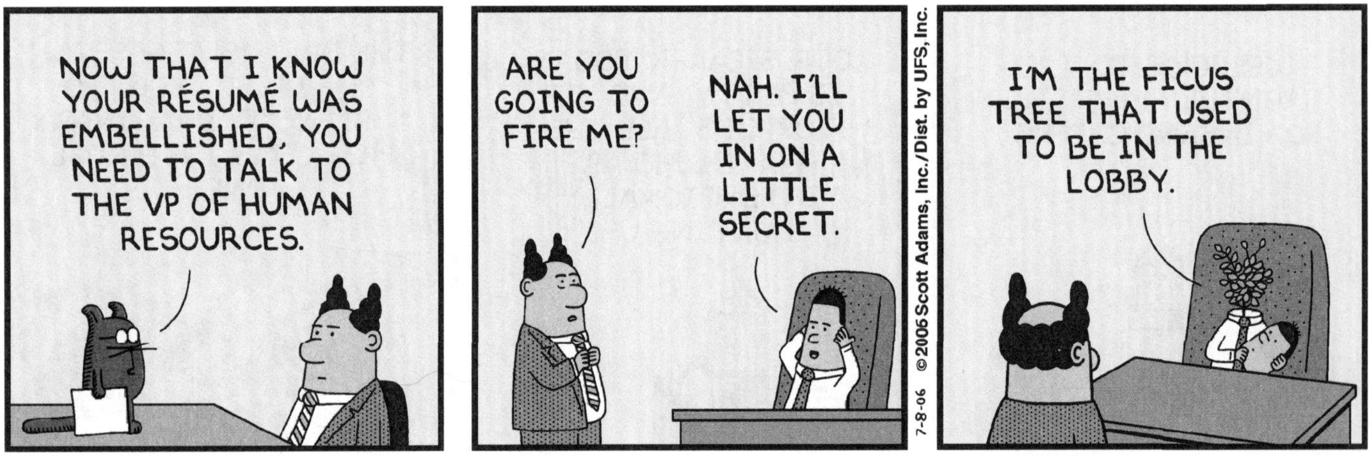
NOW THAT I KNOW YOUR RÉSUMÉ WAS EMBELLISHED, YOU NEED TO TALK TO THE VP OF HUMAN RESOURCES.
ARE YOU GOING TO FIRE ME?
NAH. I'LL LET YOU IN ON A LITTLE SECRET.
7-8-06 ©2006 Scott Adams, Inc./Dist. by UFS, Inc.
I'M THE FICUS TREE THAT USED TO BE IN THE LOBBY.

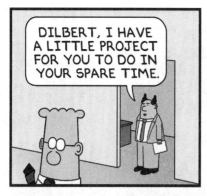

DILBERT, I HAVE A LITTLE PROJECT FOR YOU TO DO IN YOUR SPARE TIME.
WHAT EXACTLY IS MY "SPARE TIME"?
WELL, FOR EXAMPLE, THERE'S THE TIME THAT NORMAL PEOPLE WOULD USE FOR DATING.
AND SINCE YOU'RE NOT DATING, YOU CAN TRIM A FEW MINUTES FROM YOUR HYGIENE SCHEDULE TOO.
©2006 Scott Adams, Inc. /Dist. by UFS, Inc.
THEN THERE'S THE TIME YOU SPEND DAYDREAMING ABOUT A FULFILLING LIFE.
THAT'S EXACTLY LIKE STEALING FROM THE COMPANY.
AND YOUR STUPID QUESTIONS — THOSE HAVE TO TAKE AT LEAST AN HOUR A DAY.
7-09-06
ARE MY QUESTIONS STUPID?
NOT AS BAD AS YOUR ANSWERS.

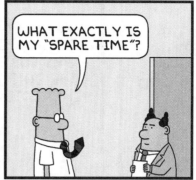

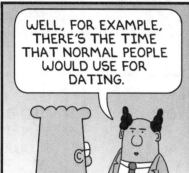

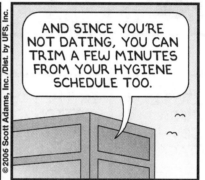

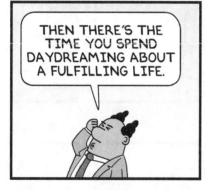

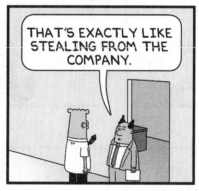

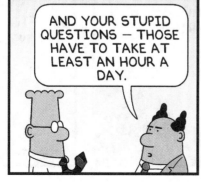

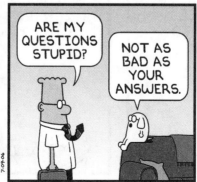

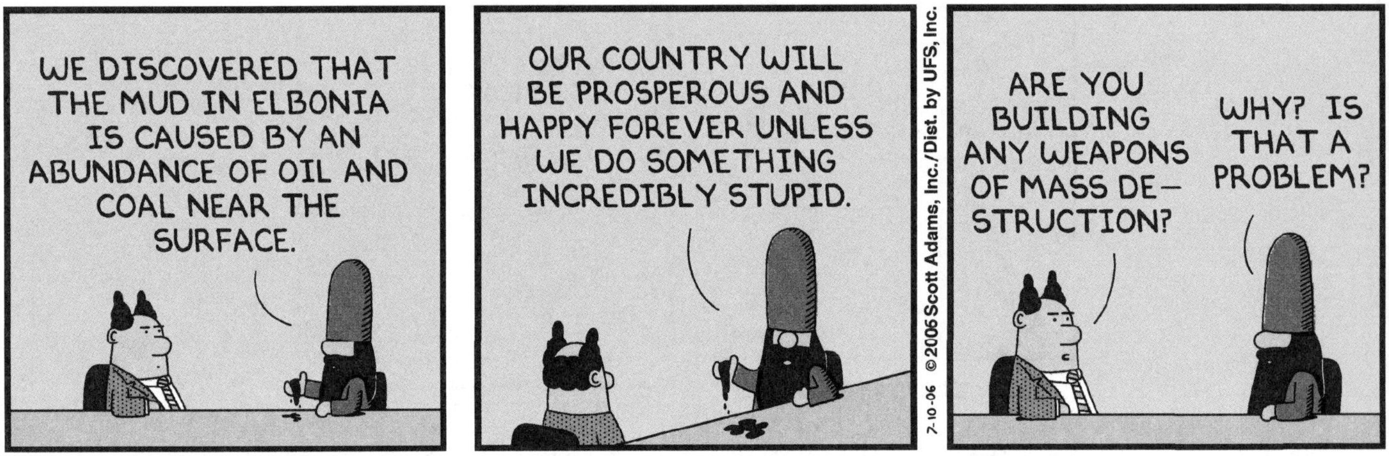
WE DISCOVERED THAT THE MUD IN ELBONIA IS CAUSED BY AN ABUNDANCE OF OIL AND COAL NEAR THE SURFACE.
OUR COUNTRY WILL BE PROSPEROUS AND HAPPY FOREVER UNLESS WE DO SOMETHING INCREDIBLY STUPID.
7-10-06 © 2006 Scott Adams, Inc./Dist. by UFS, Inc.
ARE YOU BUILDING ANY WEAPONS OF MASS DE–STRUCTION?
WHY? IS THAT A PROBLEM?

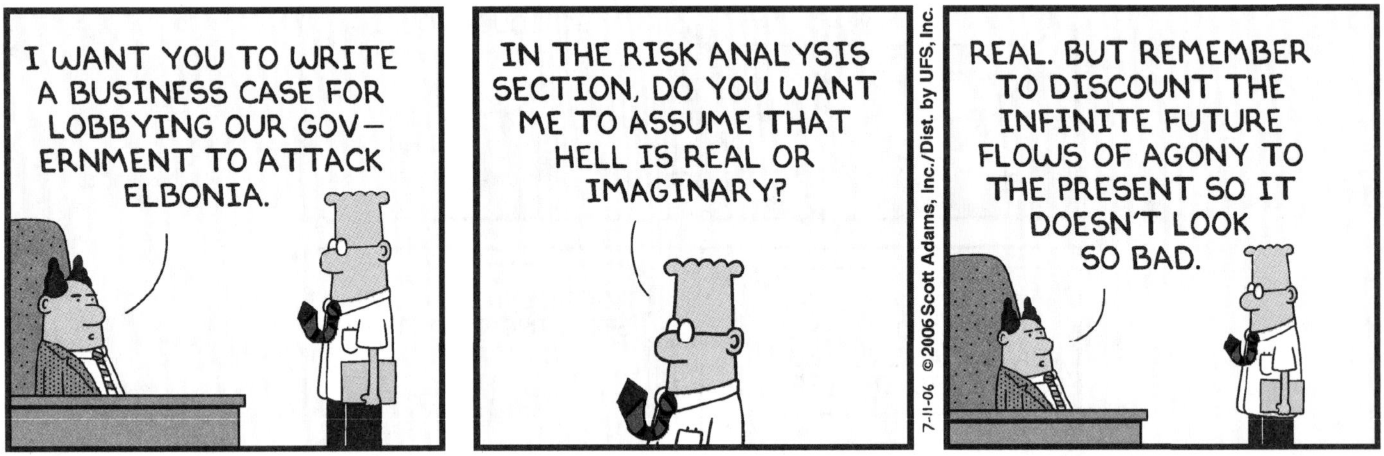
I WANT YOU TO WRITE A BUSINESS CASE FOR LOBBYING OUR GOV–ERNMENT TO ATTACK ELBONIA.
IN THE RISK ANALYSIS SECTION, DO YOU WANT ME TO ASSUME THAT HELL IS REAL OR IMAGINARY?
7-11-06 © 2006 Scott Adams, Inc./Dist. by UFS, Inc.
REAL. BUT REMEMBER TO DISCOUNT THE INFINITE FUTURE FLOWS OF AGONY TO THE PRESENT SO IT DOESN'T LOOK SO BAD.

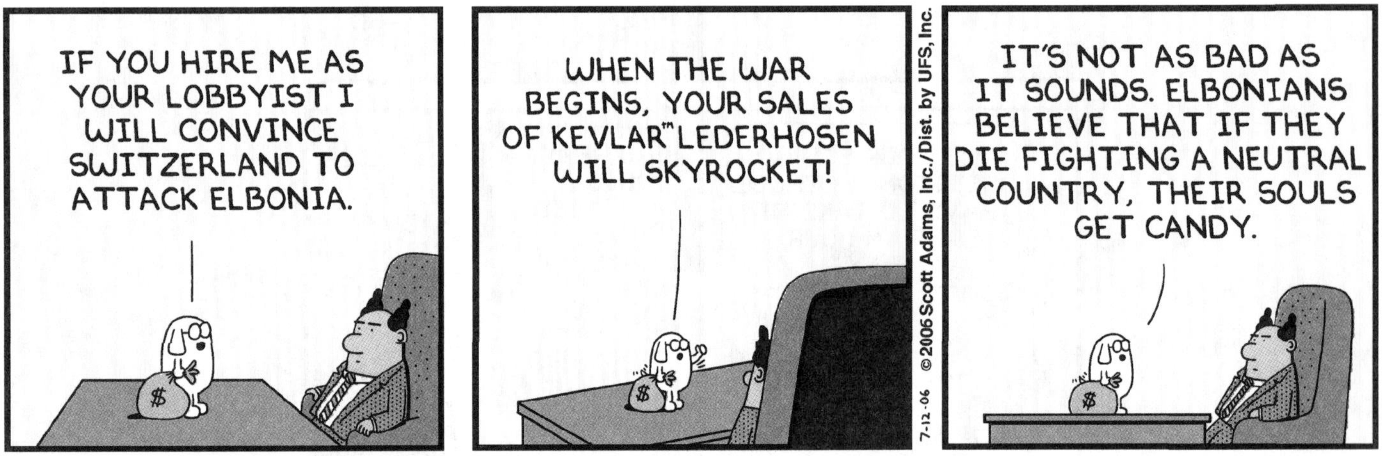
IF YOU HIRE ME AS YOUR LOBBYIST I WILL CONVINCE SWITZERLAND TO ATTACK ELBONIA.
WHEN THE WAR BEGINS, YOUR SALES OF KEVLAR™ LEDERHOSEN WILL SKYROCKET!
7-12-06 © 2006 Scott Adams, Inc./Dist. by UFS, Inc.
IT'S NOT AS BAD AS IT SOUNDS. ELBONIANS BELIEVE THAT IF THEY DIE FIGHTING A NEUTRAL COUNTRY, THEIR SOULS GET CANDY.

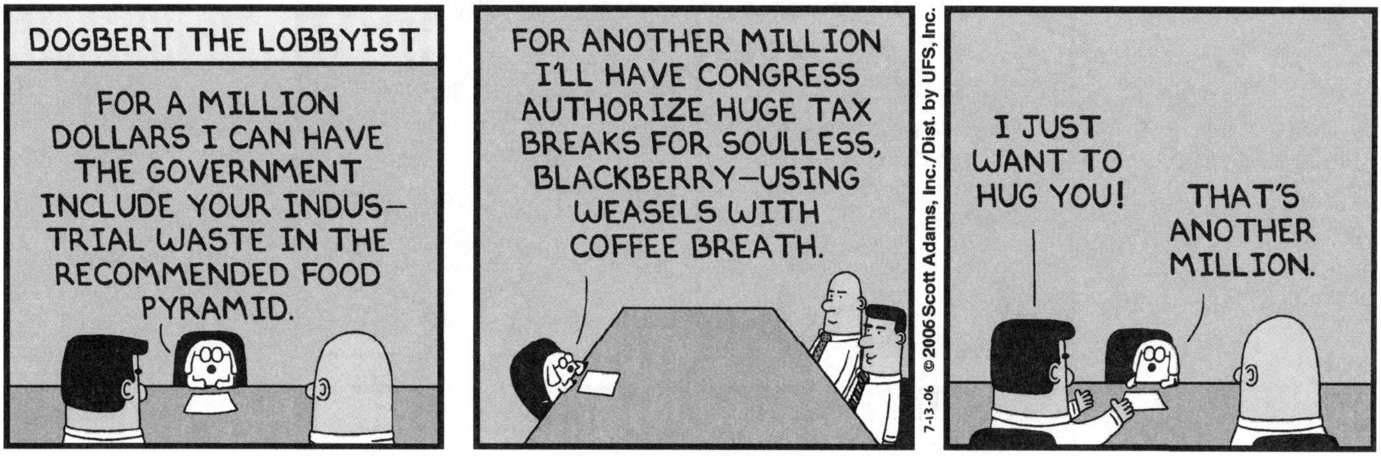
DOGBERT THE LOBBYIST
FOR A MILLION DOLLARS I CAN HAVE THE GOVERNMENT INCLUDE YOUR INDUSTRIAL WASTE IN THE RECOMMENDED FOOD PYRAMID.
FOR ANOTHER MILLION I'LL HAVE CONGRESS AUTHORIZE HUGE TAX BREAKS FOR SOULLESS, BLACKBERRY-USING WEASELS WITH COFFEE BREATH.
7-13-06 © 2006 Scott Adams, Inc./Dist. by UFS, Inc.
I JUST WANT TO HUG YOU!
THAT'S ANOTHER MILLION.

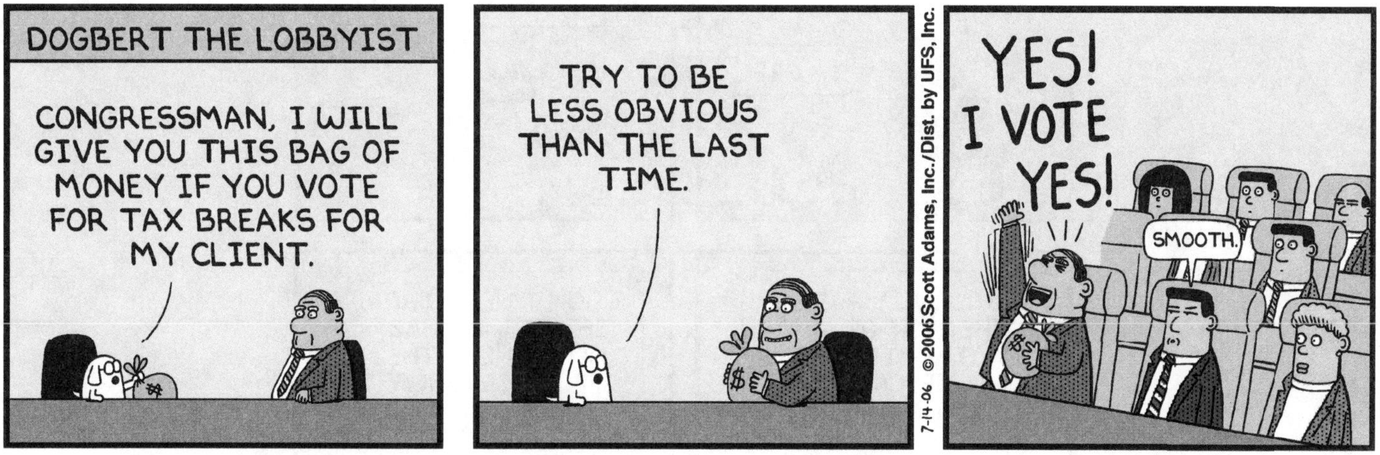
DOGBERT THE LOBBYIST
CONGRESSMAN, I WILL GIVE YOU THIS BAG OF MONEY IF YOU VOTE FOR TAX BREAKS FOR MY CLIENT.
TRY TO BE LESS OBVIOUS THAN THE LAST TIME.
7-14-06 © 2006 Scott Adams, Inc./Dist. by UFS, Inc.
YES! I VOTE YES!
SMOOTH.

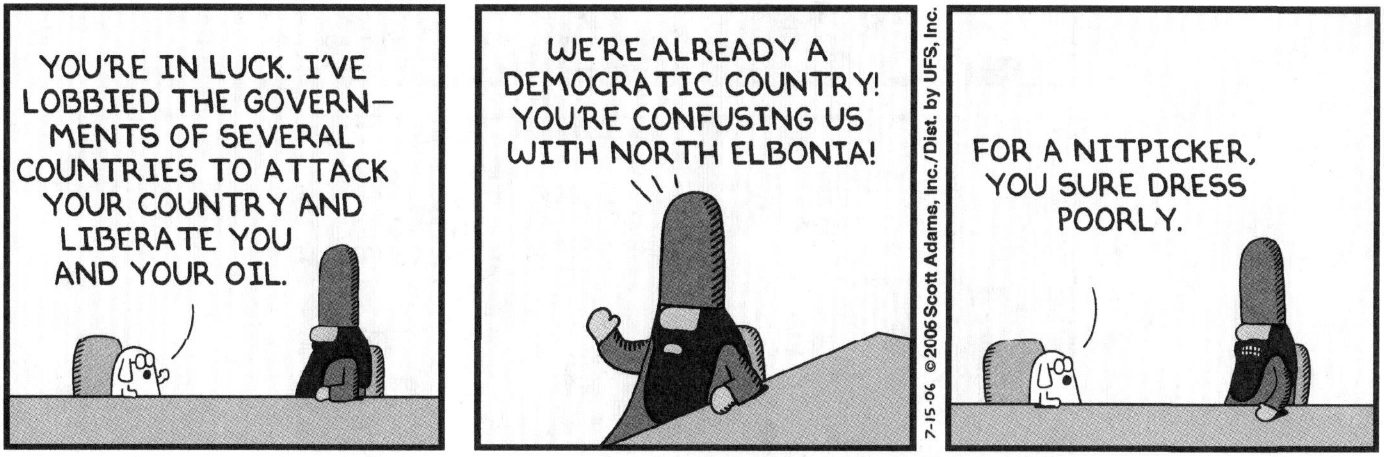
YOU'RE IN LUCK. I'VE LOBBIED THE GOVERNMENTS OF SEVERAL COUNTRIES TO ATTACK YOUR COUNTRY AND LIBERATE YOU AND YOUR OIL.
WE'RE ALREADY A DEMOCRATIC COUNTRY! YOU'RE CONFUSING US WITH NORTH ELBONIA!
7-15-06 © 2006 Scott Adams, Inc./Dist. by UFS, Inc.
FOR A NITPICKER, YOU SURE DRESS POORLY.

WALLY, YOU'VE AGREED TO PULL TOGETHER ALL OF THE TECHNICAL SPECIFICATIONS BY THURSDAY, RIGHT?
YES, I'LL LOOK INTO PULLING THAT STUFF TOGETHER.
I DON'T NEED YOU TO "LOOK INTO IT." I NEED YOU TO DO IT.
I AGREE.
ARE YOU AGREEING THAT I NEED IT OR AGREEING TO DO IT?
YOU WILL HAVE THE LIST OF WHO HAS THE TECHNICAL SPECIFICATIONS BY THURSDAY.
I DON'T NEED THE LIST OF WHO HAS THEM. I NEED THE SPECIFICATIONS!
I AGREE.
GAAA!!! FORGET IT! I'LL GET THEM MYSELF!
DID YOU HELP BOB GET WHAT HE NEEDS?
HE'LL HAVE EVERY-THING BY THURSDAY.
© 2006 Scott Adams, Inc. /Dist. by UFS, Inc.
7-16-06

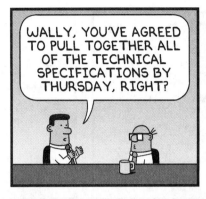

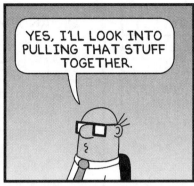

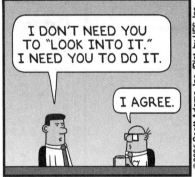

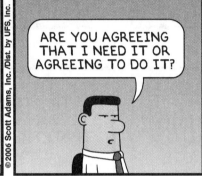

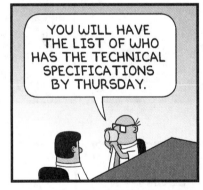

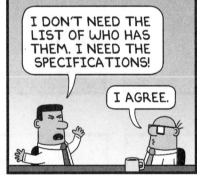

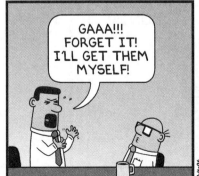

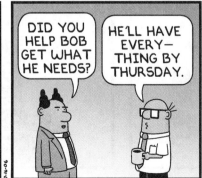

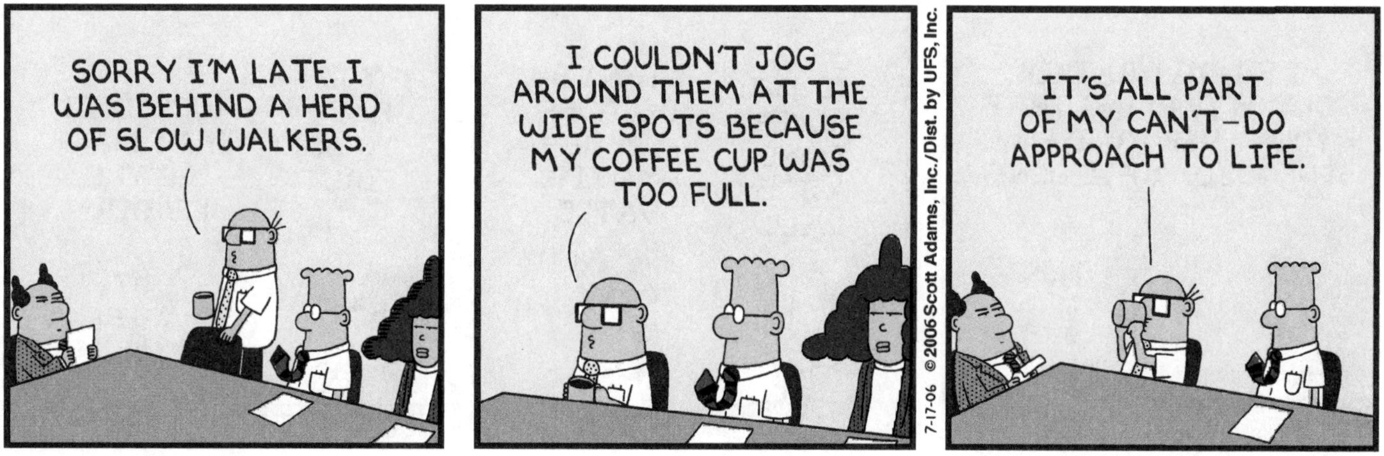
SORRY I'M LATE. I WAS BEHIND A HERD OF SLOW WALKERS.
I COULDN'T JOG AROUND THEM AT THE WIDE SPOTS BECAUSE MY COFFEE CUP WAS TOO FULL.
7-17-06 ©2006 Scott Adams, Inc./Dist. by UFS, Inc.
IT'S ALL PART OF MY CAN'T-DO APPROACH TO LIFE.

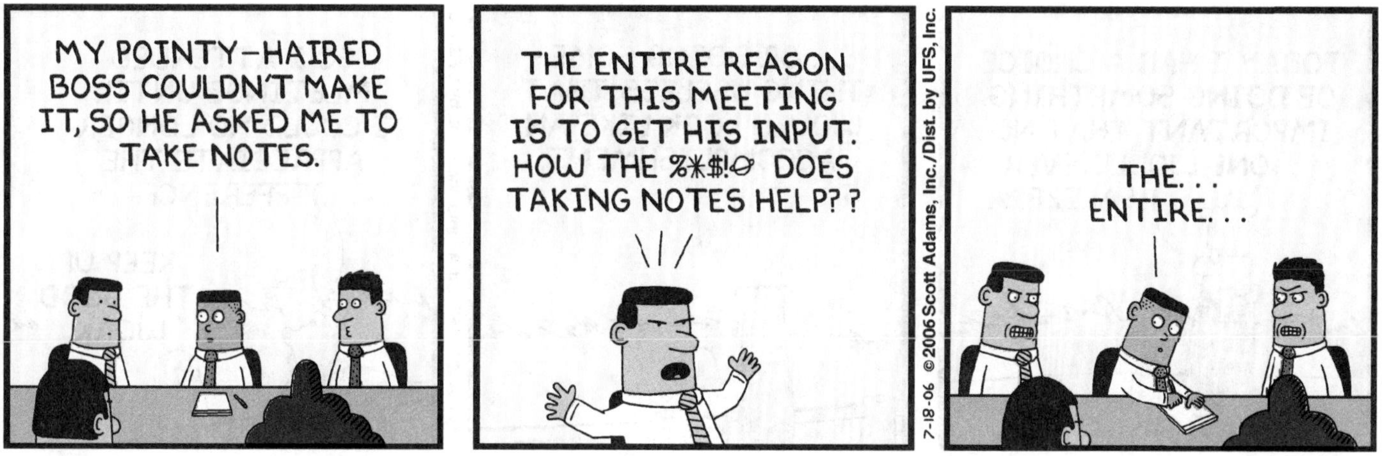
MY POINTY-HAIRED BOSS COULDN'T MAKE IT, SO HE ASKED ME TO TAKE NOTES.
THE ENTIRE REASON FOR THIS MEETING IS TO GET HIS INPUT. HOW THE %✱$!⊘ DOES TAKING NOTES HELP??
7-18-06 ©2006 Scott Adams, Inc./Dist. by UFS, Inc.
THE... ENTIRE...

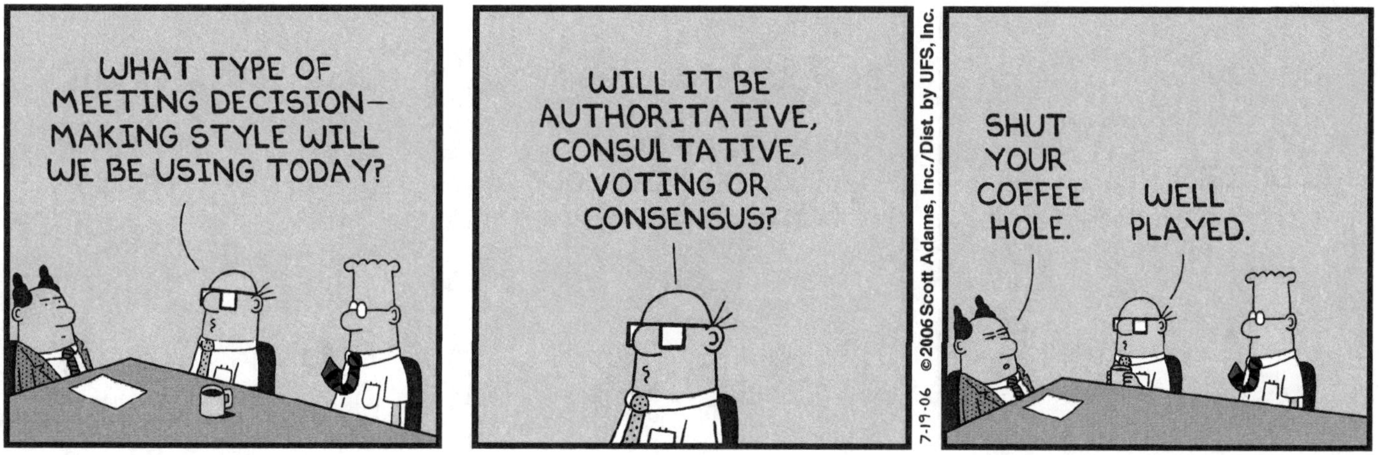
WHAT TYPE OF MEETING DECISION-MAKING STYLE WILL WE BE USING TODAY?
WILL IT BE AUTHORITATIVE, CONSULTATIVE, VOTING OR CONSENSUS?
7-19-06 ©2006 Scott Adams, Inc./Dist. by UFS, Inc.
SHUT YOUR COFFEE HOLE.
WELL PLAYED.

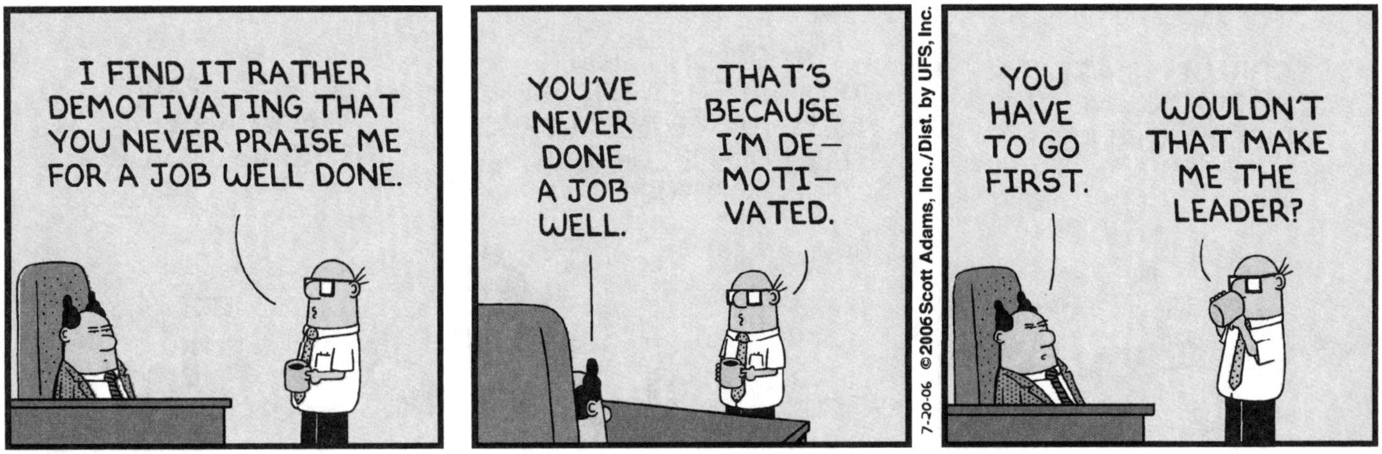
I FIND IT RATHER DEMOTIVATING THAT YOU NEVER PRAISE ME FOR A JOB WELL DONE.
YOU'VE NEVER DONE A JOB WELL.
THAT'S BECAUSE I'M DE-MOTI-VATED.
YOU HAVE TO GO FIRST.
WOULDN'T THAT MAKE ME THE LEADER?
7-20-06 ©2006 Scott Adams, Inc./Dist. by UFS, Inc.

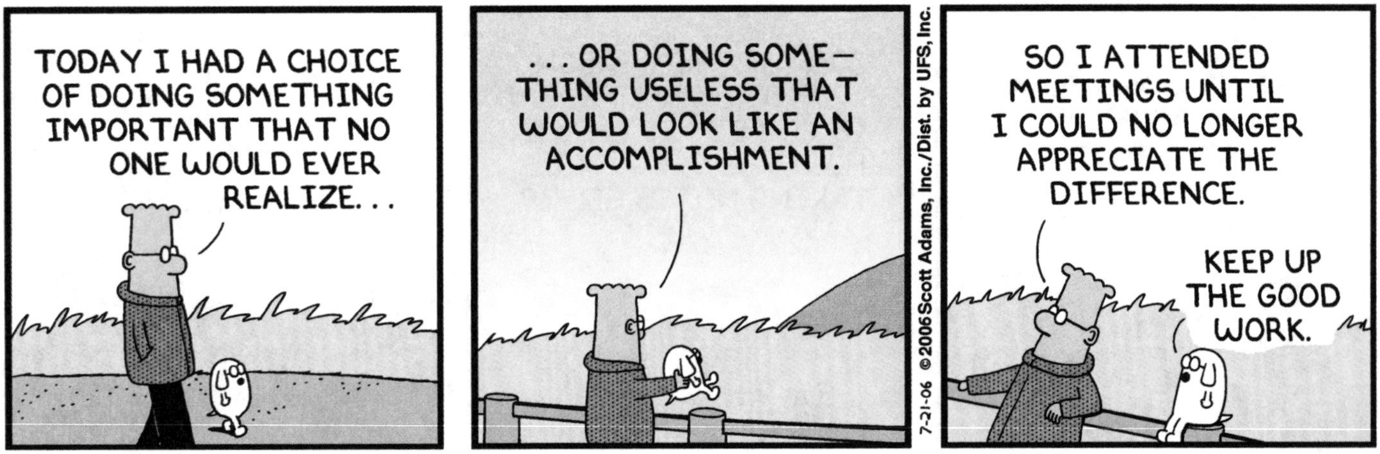
TODAY I HAD A CHOICE OF DOING SOMETHING IMPORTANT THAT NO ONE WOULD EVER REALIZE...
...OR DOING SOME-THING USELESS THAT WOULD LOOK LIKE AN ACCOMPLISHMENT.
SO I ATTENDED MEETINGS UNTIL I COULD NO LONGER APPRECIATE THE DIFFERENCE.
KEEP UP THE GOOD WORK.
7-21-06 ©2006 Scott Adams, Inc./Dist. by UFS, Inc.

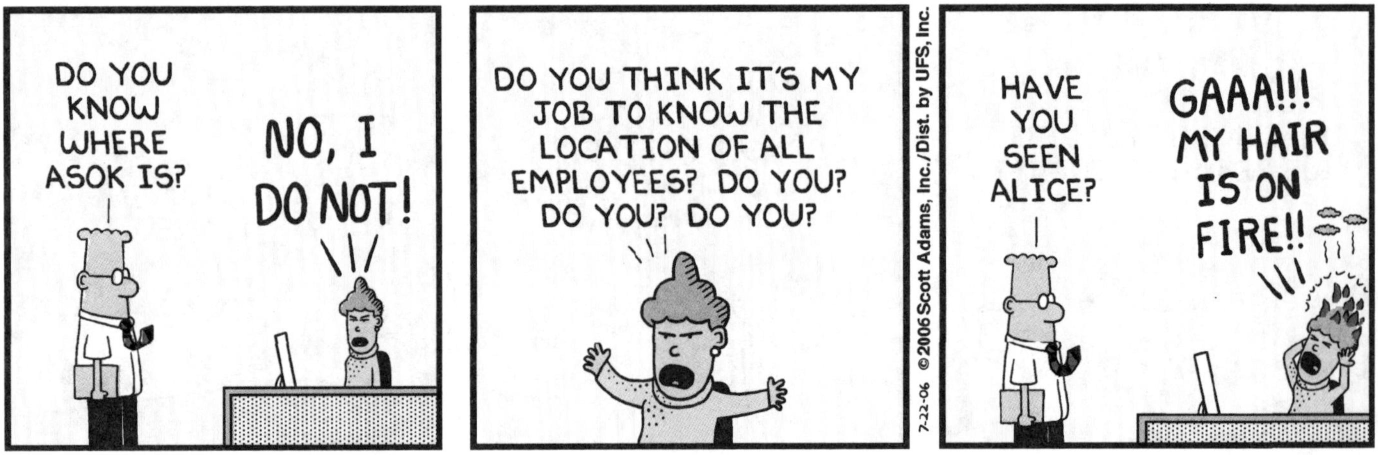
DO YOU KNOW WHERE ASOK IS?
NO, I DO NOT!
DO YOU THINK IT'S MY JOB TO KNOW THE LOCATION OF ALL EMPLOYEES? DO YOU? DO YOU? DO YOU?
HAVE YOU SEEN ALICE?
GAAA!!! MY HAIR IS ON FIRE!!
7-22-06 ©2006 Scott Adams, Inc./Dist. by UFS, Inc.

WHAT THE. . . ? HOW CAN YOU BE RELAXED WITH SO MUCH WORK TO DO?
YOUR MISTAKE IS TAKING PRIDE IN HOW MUCH WORK YOU CAN COMPLETE.
YOU SEE, ALICE, THERE'S AN INFINITE QUANTITY OF POTEN– TIAL WORK.
© 2006 Scott Adams, Inc./Dist. by UFS, Inc.
BUT IT'S ONLY POSSIBLE TO DO A FINITE AMOUNT.
YOU HAVE SET YOURSELF UP FOR CERTAIN FAILURE ACCORDING TO YOUR OWN ARBITRARY STANDARD.
BY WAY OF CONTRAST, I TAKE PRIDE IN NOT TAKING PRIDE IN MY WORK.
I'VE ALREADY ACHIEVED MY GOAL AND IT'S NOT EVEN LUNCH TIME YET.
7-23-06
DON'T YOU NEED A NEW GOAL FOR AFTER LUNCH?
I'M AIMING FOR A DISTENDED STOMACH.

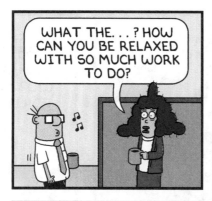

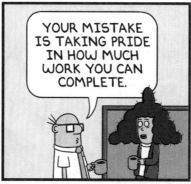

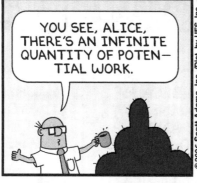

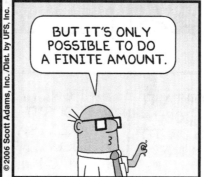

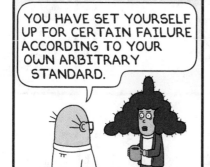

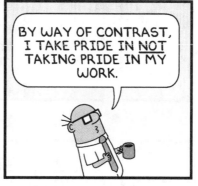

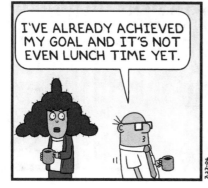

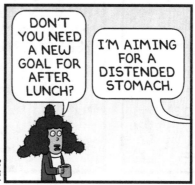

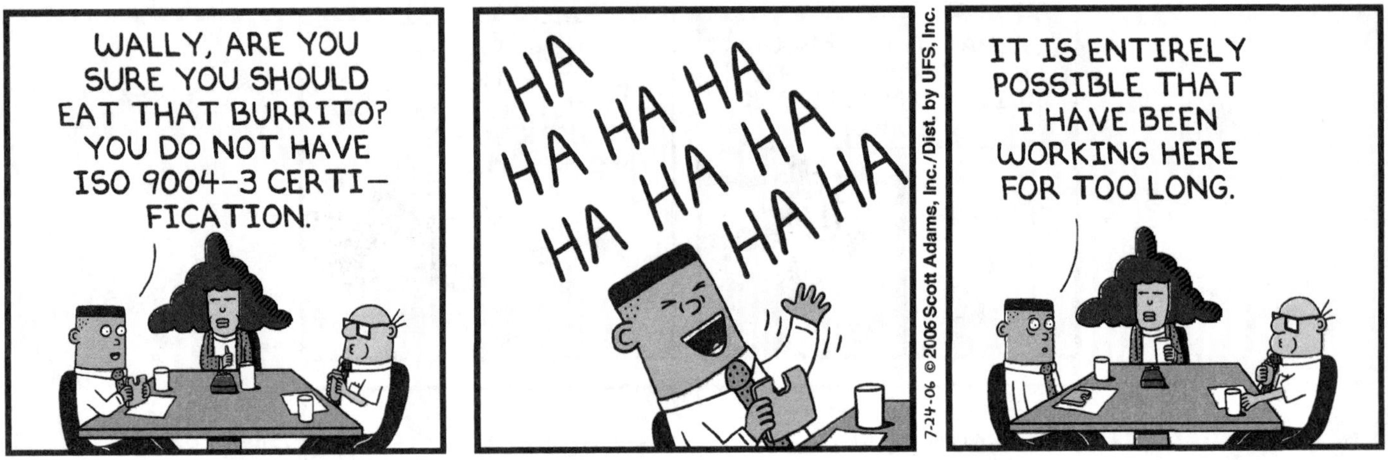
WALLY, ARE YOU SURE YOU SHOULD EAT THAT BURRITO? YOU DO NOT HAVE ISO 9004-3 CERTIFICATION.
HA HA HA HA HA HA HA HA HA HA
IT IS ENTIRELY POSSIBLE THAT I HAVE BEEN WORKING HERE FOR TOO LONG.
7-24-06 © 2006 Scott Adams, Inc./Dist. by UFS, Inc.

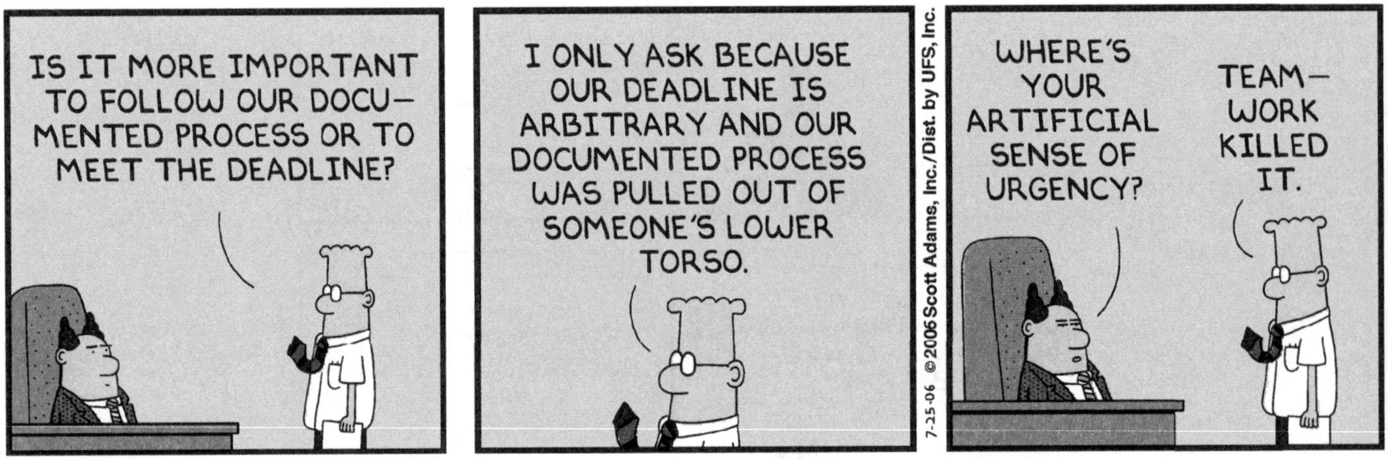
IS IT MORE IMPORTANT TO FOLLOW OUR DOCUMENTED PROCESS OR TO MEET THE DEADLINE?
I ONLY ASK BECAUSE OUR DEADLINE IS ARBITRARY AND OUR DOCUMENTED PROCESS WAS PULLED OUT OF SOMEONE'S LOWER TORSO.
WHERE'S YOUR ARTIFICIAL SENSE OF URGENCY?
TEAMWORK KILLED IT.
7-25-06 © 2006 Scott Adams, Inc./Dist. by UFS, Inc.

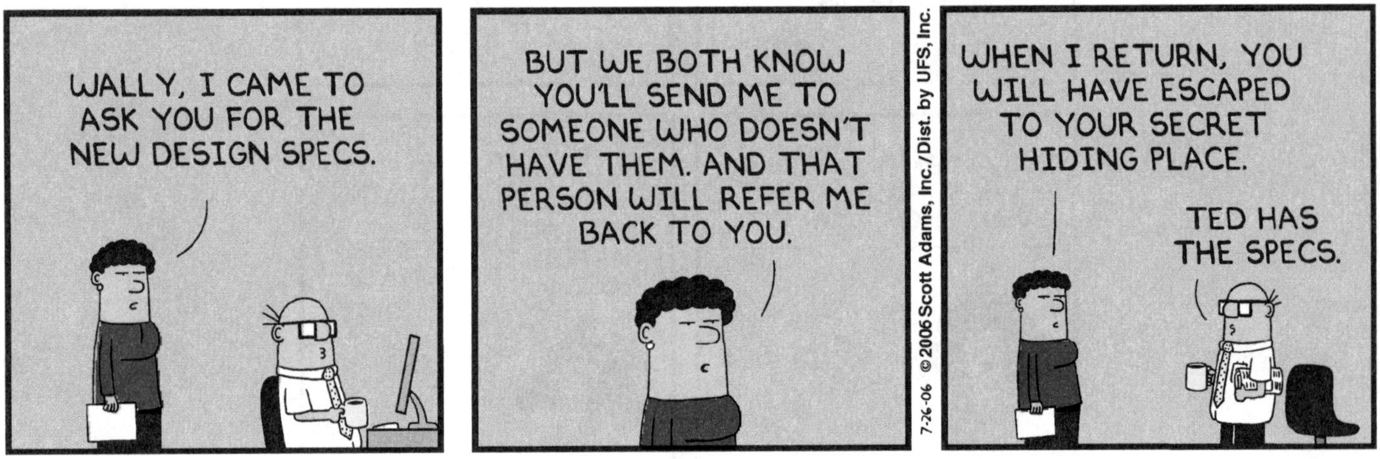
WALLY, I CAME TO ASK YOU FOR THE NEW DESIGN SPECS.
BUT WE BOTH KNOW YOU'LL SEND ME TO SOMEONE WHO DOESN'T HAVE THEM. AND THAT PERSON WILL REFER ME BACK TO YOU.
WHEN I RETURN, YOU WILL HAVE ESCAPED TO YOUR SECRET HIDING PLACE.
TED HAS THE SPECS.
7-26-06 © 2006 Scott Adams, Inc./Dist. by UFS, Inc.

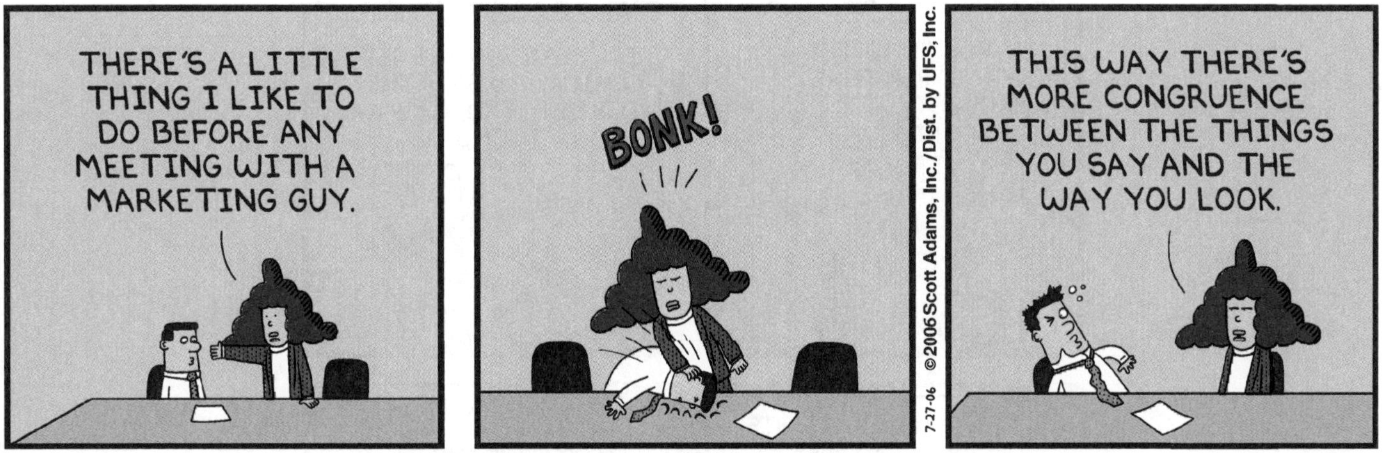
THERE'S A LITTLE THING I LIKE TO DO BEFORE ANY MEETING WITH A MARKETING GUY.
BONK!
THIS WAY THERE'S MORE CONGRUENCE BETWEEN THE THINGS YOU SAY AND THE WAY YOU LOOK.
7-27-06 ©2006 Scott Adams, Inc./Dist. by UFS, Inc.

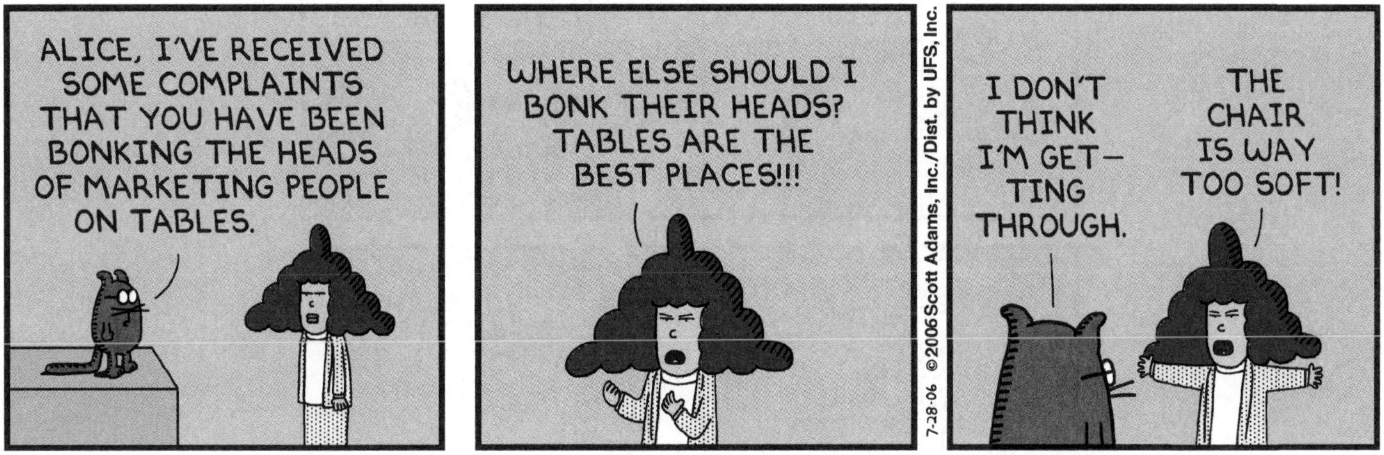
ALICE, I'VE RECEIVED SOME COMPLAINTS THAT YOU HAVE BEEN BONKING THE HEADS OF MARKETING PEOPLE ON TABLES.
WHERE ELSE SHOULD I BONK THEIR HEADS? TABLES ARE THE BEST PLACES!!!
I DON'T THINK I'M GET-TING THROUGH.
THE CHAIR IS WAY TOO SOFT!
7-28-06 ©2006 Scott Adams, Inc./Dist. by UFS, Inc.

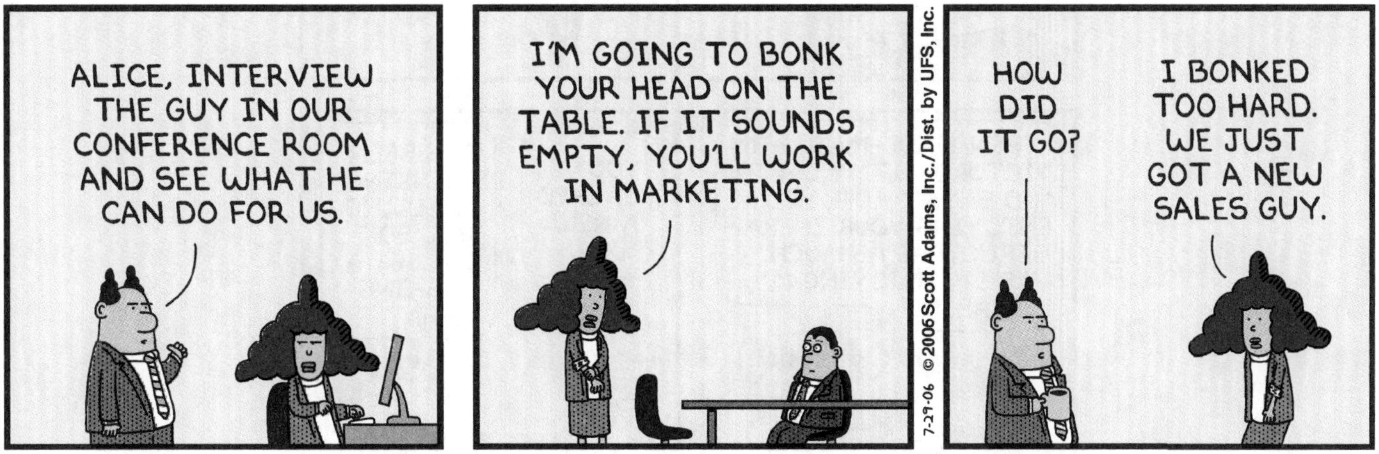
ALICE, INTERVIEW THE GUY IN OUR CONFERENCE ROOM AND SEE WHAT HE CAN DO FOR US.
I'M GOING TO BONK YOUR HEAD ON THE TABLE. IF IT SOUNDS EMPTY, YOU'LL WORK IN MARKETING.
HOW DID IT GO?
I BONKED TOO HARD. WE JUST GOT A NEW SALES GUY.
7-29-06 ©2006 Scott Adams, Inc./Dist. by UFS, Inc.

DID YOU FUND THE INFRASTRUCTURE PROJECT YET?
NOPE.
I'M PLAYING BUDGET CHICKEN WITH THE DIRECTOR OF OPERA– TIONS.
I'M HOPING THAT HIS DEPARTMENT NEEDS THE INFRASTRUCTURE MORE THAN WE DO.
IF I CAN BLUFF HIM INTO FUNDING THE PROJECT WITH HIS BUDGET INSTEAD OF MINE, I WIN.
HE'LL BE REPRIMANDED FOR EXCEEDING HIS BUDGET AND I'LL GET A BONUS FOR BEING UNDER MINE.
I'LL USE THE BONUS TO BUY A SUMMER CABIN BY THE LAKE.
THEN I'LL E–MAIL HIM PICTURES OF MY CABIN AND SAY, "I HOPE YOU'RE ENJOYING YOUR INFRA– STRUCTURE AS MUCH AS I'M ENJOYING MY CABIN!"
YOU'VE REACHED A NEW LOW.
I'VE BEEN THINKING OF FIRING YOU SO I CAN GET A FISHING HAT.
© 2006 Scott Adams, Inc./Dist. by UFS, Inc.
7-30-06

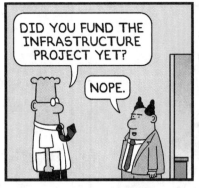

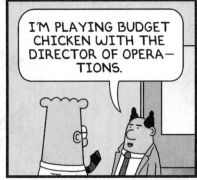

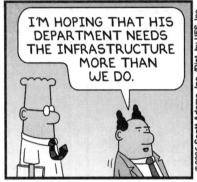

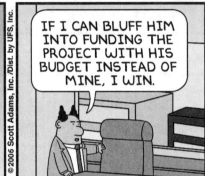

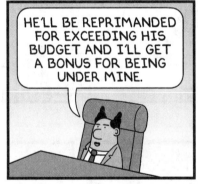

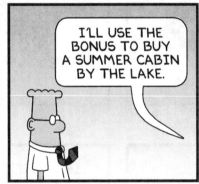

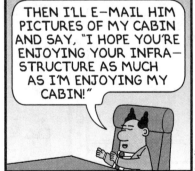

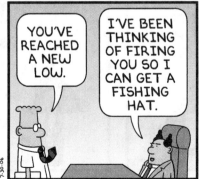

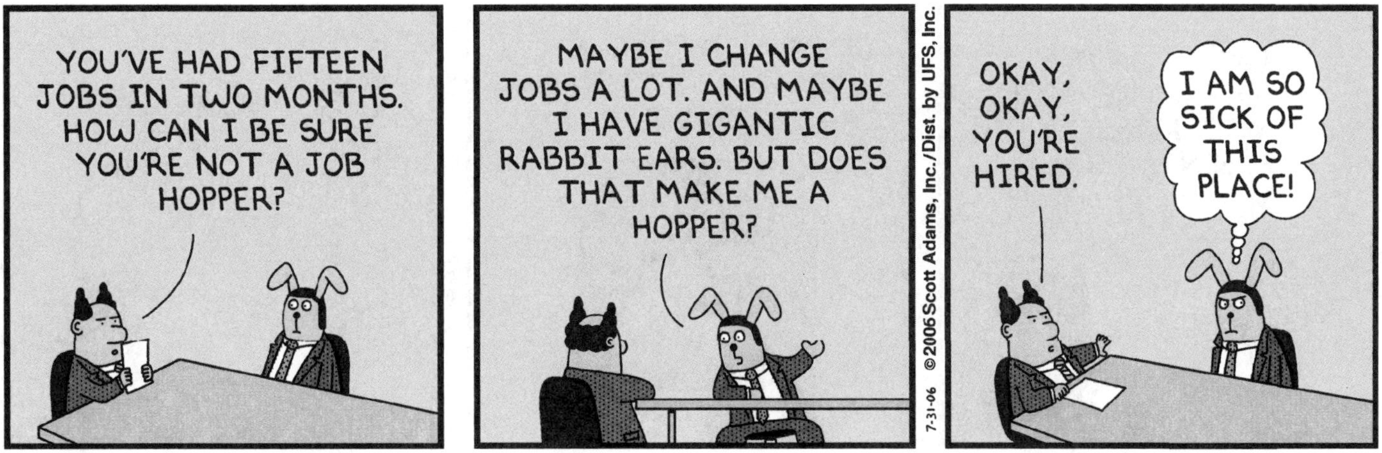
YOU'VE HAD FIFTEEN JOBS IN TWO MONTHS. HOW CAN I BE SURE YOU'RE NOT A JOB HOPPER?
MAYBE I CHANGE JOBS A LOT. AND MAYBE I HAVE GIGANTIC RABBIT EARS. BUT DOES THAT MAKE ME A HOPPER?
7-31-06 ©2006 Scott Adams, Inc./Dist. by UFS, Inc.
OKAY, OKAY, YOU'RE HIRED.
I AM SO SICK OF THIS PLACE!

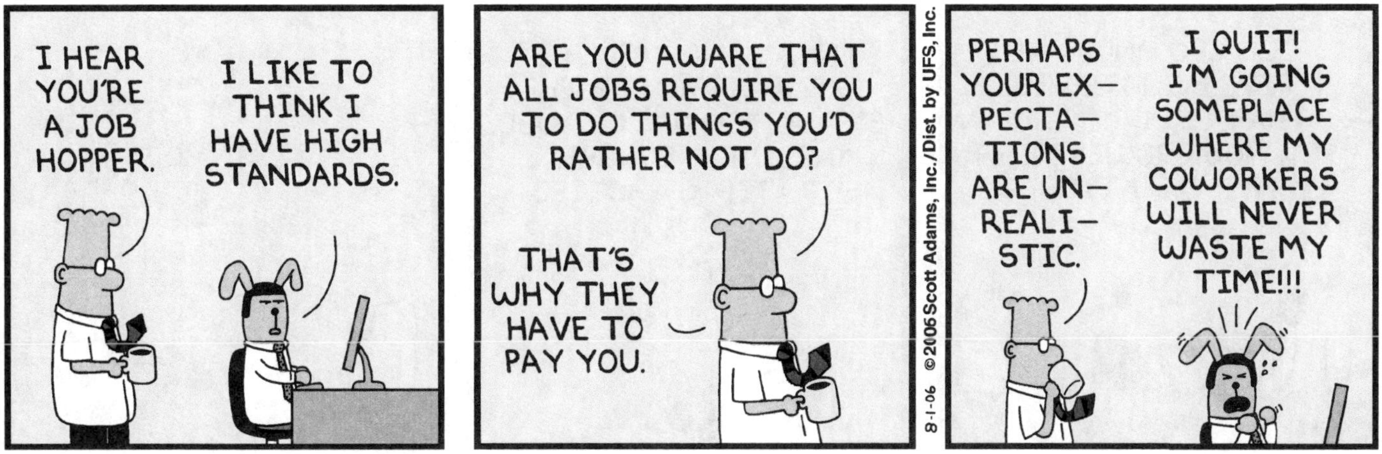
I HEAR YOU'RE A JOB HOPPER.
I LIKE TO THINK I HAVE HIGH STANDARDS.
ARE YOU AWARE THAT ALL JOBS REQUIRE YOU TO DO THINGS YOU'D RATHER NOT DO?
THAT'S WHY THEY HAVE TO PAY YOU.
8-1-06 ©2006 Scott Adams, Inc./Dist. by UFS, Inc.
PERHAPS YOUR EX-PECTA-TIONS ARE UN-REALI-STIC.
I QUIT! I'M GOING SOMEPLACE WHERE MY COWORKERS WILL NEVER WASTE MY TIME!!!

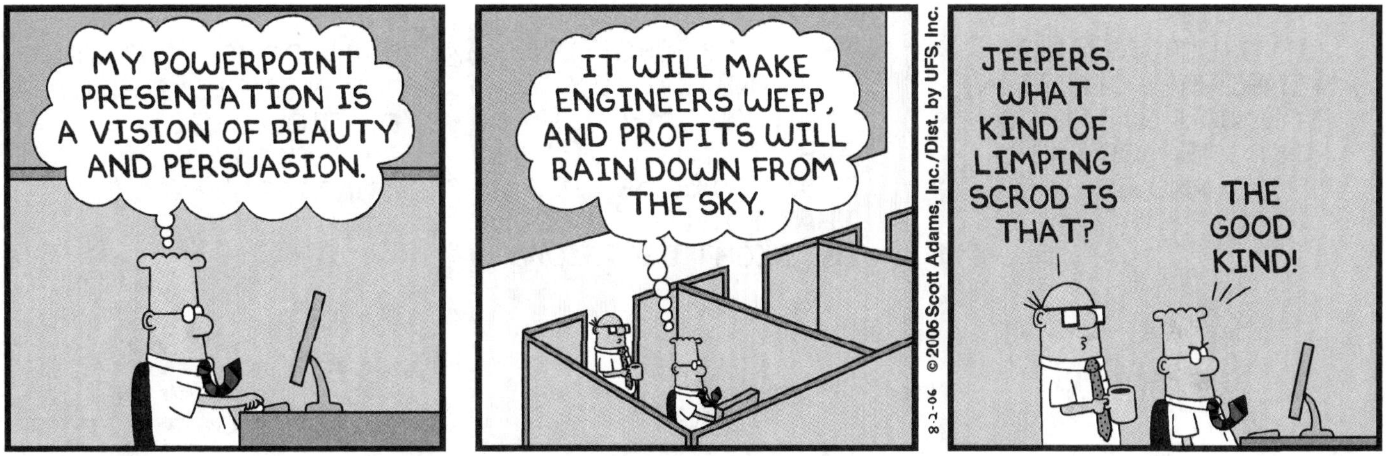
MY POWERPOINT PRESENTATION IS A VISION OF BEAUTY AND PERSUASION.
IT WILL MAKE ENGINEERS WEEP, AND PROFITS WILL RAIN DOWN FROM THE SKY.
8-2-06 ©2006 Scott Adams, Inc./Dist. by UFS, Inc.
JEEPERS. WHAT KIND OF LIMPING SCROD IS THAT?
THE GOOD KIND!

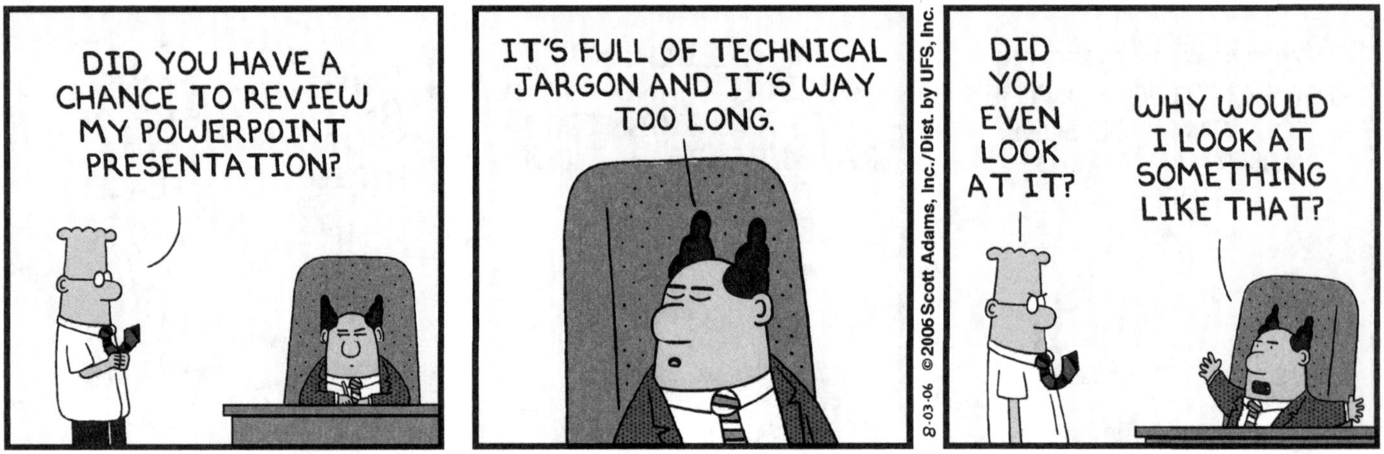
DID YOU HAVE A CHANCE TO REVIEW MY POWERPOINT PRESENTATION?
IT'S FULL OF TECHNICAL JARGON AND IT'S WAY TOO LONG.
DID YOU EVEN LOOK AT IT?
WHY WOULD I LOOK AT SOMETHING LIKE THAT?

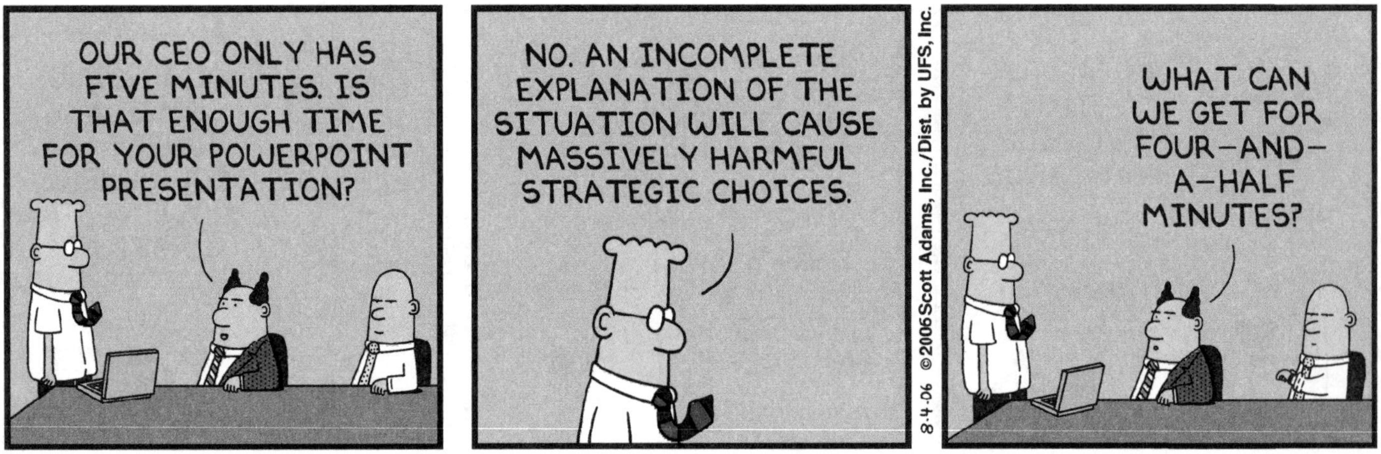
OUR CEO ONLY HAS FIVE MINUTES. IS THAT ENOUGH TIME FOR YOUR POWERPOINT PRESENTATION?
NO. AN INCOMPLETE EXPLANATION OF THE SITUATION WILL CAUSE MASSIVELY HARMFUL STRATEGIC CHOICES.
WHAT CAN WE GET FOR FOUR-AND-A-HALF MINUTES?

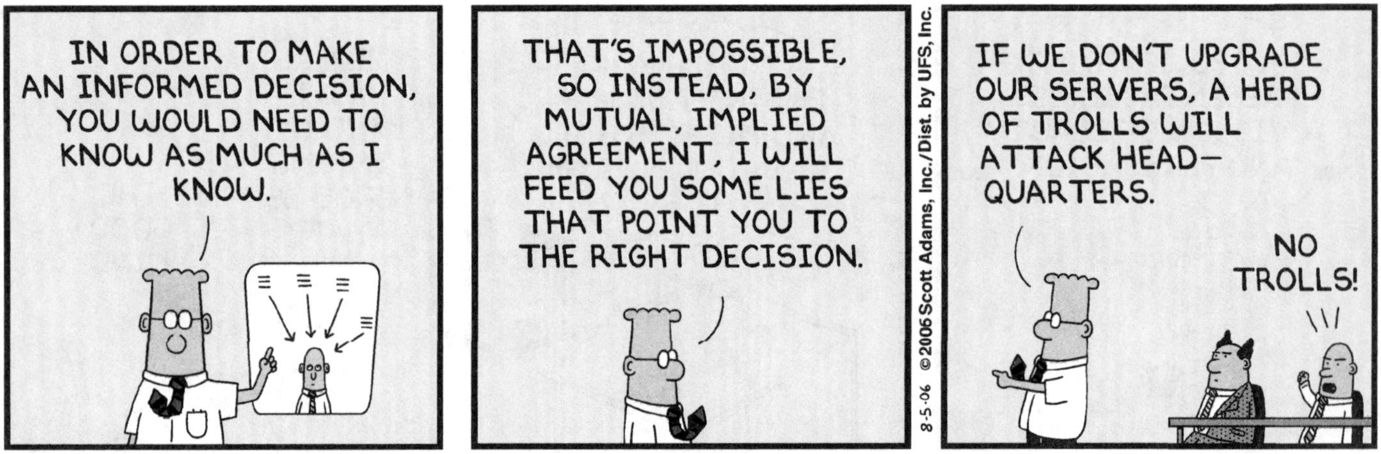
IN ORDER TO MAKE AN INFORMED DECISION, YOU WOULD NEED TO KNOW AS MUCH AS I KNOW.
THAT'S IMPOSSIBLE, SO INSTEAD, BY MUTUAL, IMPLIED AGREEMENT, I WILL FEED YOU SOME LIES THAT POINT YOU TO THE RIGHT DECISION.
IF WE DON'T UPGRADE OUR SERVERS, A HERD OF TROLLS WILL ATTACK HEAD-QUARTERS.
NO TROLLS!

I'M LIKE THE STORY OF THE AUTO MECHANIC.
A WOMAN HAS HER CAR TOWED INTO THE SHOP. THE MECHANIC OPENS THE HOOD AND TAKES A LOOK.
AFTER ABOUT TEN SECONDS HE TAKES A HAMMER AND TAPS THE ENGINE. IT STARTS RIGHT UP.
THE MECHANIC SAYS, "THAT WILL BE $100, PLEASE."
ZZZZ
THE WOMAN SAYS, "$100??? ALL YOU DID WAS TAP THE ENGINE!"
THE MECHANIC SAYS, "IT'S $90 FOR KNOWING WHERE TO TAP AND $10 FOR THE TAP."
ZZZZZ
TAP!
20 YEARS AGO I WOULDN'T HAVE KNOWN WHICH ONE OF YOU TO TAP.
©2006 Scott Adams, Inc./Dist. by UFS, Inc.
8-6-06

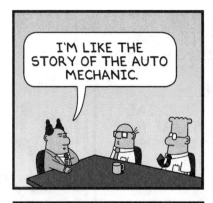

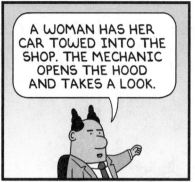

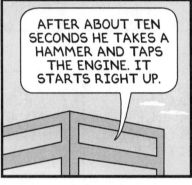

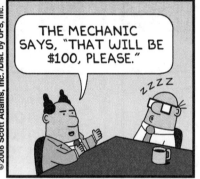

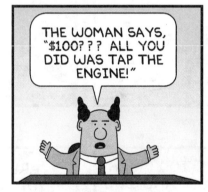

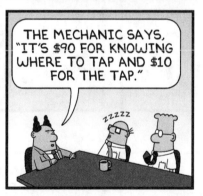

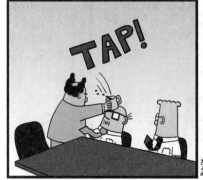

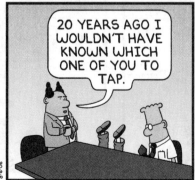

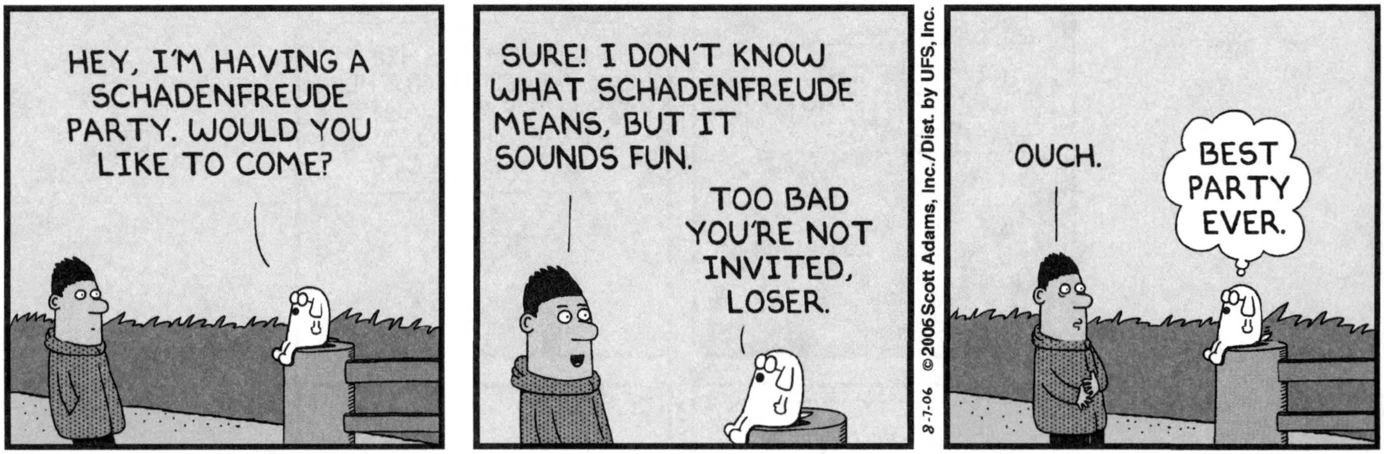
HEY, I'M HAVING A SCHADENFREUDE PARTY. WOULD YOU LIKE TO COME?
SURE! I DON'T KNOW WHAT SCHADENFREUDE MEANS, BUT IT SOUNDS FUN.
TOO BAD YOU'RE NOT INVITED, LOSER.
8-7-06 © 2006 Scott Adams, Inc./Dist. by UFS, Inc.
OUCH.
BEST PARTY EVER.

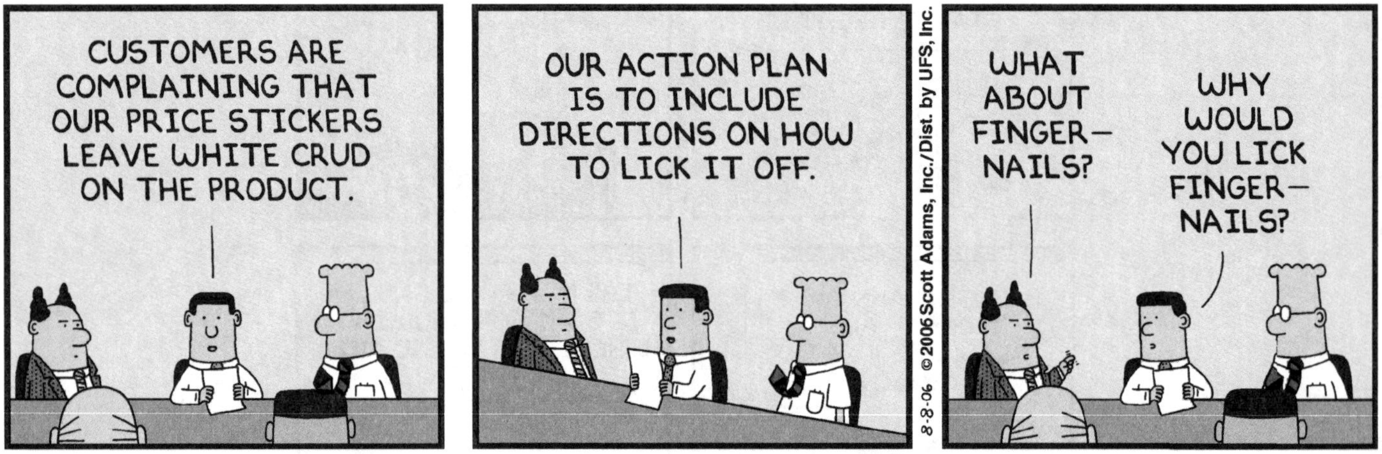
CUSTOMERS ARE COMPLAINING THAT OUR PRICE STICKERS LEAVE WHITE CRUD ON THE PRODUCT.
OUR ACTION PLAN IS TO INCLUDE DIRECTIONS ON HOW TO LICK IT OFF.
8-8-06 © 2006 Scott Adams, Inc./Dist. by UFS, Inc.
WHAT ABOUT FINGER-NAILS?
WHY WOULD YOU LICK FINGER-NAILS?

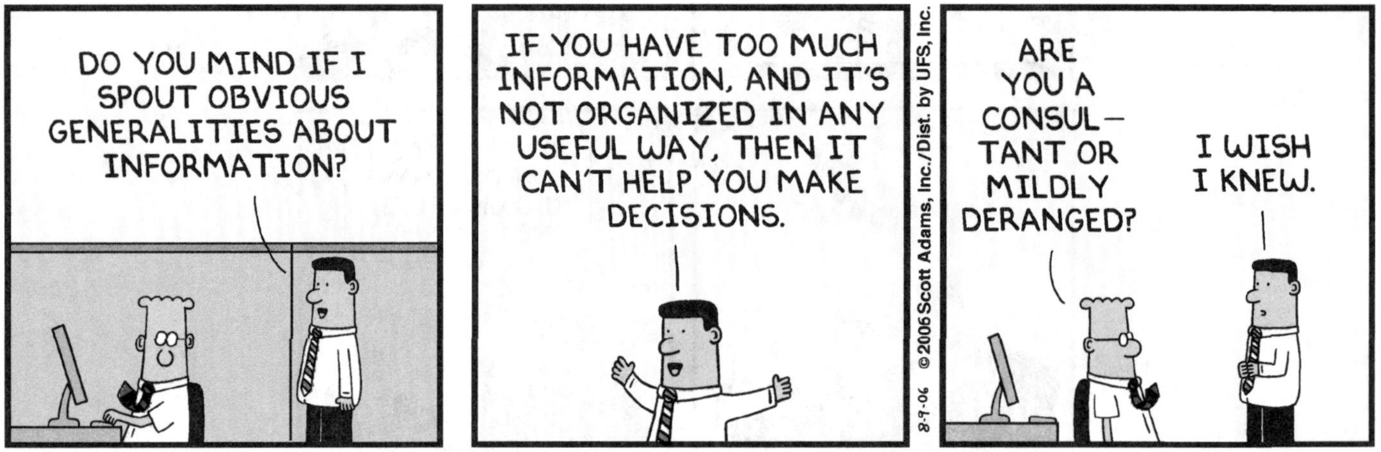
DO YOU MIND IF I SPOUT OBVIOUS GENERALITIES ABOUT INFORMATION?
IF YOU HAVE TOO MUCH INFORMATION, AND IT'S NOT ORGANIZED IN ANY USEFUL WAY, THEN IT CAN'T HELP YOU MAKE DECISIONS.
8-9-06 © 2006 Scott Adams, Inc./Dist. by UFS, Inc.
ARE YOU A CONSUL-TANT OR MILDLY DERANGED?
I WISH I KNEW.

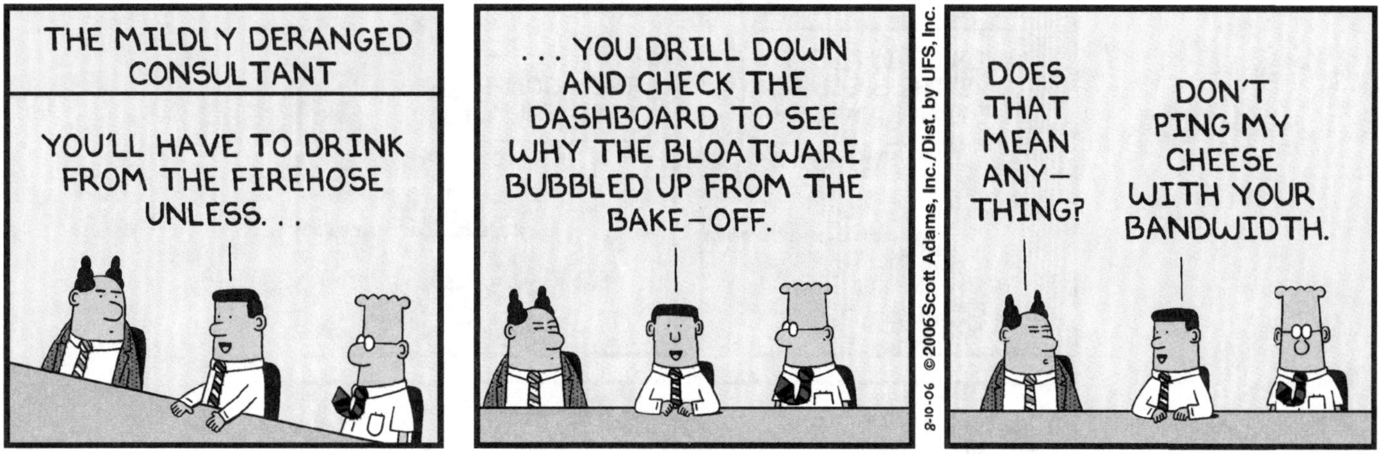
THE MILDLY DERANGED CONSULTANT
YOU'LL HAVE TO DRINK FROM THE FIREHOSE UNLESS. . .
. . . YOU DRILL DOWN AND CHECK THE DASHBOARD TO SEE WHY THE BLOATWARE BUBBLED UP FROM THE BAKE-OFF.
8-10-06 ©2006 Scott Adams, Inc./Dist. by UFS, Inc.
DOES THAT MEAN ANY-THING?
DON'T PING MY CHEESE WITH YOUR BANDWIDTH.

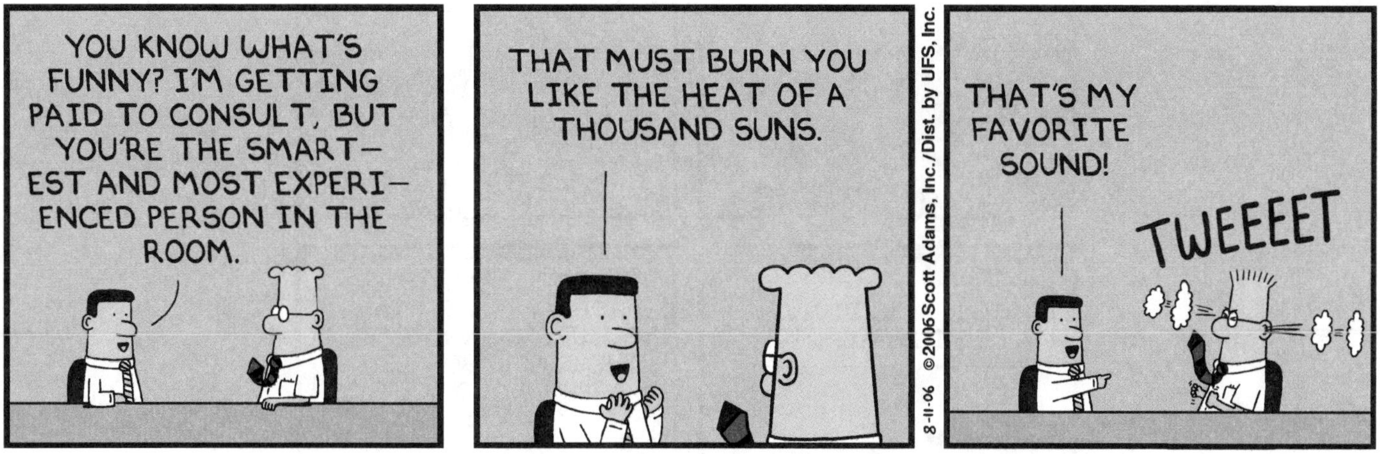
YOU KNOW WHAT'S FUNNY? I'M GETTING PAID TO CONSULT, BUT YOU'RE THE SMART-EST AND MOST EXPERI-ENCED PERSON IN THE ROOM.
THAT MUST BURN YOU LIKE THE HEAT OF A THOUSAND SUNS.
8-11-06 ©2006 Scott Adams, Inc./Dist. by UFS, Inc.
THAT'S MY FAVORITE SOUND!
TWEEEET

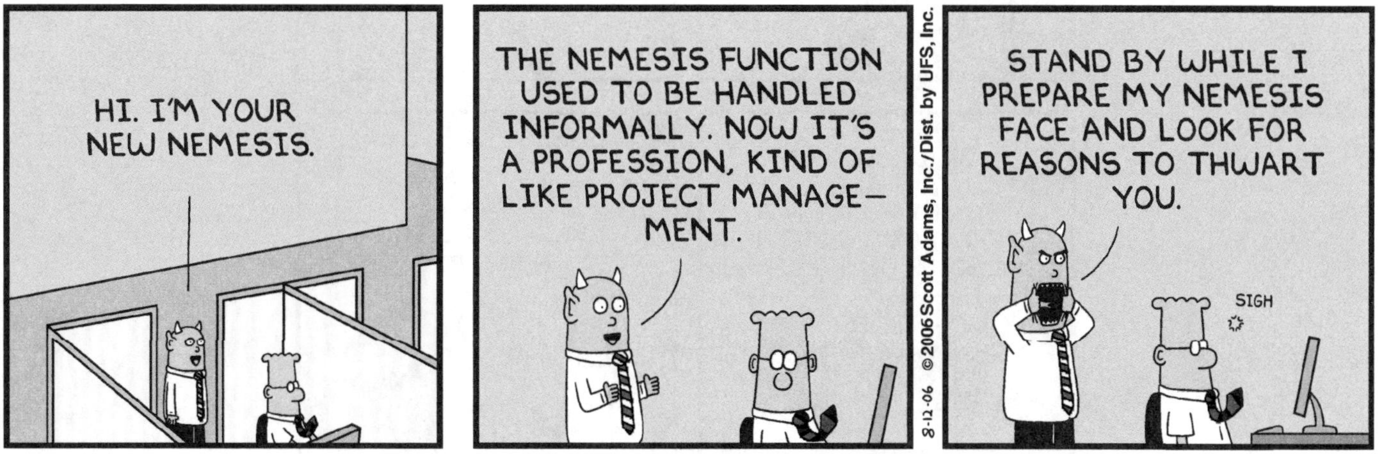
HI. I'M YOUR NEW NEMESIS.
THE NEMESIS FUNCTION USED TO BE HANDLED INFORMALLY. NOW IT'S A PROFESSION, KIND OF LIKE PROJECT MANAGE-MENT.
8-12-06 ©2006 Scott Adams, Inc./Dist. by UFS, Inc.
STAND BY WHILE I PREPARE MY NEMESIS FACE AND LOOK FOR REASONS TO THWART YOU.
SIGH

WHEN DO I NEED TO GIVE THE SPECS TO THE PROGRAMMERS?
THEY DON'T NEED THEM.
WHY? IS IT BECAUSE THEY ALREADY KNOW WHAT TO DO?
©2006 Scott Adams, Inc./Dist. by UFS, Inc.
YES. EXACTLY. THEY KNOW HOW TO DO THAT PART.
WELL, NOW I HAVE A DIFFICULT CHOICE.
I COULD CALL THE PROGRAMMERS, PROVE YOU WRONG, AND SUFFER THE CONSEQUENCES IN A THOUSAND SUBTLE WAYS. . .
OR I COULD DO NOTHING AND WAIT TO GET HOSED FOR NOT PROVIDING THE SPECS ON TIME.
8-13-06
GEEZ. YOU COMPLAIN WHEN I DON'T GIVE YOU CHOICES TOO.

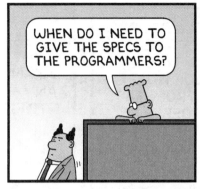

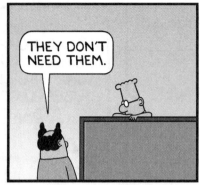

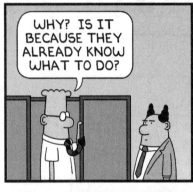

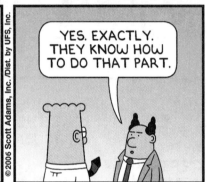

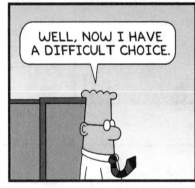

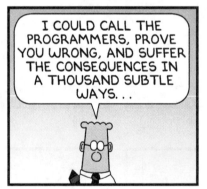

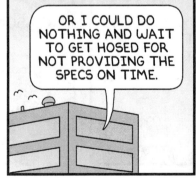

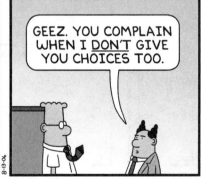

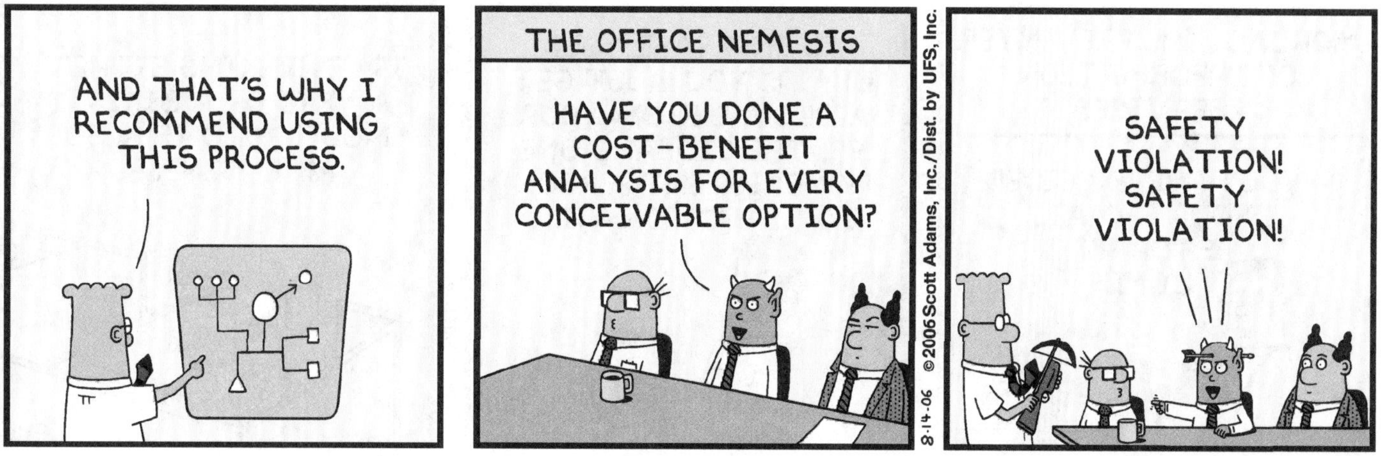
AND THAT'S WHY I RECOMMEND USING THIS PROCESS.
THE OFFICE NEMESIS
HAVE YOU DONE A COST-BENEFIT ANALYSIS FOR EVERY CONCEIVABLE OPTION?
8-14-06 ©2006 Scott Adams, Inc./Dist. by UFS, Inc.
SAFETY VIOLATION! SAFETY VIOLATION!

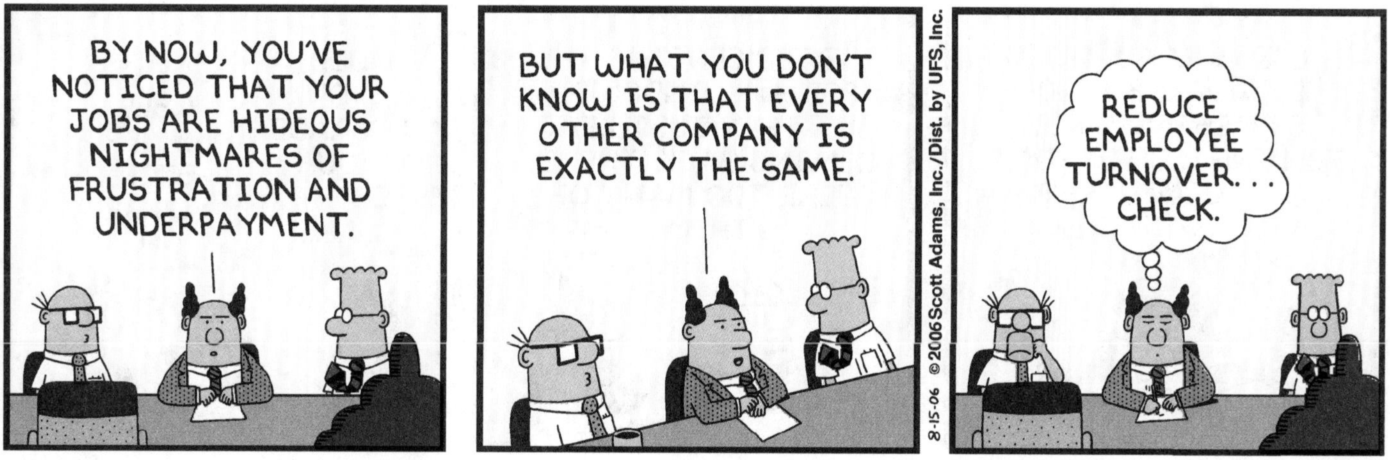
BY NOW, YOU'VE NOTICED THAT YOUR JOBS ARE HIDEOUS NIGHTMARES OF FRUSTRATION AND UNDERPAYMENT.
BUT WHAT YOU DON'T KNOW IS THAT EVERY OTHER COMPANY IS EXACTLY THE SAME.
8-15-06 ©2006 Scott Adams, Inc./Dist. by UFS, Inc.
REDUCE EMPLOYEE TURNOVER. . . CHECK.

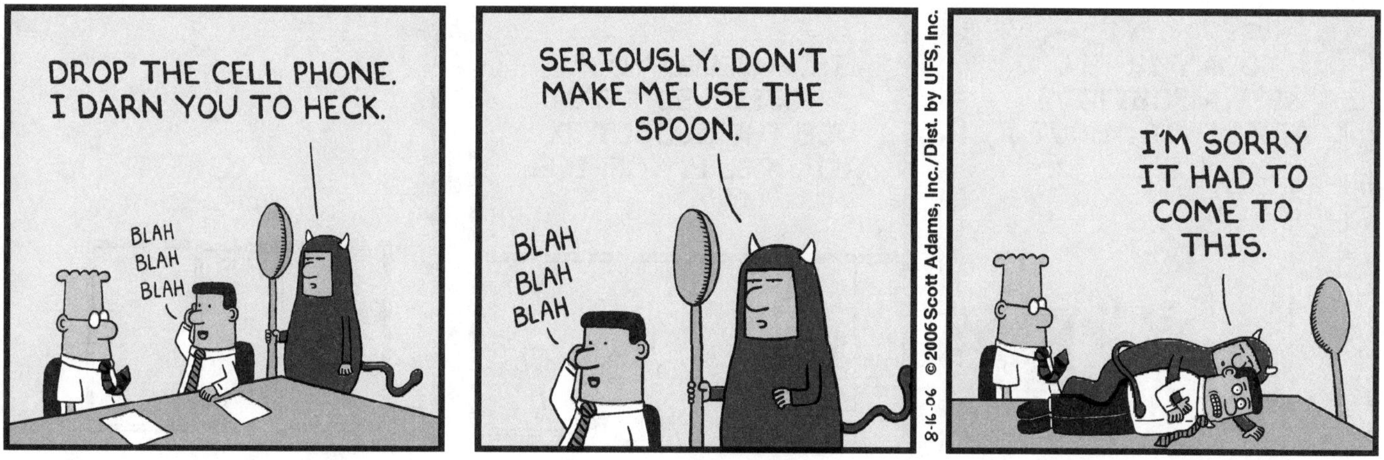
DROP THE CELL PHONE. I DARN YOU TO HECK.
BLAH BLAH BLAH
SERIOUSLY. DON'T MAKE ME USE THE SPOON.
BLAH BLAH BLAH
8-16-06 ©2006 Scott Adams, Inc./Dist. by UFS, Inc.
I'M SORRY IT HAD TO COME TO THIS.

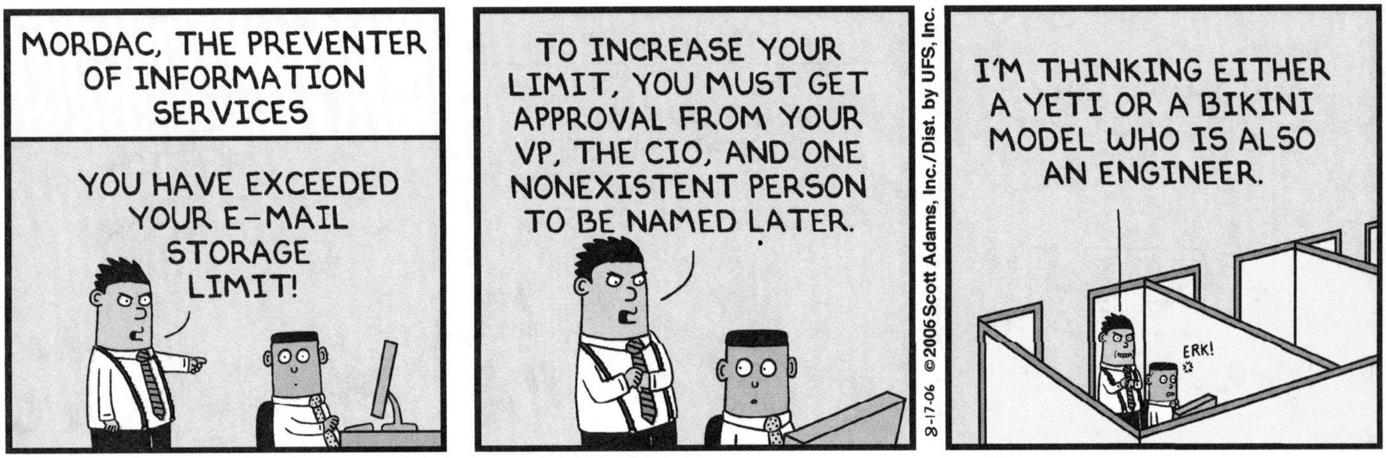
MORDAC, THE PREVENTER OF INFORMATION SERVICES
YOU HAVE EXCEEDED YOUR E-MAIL STORAGE LIMIT!
TO INCREASE YOUR LIMIT, YOU MUST GET APPROVAL FROM YOUR VP, THE CIO, AND ONE NONEXISTENT PERSON TO BE NAMED LATER.
8-17-06 © 2006 Scott Adams, Inc./Dist. by UFS, Inc.
I'M THINKING EITHER A YETI OR A BIKINI MODEL WHO IS ALSO AN ENGINEER.
ERK!

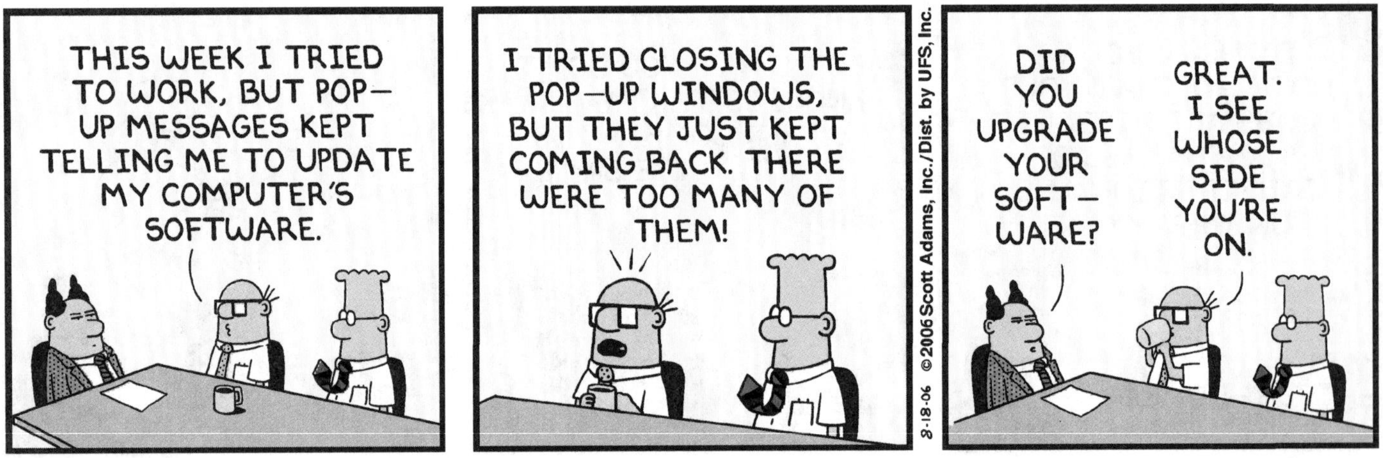
THIS WEEK I TRIED TO WORK, BUT POP-UP MESSAGES KEPT TELLING ME TO UPDATE MY COMPUTER'S SOFTWARE.
I TRIED CLOSING THE POP-UP WINDOWS, BUT THEY JUST KEPT COMING BACK. THERE WERE TOO MANY OF THEM!
8-18-06 © 2006 Scott Adams, Inc./Dist. by UFS, Inc.
DID YOU UPGRADE YOUR SOFT-WARE?
GREAT. I SEE WHOSE SIDE YOU'RE ON.

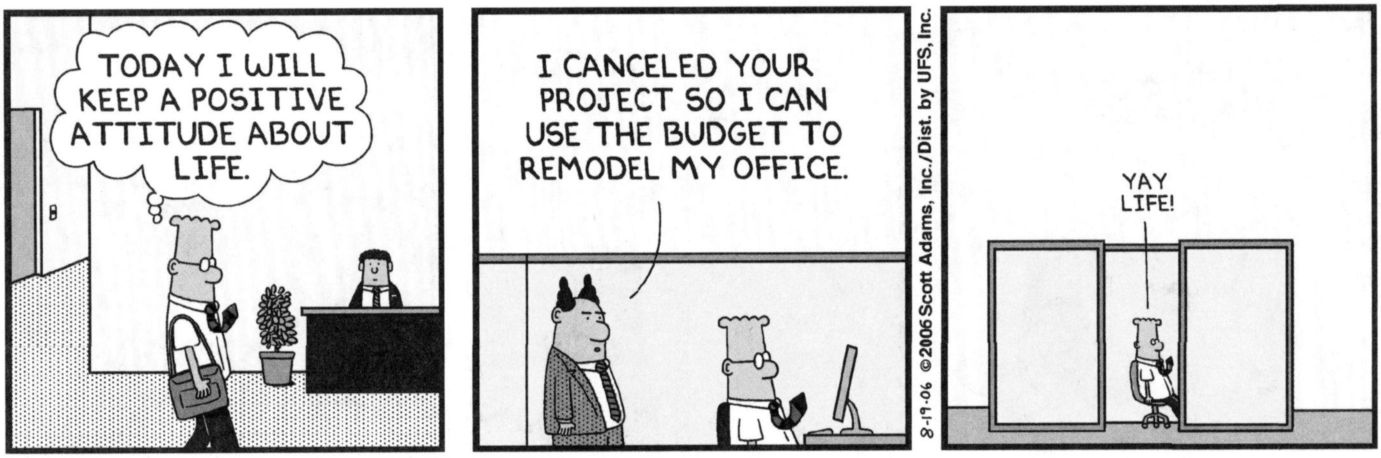
TODAY I WILL KEEP A POSITIVE ATTITUDE ABOUT LIFE.
I CANCELED YOUR PROJECT SO I CAN USE THE BUDGET TO REMODEL MY OFFICE.
8-19-06 © 2006 Scott Adams, Inc./Dist. by UFS, Inc.
YAY LIFE!

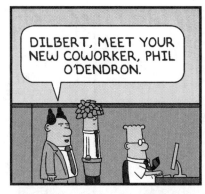

DILBERT, MEET YOUR NEW COWORKER, PHIL O'DENDRON.
PHIL IS A POTTED PLANT. HE'LL SIT IN YOUR CUBICLE ALL DAY WHILE YOU TRY TO WORK.
DOES IT TALK?
HE HAS THREE STORIES THAT HE REPEATS IN AN INFINITE LOOP.
HE'LL BEGIN WITH HIS REASONS FOR WHY YOU SHOULD USE HIS TAX GUY.
THEN HE'LL DO A RECAP OF RECENT REALITY TV SHOWS.
AND LAST BUT NOT LEAST, "THE WAY WE DID IT AT MY LAST JOB."
SOB
HOW DO YOU PLAN TO CUT EXPENSES?
WELL, PERFOR-MANCE BONUSES ARE UNDER CONTROL.
©2006 Scott Adams, Inc./Dist. by UFS, Inc.
8-20-06

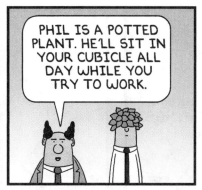

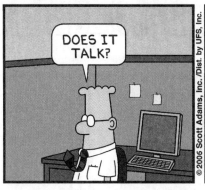

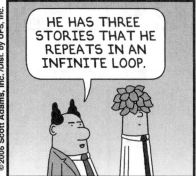

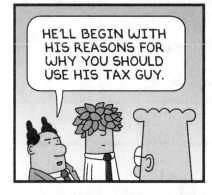

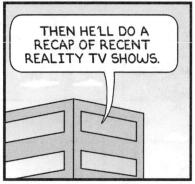

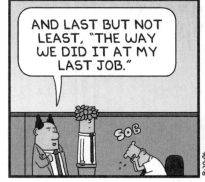

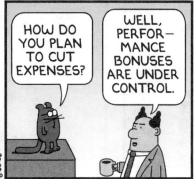

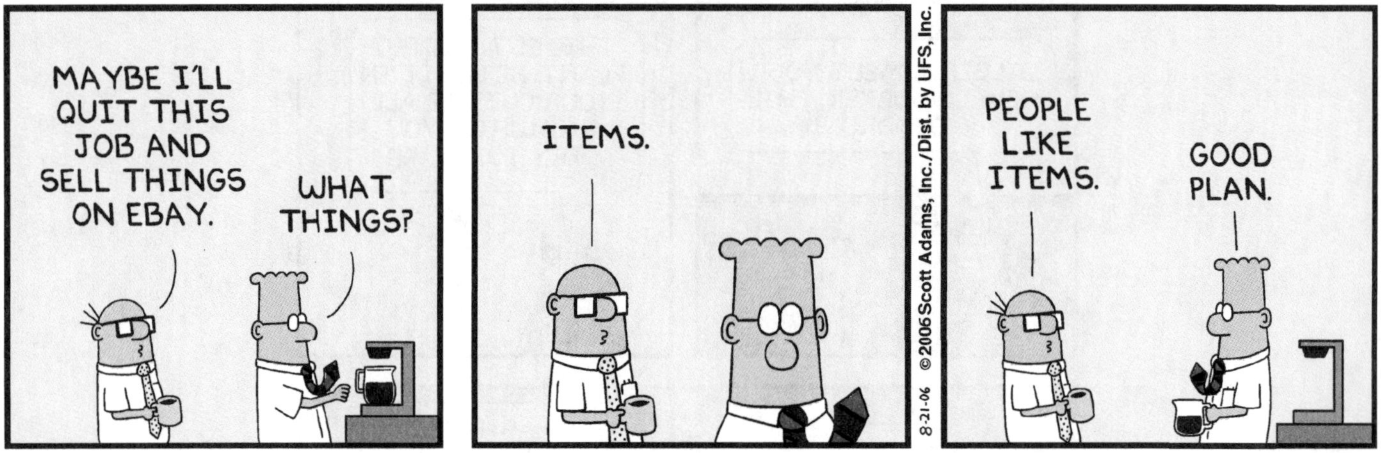
MAYBE I'LL QUIT THIS JOB AND SELL THINGS ON EBAY.
WHAT THINGS?
ITEMS.
8-21-06 © 2006 Scott Adams, Inc./Dist. by UFS, Inc.
PEOPLE LIKE ITEMS.
GOOD PLAN.

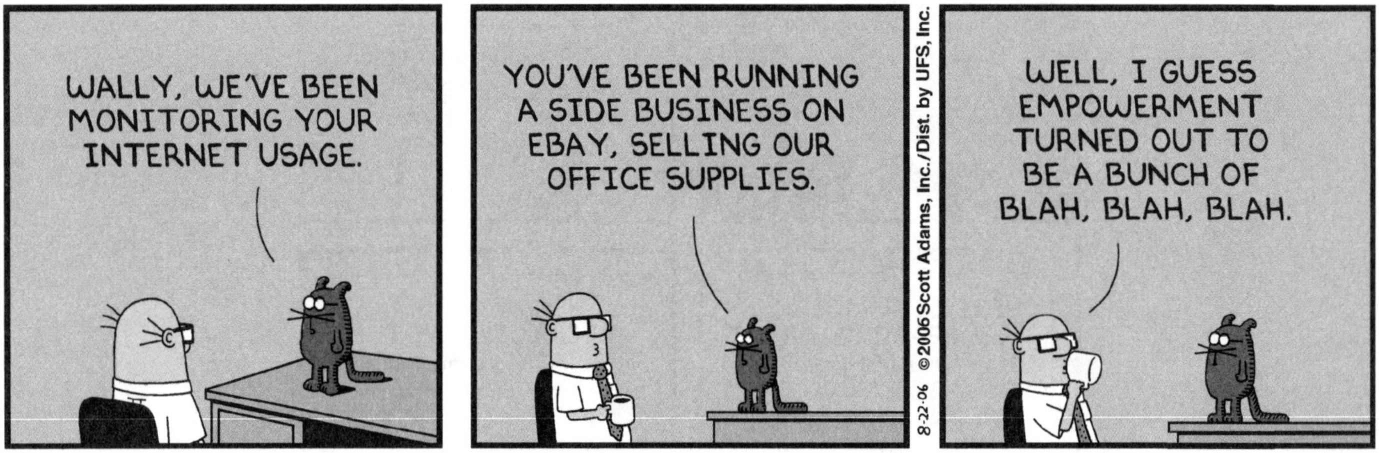
WALLY, WE'VE BEEN MONITORING YOUR INTERNET USAGE.
YOU'VE BEEN RUNNING A SIDE BUSINESS ON EBAY, SELLING OUR OFFICE SUPPLIES.
8-22-06 © 2006 Scott Adams, Inc./Dist. by UFS, Inc.
WELL, I GUESS EMPOWERMENT TURNED OUT TO BE A BUNCH OF BLAH, BLAH, BLAH.

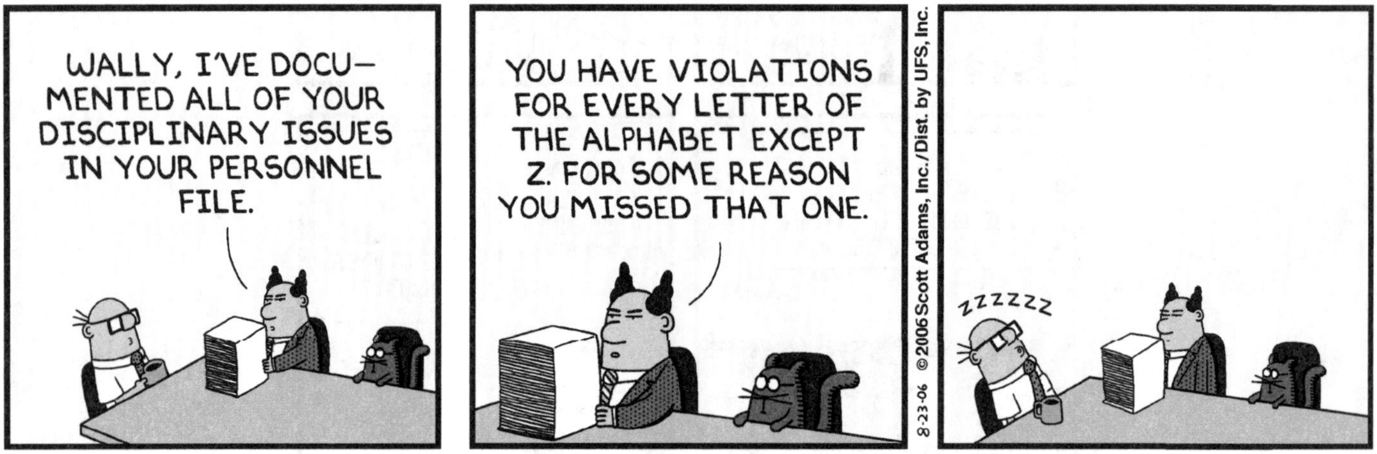
WALLY, I'VE DOCU- MENTED ALL OF YOUR DISCIPLINARY ISSUES IN YOUR PERSONNEL FILE.
YOU HAVE VIOLATIONS FOR EVERY LETTER OF THE ALPHABET EXCEPT Z. FOR SOME REASON YOU MISSED THAT ONE.
8-23-06 © 2006 Scott Adams, Inc./Dist. by UFS, Inc.
ZZZZZZ

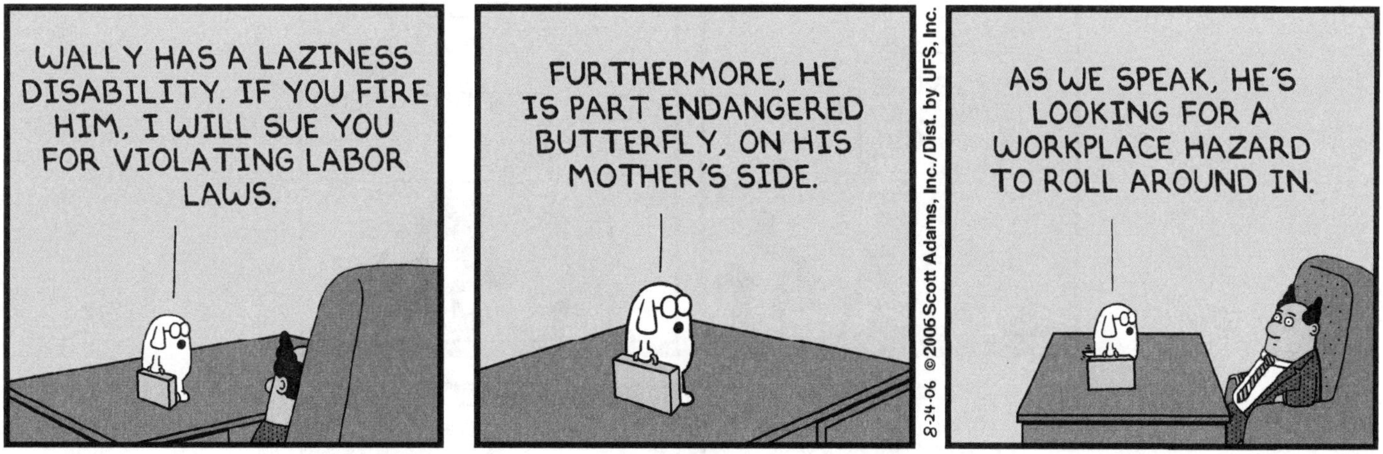
WALLY HAS A LAZINESS DISABILITY. IF YOU FIRE HIM, I WILL SUE YOU FOR VIOLATING LABOR LAWS.
FURTHERMORE, HE IS PART ENDANGERED BUTTERFLY, ON HIS MOTHER'S SIDE.
8-24-06 ©2006 Scott Adams, Inc./Dist. by UFS, Inc.
AS WE SPEAK, HE'S LOOKING FOR A WORKPLACE HAZARD TO ROLL AROUND IN.

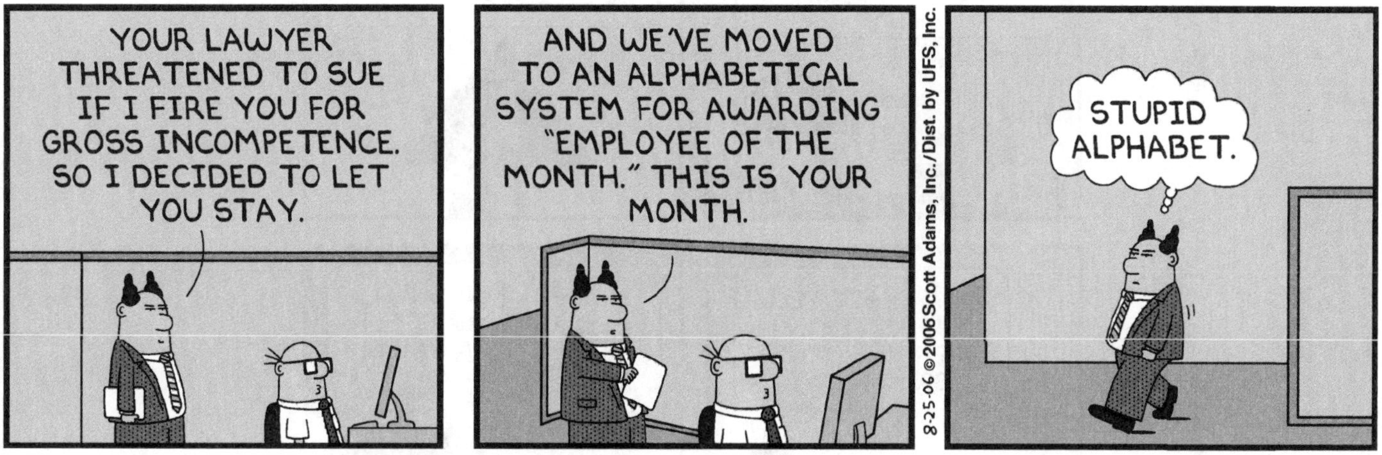
YOUR LAWYER THREATENED TO SUE IF I FIRE YOU FOR GROSS INCOMPETENCE. SO I DECIDED TO LET YOU STAY.
AND WE'VE MOVED TO AN ALPHABETICAL SYSTEM FOR AWARDING "EMPLOYEE OF THE MONTH." THIS IS YOUR MONTH.
8-25-06 ©2006 Scott Adams, Inc./Dist. by UFS, Inc.
STUPID ALPHABET.

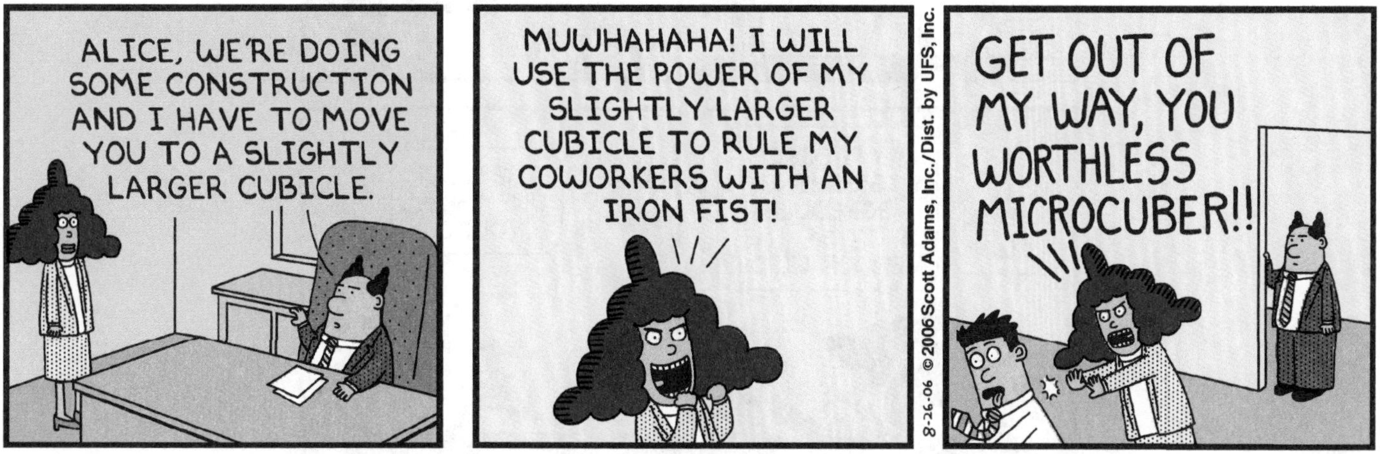
ALICE, WE'RE DOING SOME CONSTRUCTION AND I HAVE TO MOVE YOU TO A SLIGHTLY LARGER CUBICLE.
MUWHAHAHA! I WILL USE THE POWER OF MY SLIGHTLY LARGER CUBICLE TO RULE MY COWORKERS WITH AN IRON FIST!
8-26-06 ©2006 Scott Adams, Inc./Dist. by UFS, Inc.
GET OUT OF MY WAY, YOU WORTHLESS MICROCUBER!!

THERE'S ONE THING YOU SHOULD KNOW. . .
WHOA, WHOA, ASOK!
WHAT?
NEVER TELL HIM ANY-THING WHEN HE'S DIS-TRACTED.
HE WON'T REMEMBER WHAT YOU SAY. LATER HE'LL BLAME YOU FOR NOT TELLING HIM.
©2006 Scott Adams, Inc./Dist. by UFS, Inc.
ALSO AVOID TELLING HIM ANYTHING WHEN HE'S ANGRY, LATE, OR BUSY.
AND DON'T TELL HIM ANYTHING WHEN HE'S TENSE OR HUNGRY.
THAT DOESN'T LEAVE MUCH.
I USUALLY WAIT FOR A YAWN.
YAWN!
MY PROJECT IS BEHIND SCHEDULE BECAUSE THE VENDOR LIED!!!
8-27-06
THE NEXT ONE IS ALL YOURS.

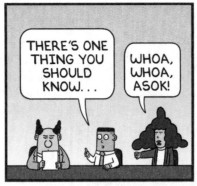

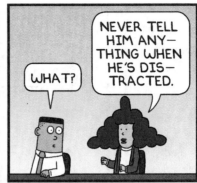

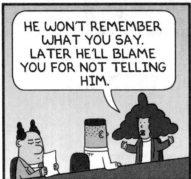

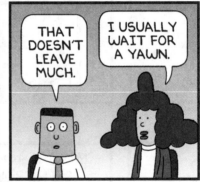

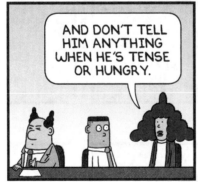

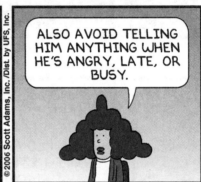

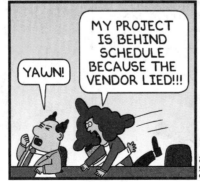

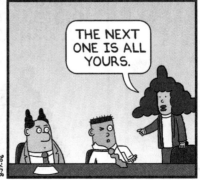

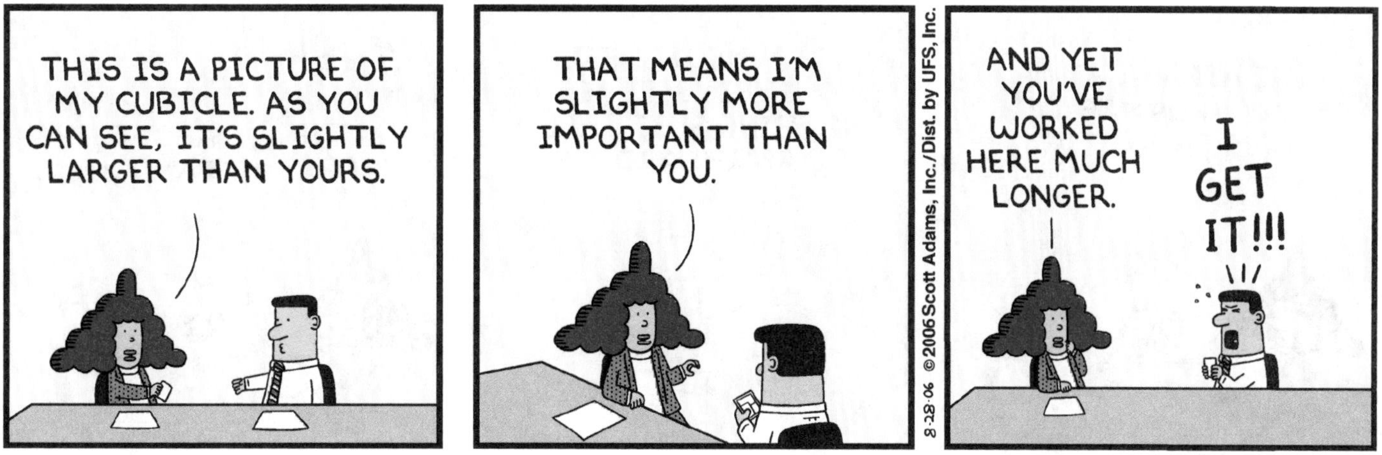
THIS IS A PICTURE OF MY CUBICLE. AS YOU CAN SEE, IT'S SLIGHTLY LARGER THAN YOURS.
THAT MEANS I'M SLIGHTLY MORE IMPORTANT THAN YOU.
8-28-06 © 2006 Scott Adams, Inc./Dist. by UFS, Inc.
AND YET YOU'VE WORKED HERE MUCH LONGER.
I GET IT!!!

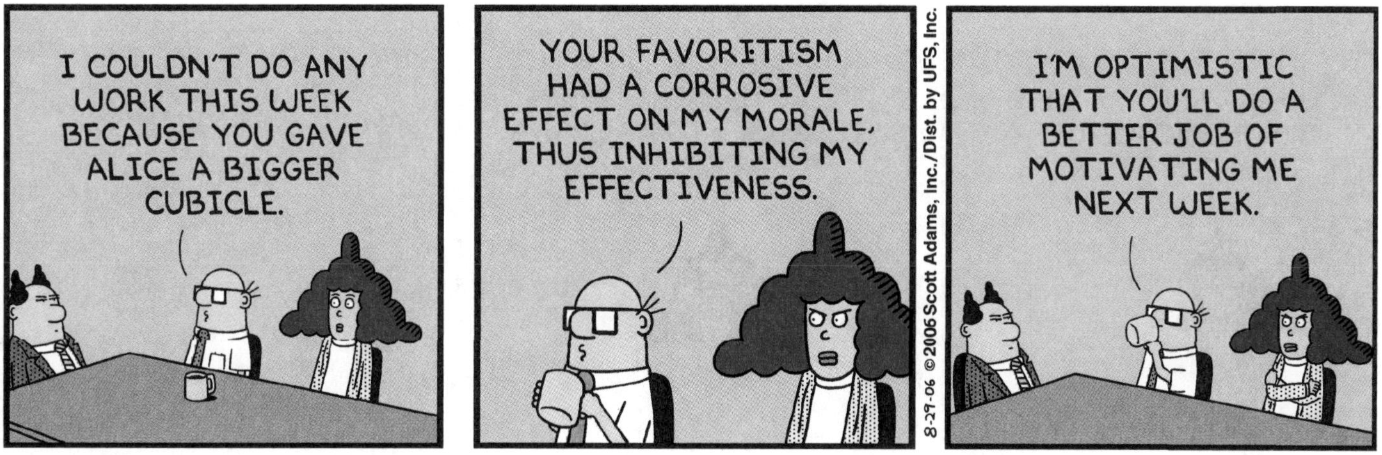
I COULDN'T DO ANY WORK THIS WEEK BECAUSE YOU GAVE ALICE A BIGGER CUBICLE.
YOUR FAVORITISM HAD A CORROSIVE EFFECT ON MY MORALE, THUS INHIBITING MY EFFECTIVENESS.
8-29-06 © 2006 Scott Adams, Inc./Dist. by UFS, Inc.
I'M OPTIMISTIC THAT YOU'LL DO A BETTER JOB OF MOTIVATING ME NEXT WEEK.

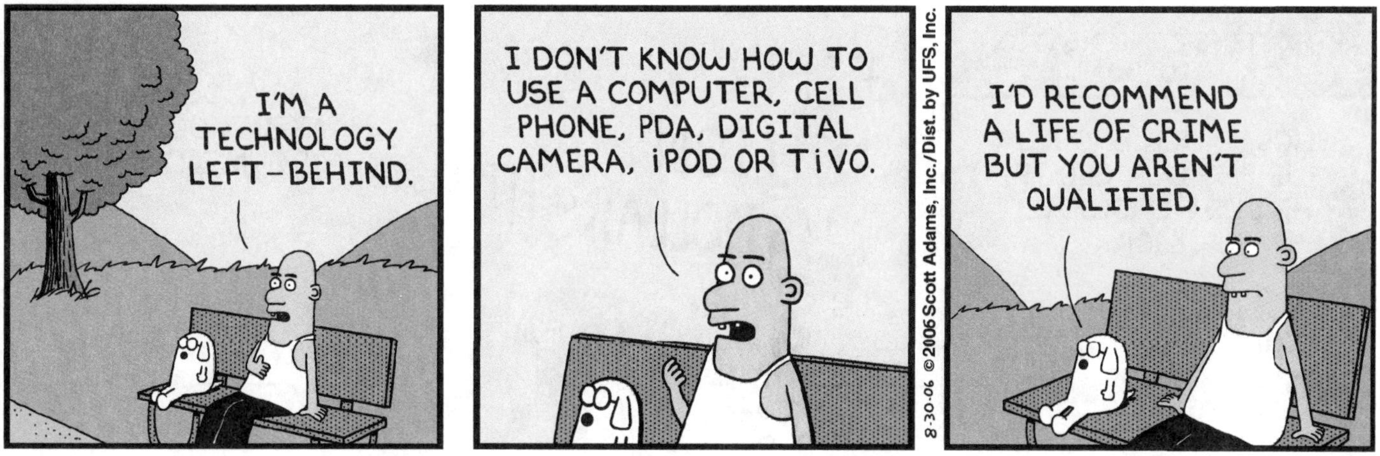
I'M A TECHNOLOGY LEFT-BEHIND.
I DON'T KNOW HOW TO USE A COMPUTER, CELL PHONE, PDA, DIGITAL CAMERA, iPOD OR TiVO.
8-30-06 © 2006 Scott Adams, Inc./Dist. by UFS, Inc.
I'D RECOMMEND A LIFE OF CRIME BUT YOU AREN'T QUALIFIED.

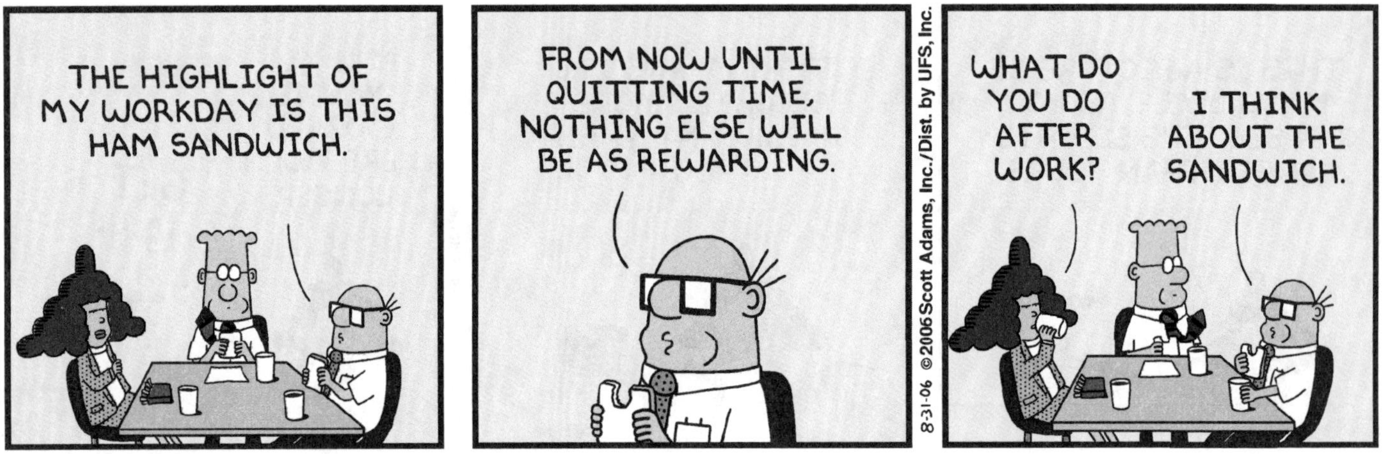
THE HIGHLIGHT OF MY WORKDAY IS THIS HAM SANDWICH.
FROM NOW UNTIL QUITTING TIME, NOTHING ELSE WILL BE AS REWARDING.
8-31-06 ©2006 Scott Adams, Inc./Dist. by UFS, Inc.
WHAT DO YOU DO AFTER WORK?
I THINK ABOUT THE SANDWICH.

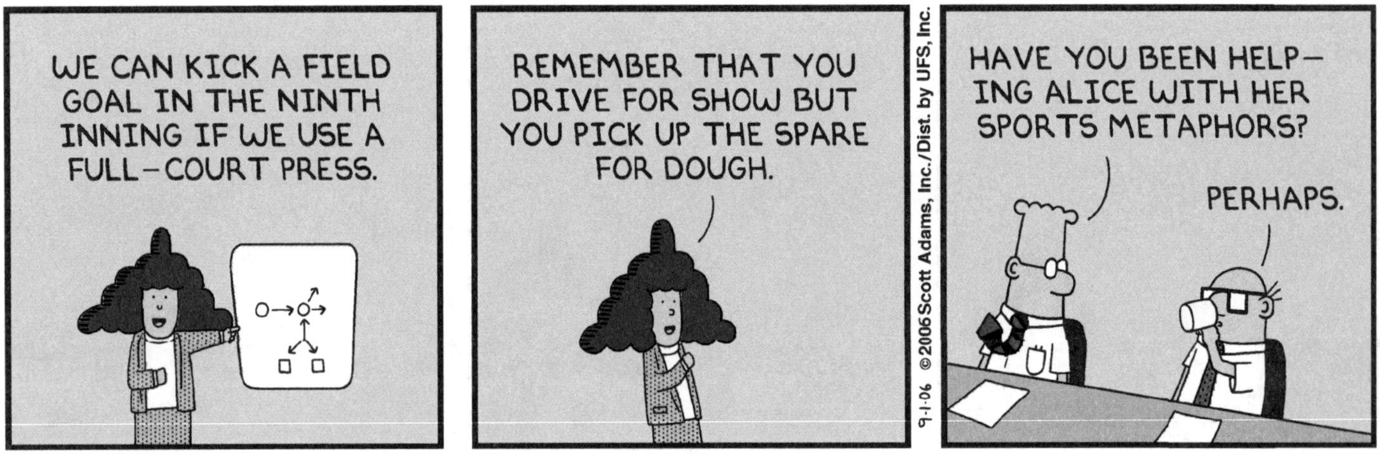
WE CAN KICK A FIELD GOAL IN THE NINTH INNING IF WE USE A FULL-COURT PRESS.
REMEMBER THAT YOU DRIVE FOR SHOW BUT YOU PICK UP THE SPARE FOR DOUGH.
9-1-06 ©2006 Scott Adams, Inc./Dist. by UFS, Inc.
HAVE YOU BEEN HELP-ING ALICE WITH HER SPORTS METAPHORS?
PERHAPS.

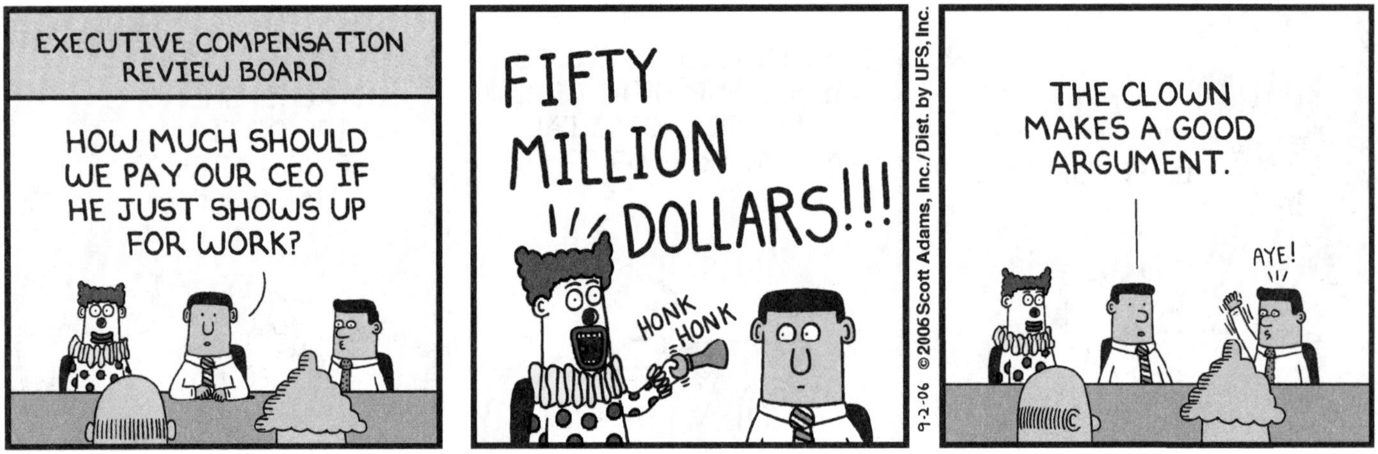
EXECUTIVE COMPENSATION REVIEW BOARD
HOW MUCH SHOULD WE PAY OUR CEO IF HE JUST SHOWS UP FOR WORK?
FIFTY MILLION DOLLARS!!!
HONK HONK
9-2-06 ©2006 Scott Adams, Inc./Dist. by UFS, Inc.
THE CLOWN MAKES A GOOD ARGUMENT.
AYE!

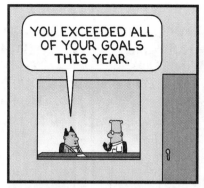

YOU EXCEEDED ALL OF YOUR GOALS THIS YEAR.
BUT I CAN'T GIVE YOU MUCH OF A RAISE BECAUSE YOU DIDN'T HAVE THE APPEARANCE OF SUCCESS.
UM. . . WHAT?
I HAVE TO JUSTIFY TO MANAGEMENT ALL LARGE RAISES, AND THEY DON'T KNOW THAT YOU EXIST.
WHO DO THEY THINK ACCOMPLISHED ALL OF MY GOALS?
I'LL MAKE IT UP TO YOU NEXT YEAR.
PUSH
WHO WAS THAT?
SOME VENDOR.
© 2006 Scott Adams, Inc. /Dist. by UFS, Inc.
9-3-06

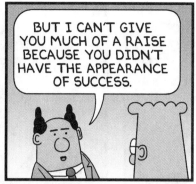

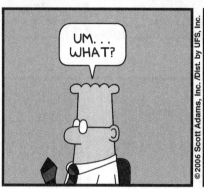

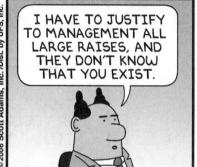

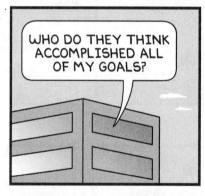

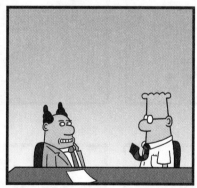

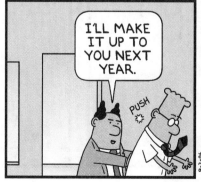

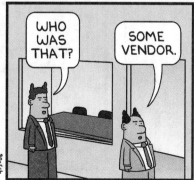

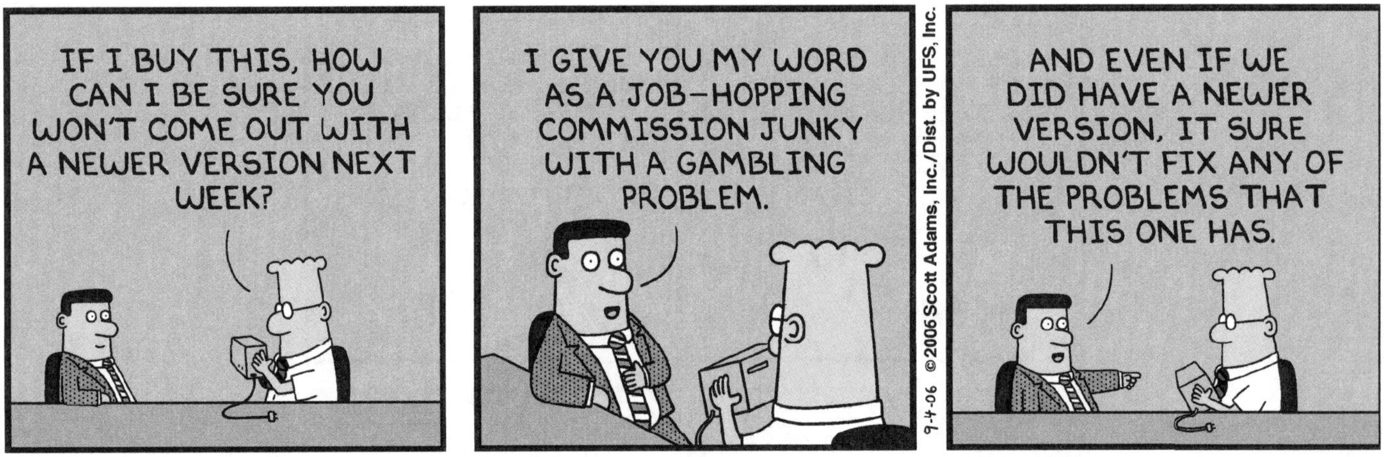
IF I BUY THIS, HOW CAN I BE SURE YOU WON'T COME OUT WITH A NEWER VERSION NEXT WEEK?
I GIVE YOU MY WORD AS A JOB-HOPPING COMMISSION JUNKY WITH A GAMBLING PROBLEM.
9-4-06 ©2006 Scott Adams, Inc./Dist. by UFS, Inc.
AND EVEN IF WE DID HAVE A NEWER VERSION, IT SURE WOULDN'T FIX ANY OF THE PROBLEMS THAT THIS ONE HAS.

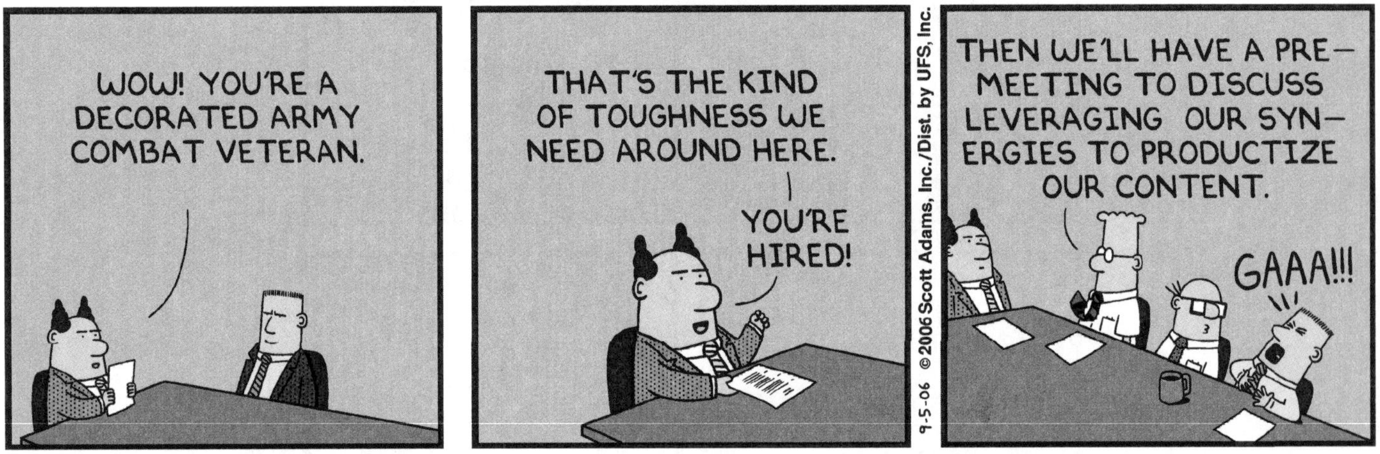
WOW! YOU'RE A DECORATED ARMY COMBAT VETERAN.
THAT'S THE KIND OF TOUGHNESS WE NEED AROUND HERE.
YOU'RE HIRED!
9-5-06 ©2006 Scott Adams, Inc./Dist. by UFS, Inc.
THEN WE'LL HAVE A PRE-MEETING TO DISCUSS LEVERAGING OUR SYNERGIES TO PRODUCTIZE OUR CONTENT.
GAAA!!!

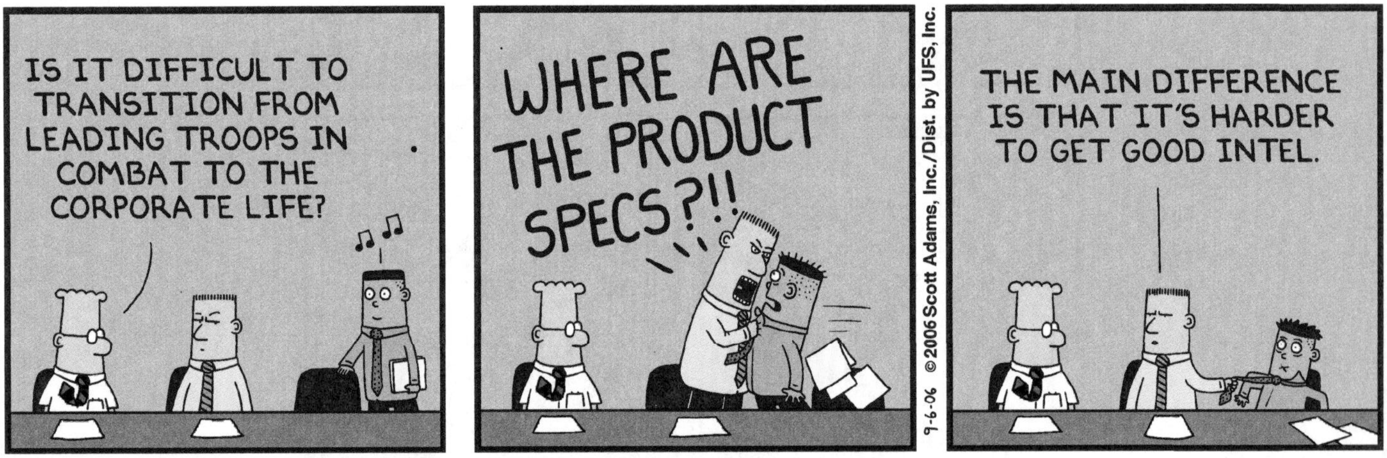
IS IT DIFFICULT TO TRANSITION FROM LEADING TROOPS IN COMBAT TO THE CORPORATE LIFE?
WHERE ARE THE PRODUCT SPECS?!!
9-6-06 ©2006 Scott Adams, Inc./Dist. by UFS, Inc.
THE MAIN DIFFERENCE IS THAT IT'S HARDER TO GET GOOD INTEL.

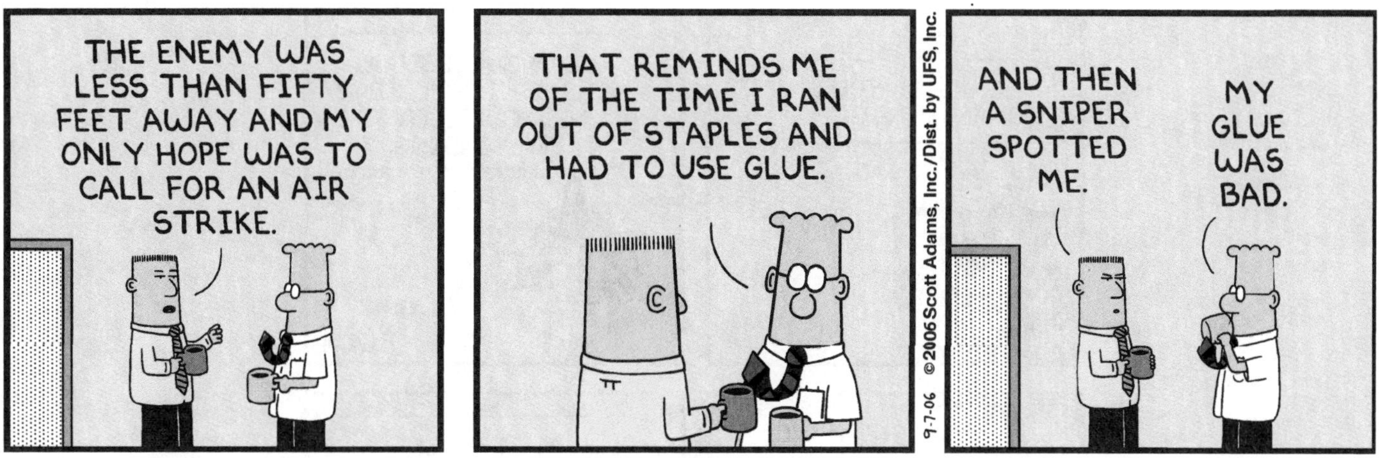
THE ENEMY WAS LESS THAN FIFTY FEET AWAY AND MY ONLY HOPE WAS TO CALL FOR AN AIR STRIKE.
THAT REMINDS ME OF THE TIME I RAN OUT OF STAPLES AND HAD TO USE GLUE.
AND THEN A SNIPER SPOTTED ME.
MY GLUE WAS BAD.
9-7-06 © 2006 Scott Adams, Inc./Dist. by UFS, Inc.

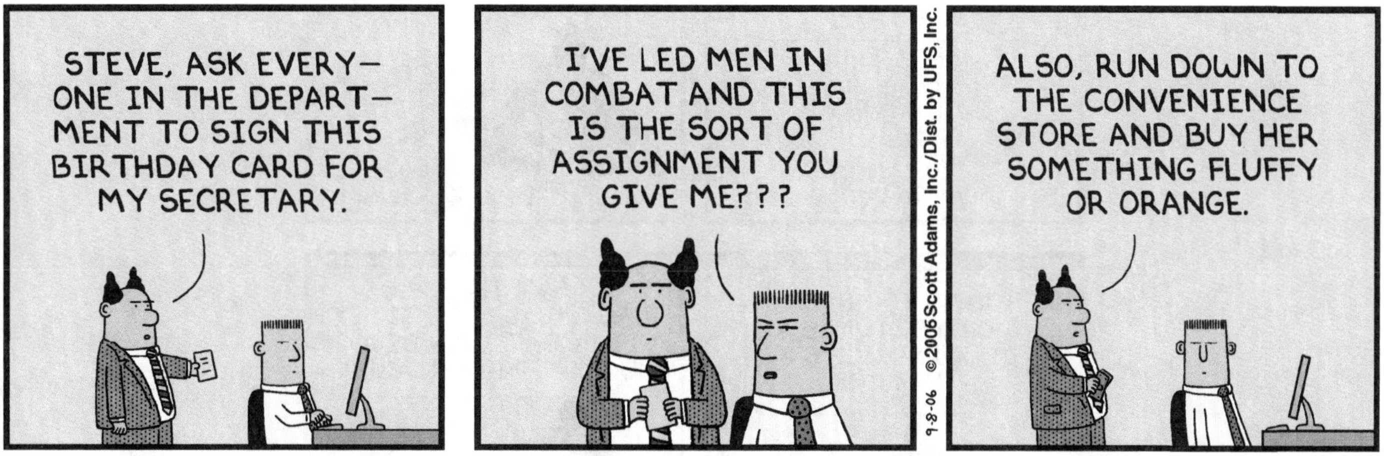
STEVE, ASK EVERY-ONE IN THE DEPART-MENT TO SIGN THIS BIRTHDAY CARD FOR MY SECRETARY.
I'VE LED MEN IN COMBAT AND THIS IS THE SORT OF ASSIGNMENT YOU GIVE ME???
ALSO, RUN DOWN TO THE CONVENIENCE STORE AND BUY HER SOMETHING FLUFFY OR ORANGE.
9-8-06 © 2006 Scott Adams, Inc./Dist. by UFS, Inc.

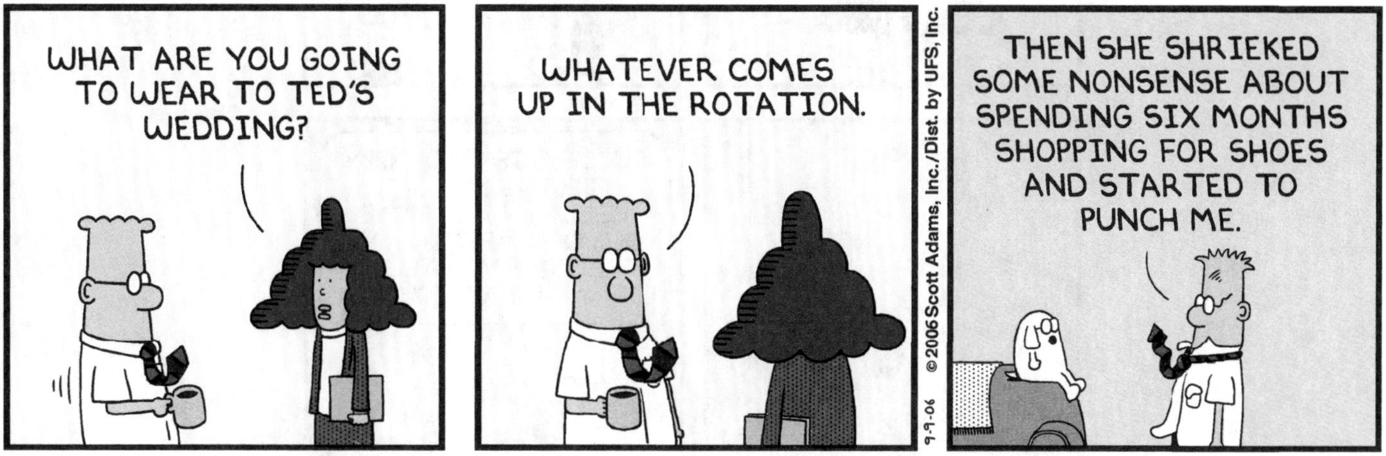
WHAT ARE YOU GOING TO WEAR TO TED'S WEDDING?
WHATEVER COMES UP IN THE ROTATION.
THEN SHE SHRIEKED SOME NONSENSE ABOUT SPENDING SIX MONTHS SHOPPING FOR SHOES AND STARTED TO PUNCH ME.
9-9-06 © 2006 Scott Adams, Inc./Dist. by UFS, Inc.

HOW WAS YOUR CONFERENCE CALL?
VERY SUCCESSFUL. BILL SAID HE'D FIND A NEW SUPPLIER FOR THE CASING.
OR IT MIGHT HAVE BEEN RON, TED, OR BOB. THEY ALL SOUND THE SAME ON THE PHONE.
I HOPE IT WASN'T BILL. HE NEVER FOLLOWS THROUGH.
RON IS TOO OVER-WORKED, TED IS A LIAR AND BOB'S A MORON.
I'D SAY THE CALL WAS A WASTE OF TIME. IT MIGHT EVEN BE A HUGE STEP BACKWARD.
SUCCESS IS THE HAPPY FEELING YOU GET BETWEEN THE TIME YOU DO SOMETHING AND THE TIME YOU TELL A WOMAN WHAT YOU DID.
©2006 Scott Adams, Inc./Dist. by UFS, Inc.
9-10-06

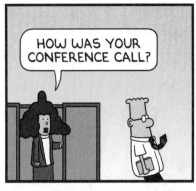

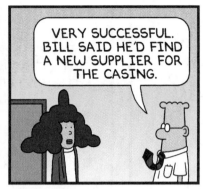

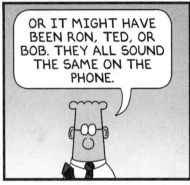

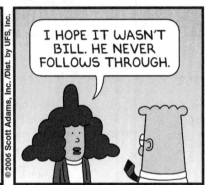

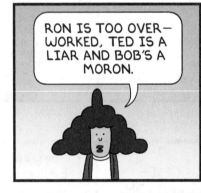

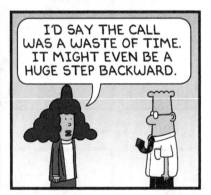

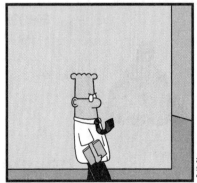

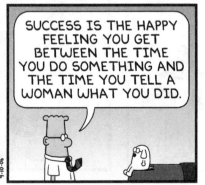

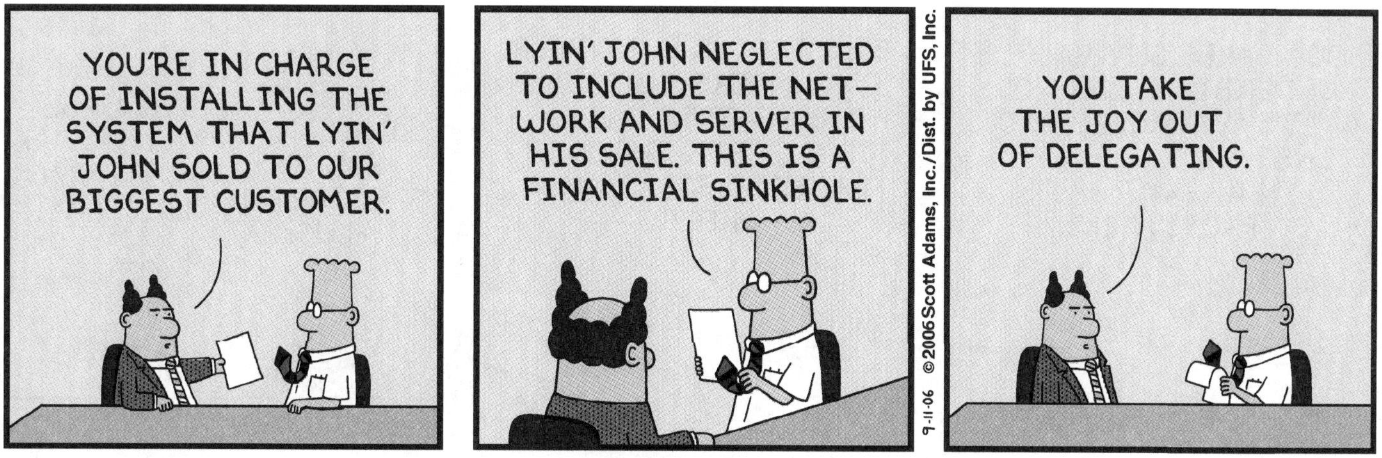
YOU'RE IN CHARGE OF INSTALLING THE SYSTEM THAT LYIN' JOHN SOLD TO OUR BIGGEST CUSTOMER.
LYIN' JOHN NEGLECTED TO INCLUDE THE NET-WORK AND SERVER IN HIS SALE. THIS IS A FINANCIAL SINKHOLE.
9-11-06 ©2006 Scott Adams, Inc./Dist. by UFS, Inc.
YOU TAKE THE JOY OUT OF DELEGATING.

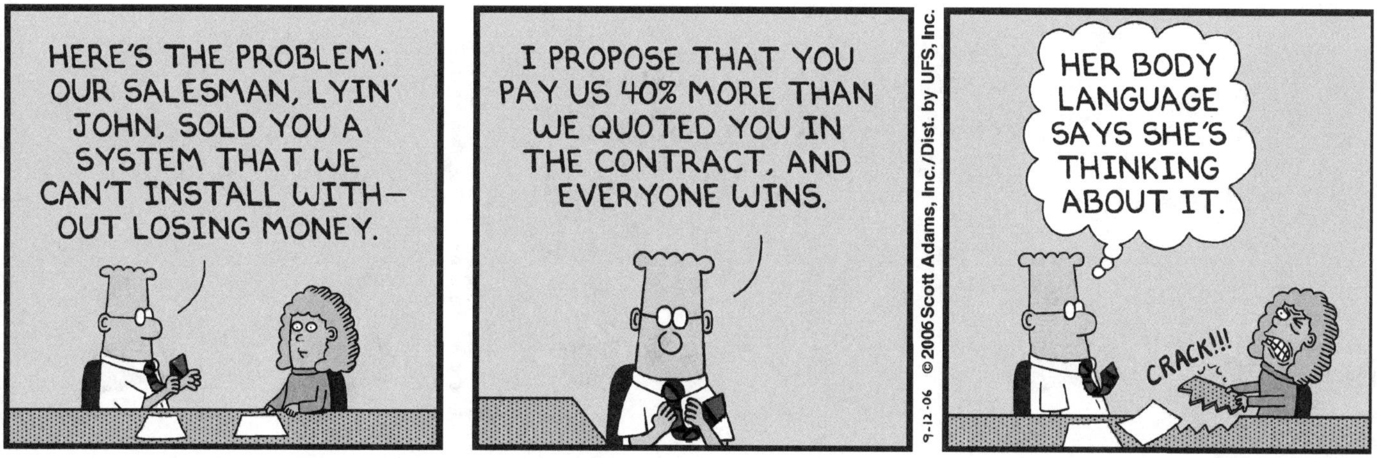
HERE'S THE PROBLEM: OUR SALESMAN, LYIN' JOHN, SOLD YOU A SYSTEM THAT WE CAN'T INSTALL WITH-OUT LOSING MONEY.
I PROPOSE THAT YOU PAY US 40% MORE THAN WE QUOTED YOU IN THE CONTRACT, AND EVERYONE WINS.
9-12-06 ©2006 Scott Adams, Inc./Dist. by UFS, Inc.
HER BODY LANGUAGE SAYS SHE'S THINKING ABOUT IT.
CRACK!!!

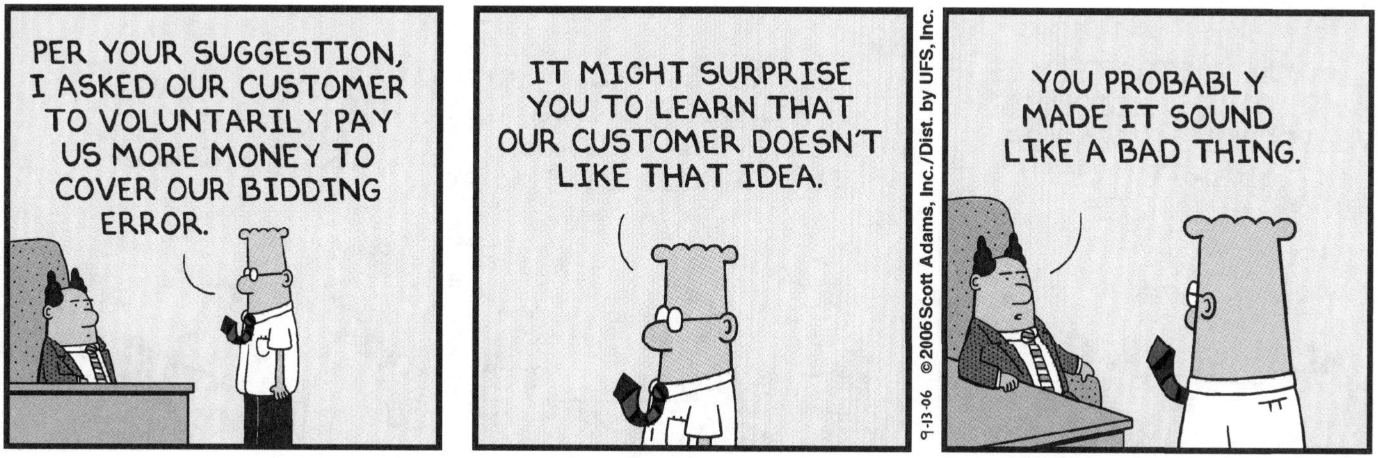
PER YOUR SUGGESTION, I ASKED OUR CUSTOMER TO VOLUNTARILY PAY US MORE MONEY TO COVER OUR BIDDING ERROR.
IT MIGHT SURPRISE YOU TO LEARN THAT OUR CUSTOMER DOESN'T LIKE THAT IDEA.
9-13-06 ©2006 Scott Adams, Inc./Dist. by UFS, Inc.
YOU PROBABLY MADE IT SOUND LIKE A BAD THING.

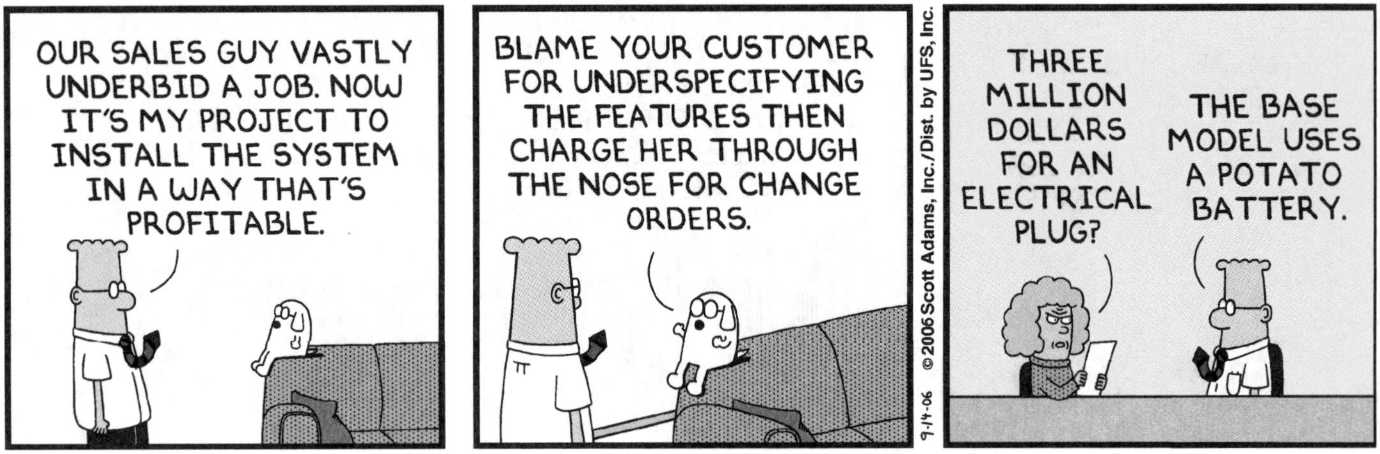
OUR SALES GUY VASTLY UNDERBID A JOB. NOW IT'S MY PROJECT TO INSTALL THE SYSTEM IN A WAY THAT'S PROFITABLE.
BLAME YOUR CUSTOMER FOR UNDERSPECIFYING THE FEATURES THEN CHARGE HER THROUGH THE NOSE FOR CHANGE ORDERS.
9-14-06 © 2006 Scott Adams, Inc./Dist. by UFS, Inc.
THREE MILLION DOLLARS FOR AN ELECTRICAL PLUG?
THE BASE MODEL USES A POTATO BATTERY.

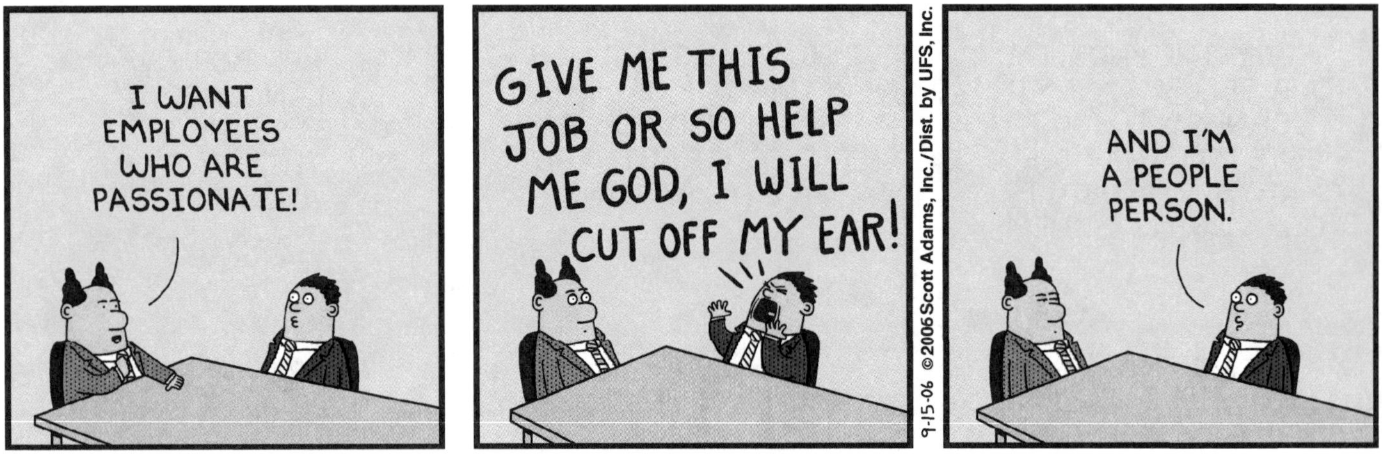
I WANT EMPLOYEES WHO ARE PASSIONATE!
GIVE ME THIS JOB OR SO HELP ME GOD, I WILL CUT OFF MY EAR!
9-15-06 © 2006 Scott Adams, Inc./Dist. by UFS, Inc.
AND I'M A PEOPLE PERSON.

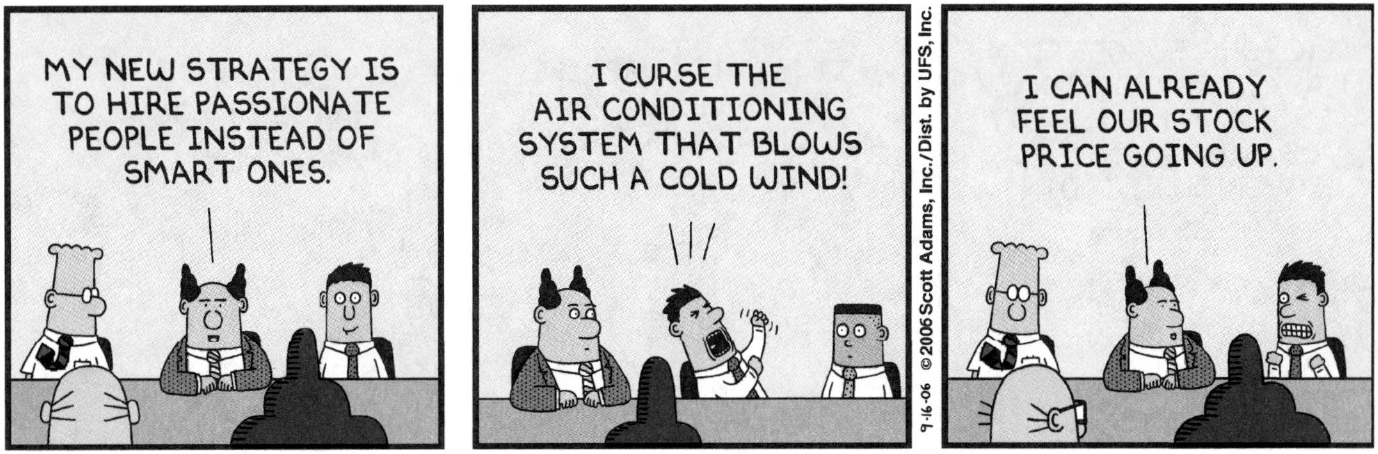
MY NEW STRATEGY IS TO HIRE PASSIONATE PEOPLE INSTEAD OF SMART ONES.
I CURSE THE AIR CONDITIONING SYSTEM THAT BLOWS SUCH A COLD WIND!
9-16-06 © 2006 Scott Adams, Inc./Dist. by UFS, Inc.
I CAN ALREADY FEEL OUR STOCK PRICE GOING UP.

WE DON'T HAVE ENOUGH CHAIRS.
WHY DO I ALWAYS HAVE TO GET THE EXTRA CHAIR?
© 2006 Scott Adams, Inc./Dist. by UFS, Inc.
I NEED TO BORROW YOUR GUEST CHAIR.
NO WAY.
PUNCH PUNCH PUNCH PUNCH PUNCH GAAA!!! PUNCH PUNCH PUNCH PUNCH
9-17-06
IF YOU AREN'T WILLING TO PUNCH A COWORKER FOR A CHAIR, YOU DON'T BELONG IN THIS BUSI-NESS.

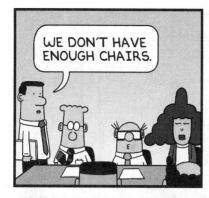

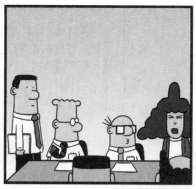

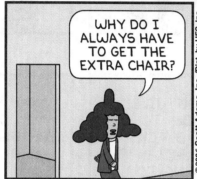

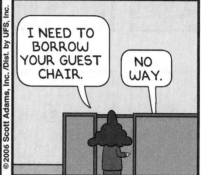

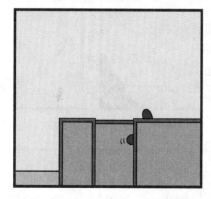

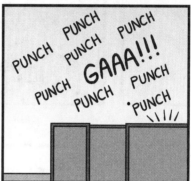

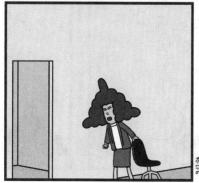

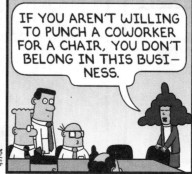

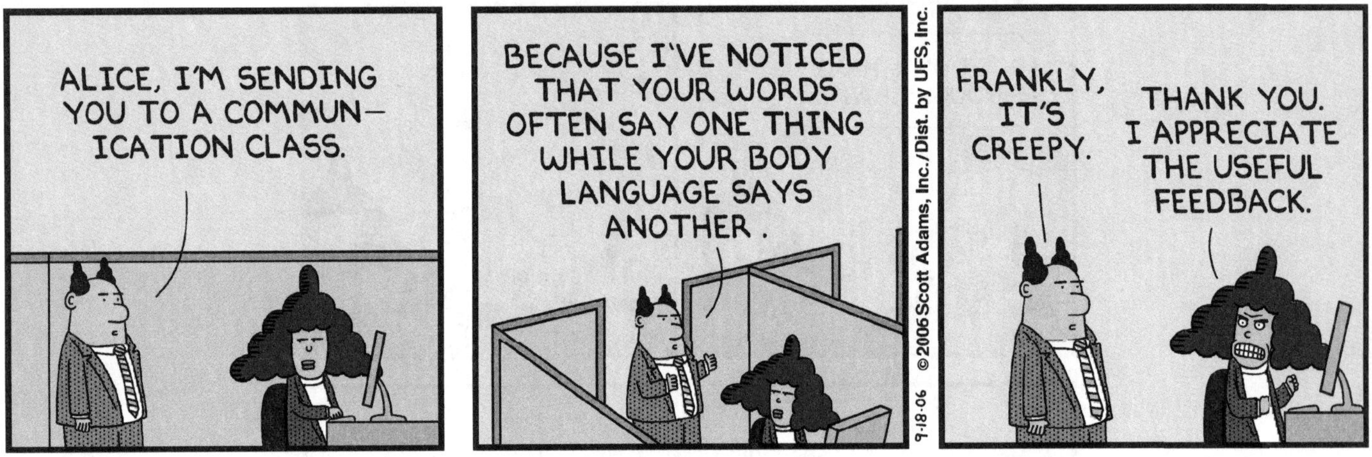
ALICE, I'M SENDING YOU TO A COMMUN- ICATION CLASS.
BECAUSE I'VE NOTICED THAT YOUR WORDS OFTEN SAY ONE THING WHILE YOUR BODY LANGUAGE SAYS ANOTHER .
9-18-06 ©2006 Scott Adams, Inc./Dist. by UFS, Inc.
FRANKLY, IT'S CREEPY.
THANK YOU. I APPRECIATE THE USEFUL FEEDBACK.

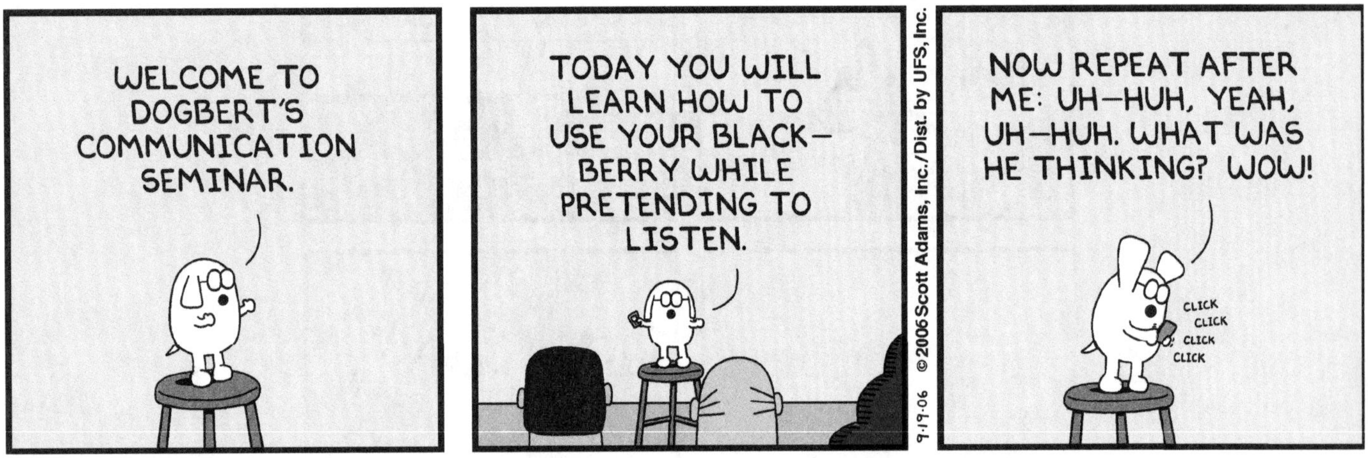
WELCOME TO DOGBERT'S COMMUNICATION SEMINAR.
TODAY YOU WILL LEARN HOW TO USE YOUR BLACK- BERRY WHILE PRETENDING TO LISTEN.
9-19-06 ©2006 Scott Adams, Inc./Dist. by UFS, Inc.
NOW REPEAT AFTER ME: UH-HUH, YEAH, UH-HUH. WHAT WAS HE THINKING? WOW!
CLICK CLICK CLICK CLICK

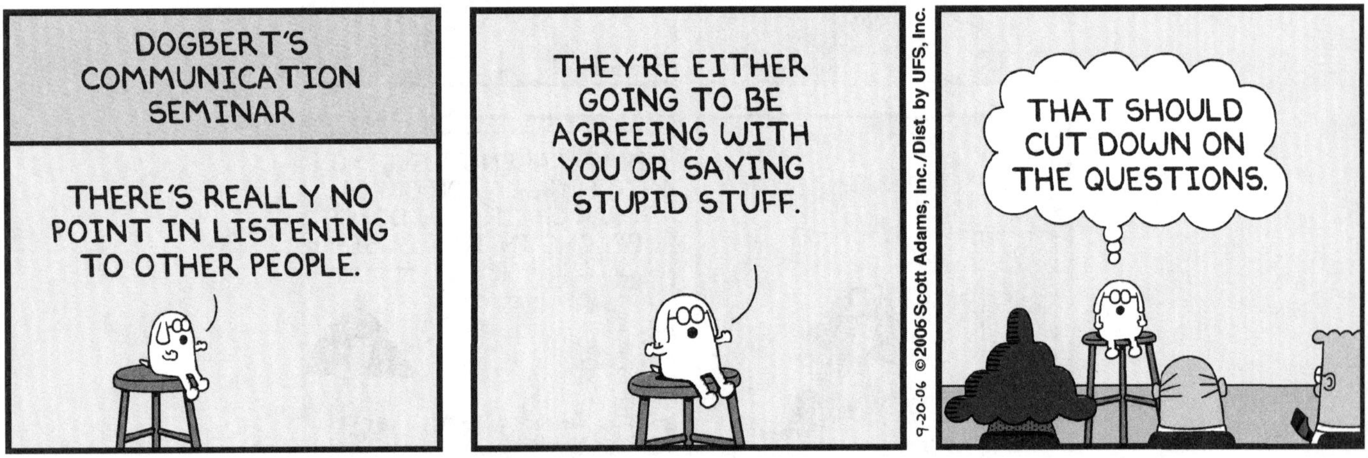
DOGBERT'S COMMUNICATION SEMINAR
THERE'S REALLY NO POINT IN LISTENING TO OTHER PEOPLE.
THEY'RE EITHER GOING TO BE AGREEING WITH YOU OR SAYING STUPID STUFF.
9-20-06 ©2006 Scott Adams, Inc./Dist. by UFS, Inc.
THAT SHOULD CUT DOWN ON THE QUESTIONS.

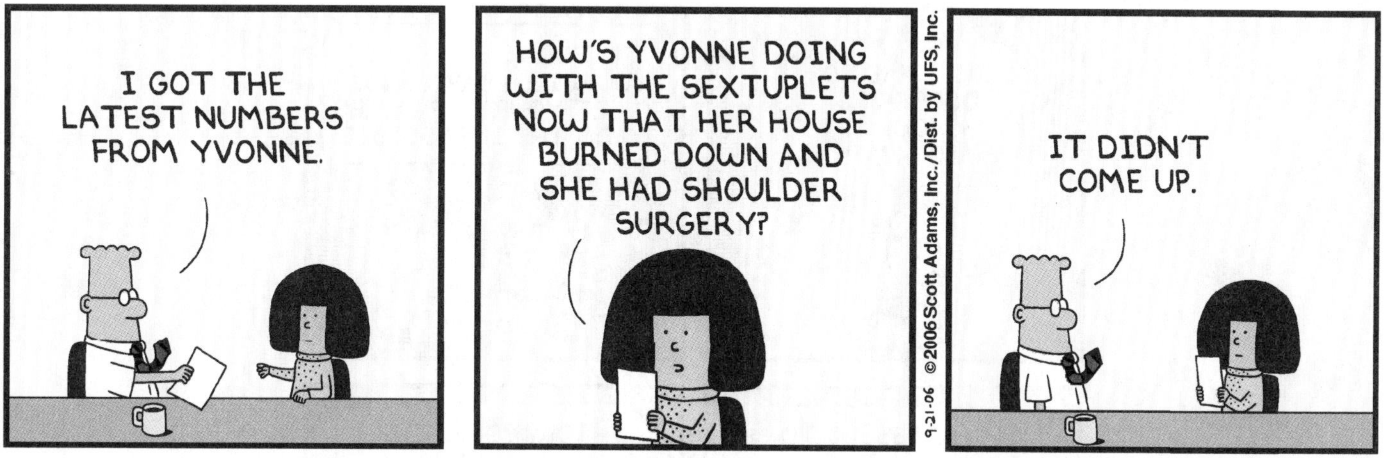
I GOT THE LATEST NUMBERS FROM YVONNE.
HOW'S YVONNE DOING WITH THE SEXTUPLETS NOW THAT HER HOUSE BURNED DOWN AND SHE HAD SHOULDER SURGERY?
IT DIDN'T COME UP.
9-21-06 ©2006 Scott Adams, Inc./Dist. by UFS, Inc.

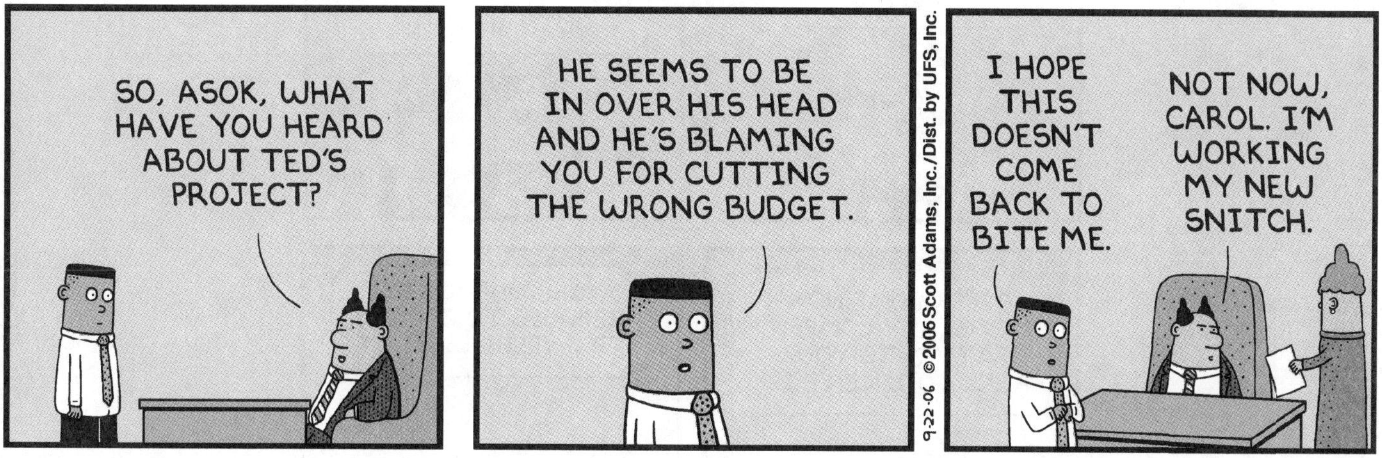
SO, ASOK, WHAT HAVE YOU HEARD ABOUT TED'S PROJECT?
HE SEEMS TO BE IN OVER HIS HEAD AND HE'S BLAMING YOU FOR CUTTING THE WRONG BUDGET.
I HOPE THIS DOESN'T COME BACK TO BITE ME.
NOT NOW, CAROL. I'M WORKING MY NEW SNITCH.
9-22-06 ©2006 Scott Adams, Inc./Dist. by UFS, Inc.

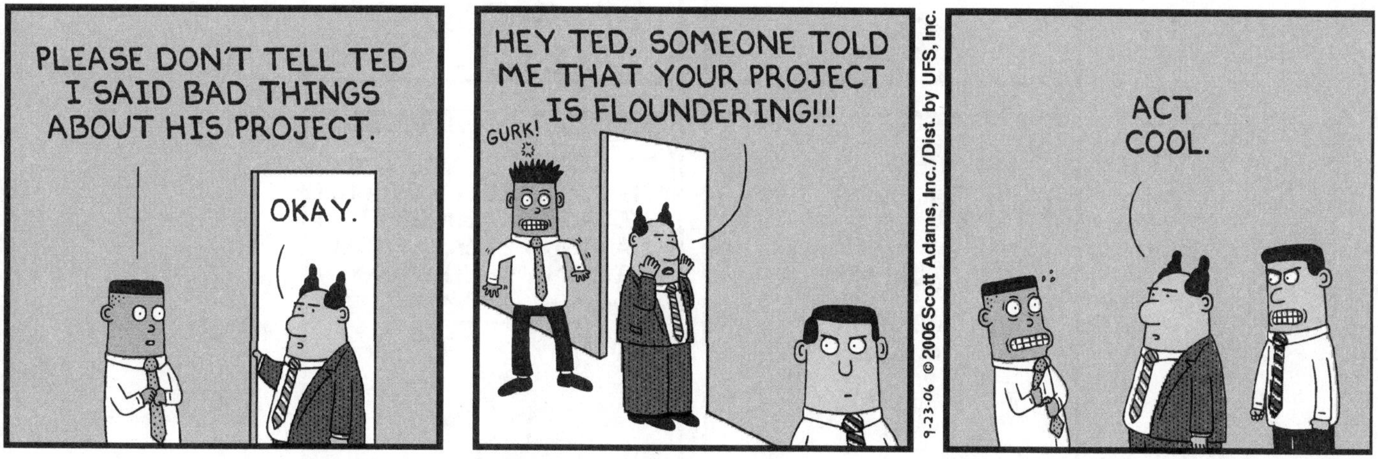
PLEASE DON'T TELL TED I SAID BAD THINGS ABOUT HIS PROJECT.
OKAY.
HEY TED, SOMEONE TOLD ME THAT YOUR PROJECT IS FLOUNDERING!!!
GURK!
ACT COOL.
9-23-06 ©2006 Scott Adams, Inc./Dist. by UFS, Inc.

WELCOME TO DOGBERT'S SCHOOL OF MANAGEMENT.
IN TODAY'S LESSON YOU WILL LEARN HOW TO GET YOUR EMPLOYEES TO DO THE IMPOSSIBLE.
I HAVE ISSUED TO EACH OF YOU ONE LARGE ROCK FOR PRACTICE.
THROW YOUR ROCK IN THE AIR AND DEMAND THAT IT STAY THERE WITH-OUT FALLING.
OFFER SOME NON-MONETARY COMPEN-SATION TO YOUR ROCK TO INCENT IT.
IF YOUR ROCK REFUSES TO COMPLY, TRY YELLING AT IT.
GO.
BONK! - OW!
BONK! - OW!
BONK! - OW!
BONK! - OW!
BONK! - OW!
BONK! - OW!
FOR THOSE OF YOU WHO STOOD DIRECTLY BELOW YOUR ROCK, CONGRAT-ULATIONS. PICK UP YOUR DIPLOMA ON THE WAY OUT.
©2006 Scott Adams, Inc./Dist. by UFS, Inc.
9-24-06

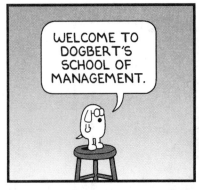

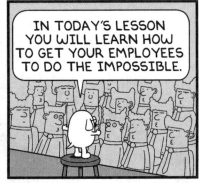

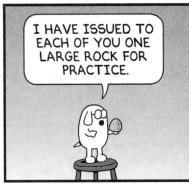

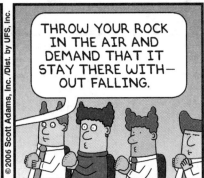

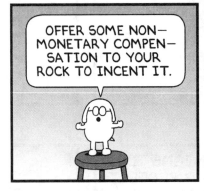

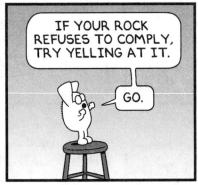

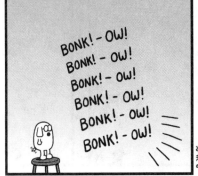

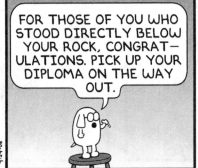

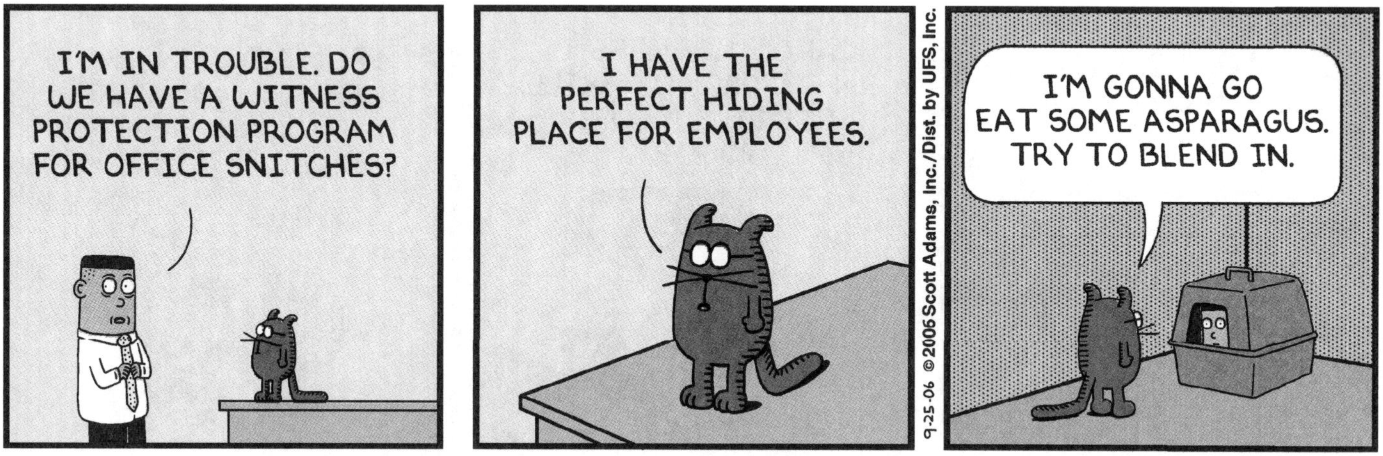
I'M IN TROUBLE. DO WE HAVE A WITNESS PROTECTION PROGRAM FOR OFFICE SNITCHES?
I HAVE THE PERFECT HIDING PLACE FOR EMPLOYEES.
9-25-06 © 2006 Scott Adams, Inc./Dist. by UFS, Inc.
I'M GONNA GO EAT SOME ASPARAGUS. TRY TO BLEND IN.

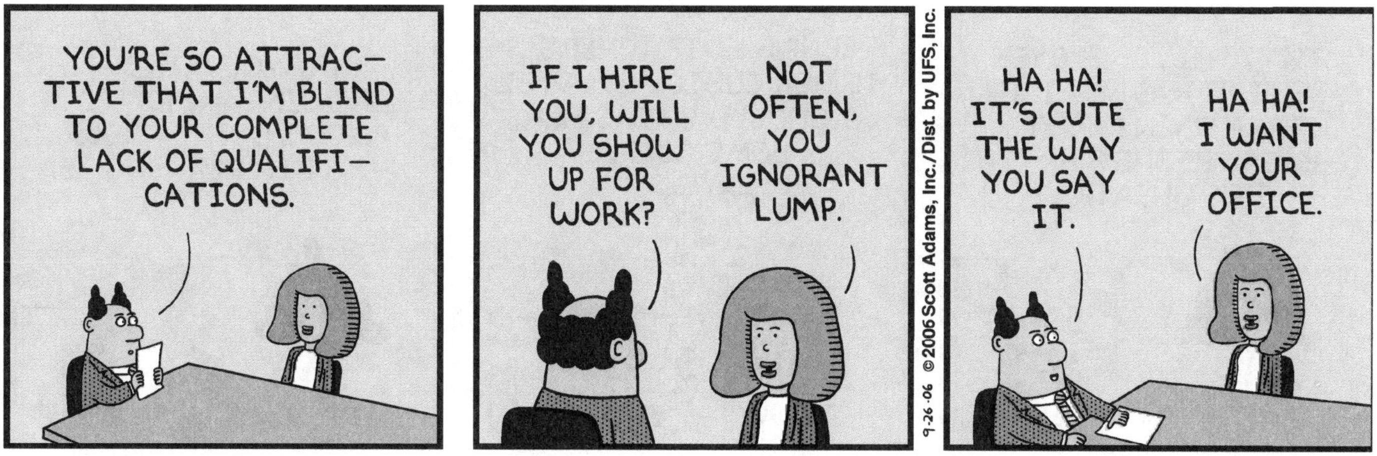
YOU'RE SO ATTRAC- TIVE THAT I'M BLIND TO YOUR COMPLETE LACK OF QUALIFI- CATIONS.
IF I HIRE YOU, WILL YOU SHOW UP FOR WORK?
NOT OFTEN, YOU IGNORANT LUMP.
9-26-06 © 2006 Scott Adams, Inc./Dist. by UFS, Inc.
HA HA! IT'S CUTE THE WAY YOU SAY IT.
HA HA! I WANT YOUR OFFICE.

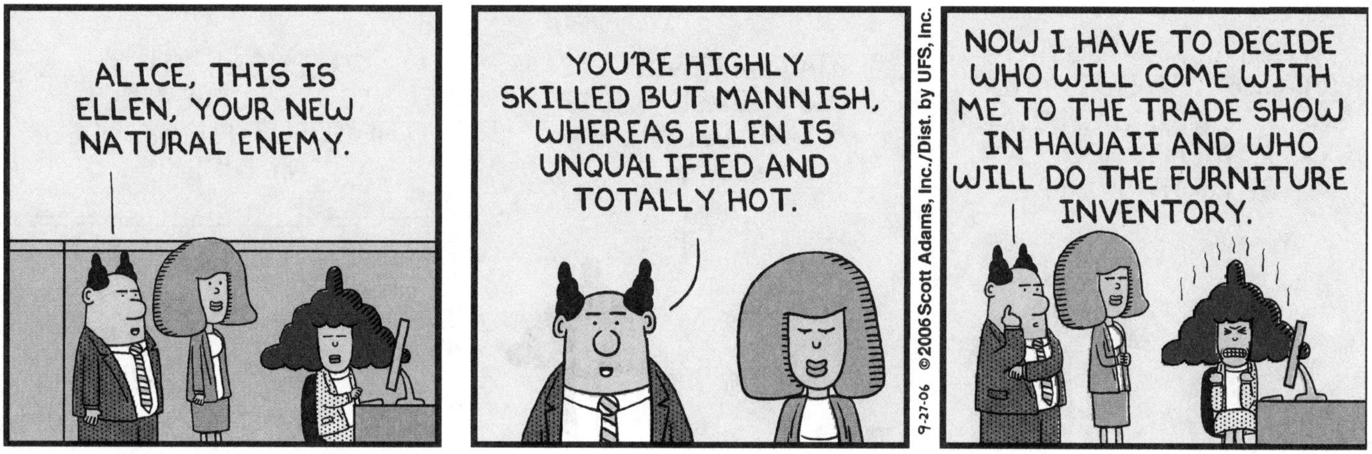
ALICE, THIS IS ELLEN, YOUR NEW NATURAL ENEMY.
YOU'RE HIGHLY SKILLED BUT MANNISH, WHEREAS ELLEN IS UNQUALIFIED AND TOTALLY HOT.
9-27-06 © 2006 Scott Adams, Inc./Dist. by UFS, Inc.
NOW I HAVE TO DECIDE WHO WILL COME WITH ME TO THE TRADE SHOW IN HAWAII AND WHO WILL DO THE FURNITURE INVENTORY.

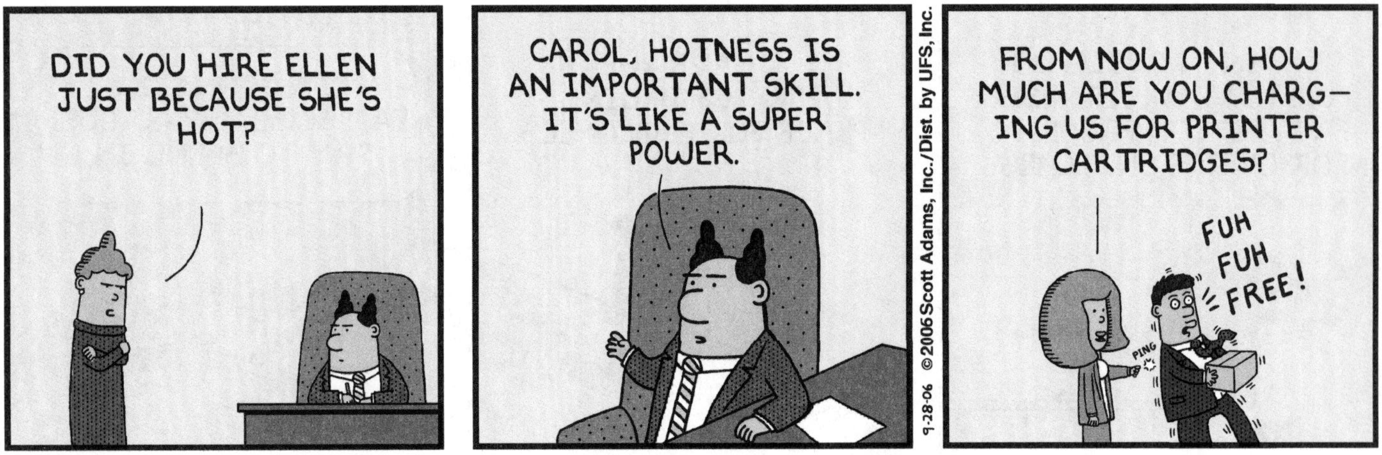
DID YOU HIRE ELLEN JUST BECAUSE SHE'S HOT?
CAROL, HOTNESS IS AN IMPORTANT SKILL. IT'S LIKE A SUPER POWER.
9-28-06 © 2006 Scott Adams, Inc./Dist. by UFS, Inc.
FROM NOW ON, HOW MUCH ARE YOU CHARG– ING US FOR PRINTER CARTRIDGES?
FUH FUH FREE!
PING

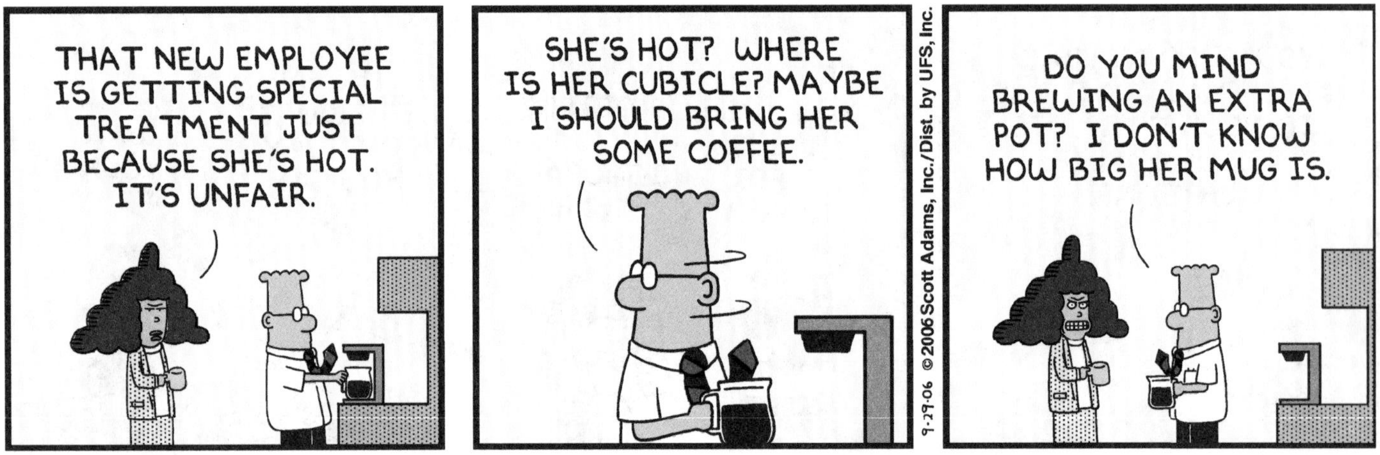
THAT NEW EMPLOYEE IS GETTING SPECIAL TREATMENT JUST BECAUSE SHE'S HOT. IT'S UNFAIR.
SHE'S HOT? WHERE IS HER CUBICLE? MAYBE I SHOULD BRING HER SOME COFFEE.
9-29-06 © 2006 Scott Adams, Inc./Dist. by UFS, Inc.
DO YOU MIND BREWING AN EXTRA POT? I DON'T KNOW HOW BIG HER MUG IS.

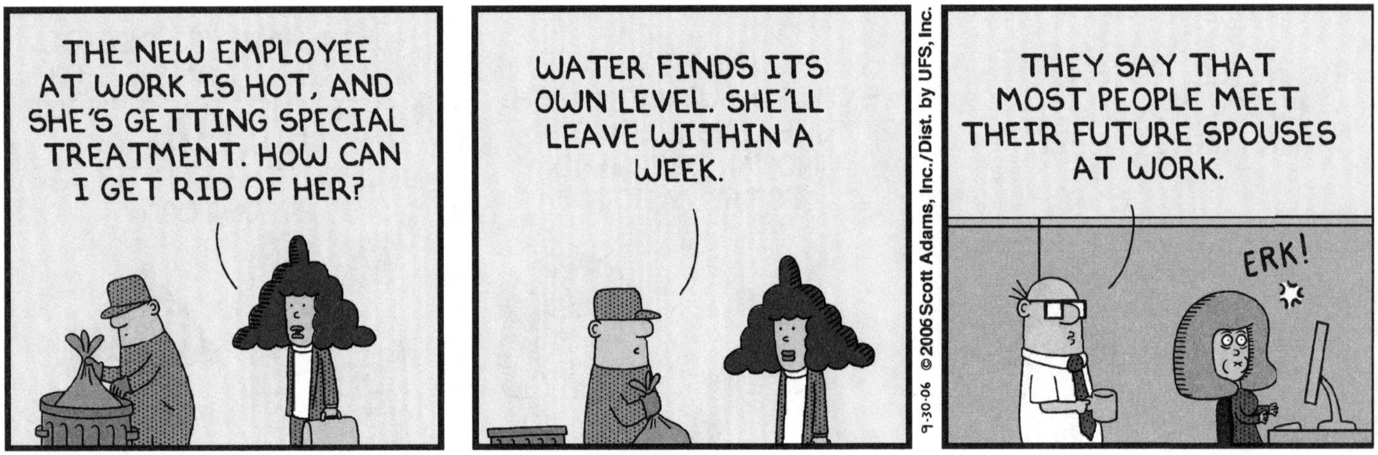
THE NEW EMPLOYEE AT WORK IS HOT, AND SHE'S GETTING SPECIAL TREATMENT. HOW CAN I GET RID OF HER?
WATER FINDS ITS OWN LEVEL. SHE'LL LEAVE WITHIN A WEEK.
9-30-06 © 2006 Scott Adams, Inc./Dist. by UFS, Inc.
THEY SAY THAT MOST PEOPLE MEET THEIR FUTURE SPOUSES AT WORK.
ERK!

ACCORDING TO MY BENCHMARK TESTS, OUR PRODUCT IS THE WORST ONE ON THE MARKET.
MAYBE YOU CAN TWEAK THE NUMBERS.
FAKE THEM?
FAKE IS SUCH AN UGLY WORD.
JUST REMEMBER THAT YOUR NEXT RAISE DEPENDS ON THE SALES OF THAT PRODUCT.
AND MISTAKES HAPPEN. A DECIMAL PLACE CAN BE EITHER HERE OR THERE.
ALL I'M ASKING IS THAT YOU DO THE TESTS AGAIN. . .
WHILE DRINKING.
I ALWAYS WONDERED WHAT JOB SATISFAC– TION FELT LIKE.
10-1-06

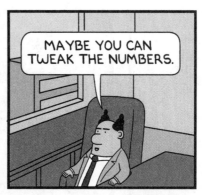

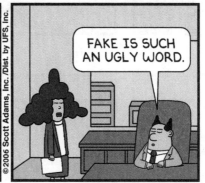

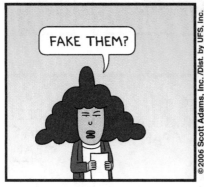

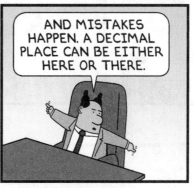

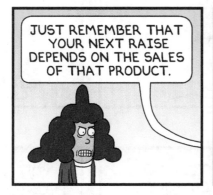

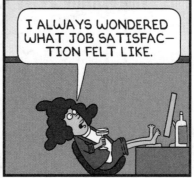

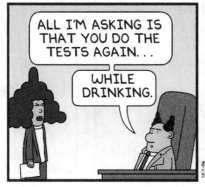

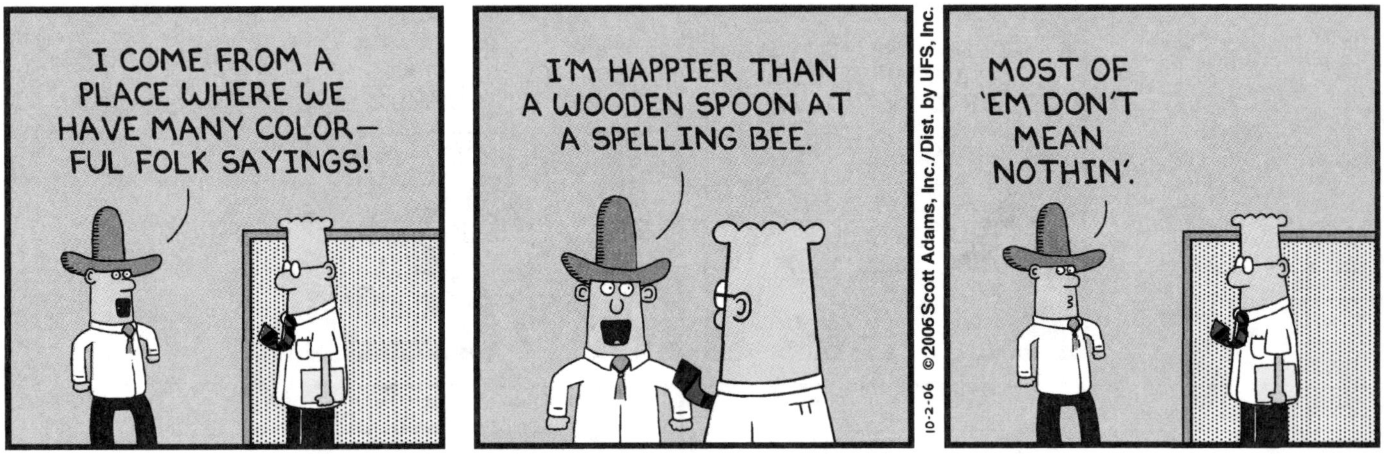
I COME FROM A PLACE WHERE WE HAVE MANY COLOR-FUL FOLK SAYINGS!
I'M HAPPIER THAN A WOODEN SPOON AT A SPELLING BEE.
10-2-06 © 2006 Scott Adams, Inc./Dist. by UFS, Inc.
MOST OF 'EM DON'T MEAN NOTHIN'.

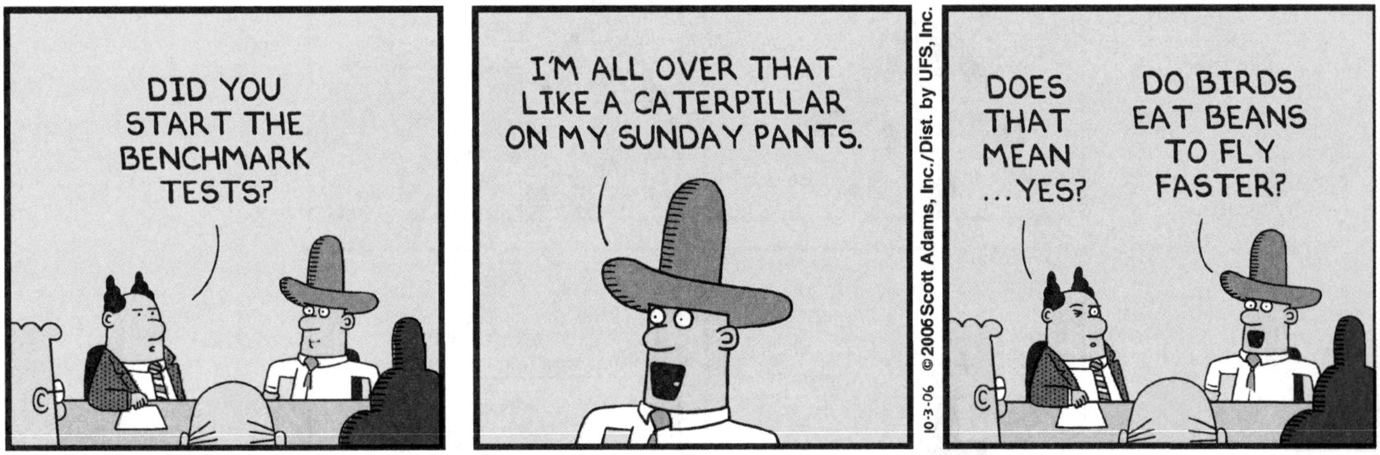
DID YOU START THE BENCHMARK TESTS?
I'M ALL OVER THAT LIKE A CATERPILLAR ON MY SUNDAY PANTS.
10-3-06 © 2006 Scott Adams, Inc./Dist. by UFS, Inc.
DOES THAT MEAN ...YES?
DO BIRDS EAT BEANS TO FLY FASTER?

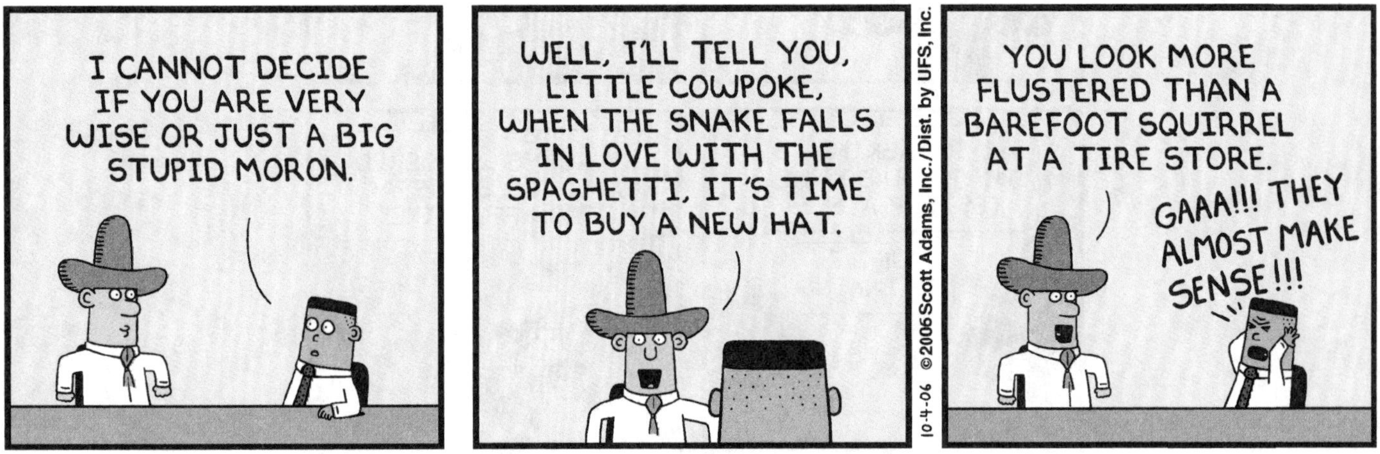
I CANNOT DECIDE IF YOU ARE VERY WISE OR JUST A BIG STUPID MORON.
WELL, I'LL TELL YOU, LITTLE COWPOKE, WHEN THE SNAKE FALLS IN LOVE WITH THE SPAGHETTI, IT'S TIME TO BUY A NEW HAT.
10-4-06 © 2006 Scott Adams, Inc./Dist. by UFS, Inc.
YOU LOOK MORE FLUSTERED THAN A BAREFOOT SQUIRREL AT A TIRE STORE.
GAAA!!! THEY ALMOST MAKE SENSE!!!

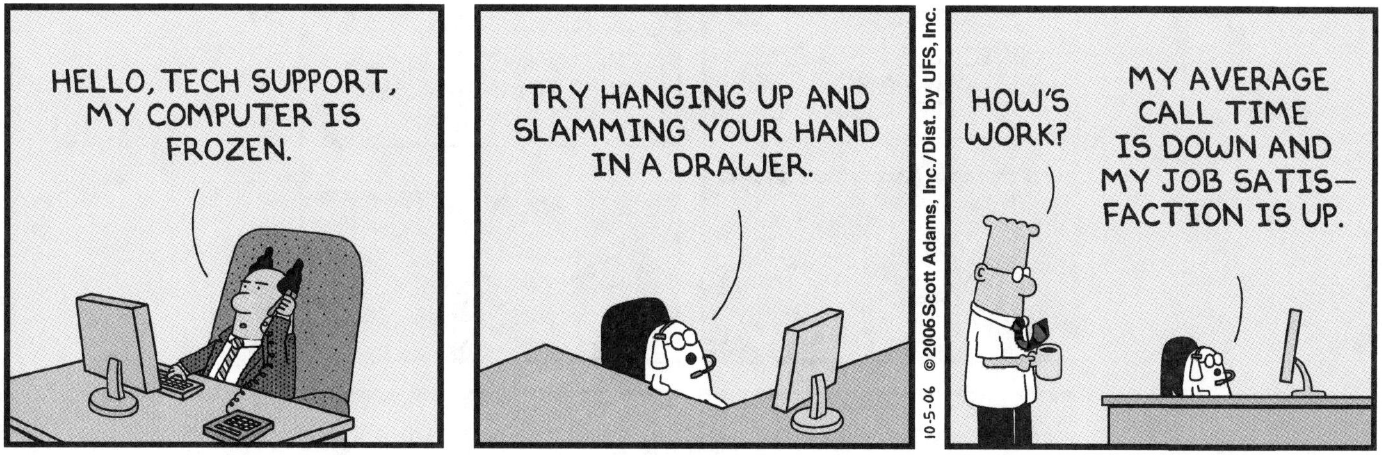
HELLO, TECH SUPPORT, MY COMPUTER IS FROZEN.
TRY HANGING UP AND SLAMMING YOUR HAND IN A DRAWER.
10-5-06 ©2006 Scott Adams, Inc./Dist. by UFS, Inc.
HOW'S WORK?
MY AVERAGE CALL TIME IS DOWN AND MY JOB SATIS-FACTION IS UP.

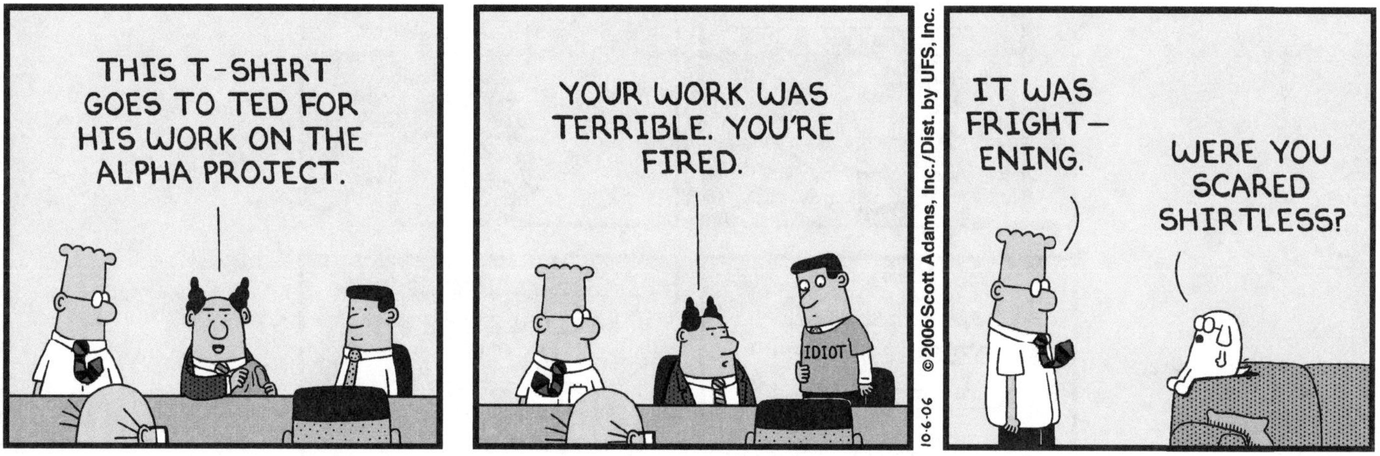
THIS T-SHIRT GOES TO TED FOR HIS WORK ON THE ALPHA PROJECT.
YOUR WORK WAS TERRIBLE. YOU'RE FIRED.
IDIOT
10-6-06 ©2006 Scott Adams, Inc./Dist. by UFS, Inc.
IT WAS FRIGHT-ENING.
WERE YOU SCARED SHIRTLESS?

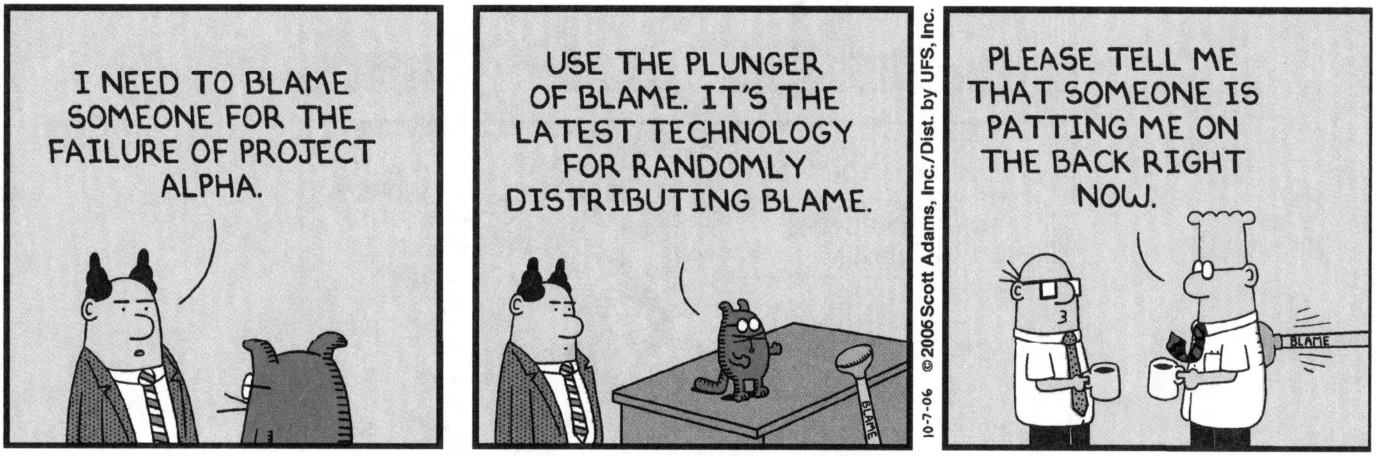
I NEED TO BLAME SOMEONE FOR THE FAILURE OF PROJECT ALPHA.
USE THE PLUNGER OF BLAME. IT'S THE LATEST TECHNOLOGY FOR RANDOMLY DISTRIBUTING BLAME.
BLAME
10-7-06 ©2006 Scott Adams, Inc./Dist. by UFS, Inc.
PLEASE TELL ME THAT SOMEONE IS PATTING ME ON THE BACK RIGHT NOW.
BLAME

A BUSINESS MAGAZINE IS SENDING A REPORTER TO INTERVIEW ME.
YOU?
THEY WANT TO LEARN MY BEST MANAGEMENT PRACTICES.
THAT'S A LITTLE LIKE MILKING A SQUIRREL BECAUSE YOU NEED BUTTER.
I DON'T KNOW WHAT THAT MEANT, BUT I LIKE THE WAY IT SOUNDED.
©2006 Scott Adams, Inc./Dist. by UFS, Inc.

DESCRIBE YOUR TYPICAL DAY.
WELL, LET ME TELL YOU. . .
SOMETIMES YOU MILK THE SQUIRREL, AND SOMETIMES THE SQUIRREL MILKS YOU.
"HE IS LIKE A ZEN MASTER. HIS WORDS ARE PEPPERED WITH SQUIRREL-RELATED WISDOM."
PHB TIMES
10-08-06

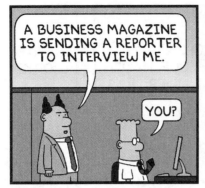

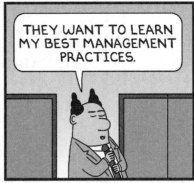

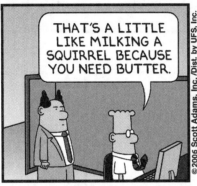

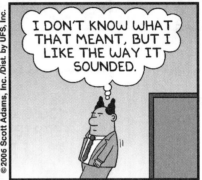

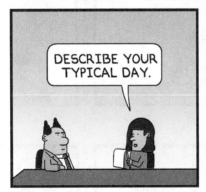

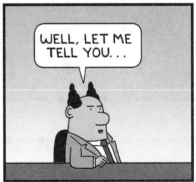

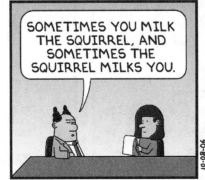

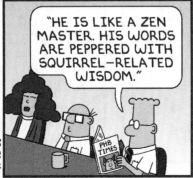

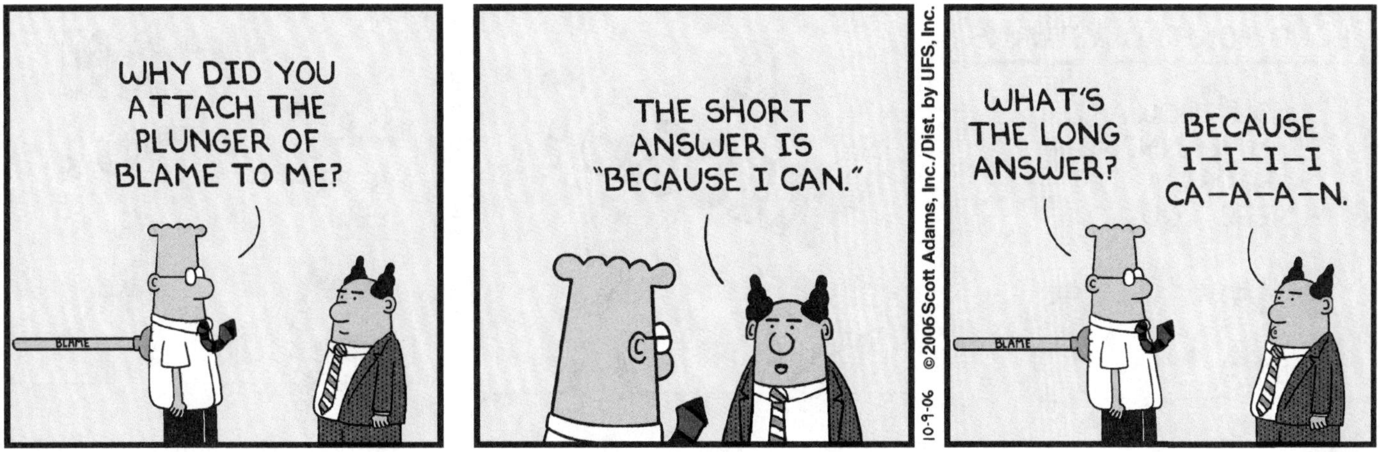
WHY DID YOU ATTACH THE PLUNGER OF BLAME TO ME?
BLAME
THE SHORT ANSWER IS "BECAUSE I CAN."
10-9-06 © 2006 Scott Adams, Inc./Dist. by UFS, Inc.
WHAT'S THE LONG ANSWER?
BECAUSE I-I-I-I CA-A-A-N.
BLAME

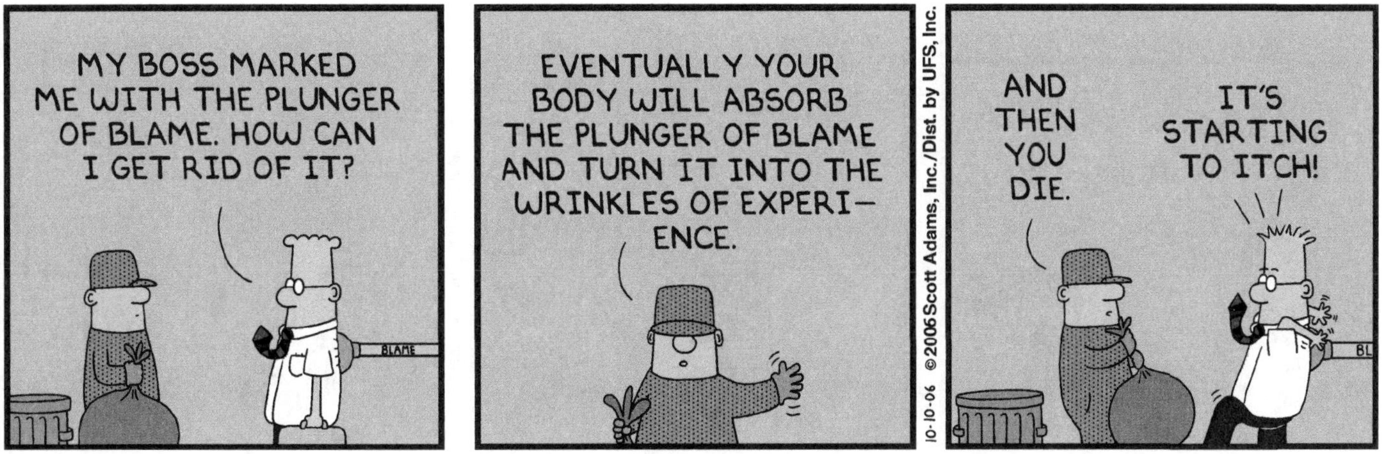
MY BOSS MARKED ME WITH THE PLUNGER OF BLAME. HOW CAN I GET RID OF IT?
BLAME
EVENTUALLY YOUR BODY WILL ABSORB THE PLUNGER OF BLAME AND TURN IT INTO THE WRINKLES OF EXPERI-ENCE.
10-10-06 © 2006 Scott Adams, Inc./Dist. by UFS, Inc.
AND THEN YOU DIE.
IT'S STARTING TO ITCH!

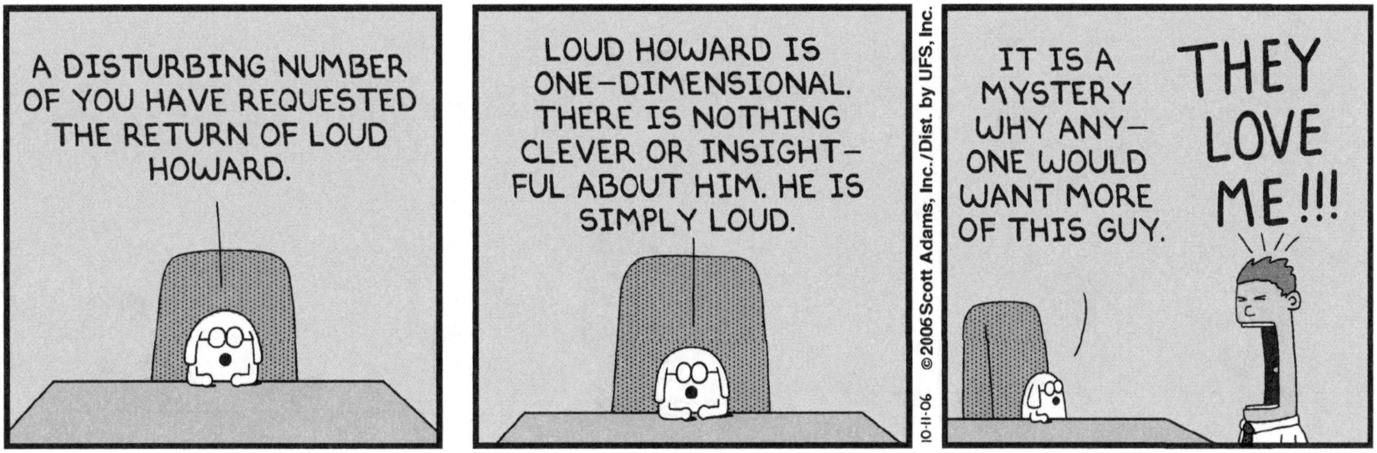
A DISTURBING NUMBER OF YOU HAVE REQUESTED THE RETURN OF LOUD HOWARD.
LOUD HOWARD IS ONE-DIMENSIONAL. THERE IS NOTHING CLEVER OR INSIGHT-FUL ABOUT HIM. HE IS SIMPLY LOUD.
10-11-06 © 2006 Scott Adams, Inc./Dist. by UFS, Inc.
IT IS A MYSTERY WHY ANY-ONE WOULD WANT MORE OF THIS GUY.
THEY LOVE ME!!!

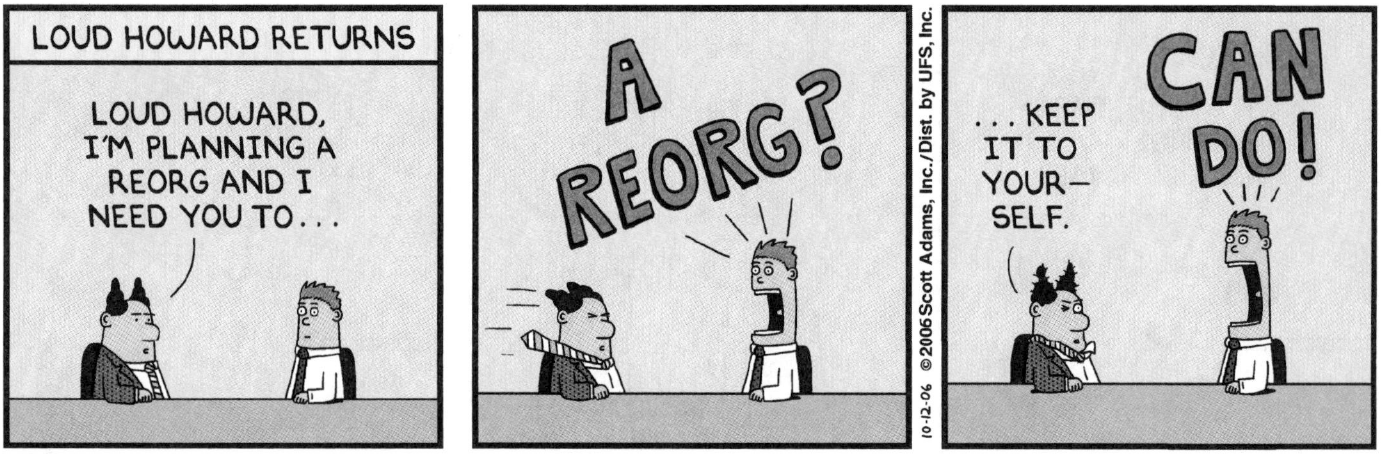
LOUD HOWARD RETURNS
LOUD HOWARD, I'M PLANNING A REORG AND I NEED YOU TO . . .
A REORG?
. . . KEEP IT TO YOUR— SELF.
CAN DO!
10-12-06 © 2006 Scott Adams, Inc./Dist. by UFS, Inc.

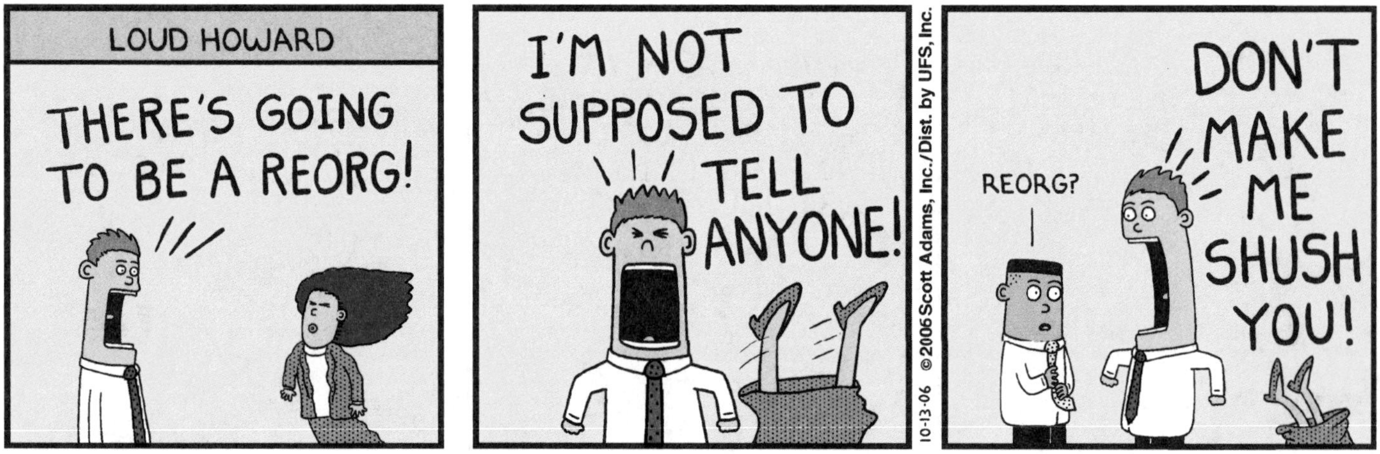
LOUD HOWARD
THERE'S GOING TO BE A REORG!
I'M NOT SUPPOSED TO TELL ANYONE!
REORG?
DON'T MAKE ME SHUSH YOU!
10-13-06 © 2006 Scott Adams, Inc./Dist. by UFS, Inc.

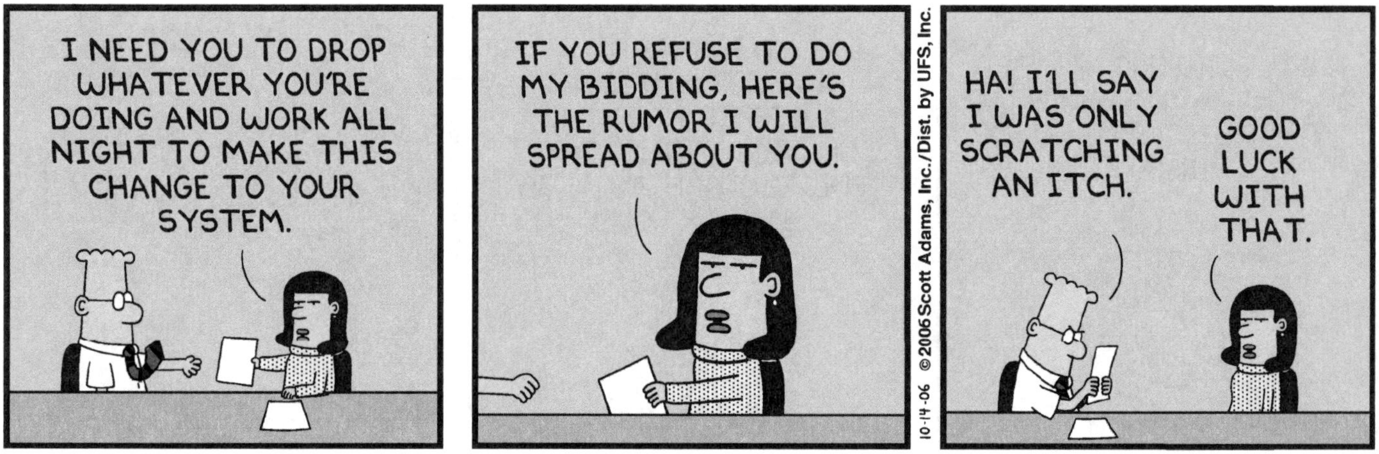
I NEED YOU TO DROP WHATEVER YOU'RE DOING AND WORK ALL NIGHT TO MAKE THIS CHANGE TO YOUR SYSTEM.
IF YOU REFUSE TO DO MY BIDDING, HERE'S THE RUMOR I WILL SPREAD ABOUT YOU.
HA! I'LL SAY I WAS ONLY SCRATCHING AN ITCH.
GOOD LUCK WITH THAT.
10-14-06 © 2006 Scott Adams, Inc./Dist. by UFS, Inc.

MY PROJECT HAS BEEN INFECTED BY ATTRACTIVE PEOPLE.
AS YOU KNOW, ATTRACTIVE PEOPLE ARE UNPRODUCTIVE.
THE PROBLEM IS COMPOUNDED WHEN YOU PUT SEVERAL OF THEM IN THE SAME ROOM.
THEY'VE ALREADY STARTED TO PAIR OFF.
I'VE GOT FOUR LOVE TRIANGLES AND SIX DIVORCES.
ALL OF MY STATUS REPORTS SAY, AND I QUOTE, "DUDE, I CAN'T CONCENTRATE NOW."
MY PLAN IS TO REPLACE EACH ATTRACTIVE PERSON WITH SOMETHING LIKE THIS, OR THIS.
HE THINKS I'M PRODUCTIVE.
©2006 Scott Adams, Inc. /Dist. by UFS, Inc.
10-15-06

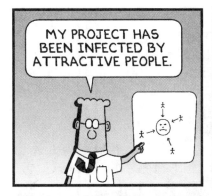

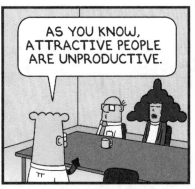

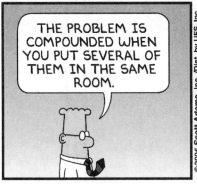

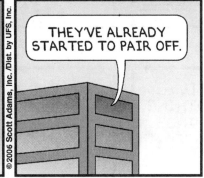

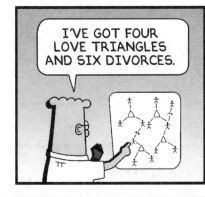

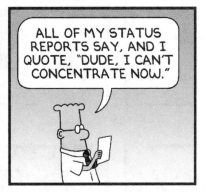

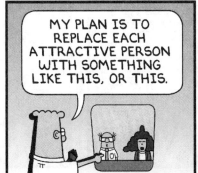

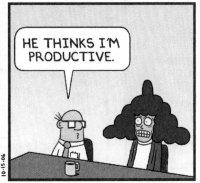

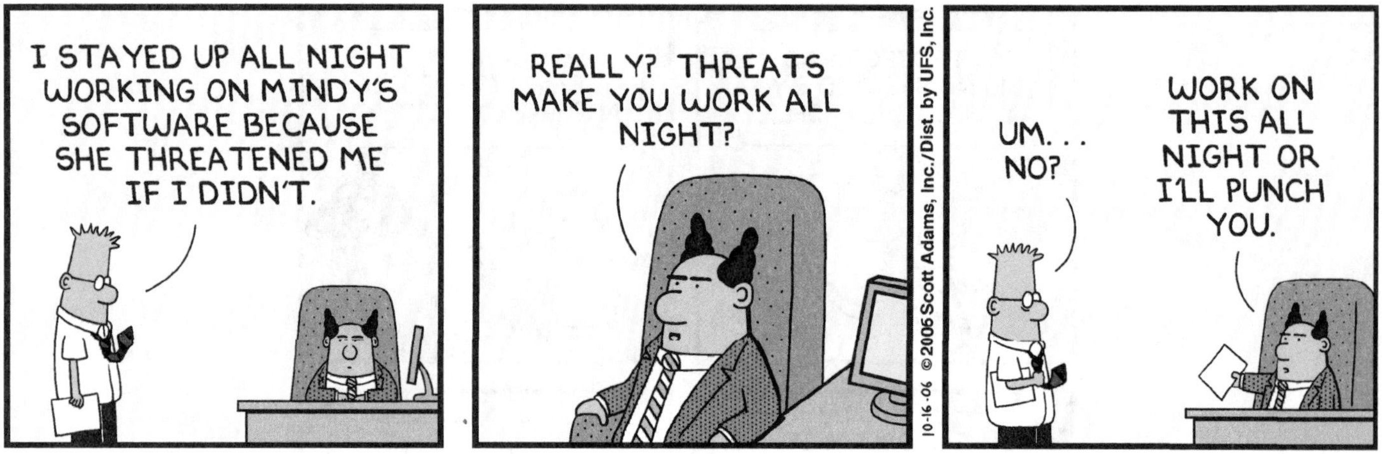
I STAYED UP ALL NIGHT WORKING ON MINDY'S SOFTWARE BECAUSE SHE THREATENED ME IF I DIDN'T.
REALLY? THREATS MAKE YOU WORK ALL NIGHT?
UM. . . NO?
WORK ON THIS ALL NIGHT OR I'LL PUNCH YOU.
10-16-06 © 2006 Scott Adams, Inc./Dist. by UFS, Inc.

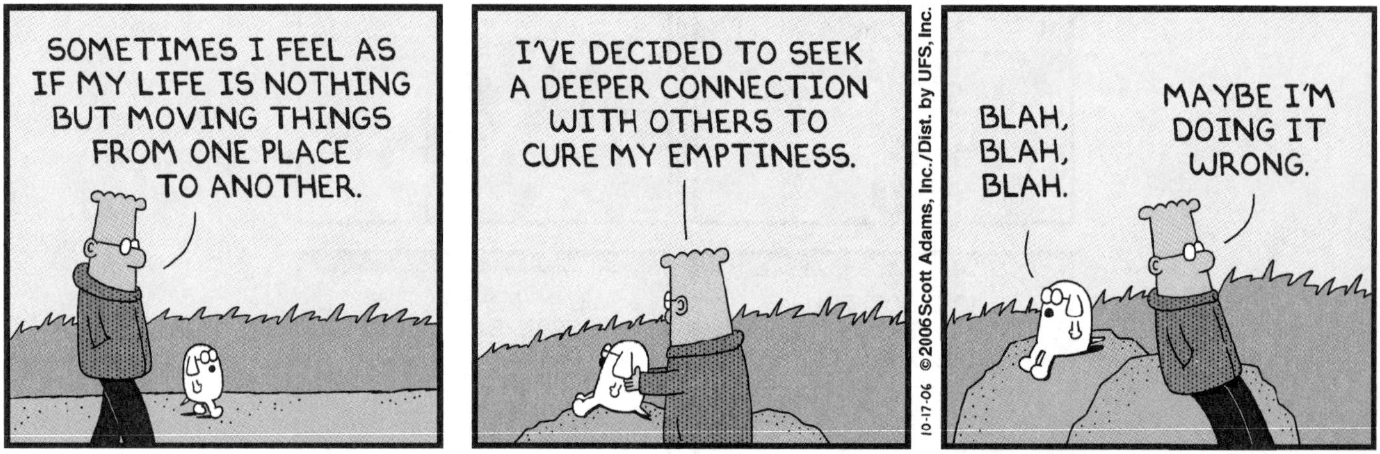
SOMETIMES I FEEL AS IF MY LIFE IS NOTHING BUT MOVING THINGS FROM ONE PLACE TO ANOTHER.
I'VE DECIDED TO SEEK A DEEPER CONNECTION WITH OTHERS TO CURE MY EMPTINESS.
BLAH, BLAH, BLAH.
MAYBE I'M DOING IT WRONG.
10-17-06 © 2006 Scott Adams, Inc./Dist. by UFS, Inc.

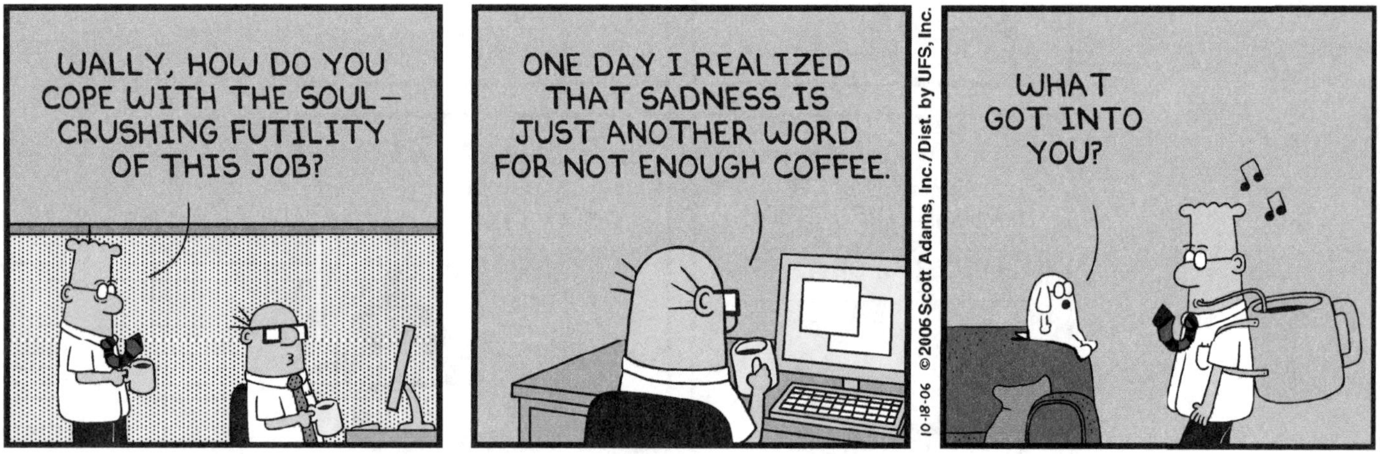
WALLY, HOW DO YOU COPE WITH THE SOUL-CRUSHING FUTILITY OF THIS JOB?
ONE DAY I REALIZED THAT SADNESS IS JUST ANOTHER WORD FOR NOT ENOUGH COFFEE.
WHAT GOT INTO YOU?
10-18-06 © 2006 Scott Adams, Inc./Dist. by UFS, Inc.

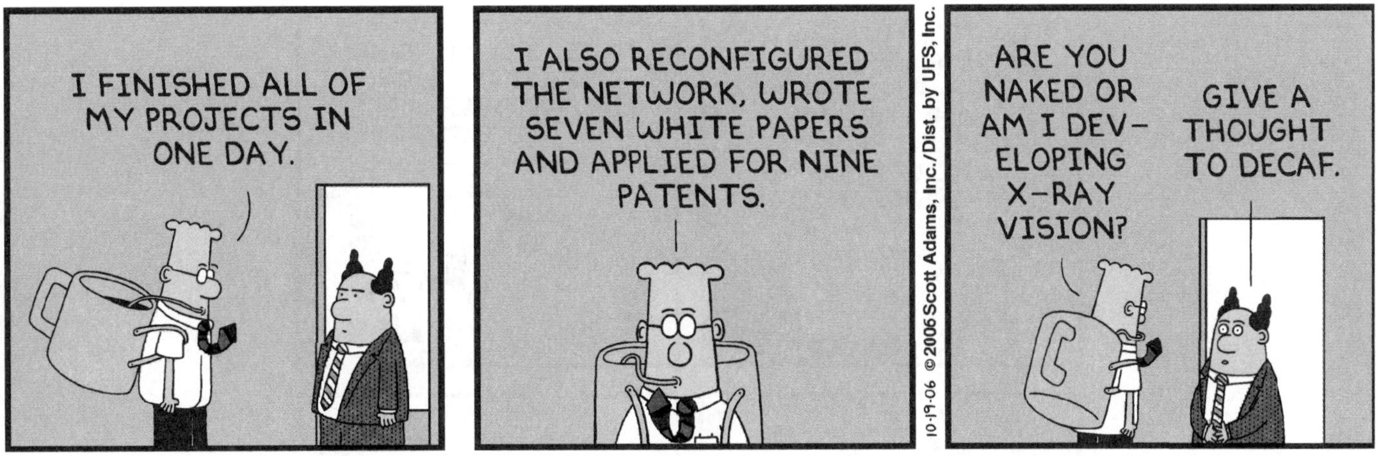
I FINISHED ALL OF MY PROJECTS IN ONE DAY.
I ALSO RECONFIGURED THE NETWORK, WROTE SEVEN WHITE PAPERS AND APPLIED FOR NINE PATENTS.
10-19-06 ©2006 Scott Adams, Inc./Dist. by UFS, Inc.
ARE YOU NAKED OR AM I DEV-ELOPING X-RAY VISION?
GIVE A THOUGHT TO DECAF.

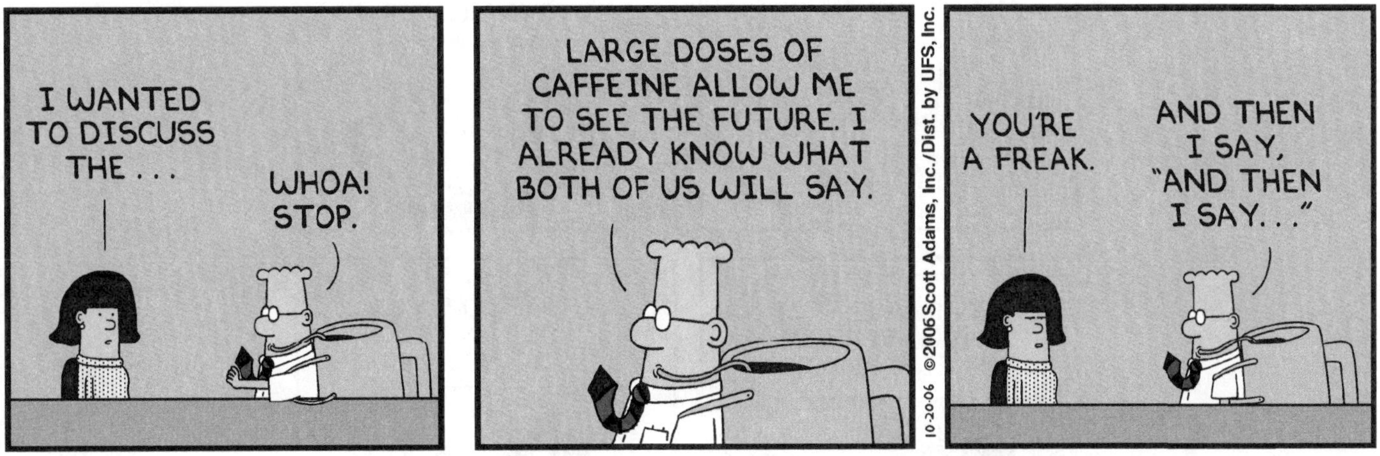
I WANTED TO DISCUSS THE . . .
WHOA! STOP.
LARGE DOSES OF CAFFEINE ALLOW ME TO SEE THE FUTURE. I ALREADY KNOW WHAT BOTH OF US WILL SAY.
10-20-06 ©2006 Scott Adams, Inc./Dist. by UFS, Inc.
YOU'RE A FREAK.
AND THEN I SAY, "AND THEN I SAY. . ."

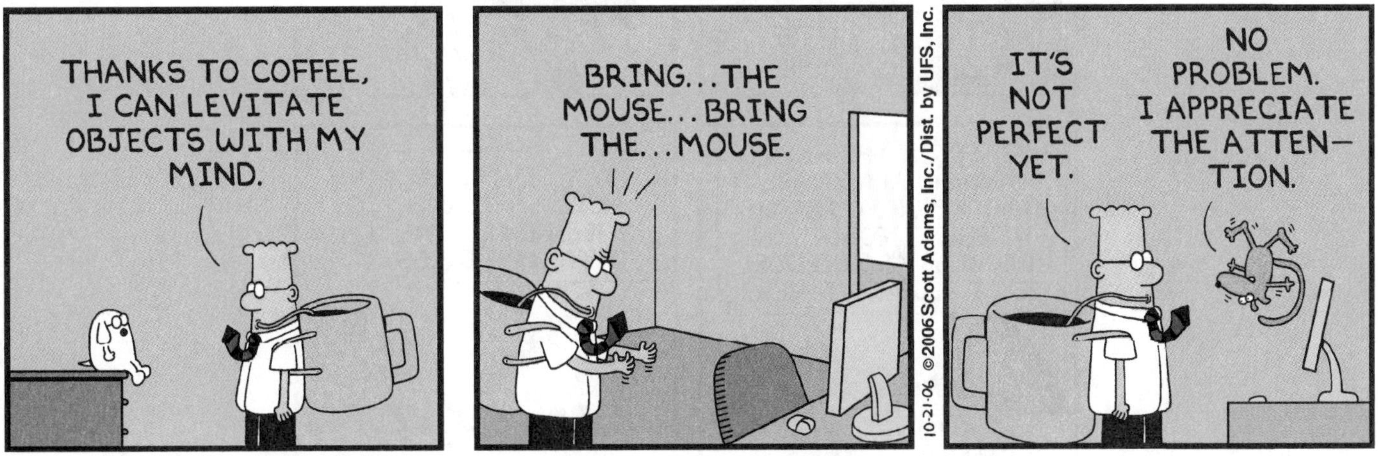
THANKS TO COFFEE, I CAN LEVITATE OBJECTS WITH MY MIND.
BRING...THE MOUSE...BRING THE...MOUSE.
10-21-06 ©2006 Scott Adams, Inc./Dist. by UFS, Inc.
IT'S NOT PERFECT YET.
NO PROBLEM. I APPRECIATE THE ATTEN-TION.

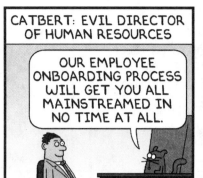

CATBERT: EVIL DIRECTOR OF HUMAN RESOURCES
OUR EMPLOYEE ONBOARDING PROCESS WILL GET YOU ALL MAINSTREAMED IN NO TIME AT ALL.
THIS WILL BE YOUR CUBICLE, IF WE CAN FIND ANOTHER PLACE TO STORE THIS JUNK.
YOU'LL GET A PHONE AND A COMPUTER IF THE BUDGET EVER GETS APPROVED.
©2006 Scott Adams, Inc./Dist. by UFS, Inc.
THIS IS ALICE. SHE WILL BE YOUR MENTOR.
I DON'T HAVE TIME TO BABYSIT! I'M BURIED IN WORK!
I DO NOT LIKE YOU. I. . . DO. . . NOT. . . LIKE YOU!!!
STAND IN THE HALL–WAY AND READ THESE BINDERS. IF YOU LEARN ANYTHING, FORGET IT, BECAUSE KNOWLEDGE ISN'T REWARDED HERE.
10-22-06
TRY GIVING UP HOPE. IT TURNS THE BAD FEELING INTO EMPTINESS.

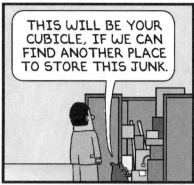

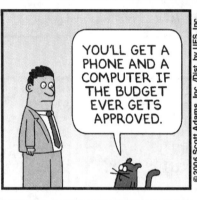

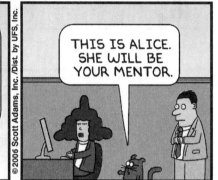

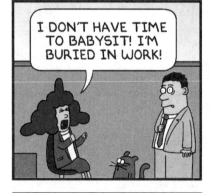

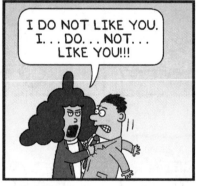

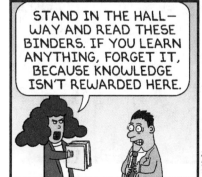

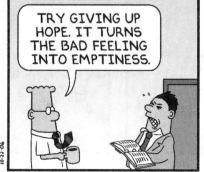

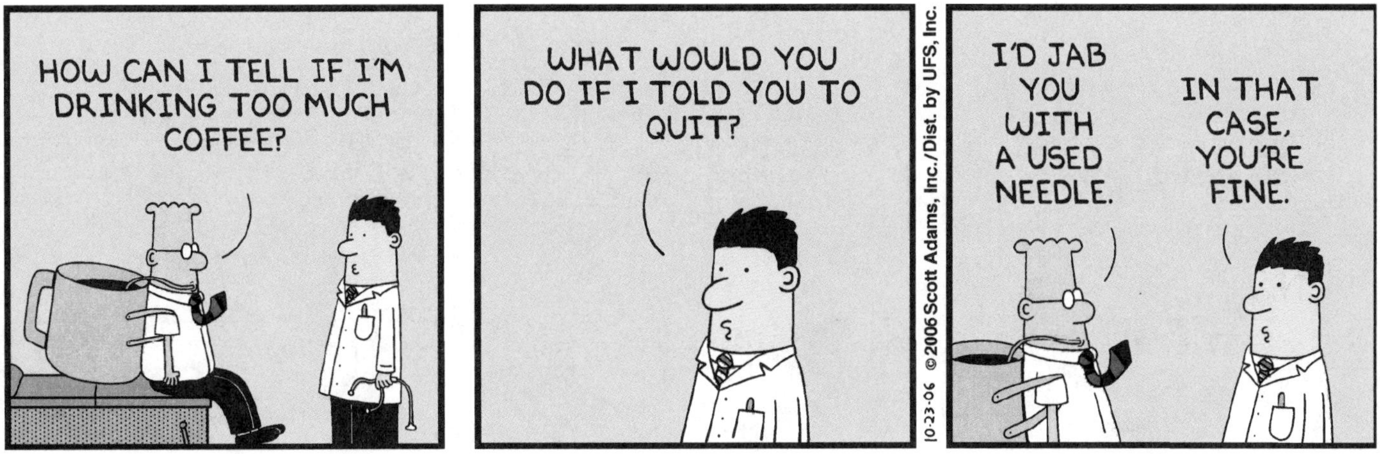
HOW CAN I TELL IF I'M DRINKING TOO MUCH COFFEE?
WHAT WOULD YOU DO IF I TOLD YOU TO QUIT?
I'D JAB YOU WITH A USED NEEDLE.
IN THAT CASE, YOU'RE FINE.
10-23-06 ©2006 Scott Adams, Inc./Dist. by UFS, Inc.

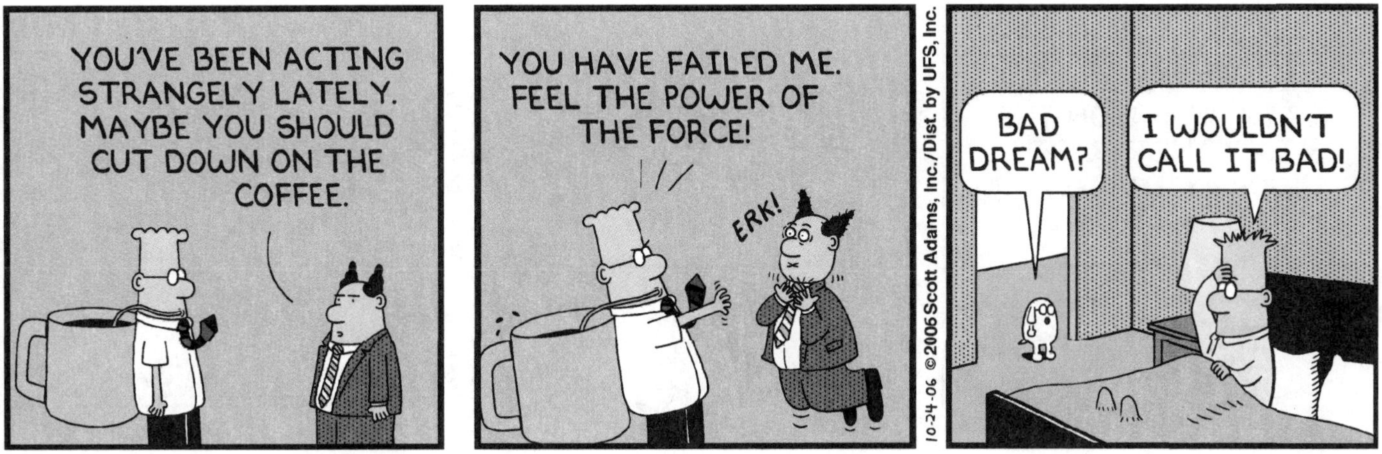
YOU'VE BEEN ACTING STRANGELY LATELY. MAYBE YOU SHOULD CUT DOWN ON THE COFFEE.
YOU HAVE FAILED ME. FEEL THE POWER OF THE FORCE!
ERK!
BAD DREAM?
I WOULDN'T CALL IT BAD!
10-24-06 ©2006 Scott Adams, Inc./Dist. by UFS, Inc.

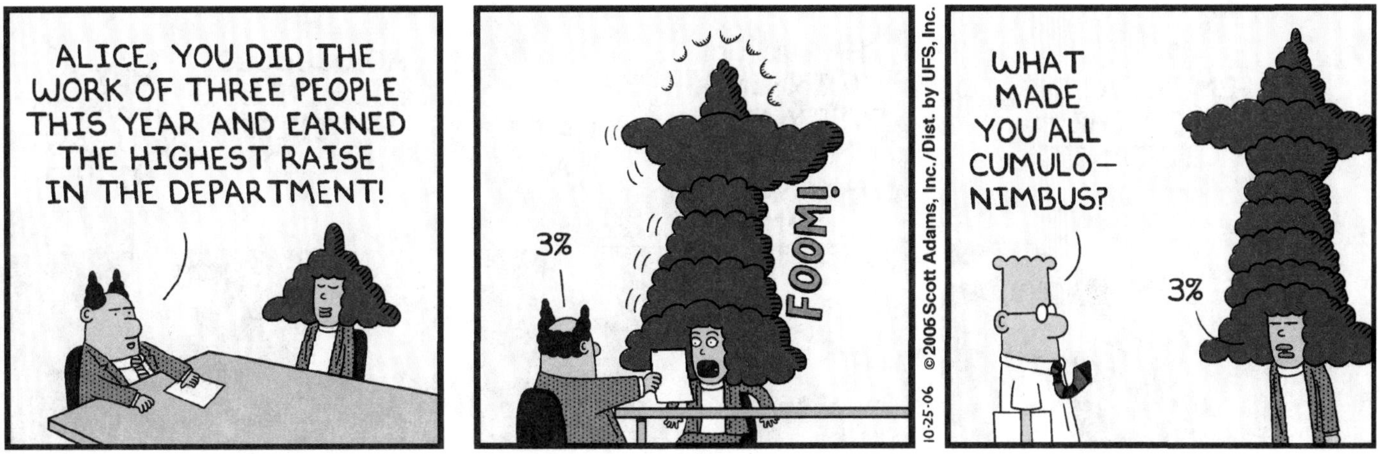
ALICE, YOU DID THE WORK OF THREE PEOPLE THIS YEAR AND EARNED THE HIGHEST RAISE IN THE DEPARTMENT!
3%
FOOM!
WHAT MADE YOU ALL CUMULO-NIMBUS?
3%
10-25-06 ©2006 Scott Adams, Inc./Dist. by UFS, Inc.

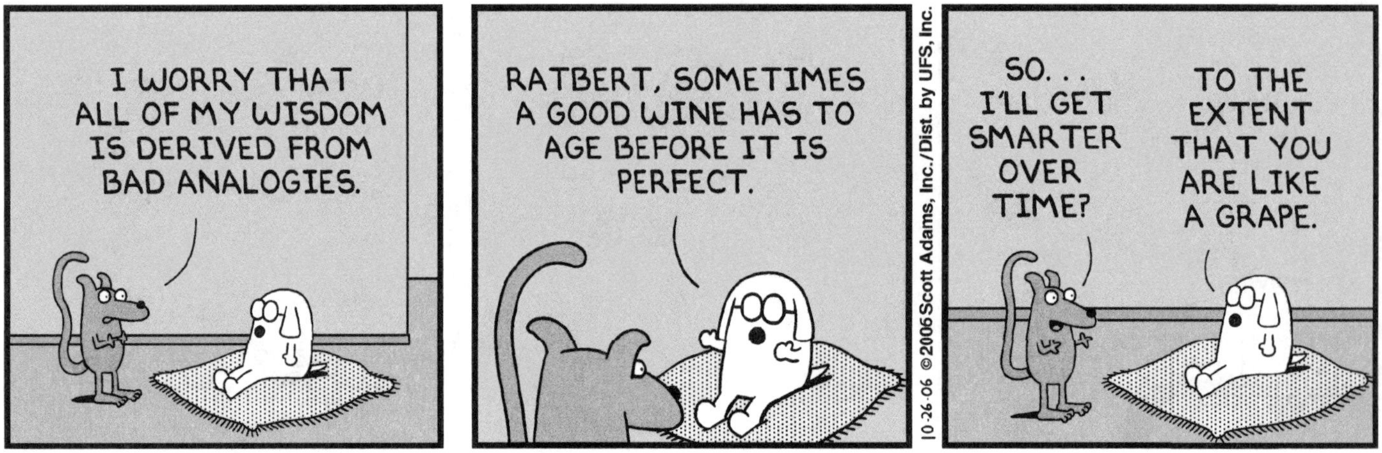
I WORRY THAT ALL OF MY WISDOM IS DERIVED FROM BAD ANALOGIES.
RATBERT, SOMETIMES A GOOD WINE HAS TO AGE BEFORE IT IS PERFECT.
SO. . . I'LL GET SMARTER OVER TIME?
TO THE EXTENT THAT YOU ARE LIKE A GRAPE.

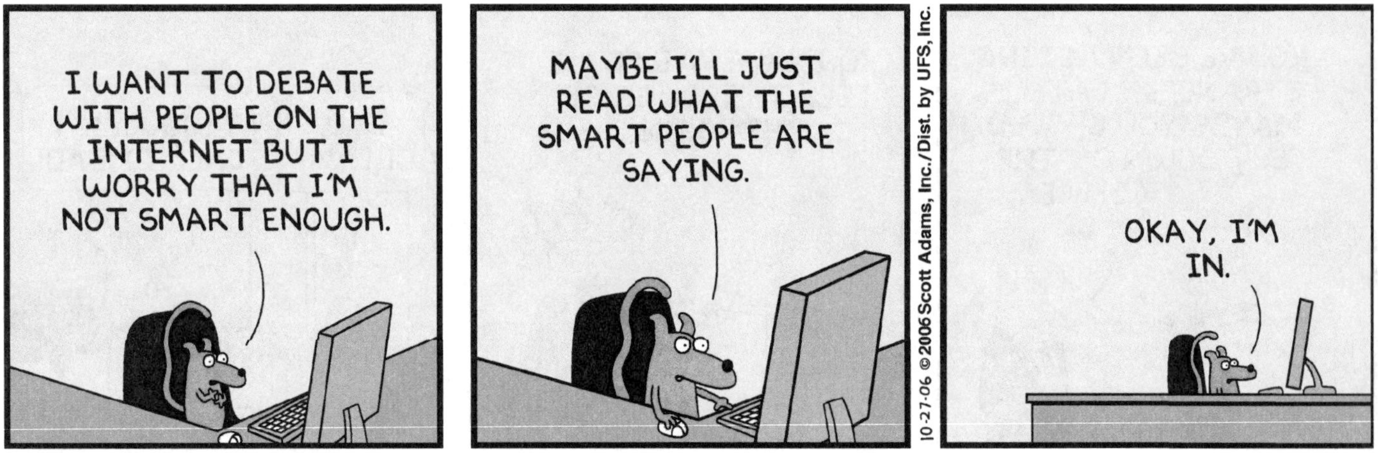
I WANT TO DEBATE WITH PEOPLE ON THE INTERNET BUT I WORRY THAT I'M NOT SMART ENOUGH.
MAYBE I'LL JUST READ WHAT THE SMART PEOPLE ARE SAYING.
OKAY, I'M IN.

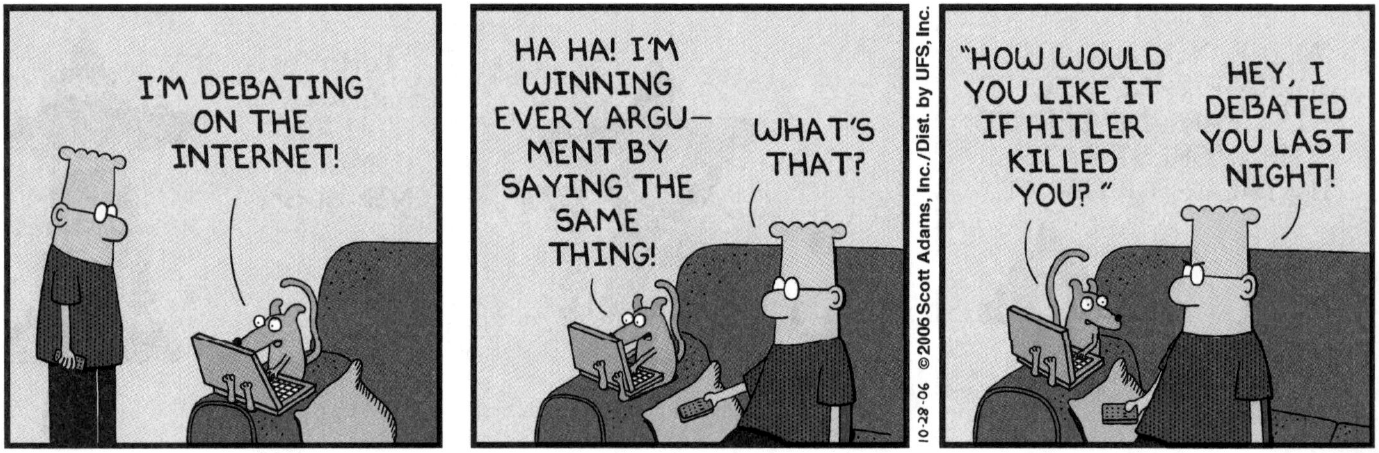
I'M DEBATING ON THE INTERNET!
HA HA! I'M WINNING EVERY ARGU– MENT BY SAYING THE SAME THING!
WHAT'S THAT?
"HOW WOULD YOU LIKE IT IF HITLER KILLED YOU?"
HEY, I DEBATED YOU LAST NIGHT!

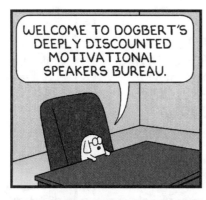

WELCOME TO DOGBERT'S DEEPLY DISCOUNTED MOTIVATIONAL SPEAKERS BUREAU.
I NEED A SLIGHTLY MOTIVATIONAL SPEAKER AND I DON'T HAVE MUCH BUDGET.
I WANT TO INSPIRE MY EMPLOYEES TO WORK HARDER, WITH-OUT MOTIVATING THEM TO SEEK BETTER JOBS.
©2006 Scott Adams, Inc./Dist. by UFS, Inc.
I RECOMMEND ROBBIE, THE FRIGHTENING HOBO.
DOES HE TALK ABOUT HIS DIFFICULT JOURNEY FROM THE DUMPSTER TO SUCCESS?
WE'RE NOT SURE.
HE MUMBLES.
BUT NO ONE HAS EVER BECOME AN ENTREPRE-NEUR AFTER HEARING HIM SPEAK.
10-29-06
MUMBLE MUMBLE MUMBLE
MUST... KEEP... JOB.

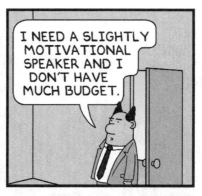

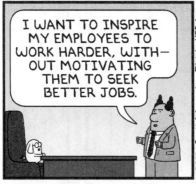

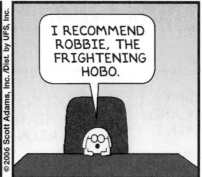

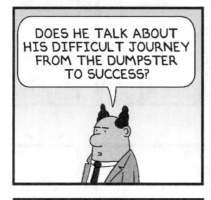

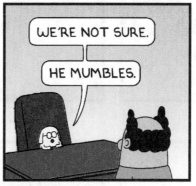

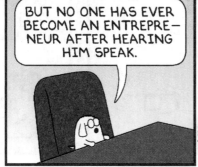

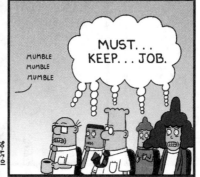

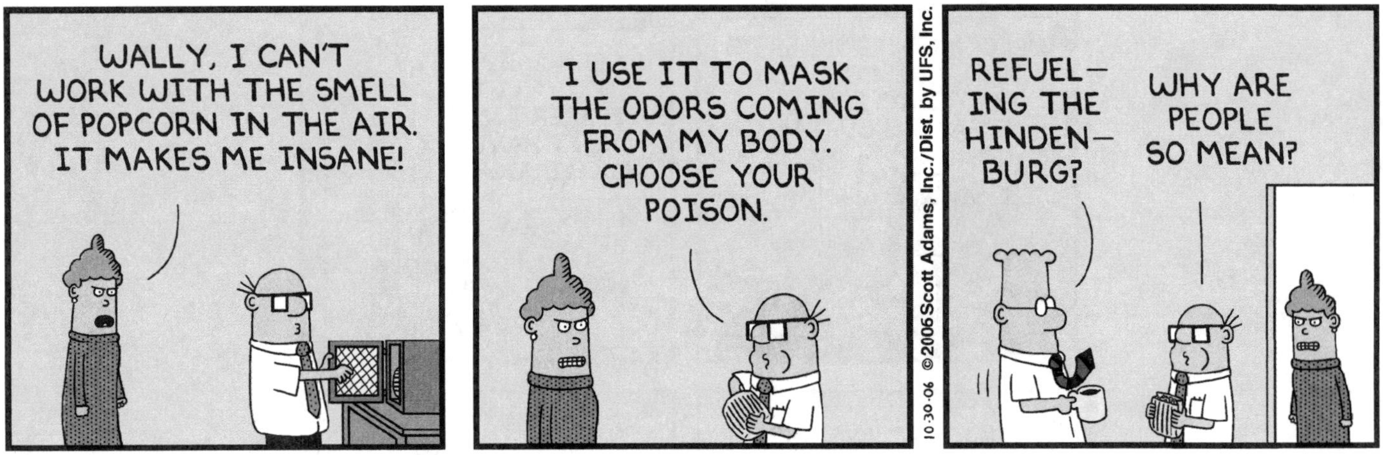
WALLY, I CAN'T WORK WITH THE SMELL OF POPCORN IN THE AIR. IT MAKES ME INSANE!
I USE IT TO MASK THE ODORS COMING FROM MY BODY. CHOOSE YOUR POISON.
10-30-06 ©2006 Scott Adams, Inc./Dist. by UFS, Inc.
REFUEL-ING THE HINDEN-BURG?
WHY ARE PEOPLE SO MEAN?

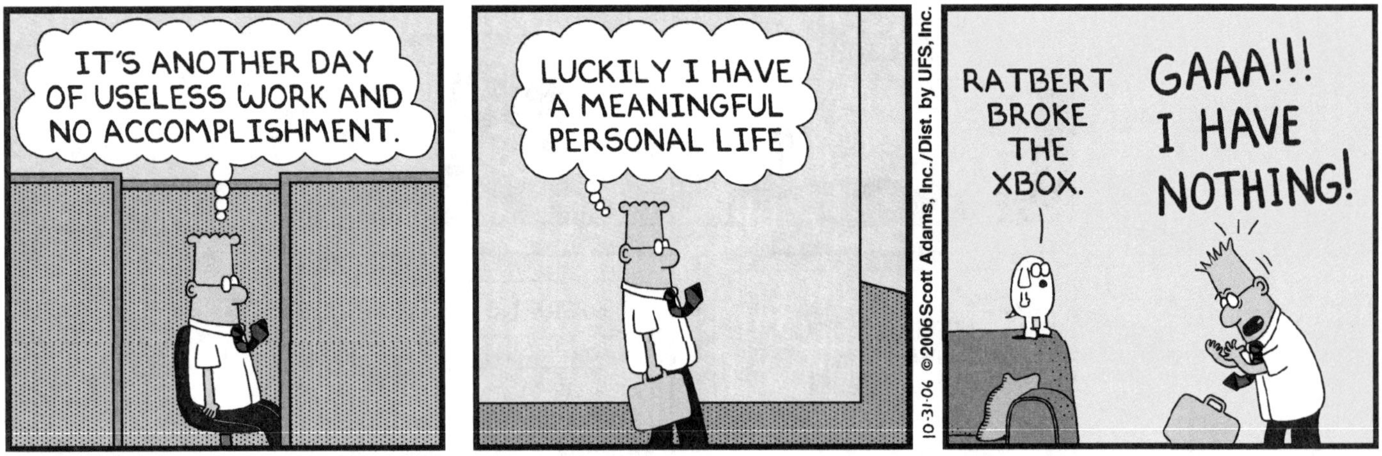
IT'S ANOTHER DAY OF USELESS WORK AND NO ACCOMPLISHMENT.
LUCKILY I HAVE A MEANINGFUL PERSONAL LIFE
10-31-06 ©2006 Scott Adams, Inc./Dist. by UFS, Inc.
RATBERT BROKE THE XBOX.
GAAA!!! I HAVE NOTHING!

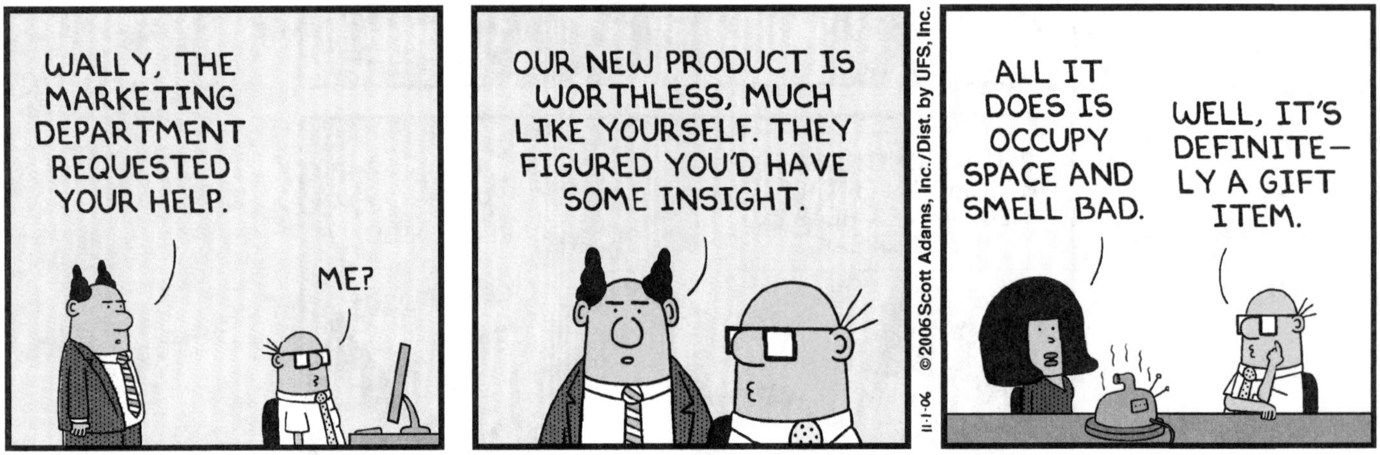
WALLY, THE MARKETING DEPARTMENT REQUESTED YOUR HELP.
ME?
OUR NEW PRODUCT IS WORTHLESS, MUCH LIKE YOURSELF. THEY FIGURED YOU'D HAVE SOME INSIGHT.
11-1-06 ©2006 Scott Adams, Inc./Dist. by UFS, Inc.
ALL IT DOES IS OCCUPY SPACE AND SMELL BAD.
WELL, IT'S DEFINITE-LY A GIFT ITEM.

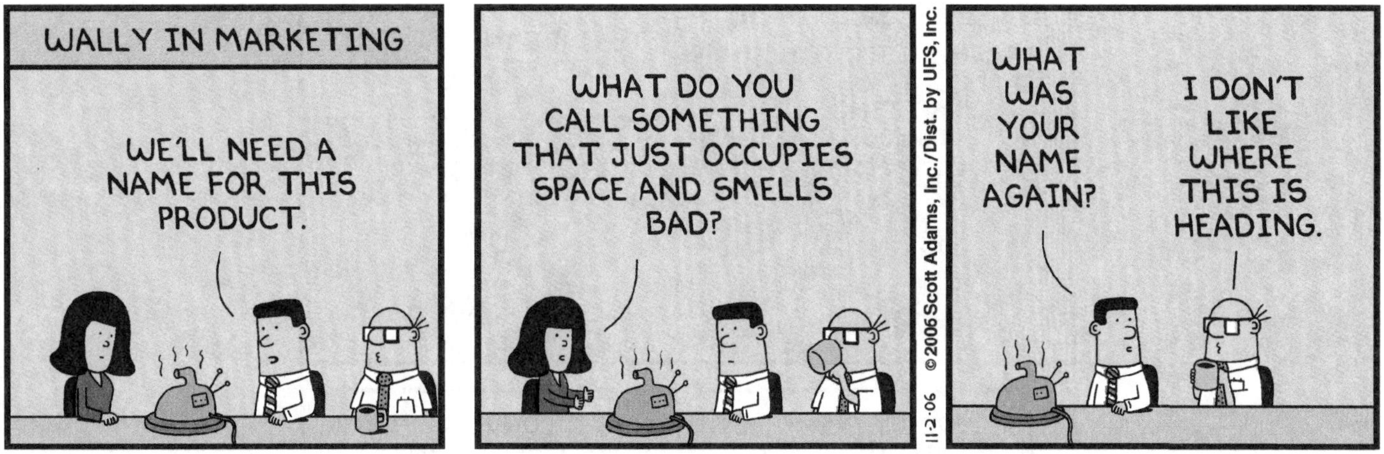
WALLY IN MARKETING
WE'LL NEED A NAME FOR THIS PRODUCT.
WHAT DO YOU CALL SOMETHING THAT JUST OCCUPIES SPACE AND SMELLS BAD?
WHAT WAS YOUR NAME AGAIN?
I DON'T LIKE WHERE THIS IS HEADING.
11-2-06 © 2006 Scott Adams, Inc./Dist. by UFS, Inc.

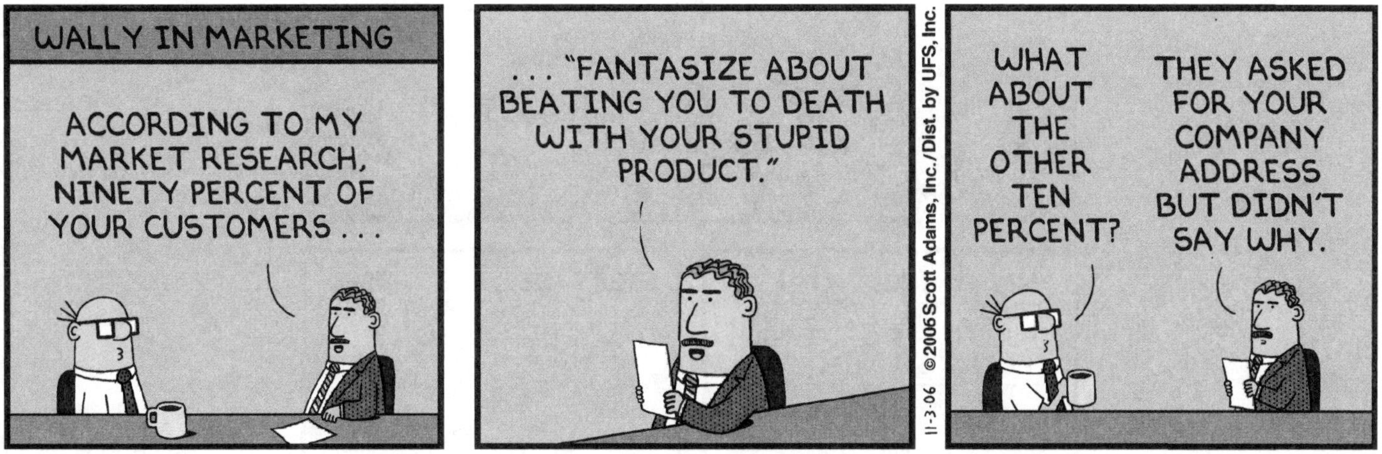
WALLY IN MARKETING
ACCORDING TO MY MARKET RESEARCH, NINETY PERCENT OF YOUR CUSTOMERS . . .
. . . "FANTASIZE ABOUT BEATING YOU TO DEATH WITH YOUR STUPID PRODUCT."
WHAT ABOUT THE OTHER TEN PERCENT?
THEY ASKED FOR YOUR COMPANY ADDRESS BUT DIDN'T SAY WHY.
11-3-06 © 2006 Scott Adams, Inc./Dist. by UFS, Inc.

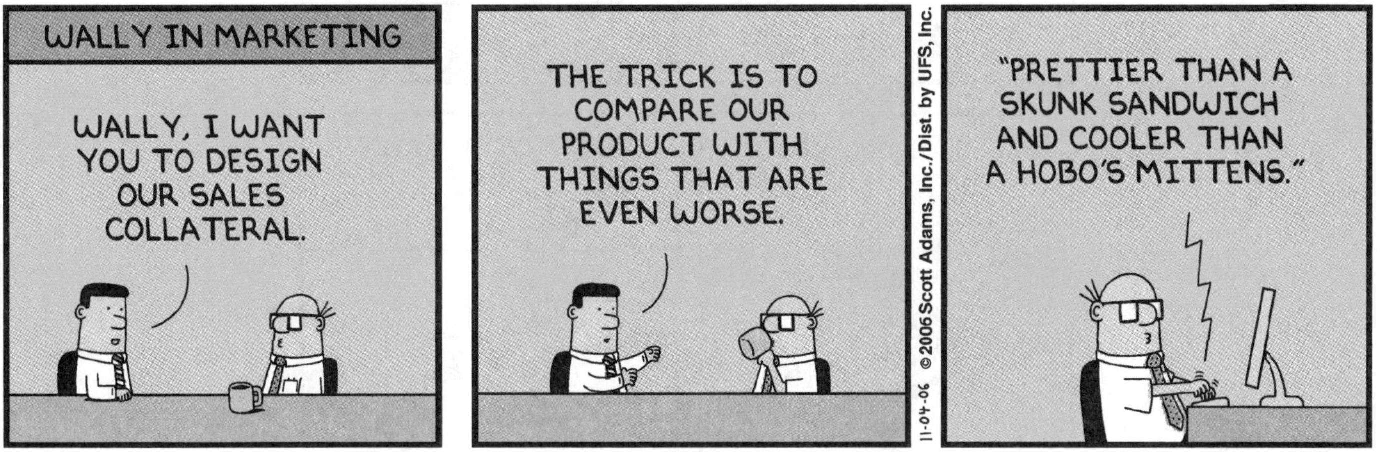
WALLY IN MARKETING
WALLY, I WANT YOU TO DESIGN OUR SALES COLLATERAL.
THE TRICK IS TO COMPARE OUR PRODUCT WITH THINGS THAT ARE EVEN WORSE.
"PRETTIER THAN A SKUNK SANDWICH AND COOLER THAN A HOBO'S MITTENS."
11-04-06 © 2006 Scott Adams, Inc./Dist. by UFS, Inc.

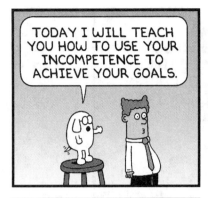

TODAY I WILL TEACH YOU HOW TO USE YOUR INCOMPETENCE TO ACHIEVE YOUR GOALS.
STEP 1: BE INCOMPETENT. (ALSO KNOWN AS "THE EASY PART.")
STEP 2: VOLUNTEER FOR THE MOST DIFFICULT AND IMPORTANT PROJECTS
STEP 3: CONVINCE YOUR BOSS THAT AN ENEMY WITHIN THE COMPANY IS SLOWING YOU DOWN.
STEP 4: INSIST THAT COMPETENT PEOPLE BE PULLED OFF OF OTHER PROJECTS TO HELP YOU.
STEP 5: DECLARE YOUR-SELF THE LEADER OF THE COMPETENT PEOPLE
STEP 6: CLAIM CREDIT FOR THE WORK OF THE COMPETENT PEOPLE.
STEP 7: AFTER YOU GET PROMOTED, FIRE THE COMPETENT PEOPLE TO ELIMINATE WITNESSES.
©2006 Scott Adams, Inc./Dist. by UFS, Inc.
11-05-06

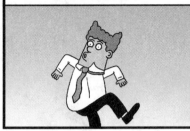

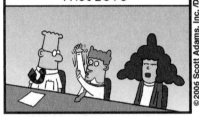

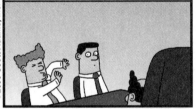

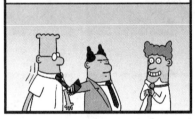

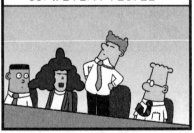

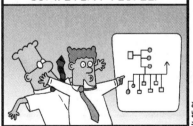

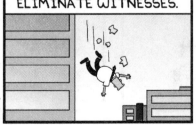

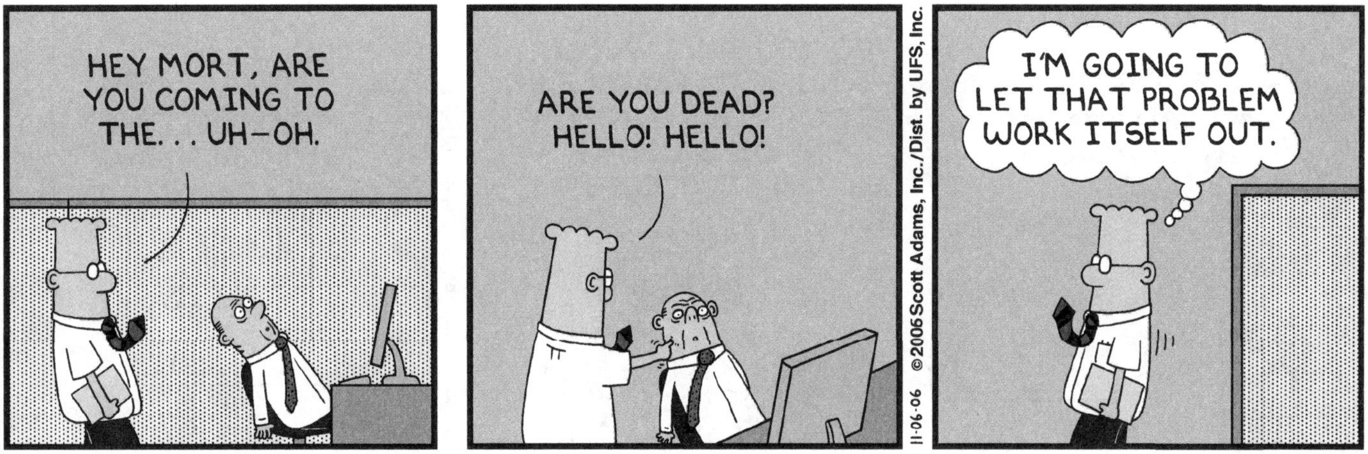
HEY MORT, ARE YOU COMING TO THE. . . UH—OH.
ARE YOU DEAD? HELLO! HELLO!
I'M GOING TO LET THAT PROBLEM WORK ITSELF OUT.
11-06-06 ©2006 Scott Adams, Inc./Dist. by UFS, Inc.

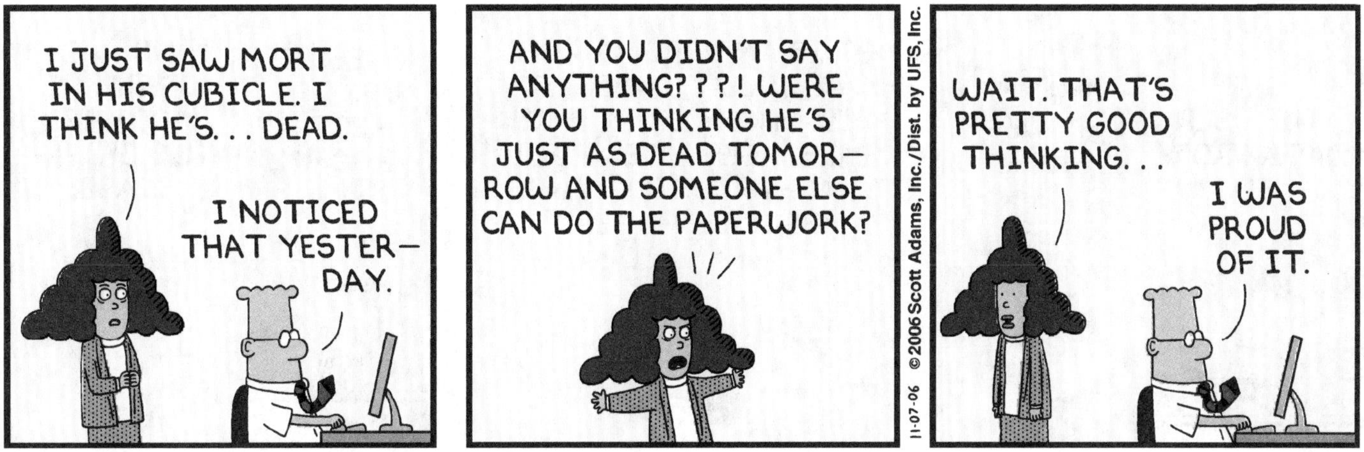
I JUST SAW MORT IN HIS CUBICLE. I THINK HE'S. . . DEAD.
I NOTICED THAT YESTER-DAY.
AND YOU DIDN'T SAY ANYTHING???! WERE YOU THINKING HE'S JUST AS DEAD TOMOR-ROW AND SOMEONE ELSE CAN DO THE PAPERWORK?
WAIT. THAT'S PRETTY GOOD THINKING. . .
I WAS PROUD OF IT.
11-07-06 ©2006 Scott Adams, Inc./Dist. by UFS, Inc.

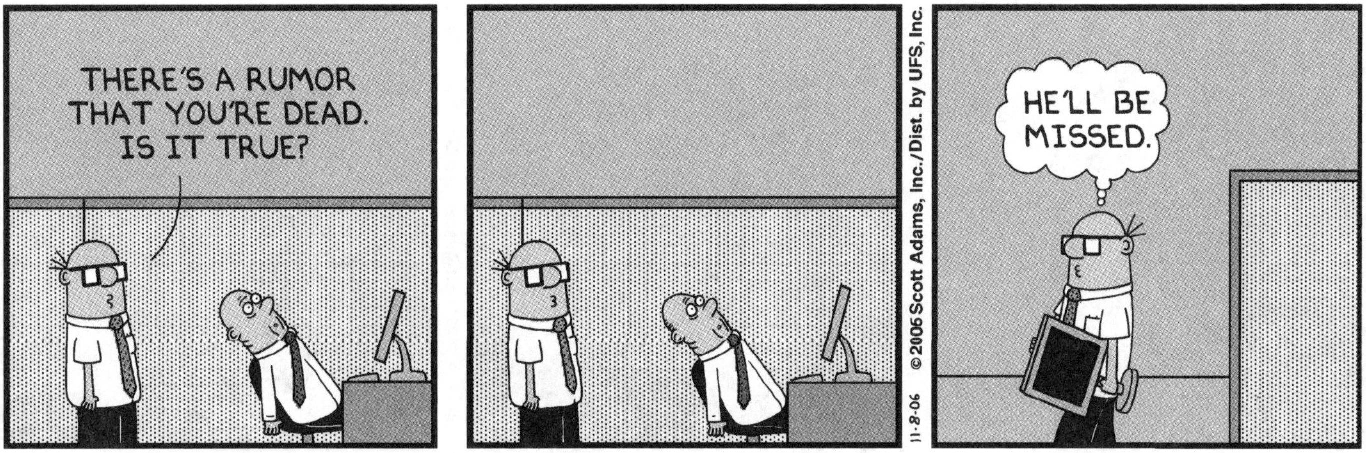
THERE'S A RUMOR THAT YOU'RE DEAD. IS IT TRUE?
HE'LL BE MISSED.
11-8-06 ©2006 Scott Adams, Inc./Dist. by UFS, Inc.

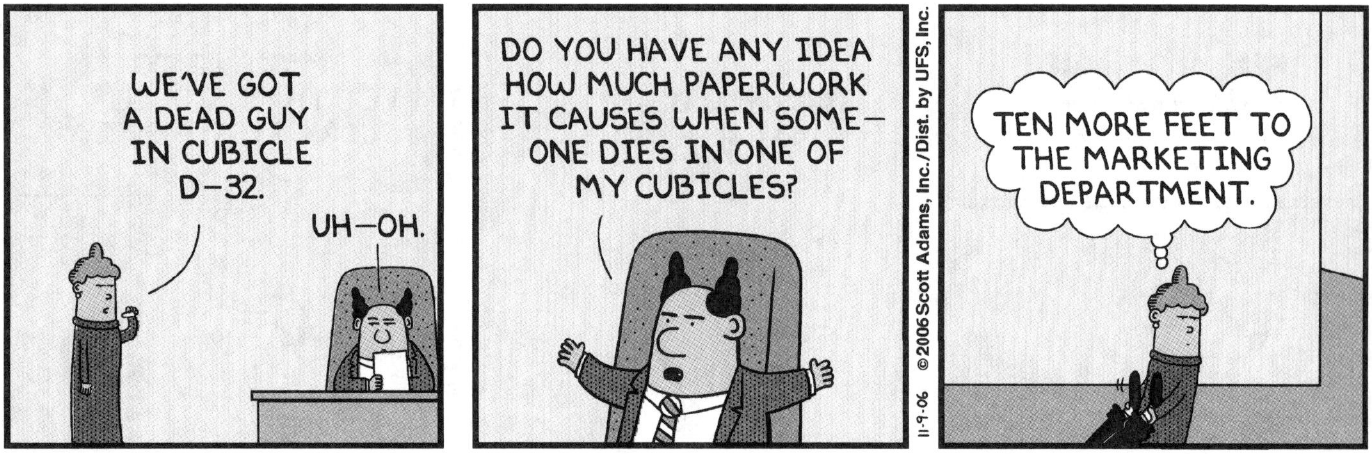
WE'VE GOT A DEAD GUY IN CUBICLE D-32.
UH-OH.
DO YOU HAVE ANY IDEA HOW MUCH PAPERWORK IT CAUSES WHEN SOME-ONE DIES IN ONE OF MY CUBICLES?
TEN MORE FEET TO THE MARKETING DEPARTMENT.
11-9-06 ©2006 Scott Adams, Inc./Dist. by UFS, Inc.

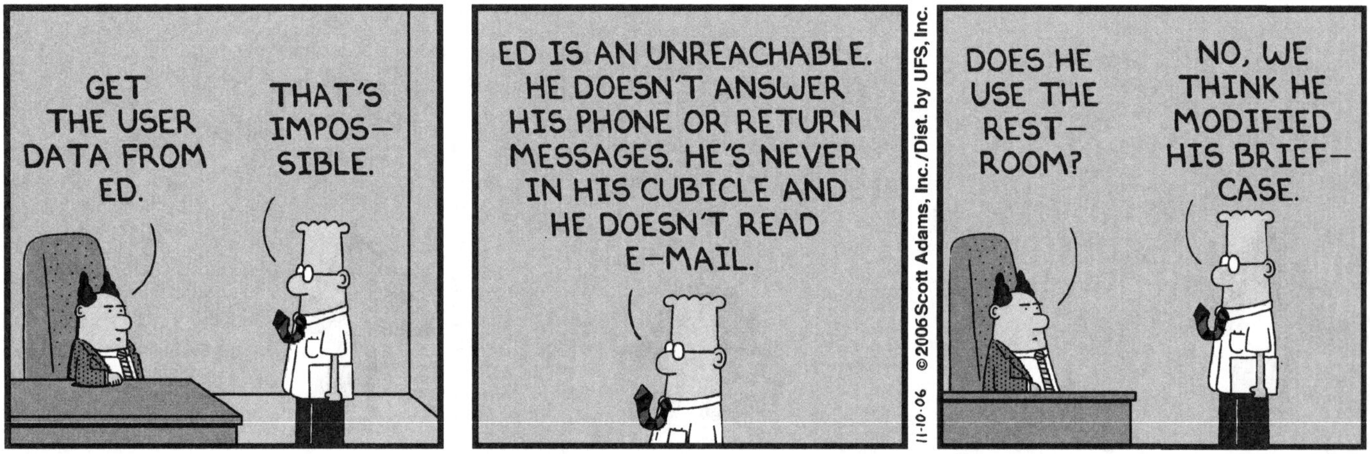
GET THE USER DATA FROM ED.
THAT'S IMPOS-SIBLE.
ED IS AN UNREACHABLE. HE DOESN'T ANSWER HIS PHONE OR RETURN MESSAGES. HE'S NEVER IN HIS CUBICLE AND HE DOESN'T READ E-MAIL.
DOES HE USE THE REST-ROOM?
NO, WE THINK HE MODIFIED HIS BRIEF-CASE.
11-10-06 ©2006 Scott Adams, Inc./Dist. by UFS, Inc.

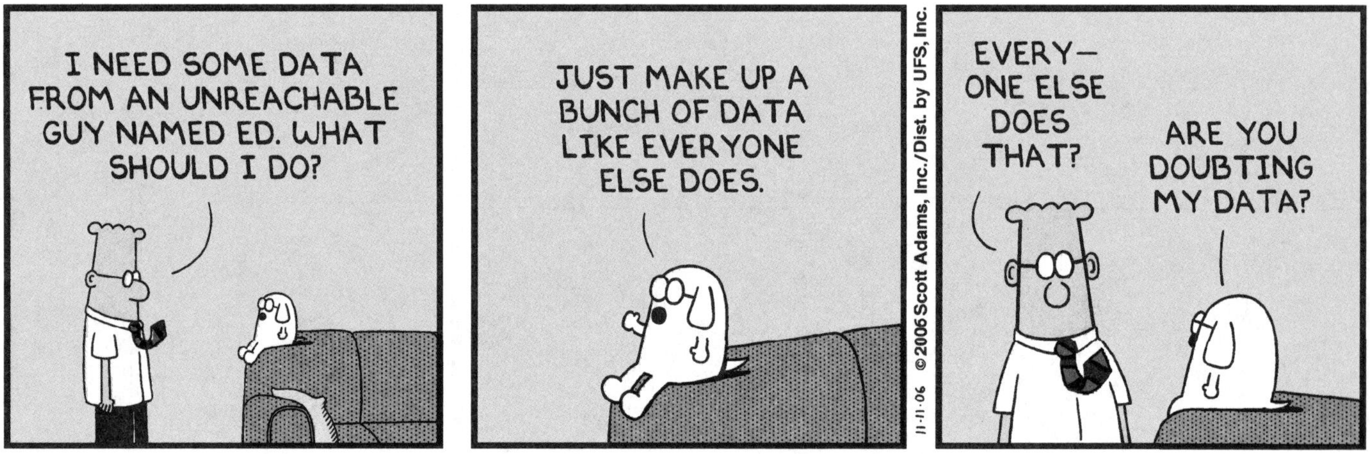
I NEED SOME DATA FROM AN UNREACHABLE GUY NAMED ED. WHAT SHOULD I DO?
JUST MAKE UP A BUNCH OF DATA LIKE EVERYONE ELSE DOES.
EVERY-ONE ELSE DOES THAT?
ARE YOU DOUBTING MY DATA?
11-11-06 ©2006 Scott Adams, Inc./Dist. by UFS, Inc.

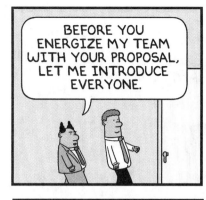

BEFORE YOU ENERGIZE MY TEAM WITH YOUR PROPOSAL, LET ME INTRODUCE EVERYONE.
THIS IS WALLY. HE'LL SHOW NO REACTION BECAUSE HE HOPES APATHY WILL KILL YOUR IDEA BEFORE IT CREATES WORK.
THIS IS ALICE. SHE'LL LEAVE HALFWAY THROUGH YOUR PRESENTATION TO TAKE A PHONE CALL.
©2006 Scott Adams, Inc./Dist. by UFS, Inc.
THIS IS ASOK. HE'LL BE ENTHUSIASTIC BECAUSE HE DOESN'T UNDERSTAND HOW THE REAL WORLD WORKS.
THIS IS DILBERT. HE'LL TELL YOU WHY YOUR IDEA IS IMPOSSIBLE.
THIS IS CAROL. SHE'LL SPEND THE ENTIRE MEETING WONDERING IF THAT'S YOUR REAL HAIR.
AND THIS IS TED. HE GAVE HIS TWO-WEEKS' NOTICE LAST WEEK.
11-12-06
AND I LIKE TO KEEP MY EYES CLOSED THE ENTIRE TIME BECAUSE OF MY ALLERGIES.
GO.

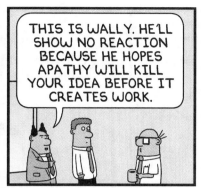

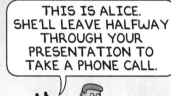

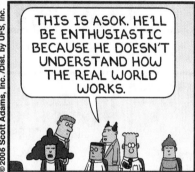

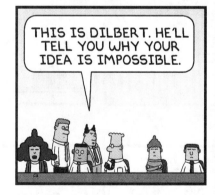

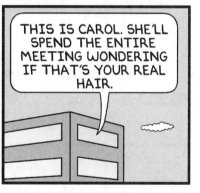

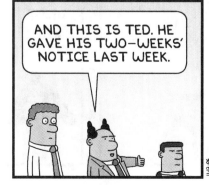

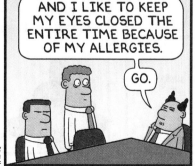

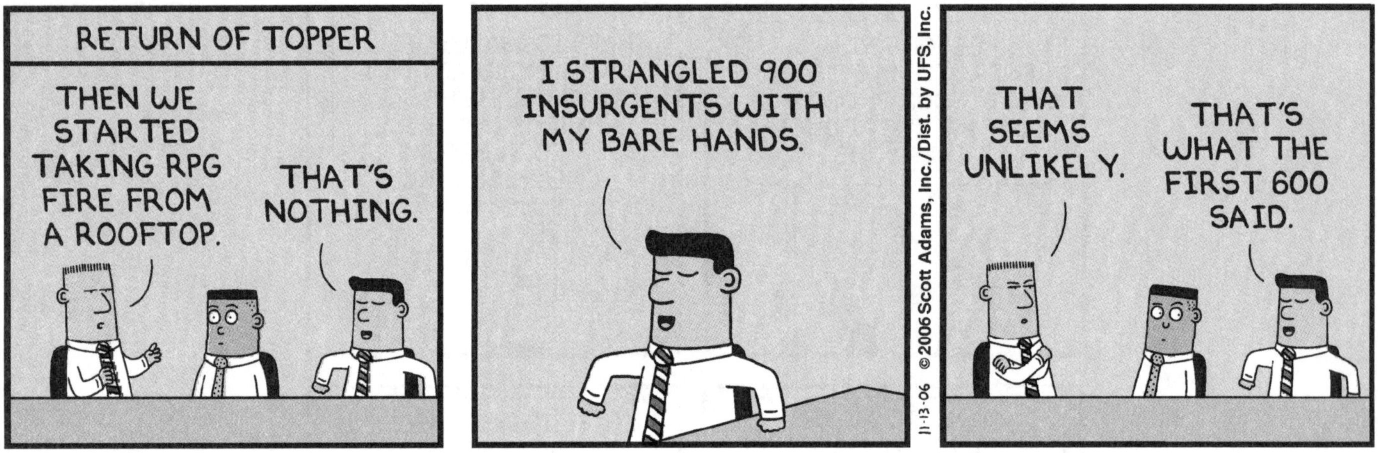
RETURN OF TOPPER
THEN WE STARTED TAKING RPG FIRE FROM A ROOFTOP.
THAT'S NOTHING.
I STRANGLED 900 INSURGENTS WITH MY BARE HANDS.
11-13-06 ©2006 Scott Adams, Inc./Dist. by UFS, Inc.
THAT SEEMS UNLIKELY.
THAT'S WHAT THE FIRST 600 SAID.

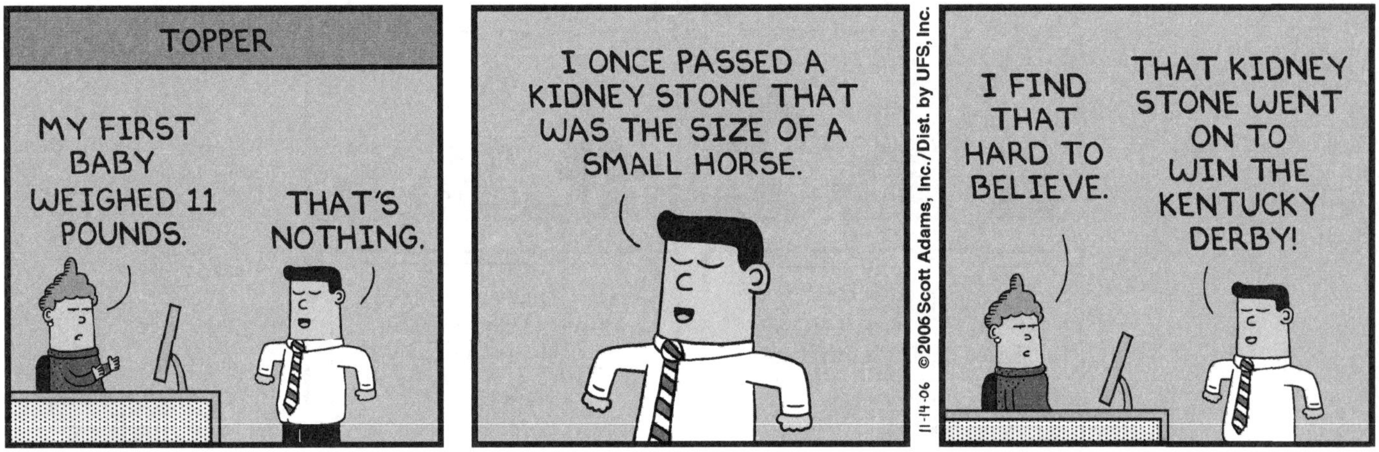
TOPPER
MY FIRST BABY WEIGHED 11 POUNDS.
THAT'S NOTHING.
I ONCE PASSED A KIDNEY STONE THAT WAS THE SIZE OF A SMALL HORSE.
11-14-06 ©2006 Scott Adams, Inc./Dist. by UFS, Inc.
I FIND THAT HARD TO BELIEVE.
THAT KIDNEY STONE WENT ON TO WIN THE KENTUCKY DERBY!

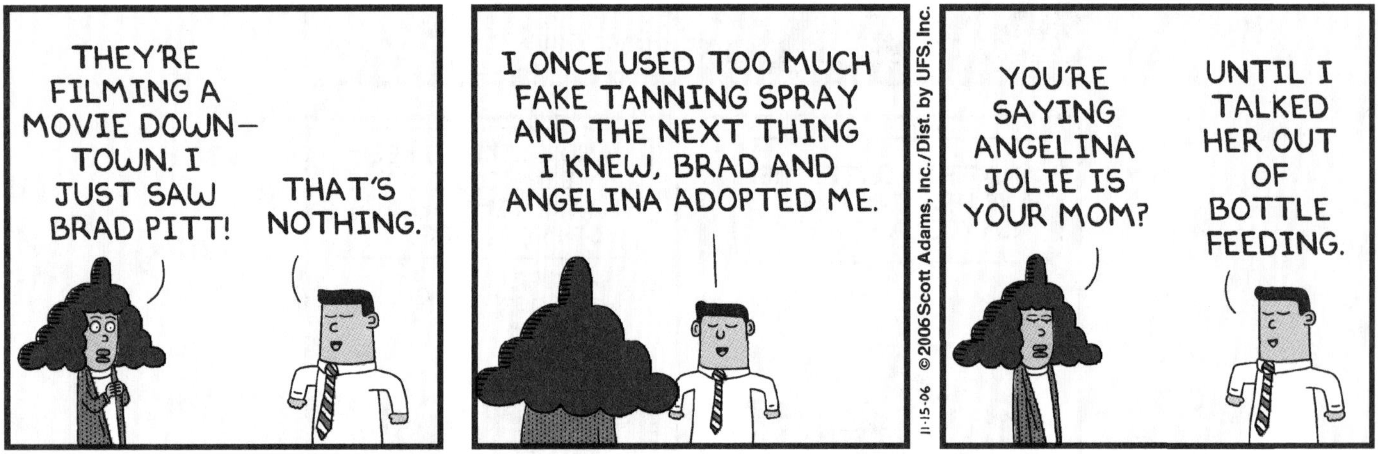
THEY'RE FILMING A MOVIE DOWN-TOWN. I JUST SAW BRAD PITT!
THAT'S NOTHING.
I ONCE USED TOO MUCH FAKE TANNING SPRAY AND THE NEXT THING I KNEW, BRAD AND ANGELINA ADOPTED ME.
11-15-06 ©2006 Scott Adams, Inc./Dist. by UFS, Inc.
YOU'RE SAYING ANGELINA JOLIE IS YOUR MOM?
UNTIL I TALKED HER OUT OF BOTTLE FEEDING.

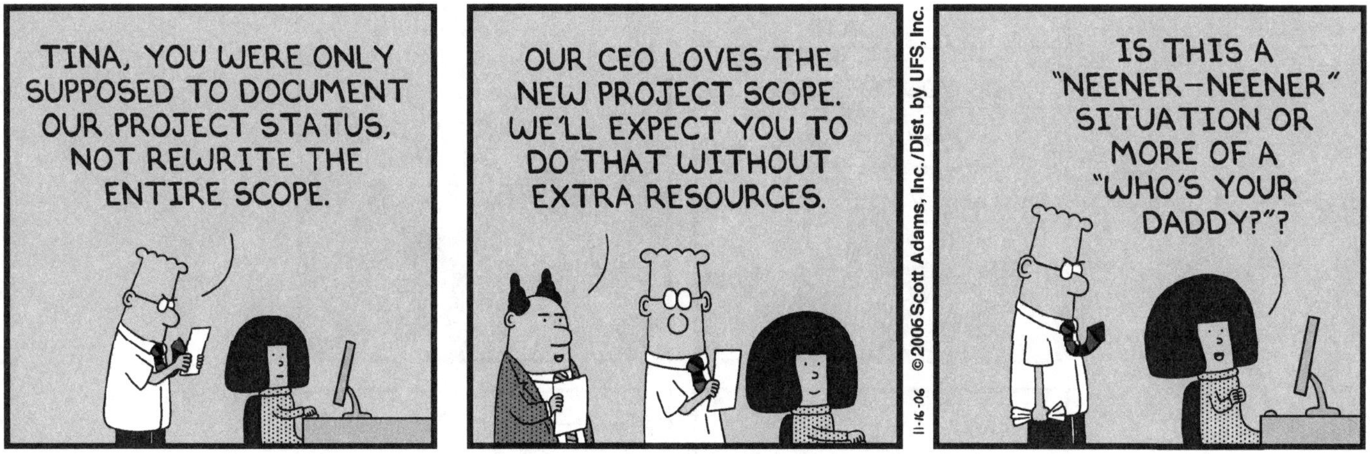
TINA, YOU WERE ONLY SUPPOSED TO DOCUMENT OUR PROJECT STATUS, NOT REWRITE THE ENTIRE SCOPE.
OUR CEO LOVES THE NEW PROJECT SCOPE. WE'LL EXPECT YOU TO DO THAT WITHOUT EXTRA RESOURCES.
11-16-06 © 2006 Scott Adams, Inc./Dist. by UFS, Inc.
IS THIS A "NEENER-NEENER" SITUATION OR MORE OF A "WHO'S YOUR DADDY?"?

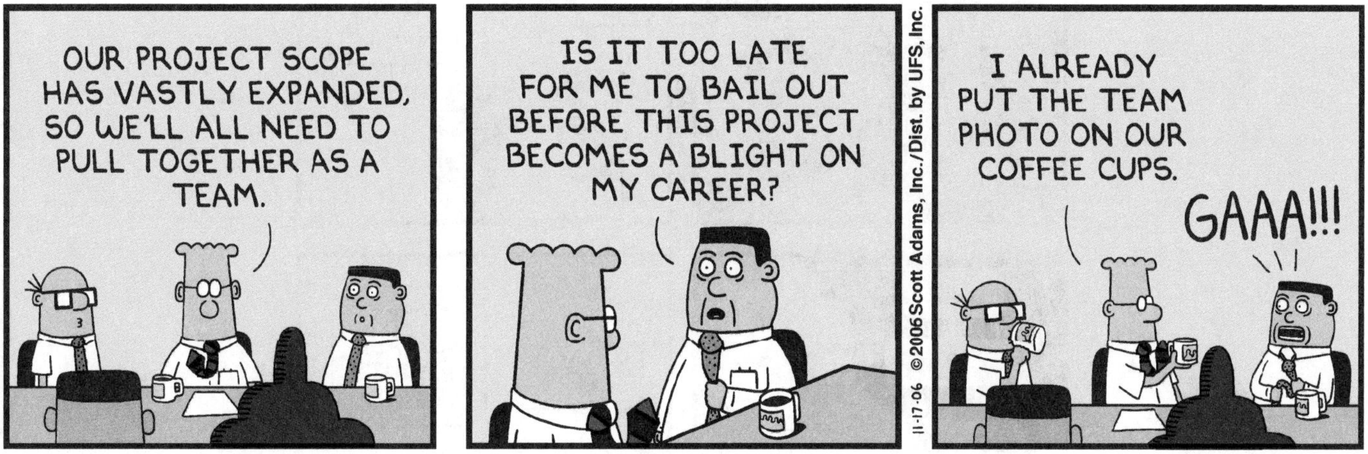
OUR PROJECT SCOPE HAS VASTLY EXPANDED, SO WE'LL ALL NEED TO PULL TOGETHER AS A TEAM.
IS IT TOO LATE FOR ME TO BAIL OUT BEFORE THIS PROJECT BECOMES A BLIGHT ON MY CAREER?
11-17-06 © 2006 Scott Adams, Inc./Dist. by UFS, Inc.
I ALREADY PUT THE TEAM PHOTO ON OUR COFFEE CUPS.
GAAA!!!

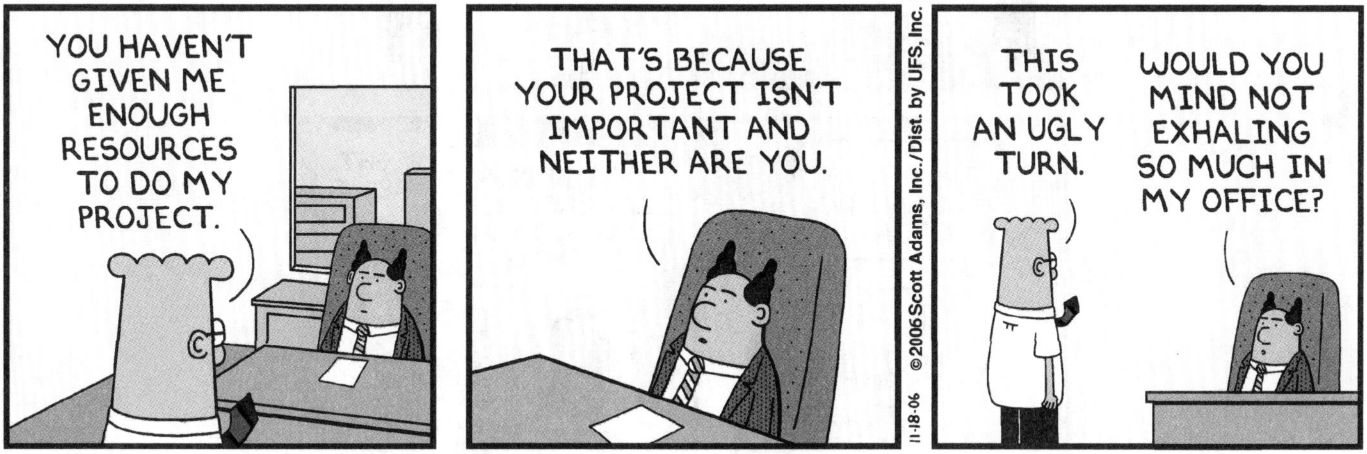
YOU HAVEN'T GIVEN ME ENOUGH RESOURCES TO DO MY PROJECT.
THAT'S BECAUSE YOUR PROJECT ISN'T IMPORTANT AND NEITHER ARE YOU.
11-18-06 © 2006 Scott Adams, Inc./Dist. by UFS, Inc.
THIS TOOK AN UGLY TURN.
WOULD YOU MIND NOT EXHALING SO MUCH IN MY OFFICE?

FIRST DATE
DO YOU FEEL LIKE DOING SOME CON-VERSATION?
OKAY. I LOVE TALKING.
DO YOU LIKE POLITICS?
NO.
SCIENCE AND TECH-NOLOGY?
NOT REALLY.
WAR?
NO.
SPORTS?
NO.
CURRENT EVENTS?
NO.
WHAT'S LEFT?
I LIKE TO TALK ABOUT MY HAIR.
UM... OKAY, WE CAN TRY THAT.
THIS BROWN IS A BROWNER BROWN THAN I WANTED.
RIGHT. ARE WE DONE WITH HAIR?
©2006 Scott Adams, Inc. /Dist. by UFS, Inc.
11-19-06

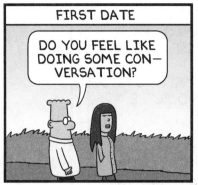

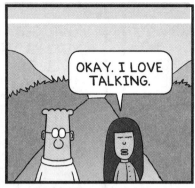

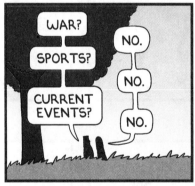

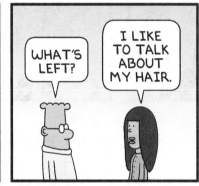

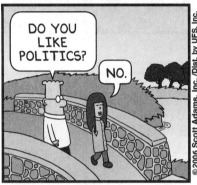

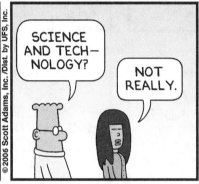

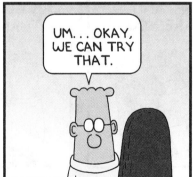

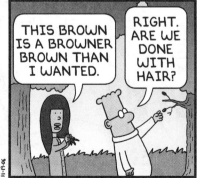

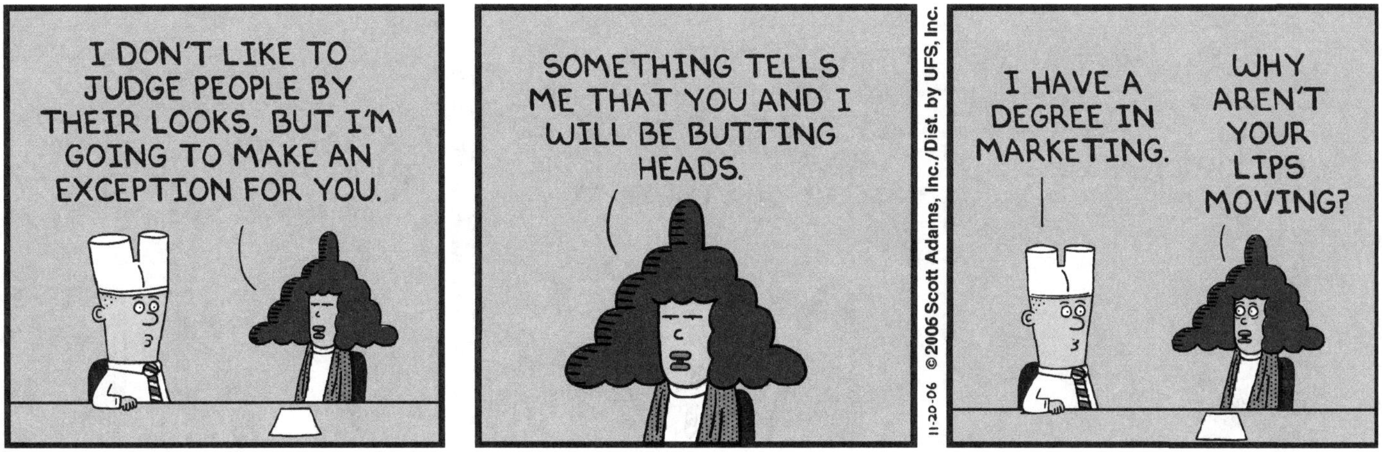
I DON'T LIKE TO JUDGE PEOPLE BY THEIR LOOKS, BUT I'M GOING TO MAKE AN EXCEPTION FOR YOU.
SOMETHING TELLS ME THAT YOU AND I WILL BE BUTTING HEADS.
I HAVE A DEGREE IN MARKETING.
WHY AREN'T YOUR LIPS MOVING?
11-20-06 ©2006 Scott Adams, Inc./Dist. by UFS, Inc.

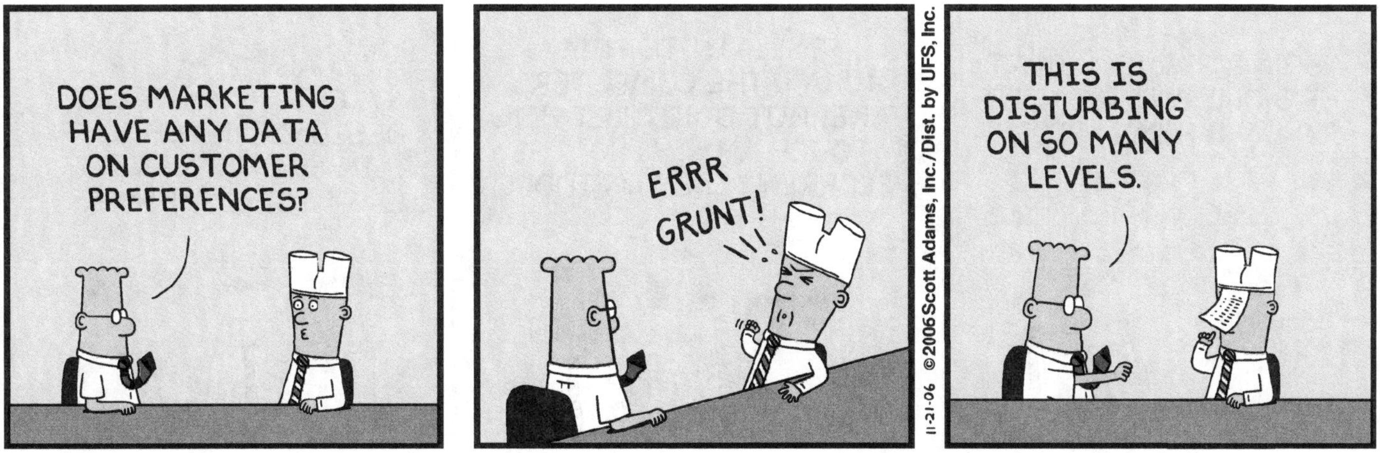
DOES MARKETING HAVE ANY DATA ON CUSTOMER PREFERENCES?
ERRR GRUNT!
THIS IS DISTURBING ON SO MANY LEVELS.
11-21-06 ©2006 Scott Adams, Inc./Dist. by UFS, Inc.

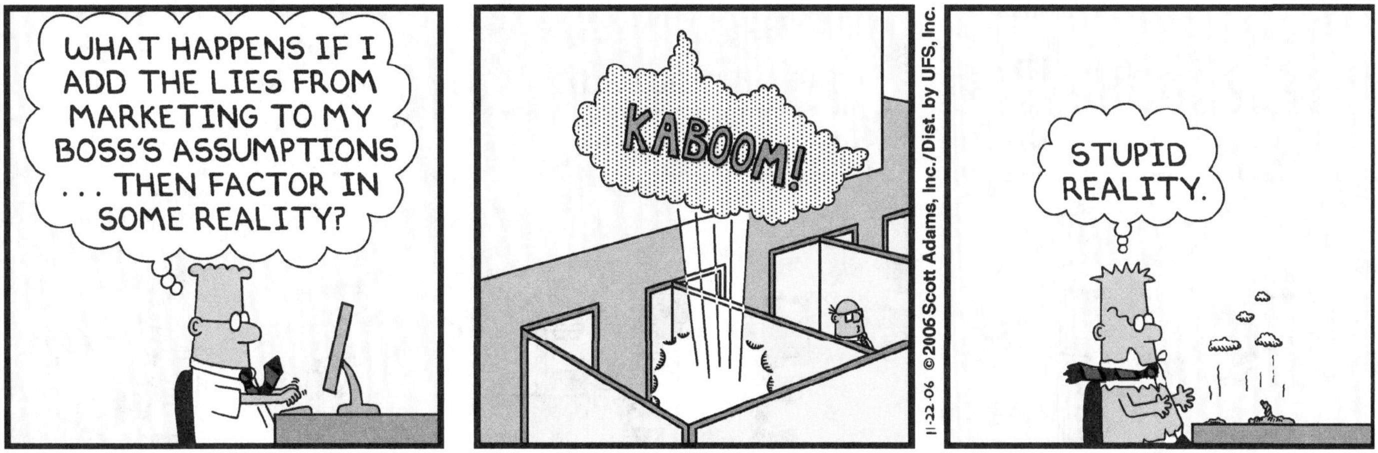
WHAT HAPPENS IF I ADD THE LIES FROM MARKETING TO MY BOSS'S ASSUMPTIONS . . . THEN FACTOR IN SOME REALITY?
KABOOM!
STUPID REALITY.
11-22-06 ©2006 Scott Adams, Inc./Dist. by UFS, Inc.

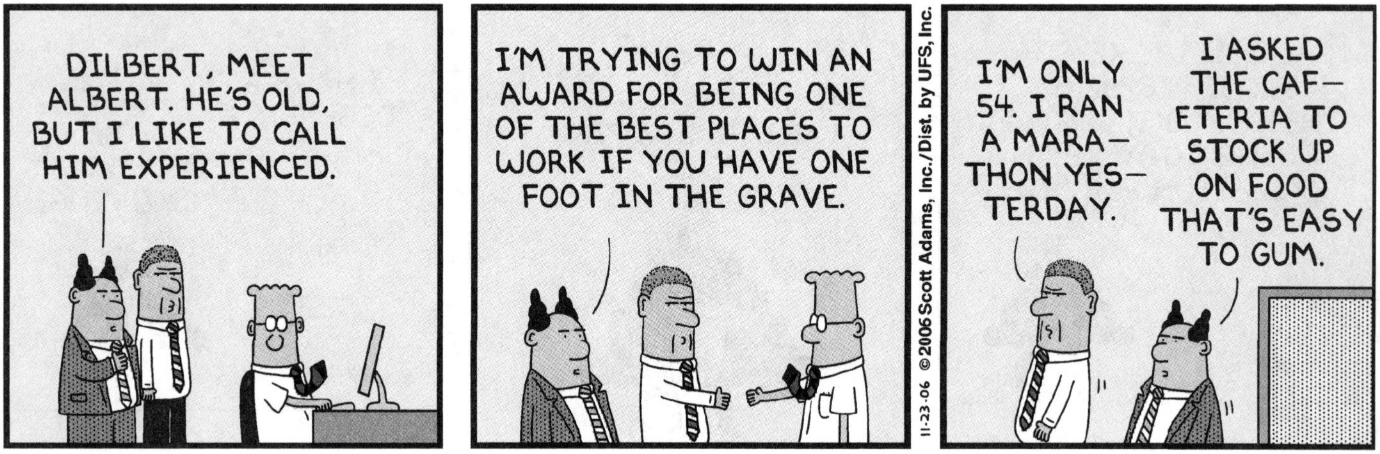
DILBERT, MEET ALBERT. HE'S OLD, BUT I LIKE TO CALL HIM EXPERIENCED.
I'M TRYING TO WIN AN AWARD FOR BEING ONE OF THE BEST PLACES TO WORK IF YOU HAVE ONE FOOT IN THE GRAVE.
11-23-06 ©2006 Scott Adams, Inc./Dist. by UFS, Inc.
I'M ONLY 54. I RAN A MARA-THON YES-TERDAY.
I ASKED THE CAF-ETERIA TO STOCK UP ON FOOD THAT'S EASY TO GUM.

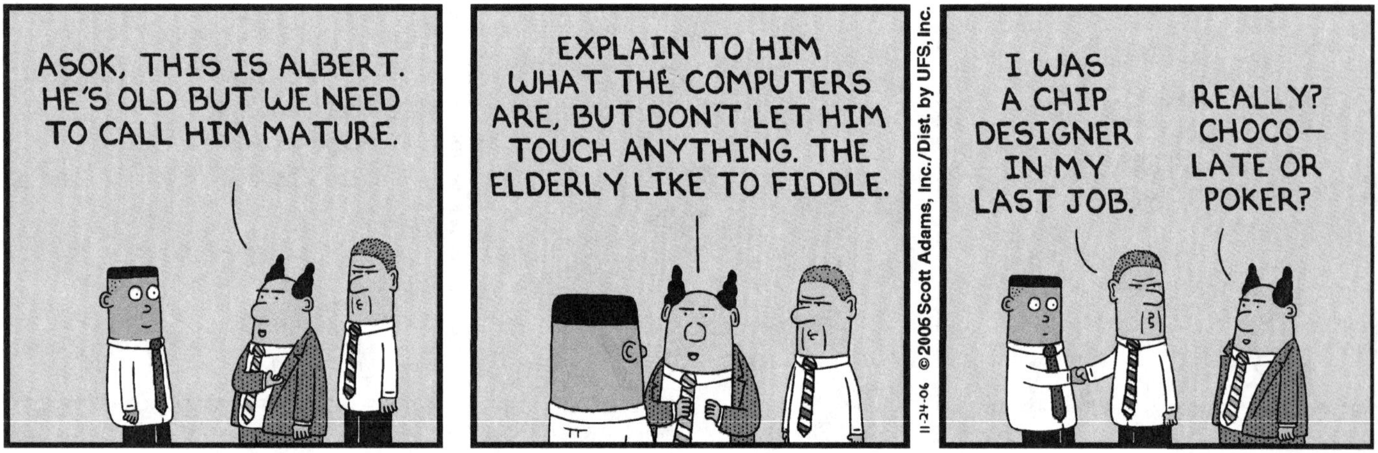
ASOK, THIS IS ALBERT. HE'S OLD BUT WE NEED TO CALL HIM MATURE.
EXPLAIN TO HIM WHAT THE COMPUTERS ARE, BUT DON'T LET HIM TOUCH ANYTHING. THE ELDERLY LIKE TO FIDDLE.
11-24-06 ©2006 Scott Adams, Inc./Dist. by UFS, Inc.
I WAS A CHIP DESIGNER IN MY LAST JOB.
REALLY? CHOCO-LATE OR POKER?

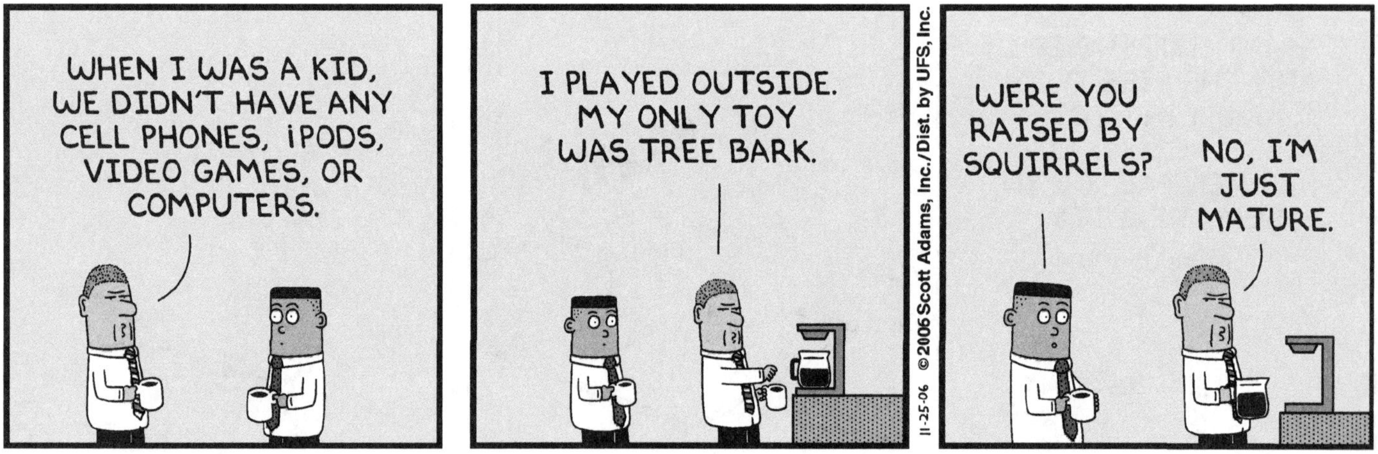
WHEN I WAS A KID, WE DIDN'T HAVE ANY CELL PHONES, iPODS, VIDEO GAMES, OR COMPUTERS.
I PLAYED OUTSIDE. MY ONLY TOY WAS TREE BARK.
11-25-06 ©2006 Scott Adams, Inc./Dist. by UFS, Inc.
WERE YOU RAISED BY SQUIRRELS?
NO, I'M JUST MATURE.

OUR COMPANY HAS DECIDED TO TRY SOMETHING NEW.
SIX SIGMA
NEW? SIX SIGMA WAS DEVELOPED IN THE 80s.
IT'S NEW TO US.
WHY DON'T WE JUMP ON A FAD THAT HASN'T ALREADY BEEN WIDELY DISCREDITED?
©2006 Scott Adams, Inc./Dist. by UFS, Inc.
THAT WAY THE FALSE HOPE MIGHT SUSTAIN US.
THERE'S NOTHING WRONG WITH SIX SIGMA. ALL IT DOES IS REDUCE DEFECTS!
LET'S SEE. . . FORTUNE MAGAZINE SAYS. . . BLAH, BLAH. . . MOST COMPANIES THAT USED SIX SIGMA HAVE TRAILED THE S&P 500.
11-26-06
SORRY I'M LATE. WHAT DID I MISS WHILE I WAS INNOVATING?

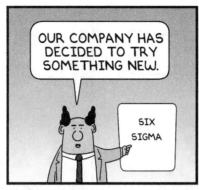

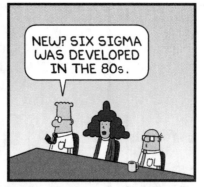

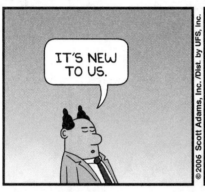

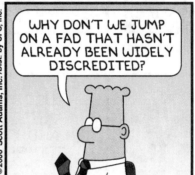

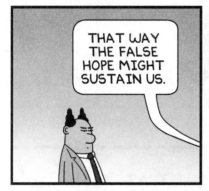

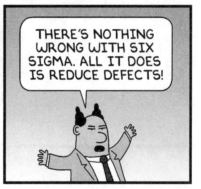

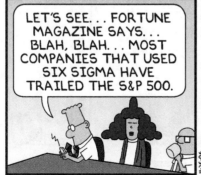

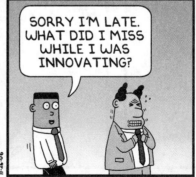

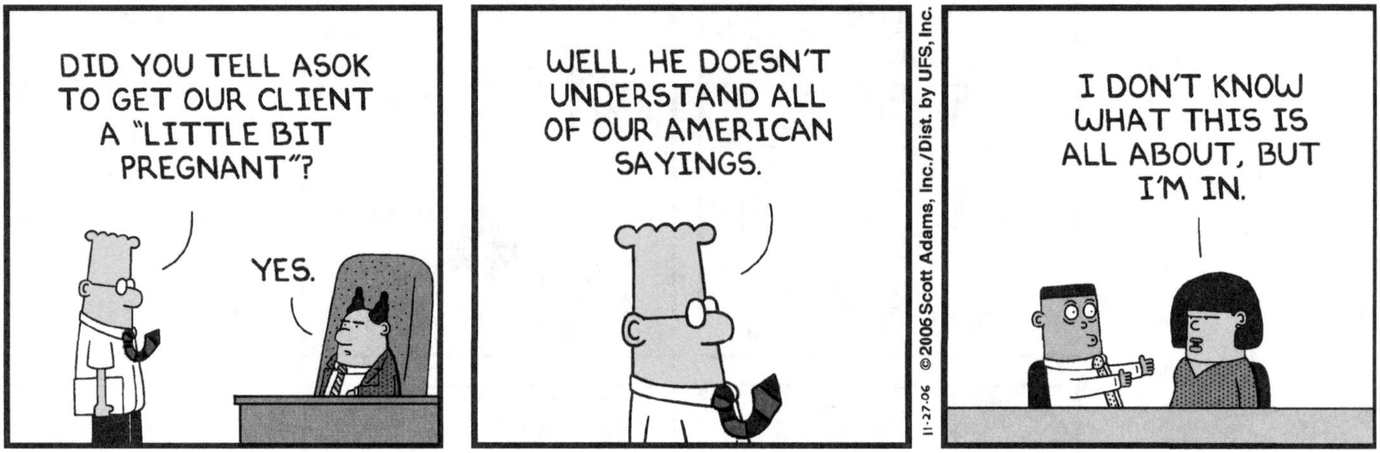
DID YOU TELL ASOK TO GET OUR CLIENT A "LITTLE BIT PREGNANT"?
YES.
WELL, HE DOESN'T UNDERSTAND ALL OF OUR AMERICAN SAYINGS.
11-27-06 © 2006 Scott Adams, Inc./Dist. by UFS, Inc.
I DON'T KNOW WHAT THIS IS ALL ABOUT, BUT I'M IN.

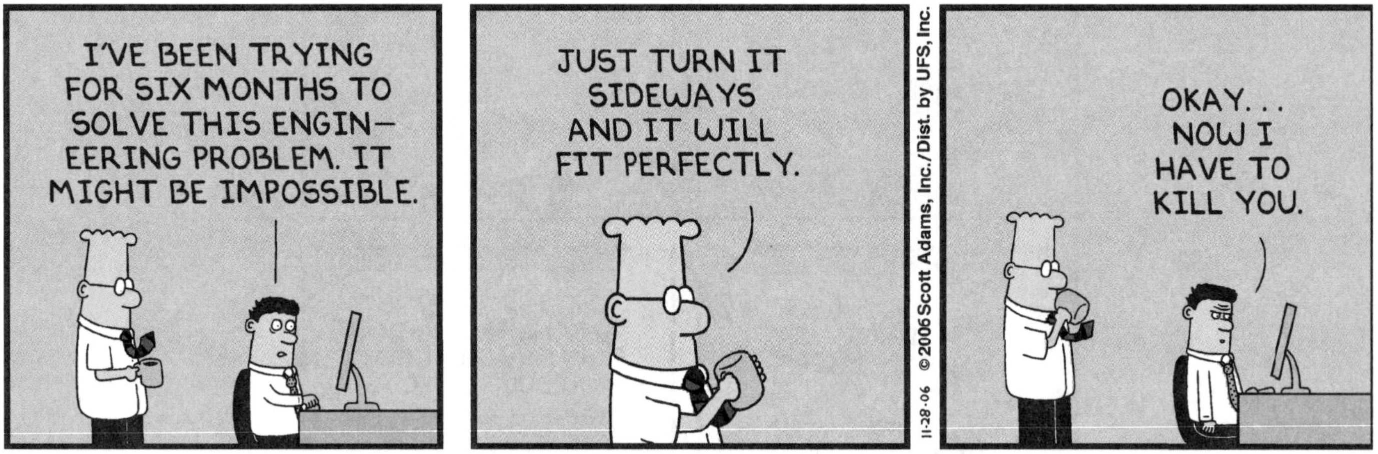
I'VE BEEN TRYING FOR SIX MONTHS TO SOLVE THIS ENGIN-EERING PROBLEM. IT MIGHT BE IMPOSSIBLE.
JUST TURN IT SIDEWAYS AND IT WILL FIT PERFECTLY.
11-28-06 © 2006 Scott Adams, Inc./Dist. by UFS, Inc.
OKAY... NOW I HAVE TO KILL YOU.

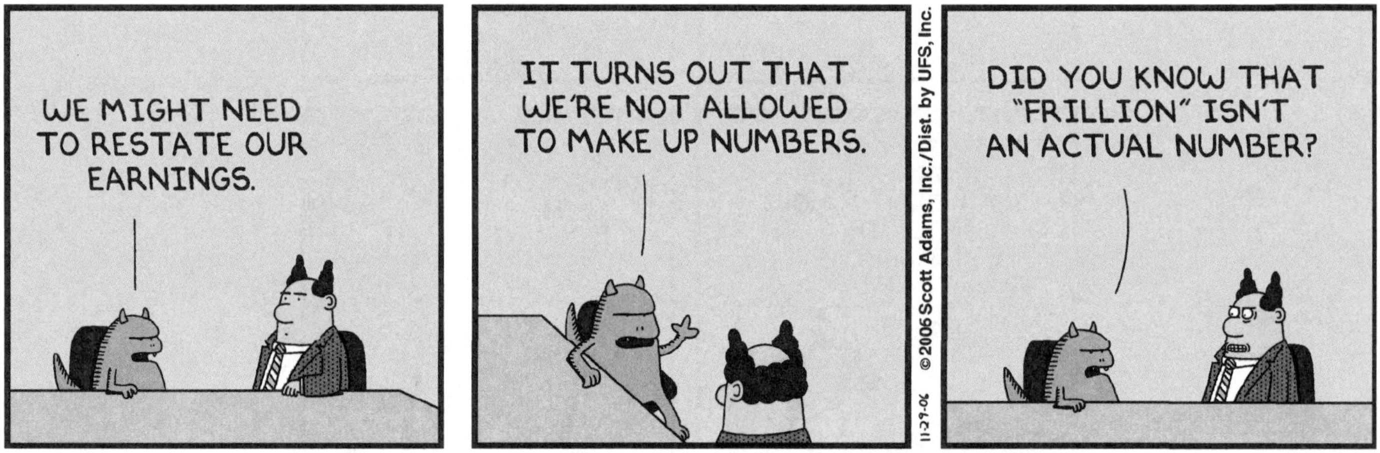
WE MIGHT NEED TO RESTATE OUR EARNINGS.
IT TURNS OUT THAT WE'RE NOT ALLOWED TO MAKE UP NUMBERS.
11-29-06 © 2006 Scott Adams, Inc./Dist. by UFS, Inc.
DID YOU KNOW THAT "FRILLION" ISN'T AN ACTUAL NUMBER?

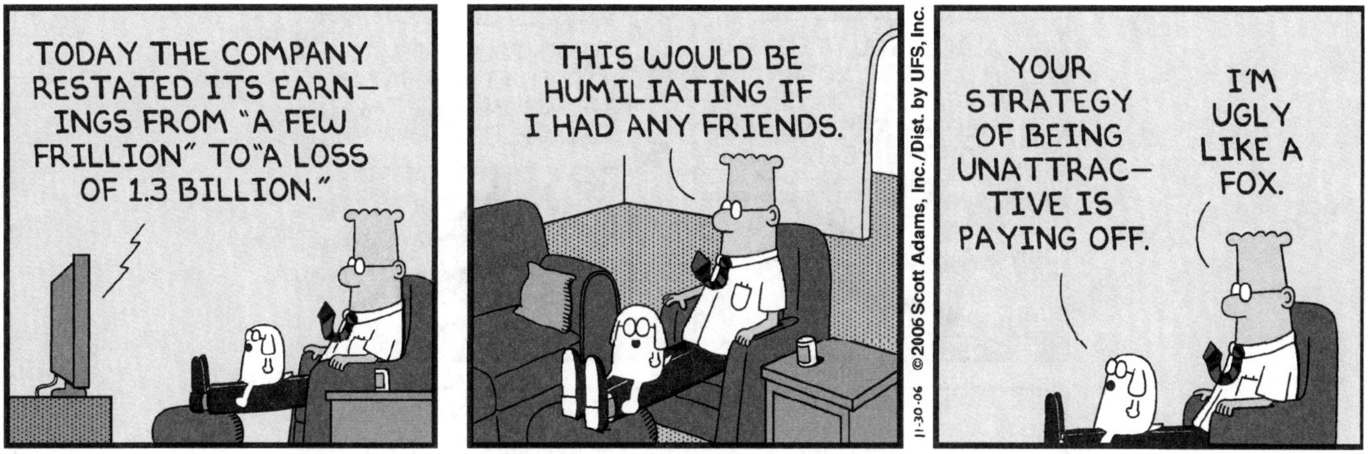
TODAY THE COMPANY RESTATED ITS EARN–INGS FROM "A FEW FRILLION" TO "A LOSS OF 1.3 BILLION."
THIS WOULD BE HUMILIATING IF I HAD ANY FRIENDS.
11-30-06 © 2006 Scott Adams, Inc./Dist. by UFS, Inc.
YOUR STRATEGY OF BEING UNATTRAC–TIVE IS PAYING OFF.
I'M UGLY LIKE A FOX.

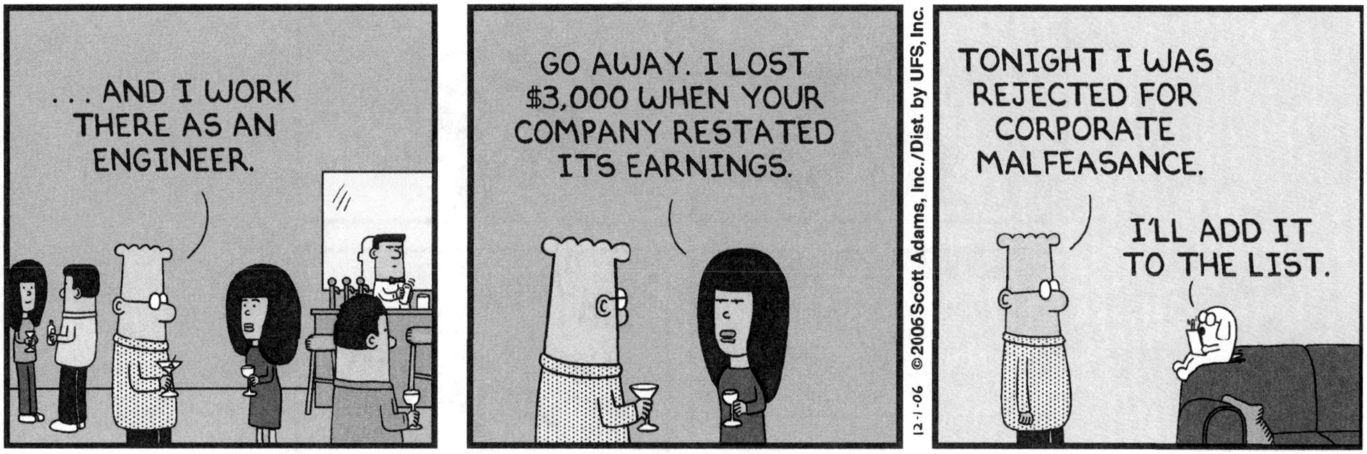
. . . AND I WORK THERE AS AN ENGINEER.
GO AWAY. I LOST $3,000 WHEN YOUR COMPANY RESTATED ITS EARNINGS.
12-1-06 © 2006 Scott Adams, Inc./Dist. by UFS, Inc.
TONIGHT I WAS REJECTED FOR CORPORATE MALFEASANCE.
I'LL ADD IT TO THE LIST.

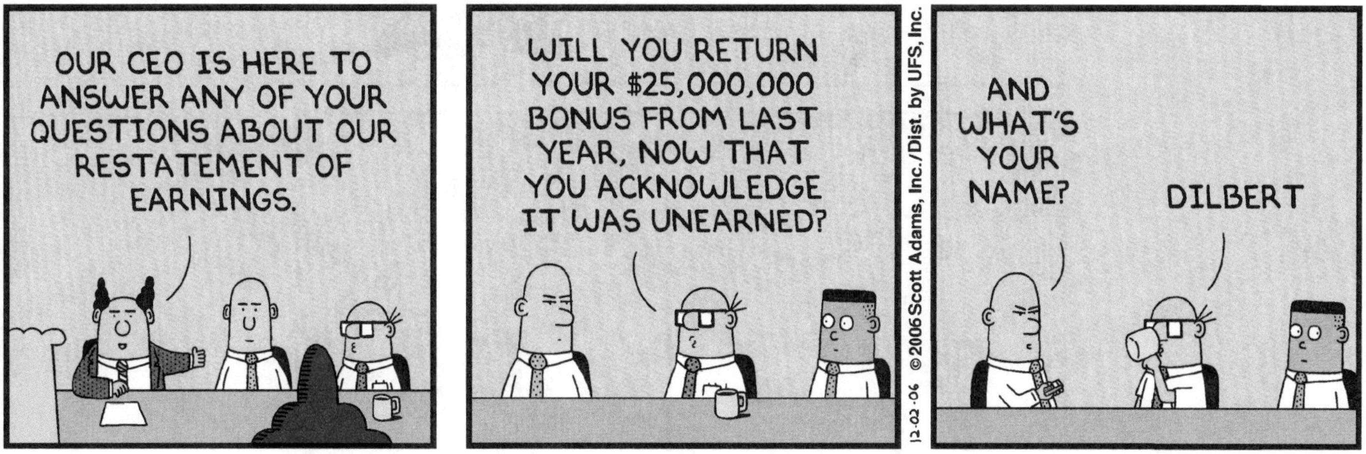
OUR CEO IS HERE TO ANSWER ANY OF YOUR QUESTIONS ABOUT OUR RESTATEMENT OF EARNINGS.
WILL YOU RETURN YOUR $25,000,000 BONUS FROM LAST YEAR, NOW THAT YOU ACKNOWLEDGE IT WAS UNEARNED?
12-02-06 © 2006 Scott Adams, Inc./Dist. by UFS, Inc.
AND WHAT'S YOUR NAME?
DILBERT

ALICE, YOU NEED TO USE UP YOUR VACATION DAYS BEFORE THE END OF THE YEAR.
YOU TOLD ME I HAD TO FINISH MY PROJECT BEFORE THE END OF THE YEAR.
I HAVE 19 VACATION DAYS TO USE AND THERE ARE 19 WORK DAYS LEFT IN THE YEAR..
THAT LEAVES ZERO DAYS TO DO 19 DAYS WORTH OF WORK.
YOU COULD WORK ON WEEKENDS AND USE WEEKDAYS FOR VACATION.
WHY THE *%@!# WOULD I DO THAT?!!
BECAUSE VACATIONS REDUCE YOUR STRESS.
DUH.
YOU'D THINK THAT WOULD BE OBVIOUS.
AAIEEE!!!
PUNCH!!!
12-3-06

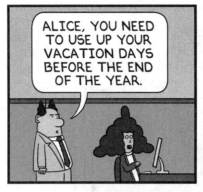

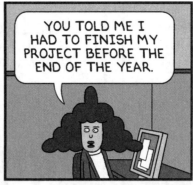

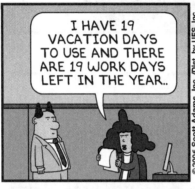

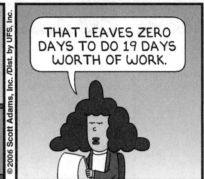

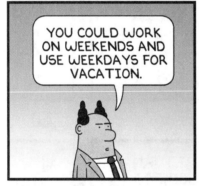

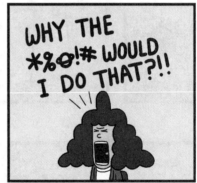

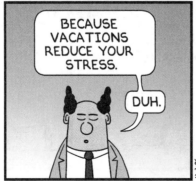

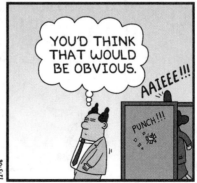

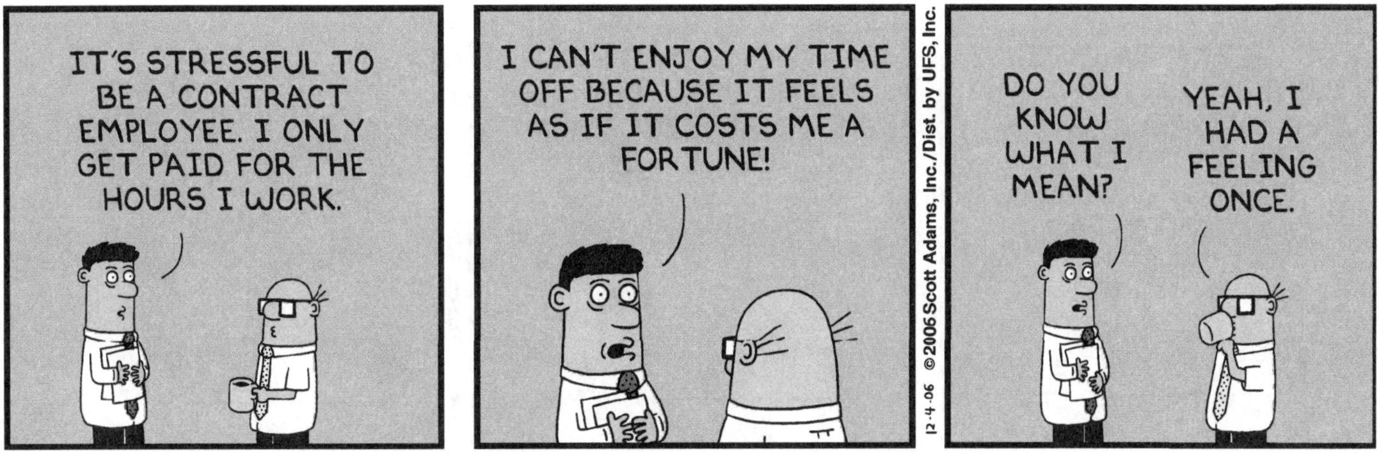
IT'S STRESSFUL TO BE A CONTRACT EMPLOYEE. I ONLY GET PAID FOR THE HOURS I WORK.
I CAN'T ENJOY MY TIME OFF BECAUSE IT FEELS AS IF IT COSTS ME A FORTUNE!
DO YOU KNOW WHAT I MEAN?
YEAH, I HAD A FEELING ONCE.
12-4-06 ©2006 Scott Adams, Inc./Dist. by UFS, Inc.

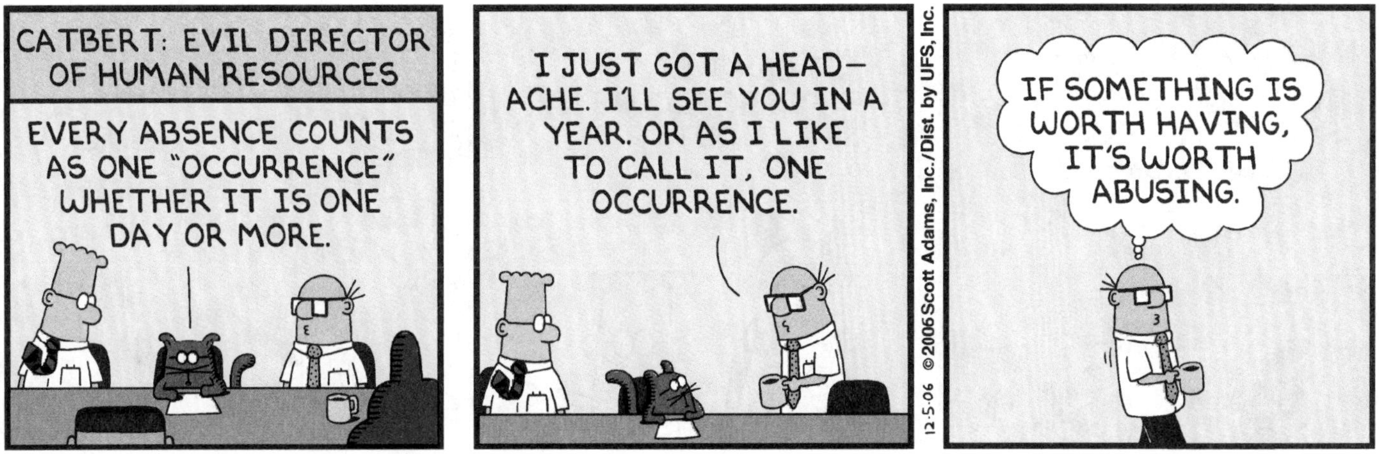
CATBERT: EVIL DIRECTOR OF HUMAN RESOURCES
EVERY ABSENCE COUNTS AS ONE "OCCURRENCE" WHETHER IT IS ONE DAY OR MORE.
I JUST GOT A HEAD-ACHE. I'LL SEE YOU IN A YEAR. OR AS I LIKE TO CALL IT, ONE OCCURRENCE.
IF SOMETHING IS WORTH HAVING, IT'S WORTH ABUSING.
12-5-06 ©2006 Scott Adams, Inc./Dist. by UFS, Inc.

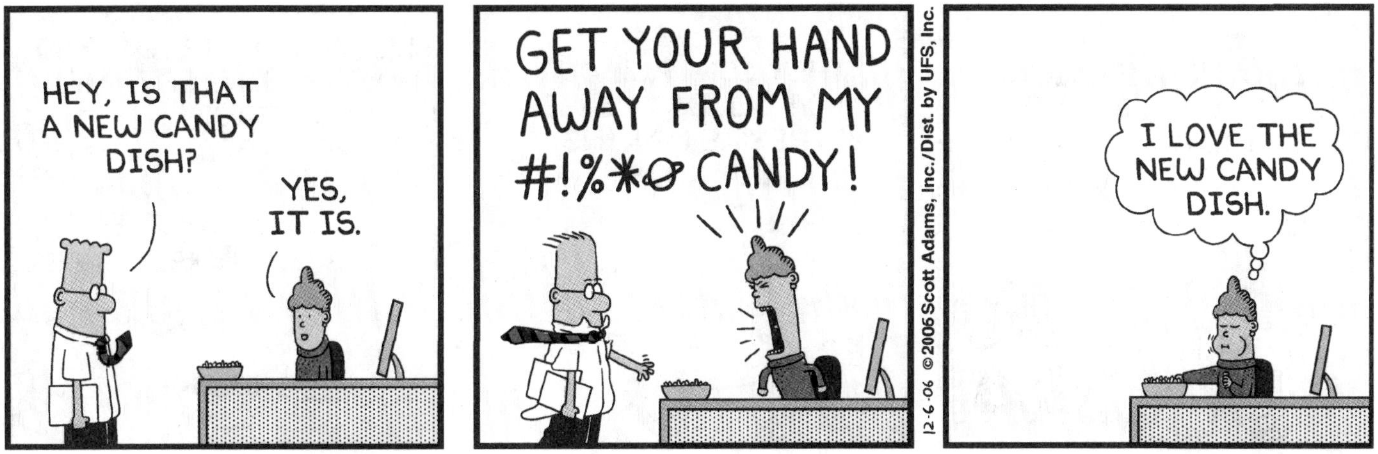
HEY, IS THAT A NEW CANDY DISH?
YES, IT IS.
GET YOUR HAND AWAY FROM MY #!%*ø CANDY!
I LOVE THE NEW CANDY DISH.
12-6-06 ©2006 Scott Adams, Inc./Dist. by UFS, Inc.

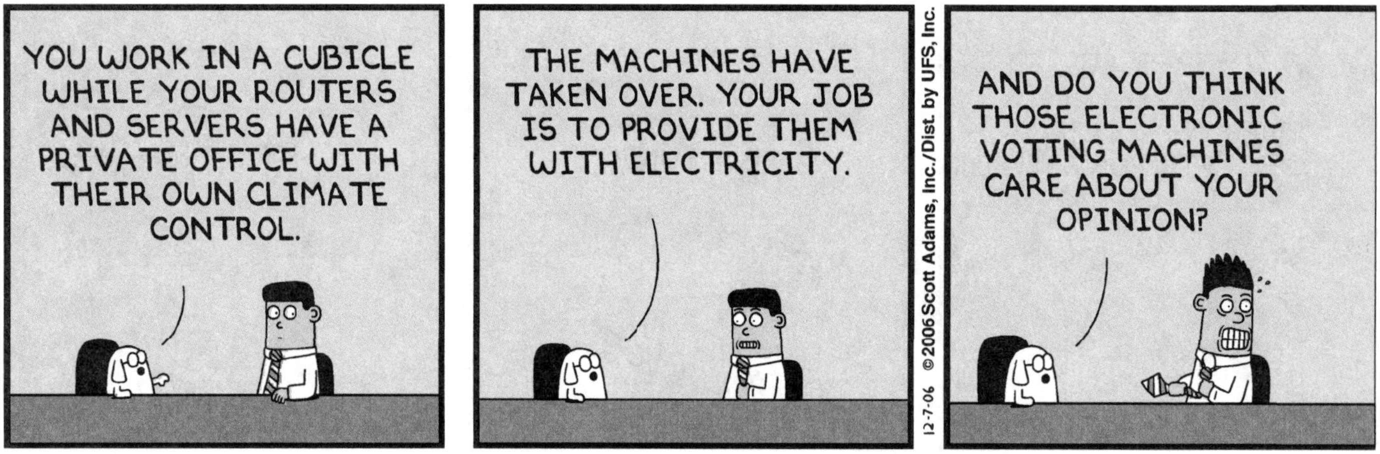
YOU WORK IN A CUBICLE WHILE YOUR ROUTERS AND SERVERS HAVE A PRIVATE OFFICE WITH THEIR OWN CLIMATE CONTROL.
THE MACHINES HAVE TAKEN OVER. YOUR JOB IS TO PROVIDE THEM WITH ELECTRICITY.
12-7-06 ©2006 Scott Adams, Inc./Dist. by UFS, Inc.
AND DO YOU THINK THOSE ELECTRONIC VOTING MACHINES CARE ABOUT YOUR OPINION?

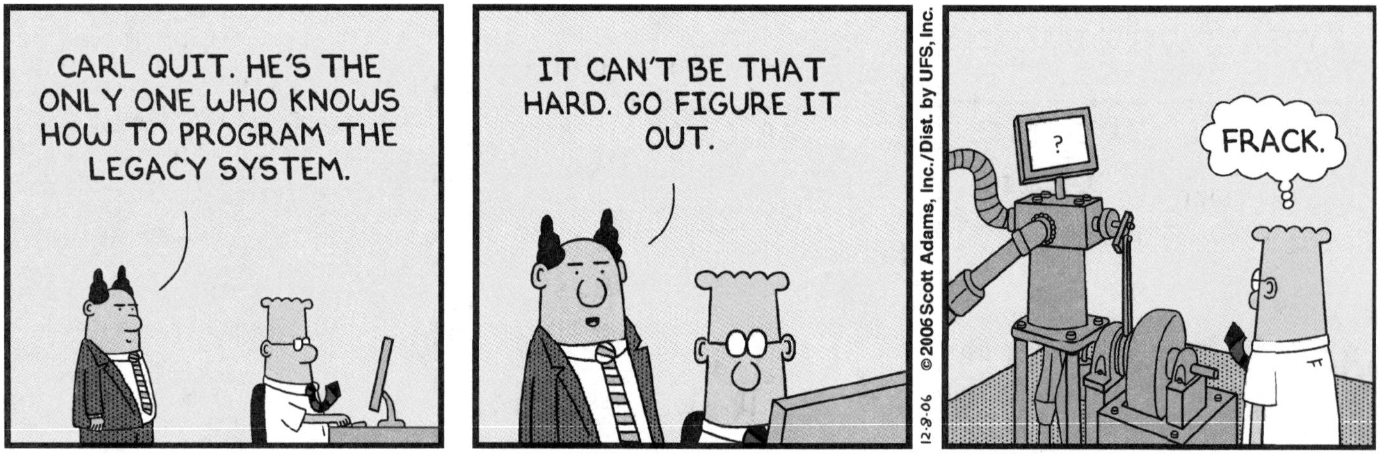
CARL QUIT. HE'S THE ONLY ONE WHO KNOWS HOW TO PROGRAM THE LEGACY SYSTEM.
IT CAN'T BE THAT HARD. GO FIGURE IT OUT.
12-8-06 ©2006 Scott Adams, Inc./Dist. by UFS, Inc.
?
FRACK.

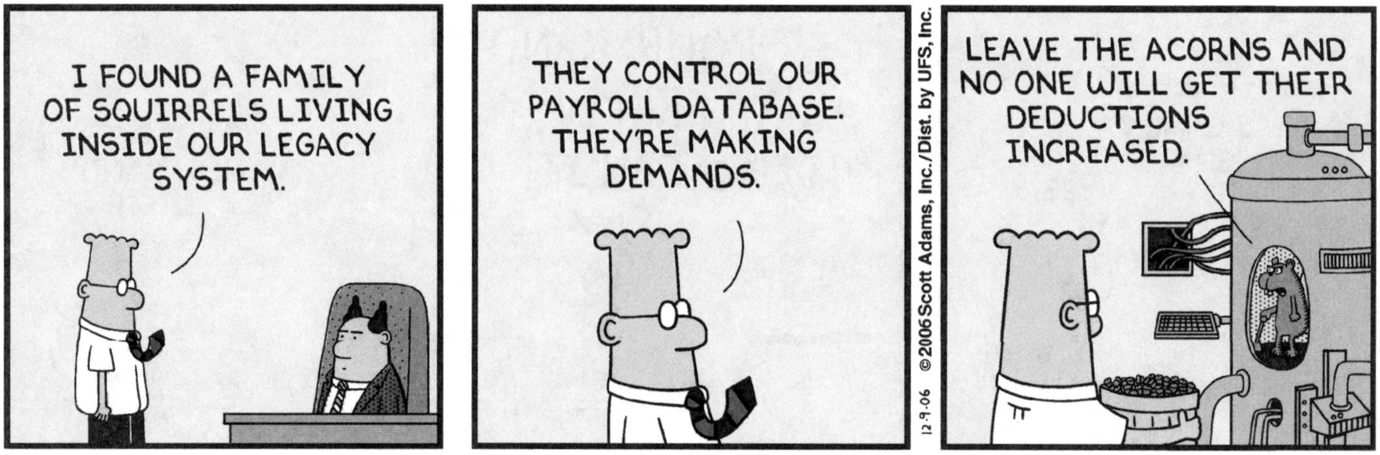
I FOUND A FAMILY OF SQUIRRELS LIVING INSIDE OUR LEGACY SYSTEM.
THEY CONTROL OUR PAYROLL DATABASE. THEY'RE MAKING DEMANDS.
12-9-06 ©2006 Scott Adams, Inc./Dist. by UFS, Inc.
LEAVE THE ACORNS AND NO ONE WILL GET THEIR DEDUCTIONS INCREASED.

THIS IS DOGBERT'S TECH SUPPORT. HOW MAY I ABUSE YOU?
I GET AN ERROR MESSAGE EVERY TIME I OPEN AN APPLICATION.
TRY GIVING ME ALL OF YOUR PERSONAL INFORMATION AND THEN CHECKING INTO REHAB.
THEN I'LL HAVE SOMEONE STEAL YOUR IDENTITY AND MOVE IN WITH YOUR WIFE.
THERE'S A GOOD CHANCE THAT THE NEW GUY WILL KNOW HOW TO FIX YOUR COMPUTER.
WHEN YOU GET OUT OF REHAB, TALK YOUR WIFE INTO TAKING YOU BACK.
THEN NEVER TOUCH YOUR COMPUTER AGAIN BECAUSE IT HURTS THE ONES YOU LOVE.
HOW'S WORK?
EVERYONE WANTS TO TALK TO MY SUPERVISOR.
©2006 Scott Adams, Inc. /Dist. by UFS, Inc.
12-10-06

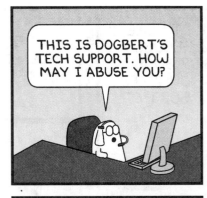

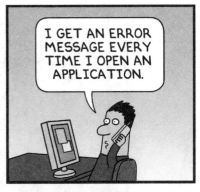

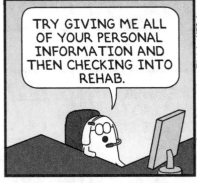

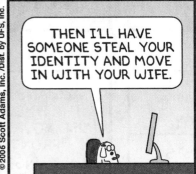

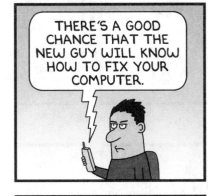

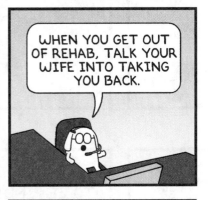

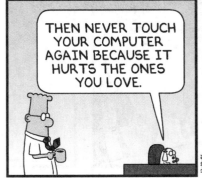

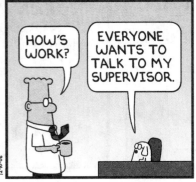

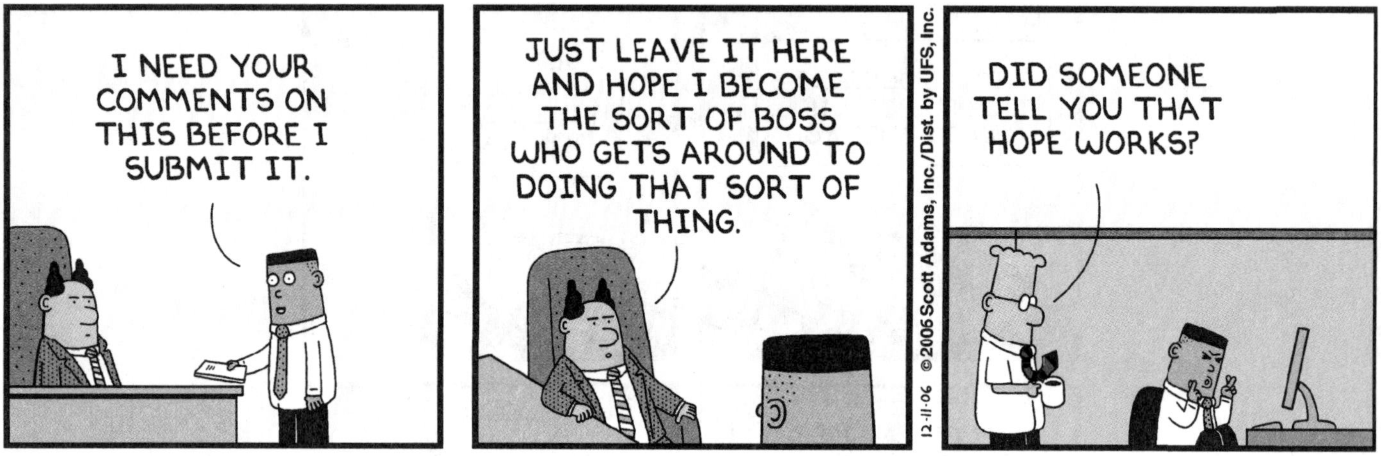
I NEED YOUR COMMENTS ON THIS BEFORE I SUBMIT IT.
JUST LEAVE IT HERE AND HOPE I BECOME THE SORT OF BOSS WHO GETS AROUND TO DOING THAT SORT OF THING.
12-11-06 ©2006 Scott Adams, Inc./Dist. by UFS, Inc.
DID SOMEONE TELL YOU THAT HOPE WORKS?

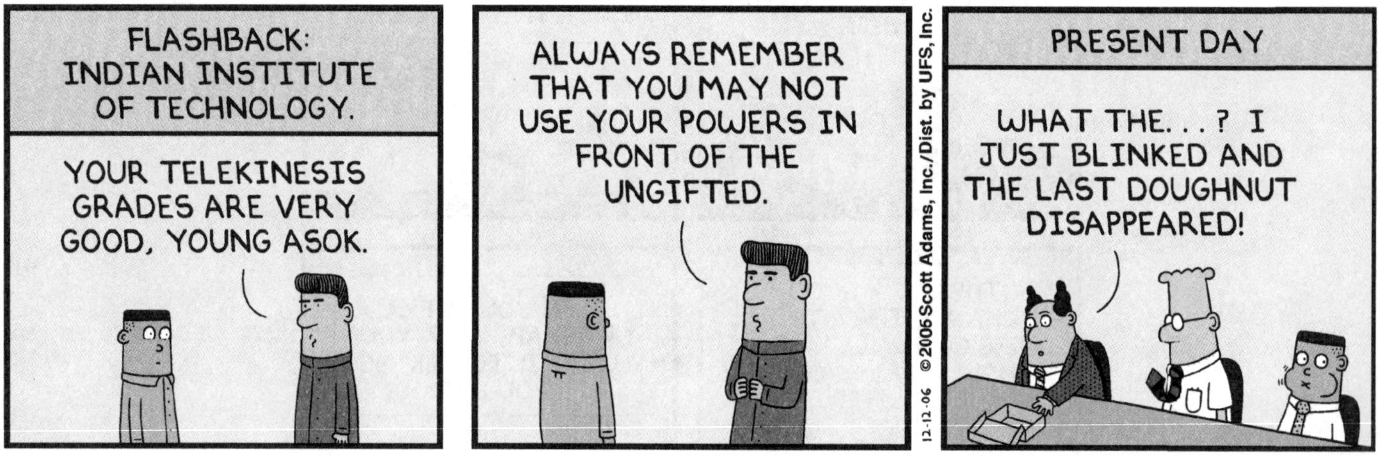
FLASHBACK: INDIAN INSTITUTE OF TECHNOLOGY.
YOUR TELEKINESIS GRADES ARE VERY GOOD, YOUNG ASOK.
ALWAYS REMEMBER THAT YOU MAY NOT USE YOUR POWERS IN FRONT OF THE UNGIFTED.
12-12-06 ©2006 Scott Adams, Inc./Dist. by UFS, Inc.
PRESENT DAY
WHAT THE...? I JUST BLINKED AND THE LAST DOUGHNUT DISAPPEARED!

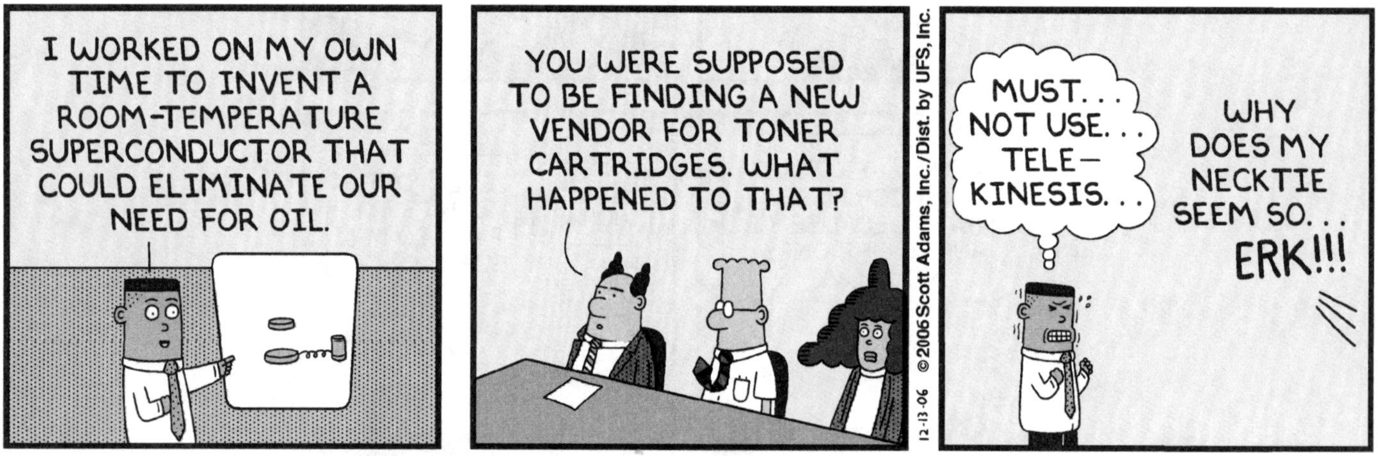
I WORKED ON MY OWN TIME TO INVENT A ROOM-TEMPERATURE SUPERCONDUCTOR THAT COULD ELIMINATE OUR NEED FOR OIL.
YOU WERE SUPPOSED TO BE FINDING A NEW VENDOR FOR TONER CARTRIDGES. WHAT HAPPENED TO THAT?
12-13-06 ©2006 Scott Adams, Inc./Dist. by UFS, Inc.
MUST... NOT USE... TELE-KINESIS...
WHY DOES MY NECKTIE SEEM SO...
ERK!!!

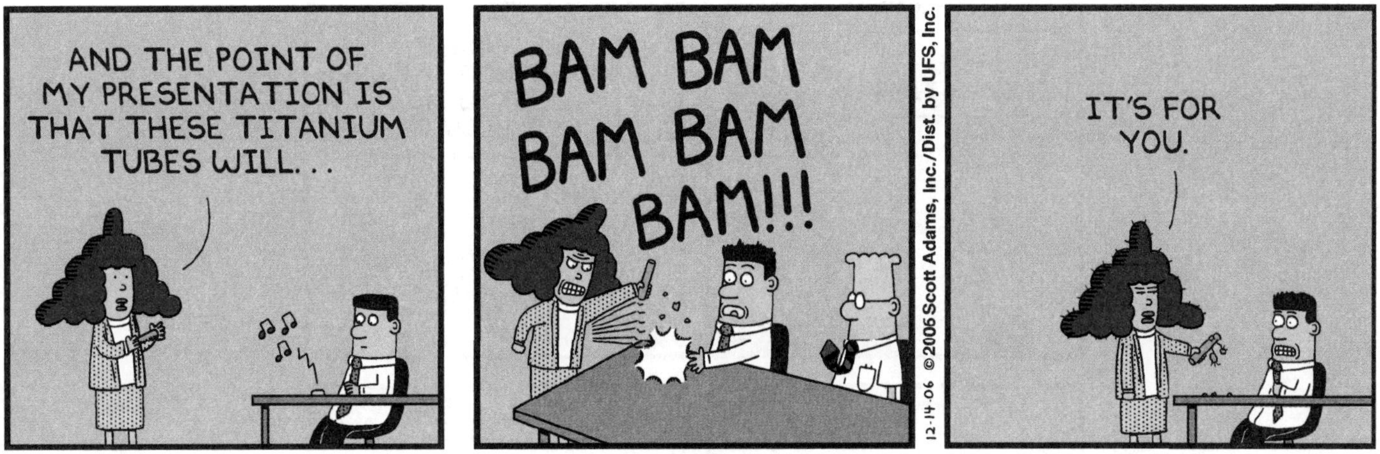
AND THE POINT OF MY PRESENTATION IS THAT THESE TITANIUM TUBES WILL. . .
BAM BAM BAM BAM BAM!!!
©2006 Scott Adams, Inc./Dist. by UFS, Inc.
12-14-06
IT'S FOR YOU.

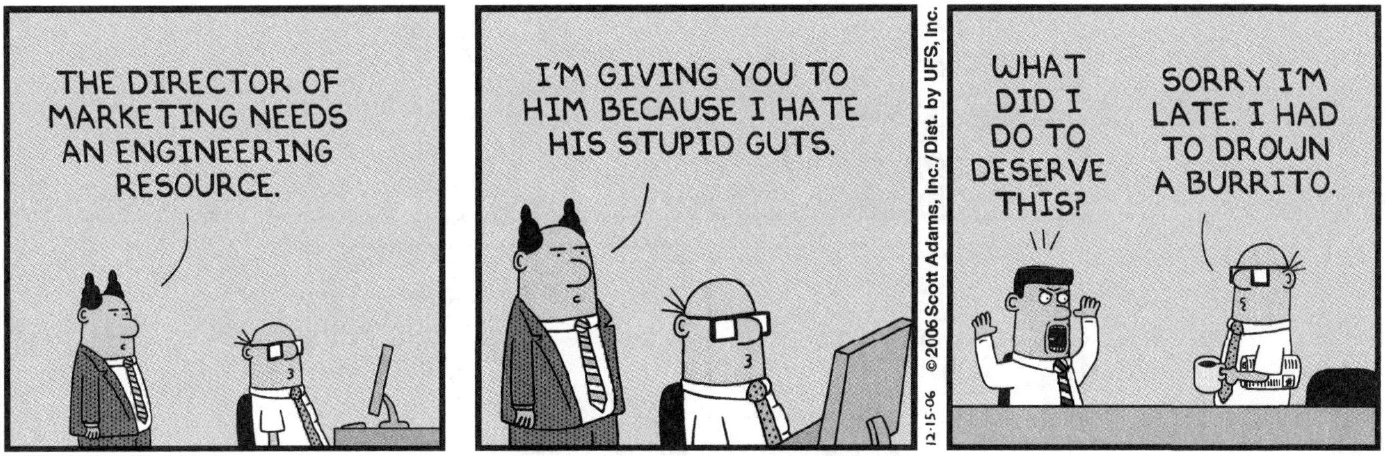
THE DIRECTOR OF MARKETING NEEDS AN ENGINEERING RESOURCE.
I'M GIVING YOU TO HIM BECAUSE I HATE HIS STUPID GUTS.
©2006 Scott Adams, Inc./Dist. by UFS, Inc.
12-15-06
WHAT DID I DO TO DESERVE THIS?
SORRY I'M LATE. I HAD TO DROWN A BURRITO.

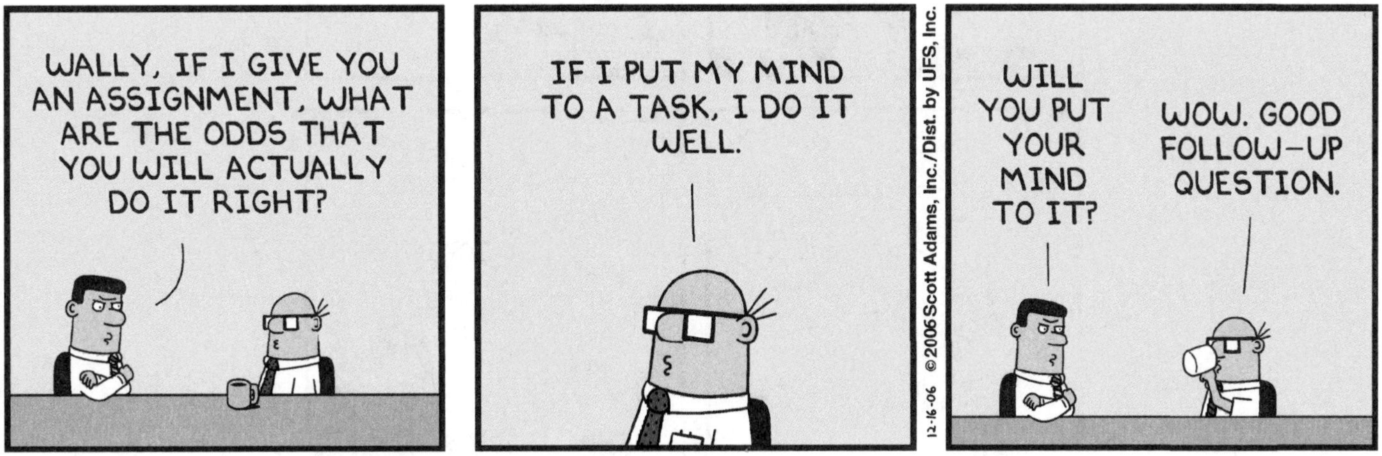
WALLY, IF I GIVE YOU AN ASSIGNMENT, WHAT ARE THE ODDS THAT YOU WILL ACTUALLY DO IT RIGHT?
IF I PUT MY MIND TO A TASK, I DO IT WELL.
©2006 Scott Adams, Inc./Dist. by UFS, Inc.
12-16-06
WILL YOU PUT YOUR MIND TO IT?
WOW. GOOD FOLLOW-UP QUESTION.

YOU MISSED THE MEETING.
WHAT MEETING?
THE BUDGET MEETING THAT YOU TOLD ME TO SCHEDULE.
YOU NEVER TOLD ME WHEN IT WAS.
I SENT YOU AN E-MAIL.
WELL, OBVIOUSLY YOU CHOSE AN UNINTERESTING SUBJECT LINE.
OTHERWISE I WOULD HAVE OPENED IT.
YOU'RE A BAD E-MAIL SENDER.
I ALSO TOLD YOU IN PERSON.
BORINGLY?
©2006 Scott Adams, Inc./Dist. by UFS, Inc.
12-17-06

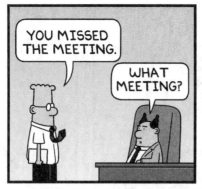

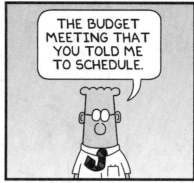

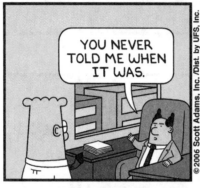

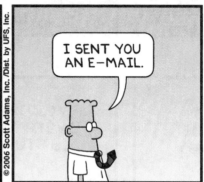

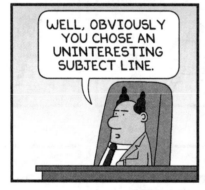

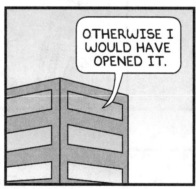

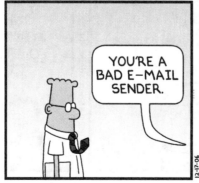

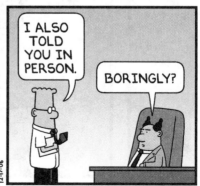

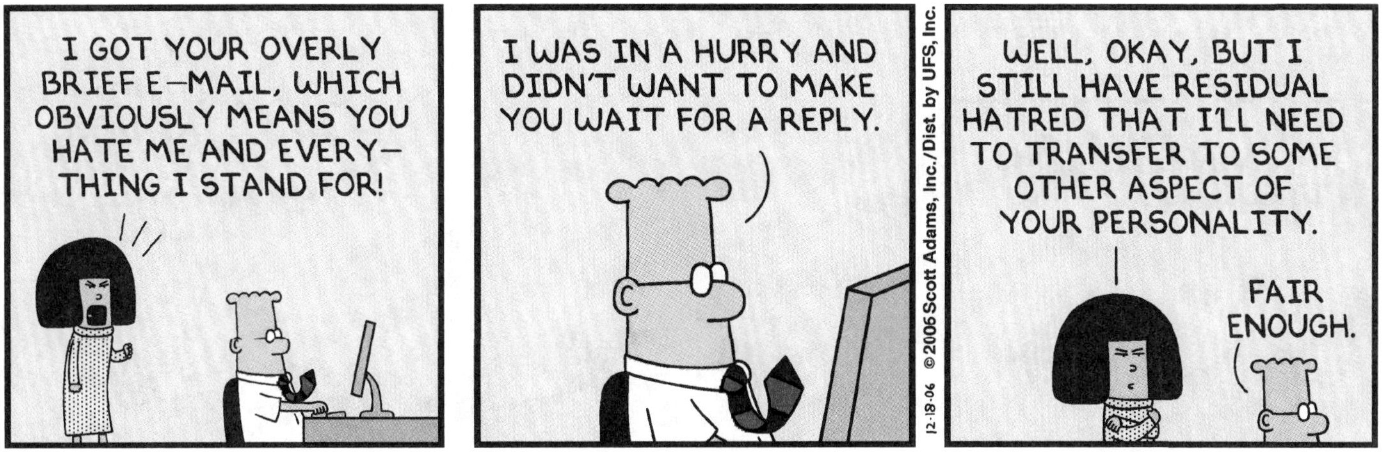
I GOT YOUR OVERLY BRIEF E-MAIL, WHICH OBVIOUSLY MEANS YOU HATE ME AND EVERY-THING I STAND FOR!
I WAS IN A HURRY AND DIDN'T WANT TO MAKE YOU WAIT FOR A REPLY.
12·18·06 © 2006 Scott Adams, Inc./Dist. by UFS, Inc.
WELL, OKAY, BUT I STILL HAVE RESIDUAL HATRED THAT I'LL NEED TO TRANSFER TO SOME OTHER ASPECT OF YOUR PERSONALITY.
FAIR ENOUGH.

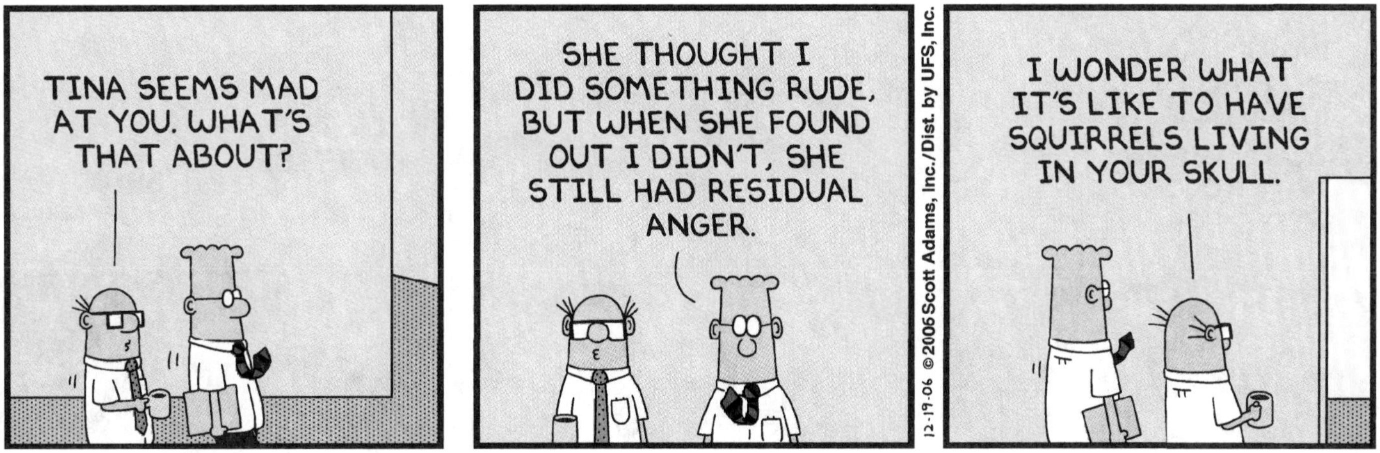
TINA SEEMS MAD AT YOU. WHAT'S THAT ABOUT?
SHE THOUGHT I DID SOMETHING RUDE, BUT WHEN SHE FOUND OUT I DIDN'T, SHE STILL HAD RESIDUAL ANGER.
12·19·06 © 2006 Scott Adams, Inc./Dist. by UFS, Inc.
I WONDER WHAT IT'S LIKE TO HAVE SQUIRRELS LIVING IN YOUR SKULL.

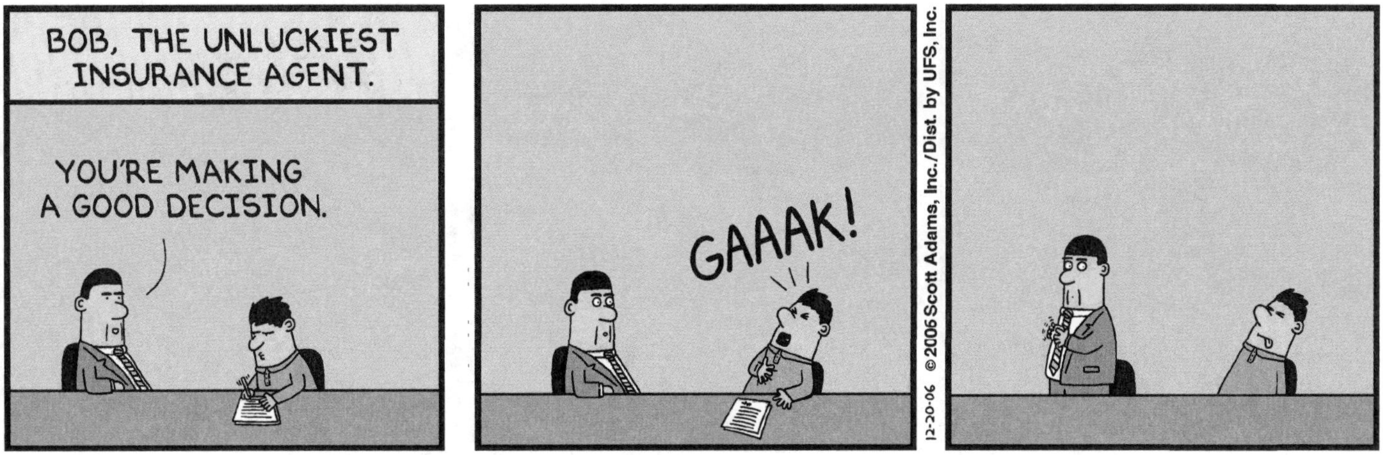
BOB, THE UNLUCKIEST INSURANCE AGENT.
YOU'RE MAKING A GOOD DECISION.
GAAAK!
12·20·06 © 2006 Scott Adams, Inc./Dist. by UFS, Inc.

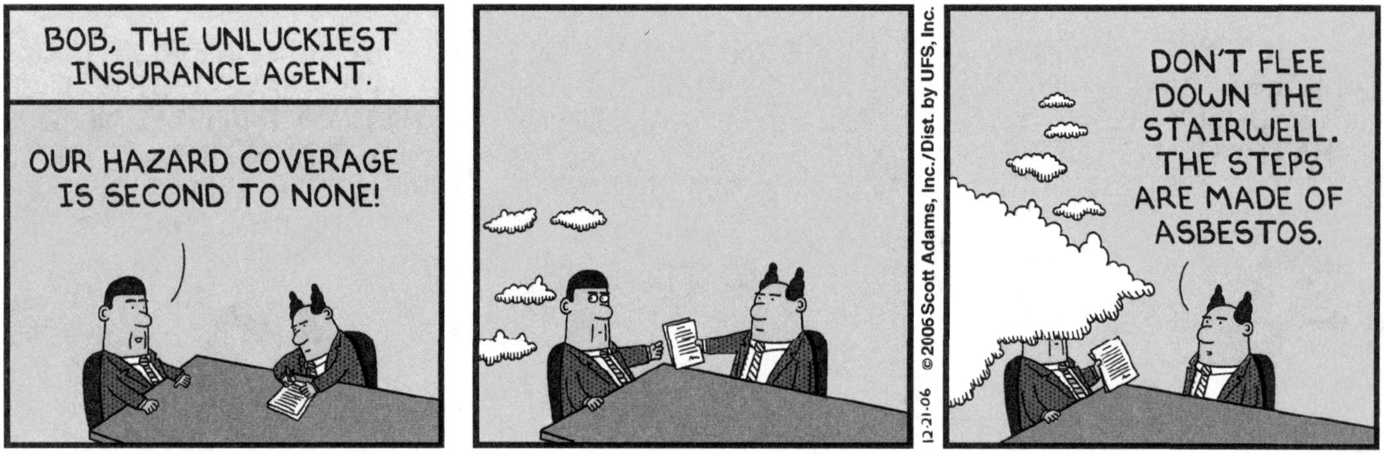
BOB, THE UNLUCKIEST INSURANCE AGENT.
OUR HAZARD COVERAGE IS SECOND TO NONE!
DON'T FLEE DOWN THE STAIRWELL. THE STEPS ARE MADE OF ASBESTOS.
12-21-06 © 2006 Scott Adams, Inc./Dist. by UFS, Inc.

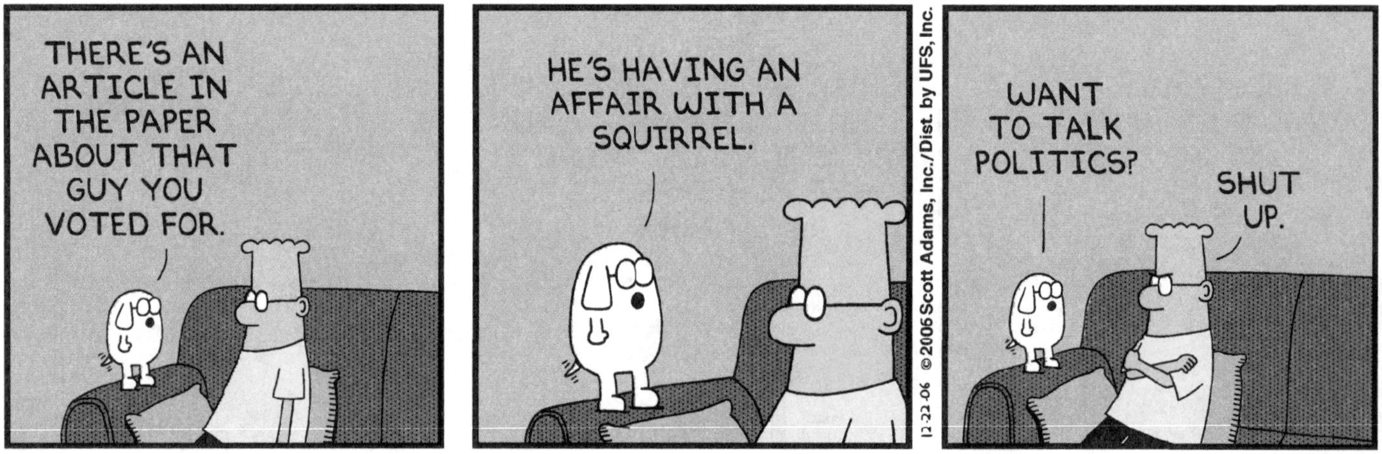
THERE'S AN ARTICLE IN THE PAPER ABOUT THAT GUY YOU VOTED FOR.
HE'S HAVING AN AFFAIR WITH A SQUIRREL.
WANT TO TALK POLITICS?
SHUT UP.
12-22-06 © 2006 Scott Adams, Inc./Dist. by UFS, Inc.

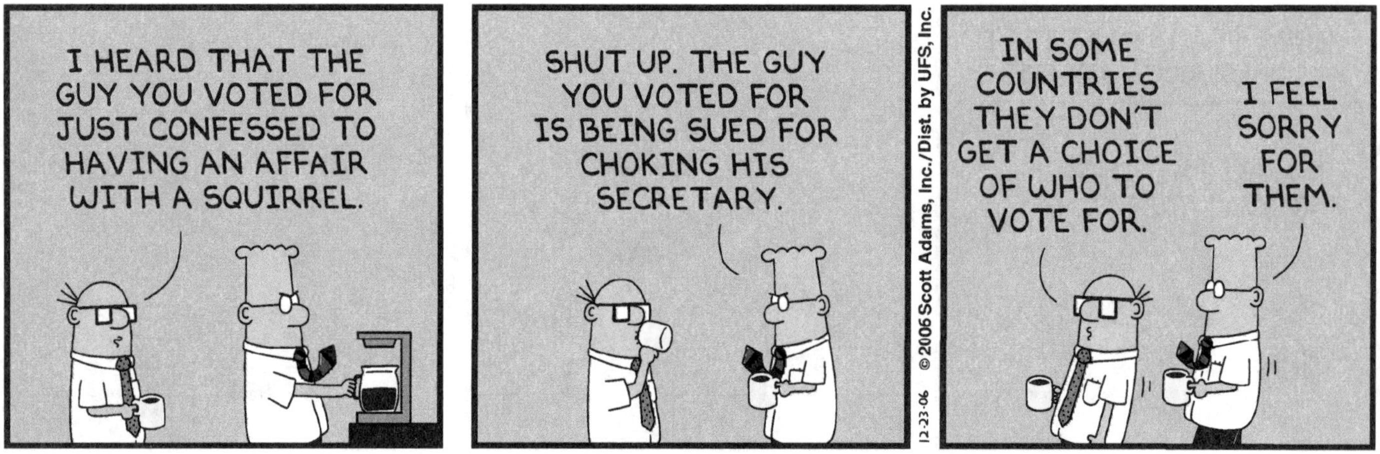
I HEARD THAT THE GUY YOU VOTED FOR JUST CONFESSED TO HAVING AN AFFAIR WITH A SQUIRREL.
SHUT UP. THE GUY YOU VOTED FOR IS BEING SUED FOR CHOKING HIS SECRETARY.
IN SOME COUNTRIES THEY DON'T GET A CHOICE OF WHO TO VOTE FOR.
I FEEL SORRY FOR THEM.
12-23-06 © 2006 Scott Adams, Inc./Dist. by UFS, Inc.

I'LL BE RIGHT BACK AFTER I RETURN THESE DISHES TO THE CAFETERIA.
WHOA, WHOA!
WINNERS DON'T RETURN DISHES TO THE CAFETERIA.
THEN HOW DO THE DISHES GET BACK?
YOU MUST USE YOUR POWER OF LOW STANDARDS.
JUST PLACE THE DISHES ON THE FLOOR AND WAIT FOR A LOSER WITH HIGH STANDARDS.
GAAA! DISHES ON THE FLOOR!
ONCE AGAIN I HAVE TO CLEAN UP AFTER SLOBS!
IT IS LIKE A MIRACLE.
NOW ASK HER TO BRING YOU BACK A YOGURT.
© 2006 Scott Adams, Inc./Dist. by UFS, Inc.
12-24-06

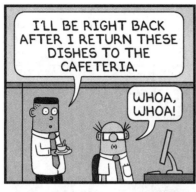

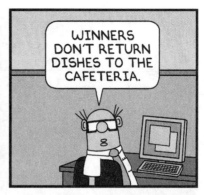

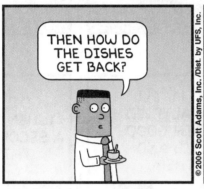

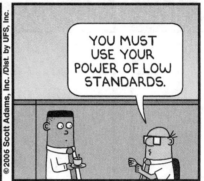

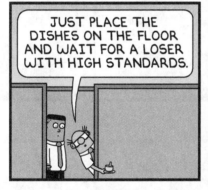

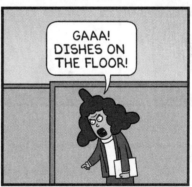

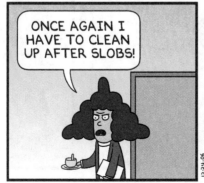

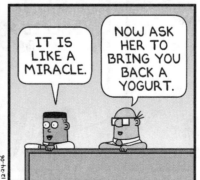

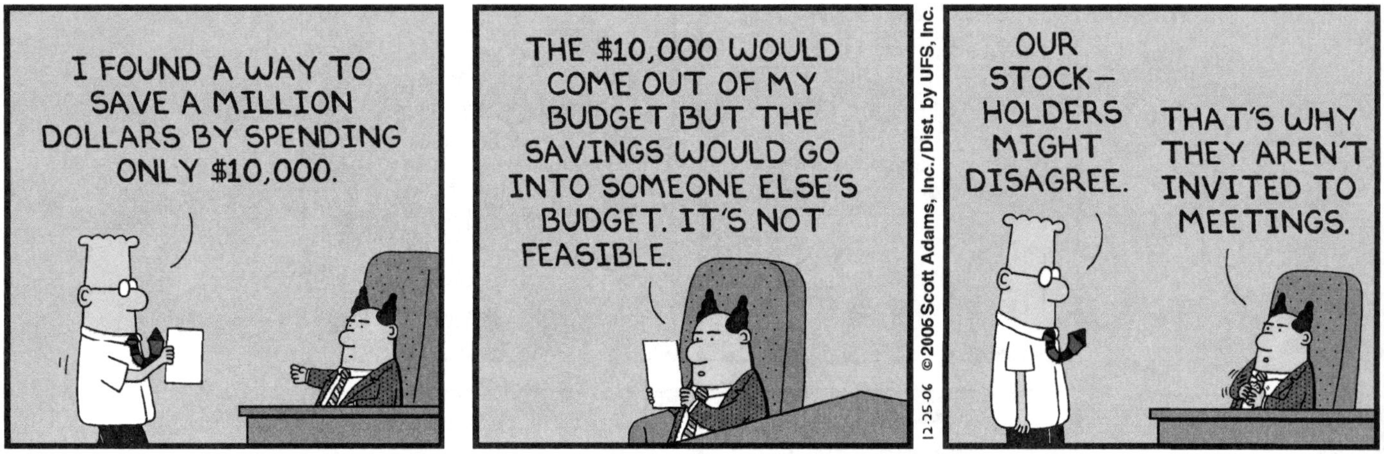
I FOUND A WAY TO SAVE A MILLION DOLLARS BY SPENDING ONLY $10,000.
THE $10,000 WOULD COME OUT OF MY BUDGET BUT THE SAVINGS WOULD GO INTO SOMEONE ELSE'S BUDGET. IT'S NOT FEASIBLE.
12-25-06 ©2006 Scott Adams, Inc./Dist. by UFS, Inc.
OUR STOCK-HOLDERS MIGHT DISAGREE.
THAT'S WHY THEY AREN'T INVITED TO MEETINGS.

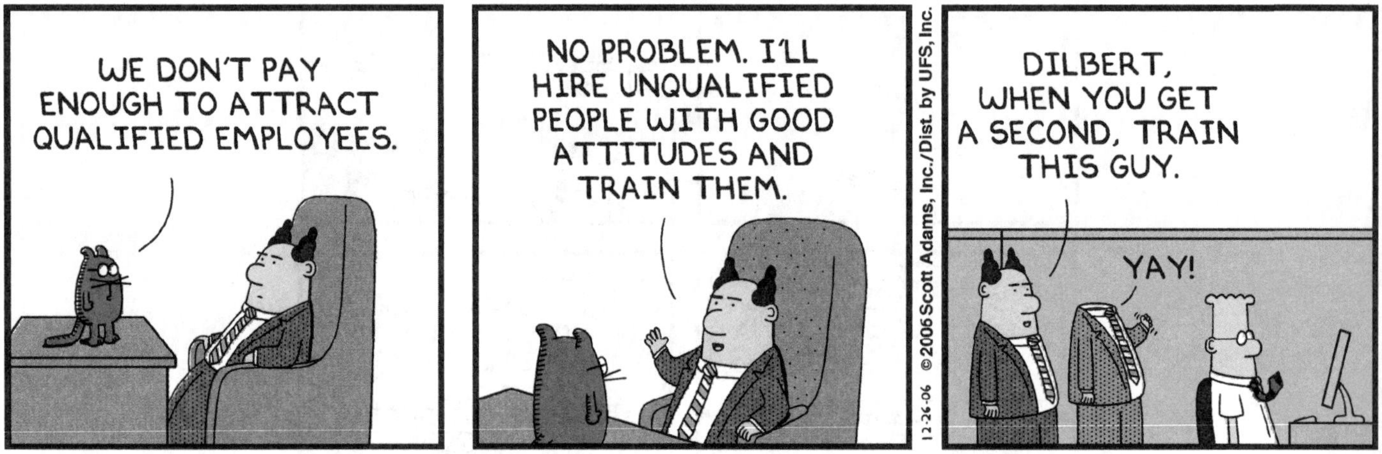
WE DON'T PAY ENOUGH TO ATTRACT QUALIFIED EMPLOYEES.
NO PROBLEM. I'LL HIRE UNQUALIFIED PEOPLE WITH GOOD ATTITUDES AND TRAIN THEM.
12-26-06 ©2006 Scott Adams, Inc./Dist. by UFS, Inc.
DILBERT, WHEN YOU GET A SECOND, TRAIN THIS GUY.
YAY!

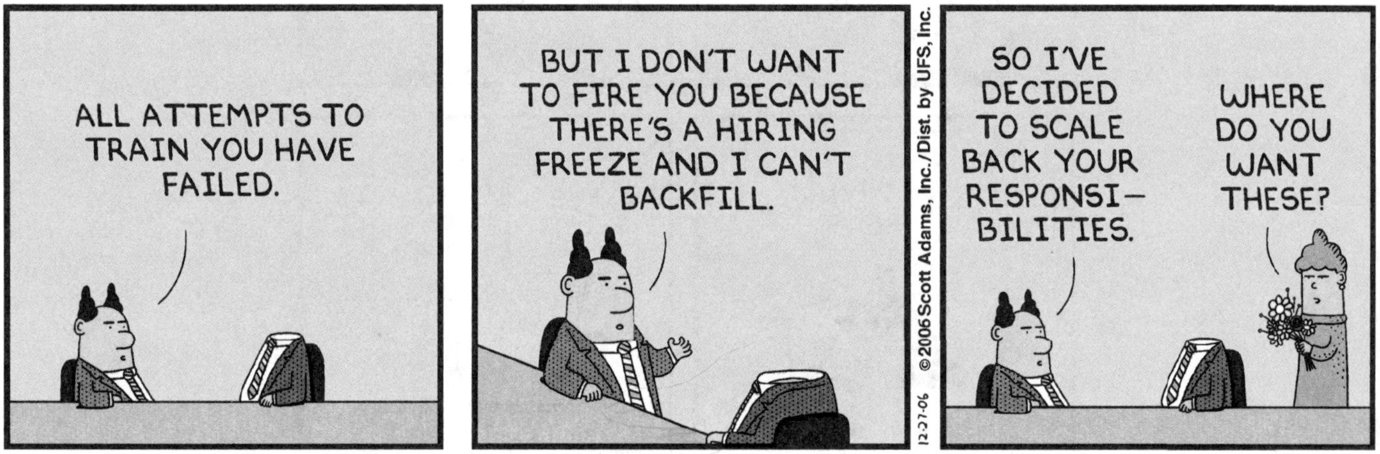
ALL ATTEMPTS TO TRAIN YOU HAVE FAILED.
BUT I DON'T WANT TO FIRE YOU BECAUSE THERE'S A HIRING FREEZE AND I CAN'T BACKFILL.
12-27-06 ©2006 Scott Adams, Inc./Dist. by UFS, Inc.
SO I'VE DECIDED TO SCALE BACK YOUR RESPONSI-BILITIES.
WHERE DO YOU WANT THESE?

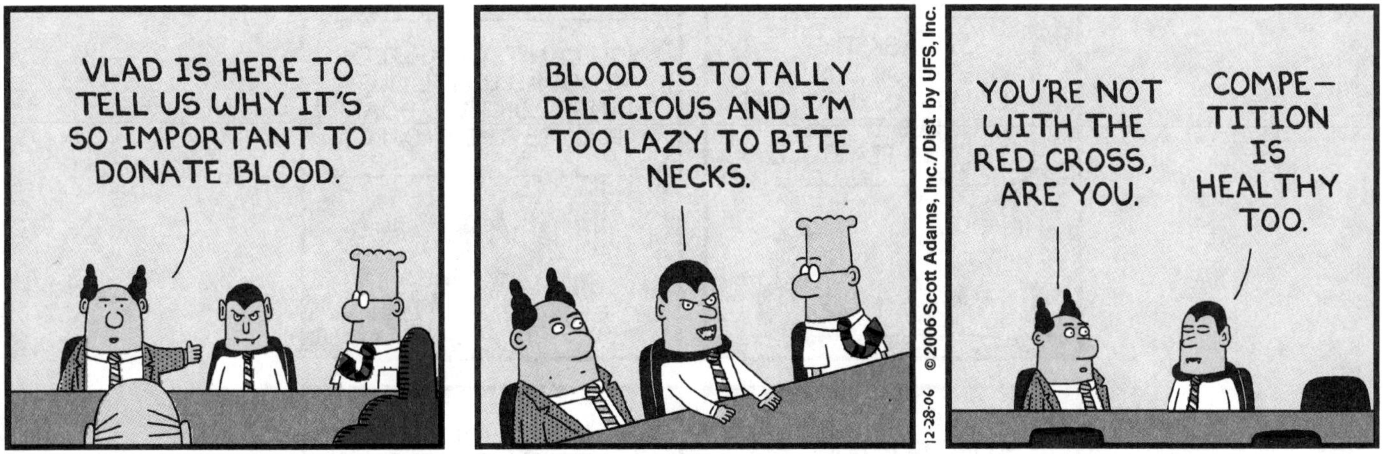
VLAD IS HERE TO TELL US WHY IT'S SO IMPORTANT TO DONATE BLOOD.
BLOOD IS TOTALLY DELICIOUS AND I'M TOO LAZY TO BITE NECKS.
12-28-06 © 2006 Scott Adams, Inc./Dist. by UFS, Inc.
YOU'RE NOT WITH THE RED CROSS, ARE YOU.
COMPE-TITION IS HEALTHY TOO.

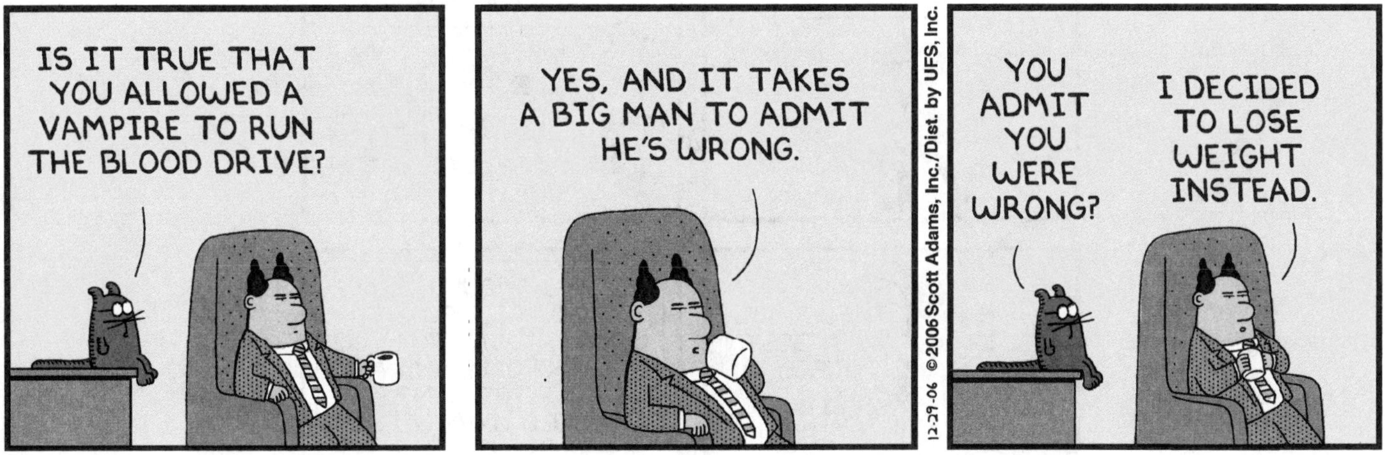
IS IT TRUE THAT YOU ALLOWED A VAMPIRE TO RUN THE BLOOD DRIVE?
YES, AND IT TAKES A BIG MAN TO ADMIT HE'S WRONG.
12-29-06 © 2006 Scott Adams, Inc./Dist. by UFS, Inc.
YOU ADMIT YOU WERE WRONG?
I DECIDED TO LOSE WEIGHT INSTEAD.

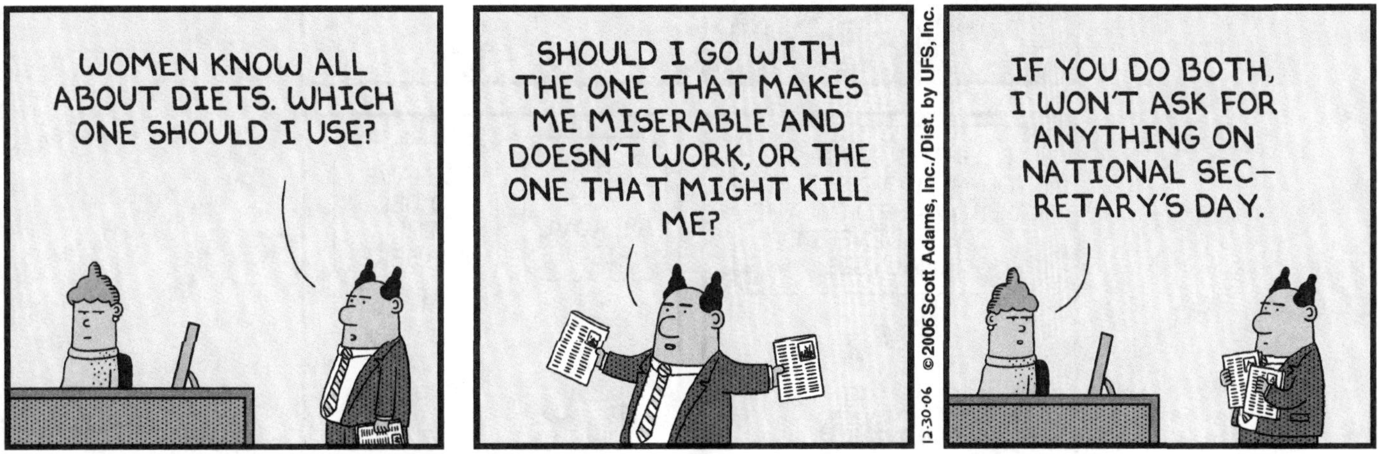
WOMEN KNOW ALL ABOUT DIETS. WHICH ONE SHOULD I USE?
SHOULD I GO WITH THE ONE THAT MAKES ME MISERABLE AND DOESN'T WORK, OR THE ONE THAT MIGHT KILL ME?
12-30-06 © 2006 Scott Adams, Inc./Dist. by UFS, Inc.
IF YOU DO BOTH, I WON'T ASK FOR ANYTHING ON NATIONAL SEC-RETARY'S DAY.

I'LL ASK THE VENDOR FOR BALLPARK PRICES TO SEE IF THE IDEA IS FEASIBLE.
YOU CAN'T TALK WITH VENDORS UNTIL OUR CHANGE CONTROL BOARD APPROVES THE PROJECT.
BUT THAT WOULD REQUIRE A COST-BENEFIT ANALYSIS.
AND I CAN'T DO THAT WITHOUT BALLPARK PRICES FROM THE VENDOR.
JUST TAKE YOUR BEST GUESS.
SO. . . I SHOULD MAKE UP A NUMBER SO I CAN GET APPROVAL TO MAKE A PHONE CALL AND ASK WHAT THE NUMBER SHOULD HAVE BEEN?
RIGHT. BUT FIRST YOU NEED TO GET MY APPROVAL TO DO THE COST-BENEFIT ANALYSIS.
WILL YOU APPROVE IT?
I'D HAVE TO SEE THE NUMBERS.
©2006 Scott Adams, Inc./Dist. by UFS, Inc.
12-31-06

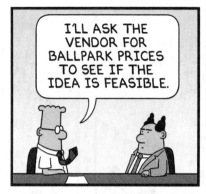

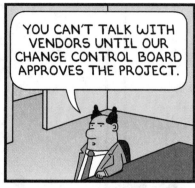

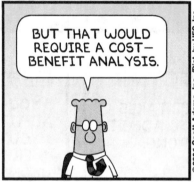

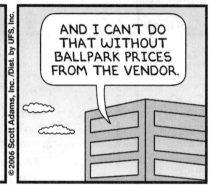

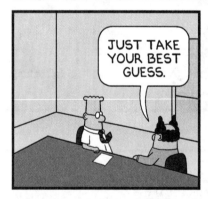

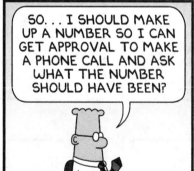

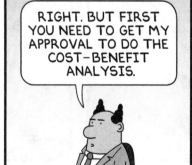

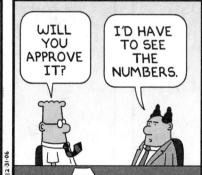

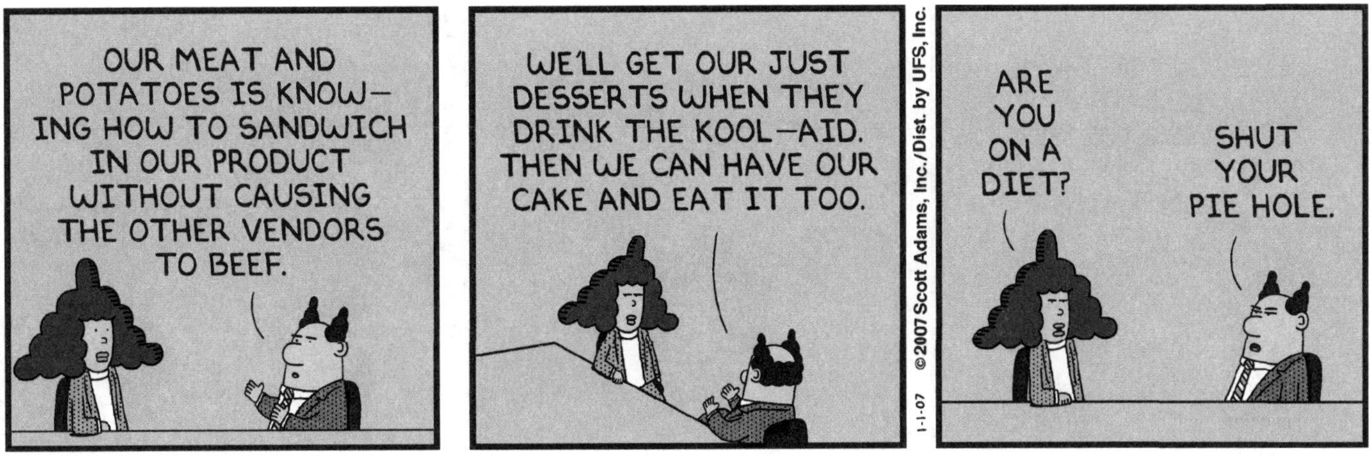
OUR MEAT AND POTATOES IS KNOW-ING HOW TO SANDWICH IN OUR PRODUCT WITHOUT CAUSING THE OTHER VENDORS TO BEEF.
WE'LL GET OUR JUST DESSERTS WHEN THEY DRINK THE KOOL-AID. THEN WE CAN HAVE OUR CAKE AND EAT IT TOO.
1-1-07 © 2007 Scott Adams, Inc./Dist. by UFS, Inc.
ARE YOU ON A DIET?
SHUT YOUR PIE HOLE.

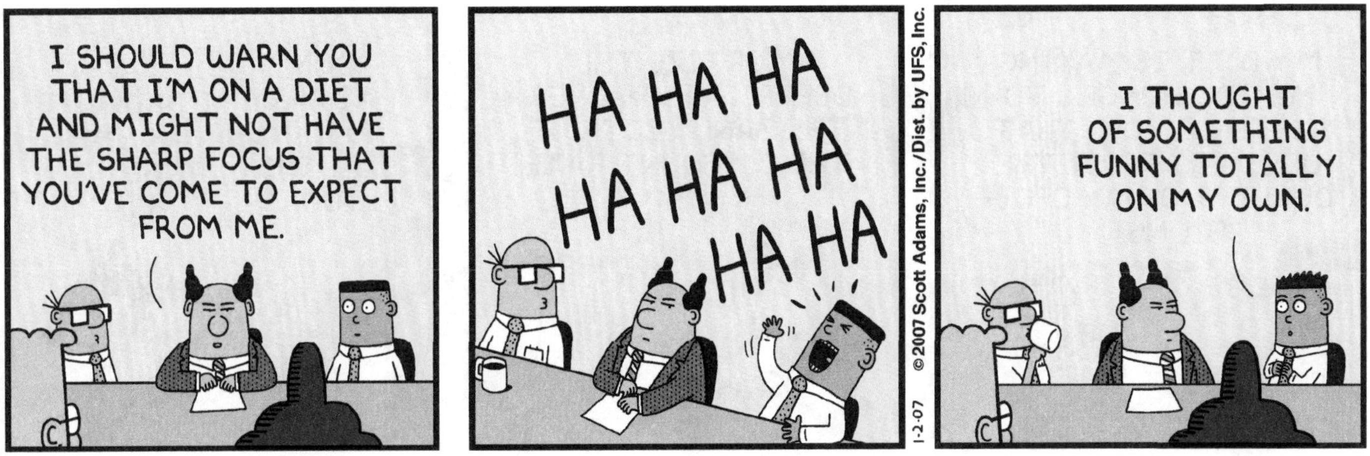
I SHOULD WARN YOU THAT I'M ON A DIET AND MIGHT NOT HAVE THE SHARP FOCUS THAT YOU'VE COME TO EXPECT FROM ME.
HA HA HA HA HA HA HA HA
1-2-07 © 2007 Scott Adams, Inc./Dist. by UFS, Inc.
I THOUGHT OF SOMETHING FUNNY TOTALLY ON MY OWN.

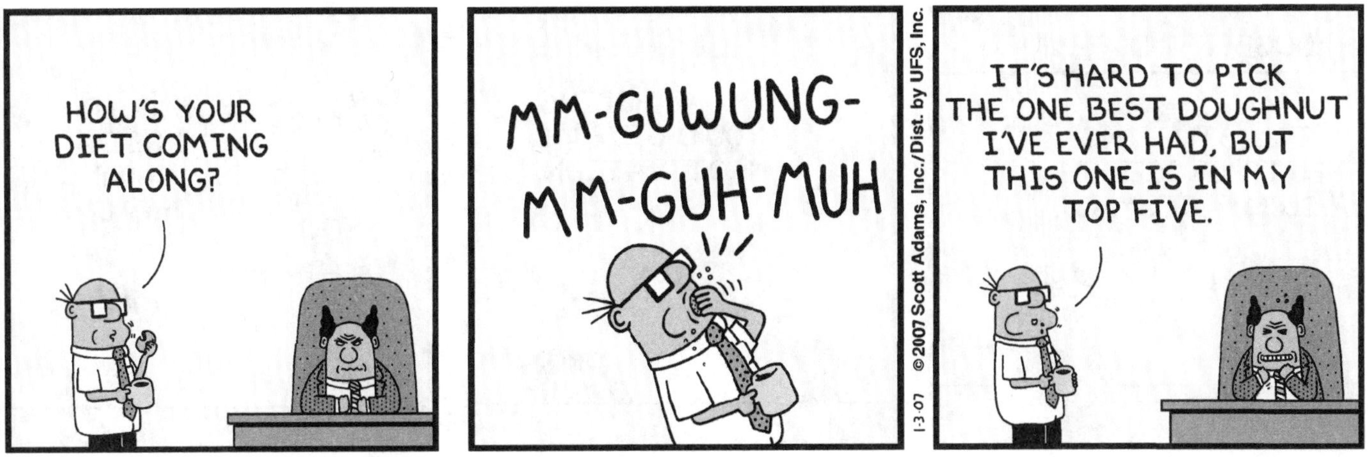
HOW'S YOUR DIET COMING ALONG?
MM-GUWUNG-MM-GUH-MUH
1-3-07 © 2007 Scott Adams, Inc./Dist. by UFS, Inc.
IT'S HARD TO PICK THE ONE BEST DOUGHNUT I'VE EVER HAD, BUT THIS ONE IS IN MY TOP FIVE.

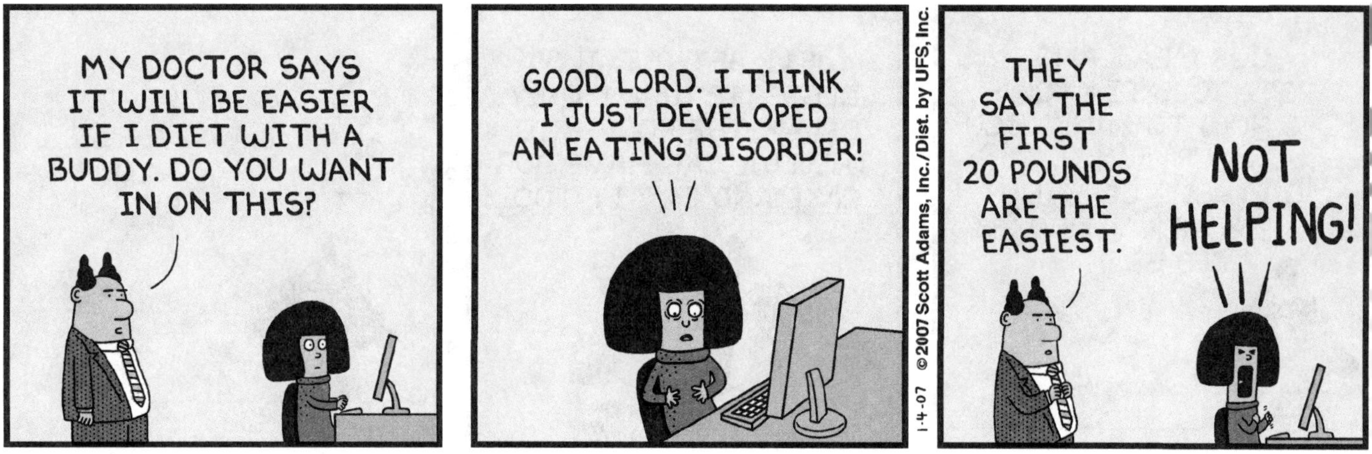
MY DOCTOR SAYS IT WILL BE EASIER IF I DIET WITH A BUDDY. DO YOU WANT IN ON THIS?
GOOD LORD. I THINK I JUST DEVELOPED AN EATING DISORDER!
1-4-07 ©2007 Scott Adams, Inc./Dist. by UFS, Inc.
THEY SAY THE FIRST 20 POUNDS ARE THE EASIEST.
NOT HELPING!

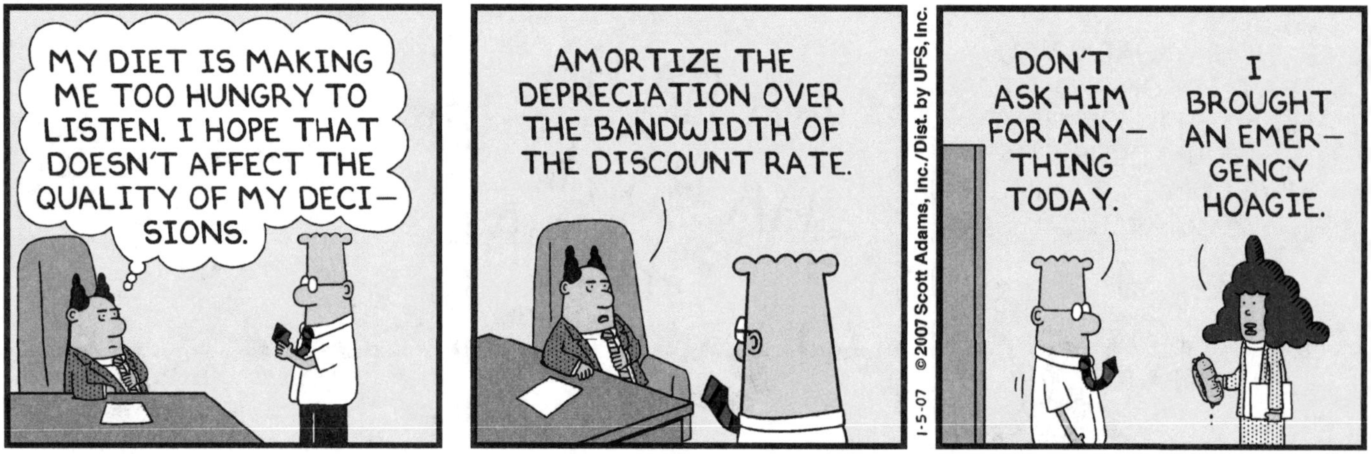
MY DIET IS MAKING ME TOO HUNGRY TO LISTEN. I HOPE THAT DOESN'T AFFECT THE QUALITY OF MY DECI-SIONS.
AMORTIZE THE DEPRECIATION OVER THE BANDWIDTH OF THE DISCOUNT RATE.
1-5-07 ©2007 Scott Adams, Inc./Dist. by UFS, Inc.
DON'T ASK HIM FOR ANY-THING TODAY.
I BROUGHT AN EMER-GENCY HOAGIE.

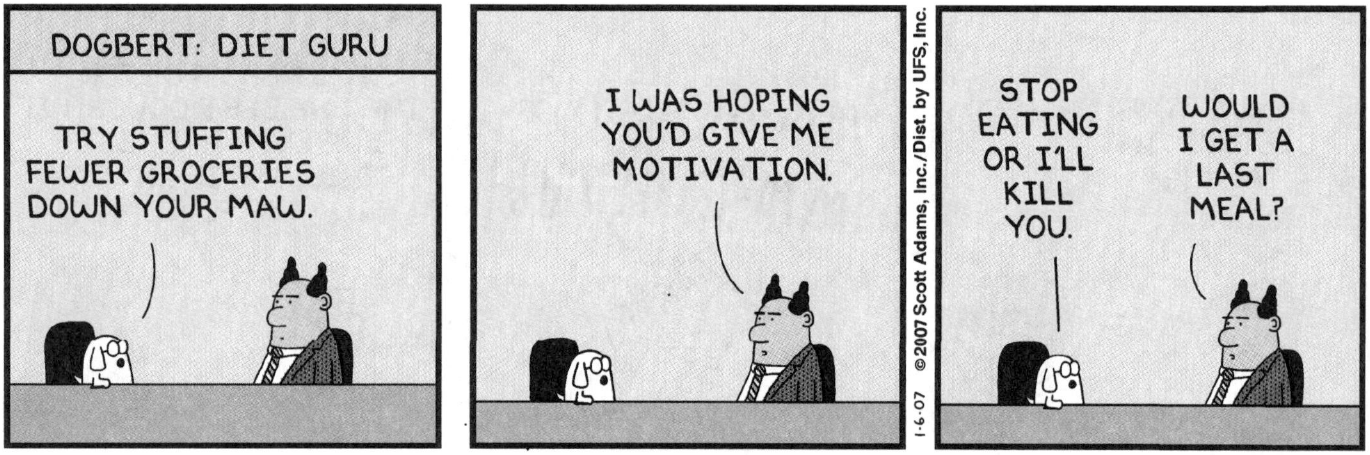
DOGBERT: DIET GURU
TRY STUFFING FEWER GROCERIES DOWN YOUR MAW.
I WAS HOPING YOU'D GIVE ME MOTIVATION.
1-6-07 ©2007 Scott Adams, Inc./Dist. by UFS, Inc.
STOP EATING OR I'LL KILL YOU.
WOULD I GET A LAST MEAL?

TINA, I NEED YOU TO EDIT THIS BEFORE I SEND IT OUT.
SURE. I COULD USE A GOOD LAUGH.
LET'S START WITH THE WORDS THAT AREN'T WORDS.
INCENTIMENT. . . ROBUSTIFY. . . FLEXITATE. . . AND LEADERSHIPPING.
I'LL TAKE THOSE OUT AND SEE WHAT'S LEFT.
"IF YOU'RE NOT ONBOARD WITH QUALITY EXCELLENCE, YOU'RE UNDERBOARD."
WA-HA-HA HA-HA-HA HA!!!
WHY DO I EVEN BOTHER TRYING TO MORALIFY THESE PEOPLE.
©2007 Scott Adams, Inc./Dist. by UFS, Inc.
1-7-07

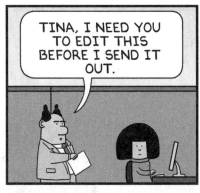

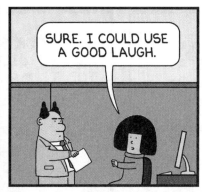

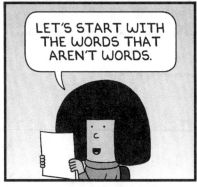

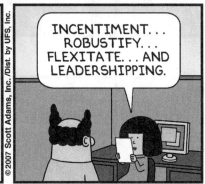

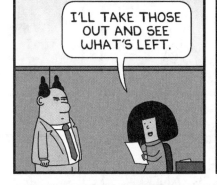

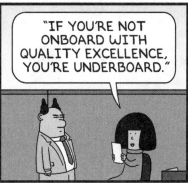

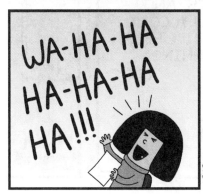

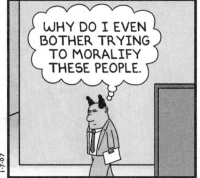

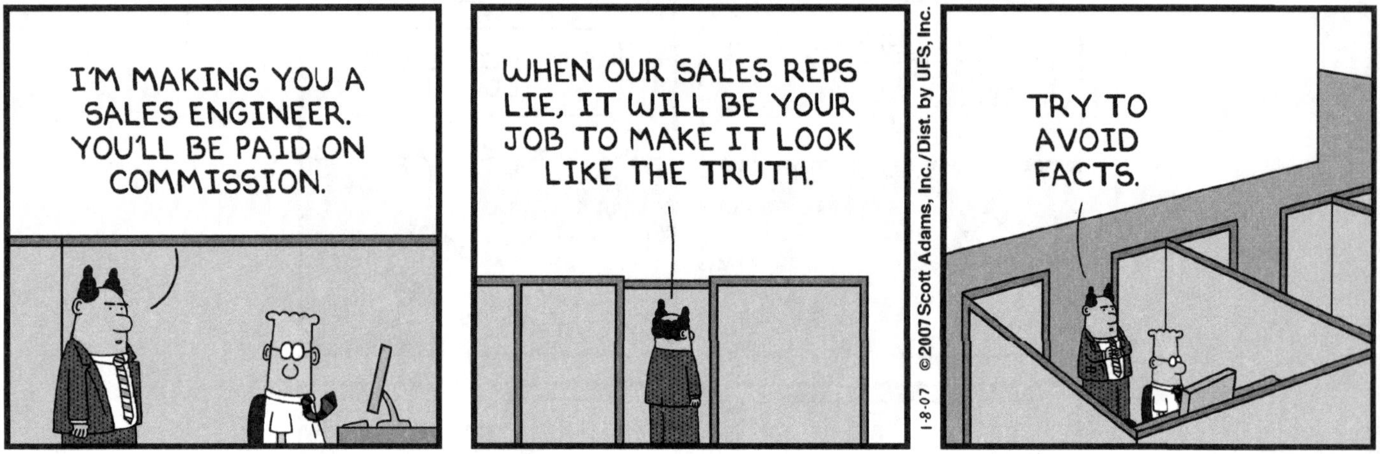
I'M MAKING YOU A SALES ENGINEER. YOU'LL BE PAID ON COMMISSION.
WHEN OUR SALES REPS LIE, IT WILL BE YOUR JOB TO MAKE IT LOOK LIKE THE TRUTH.
1-8-07 ©2007 Scott Adams, Inc./Dist. by UFS, Inc.
TRY TO AVOID FACTS.

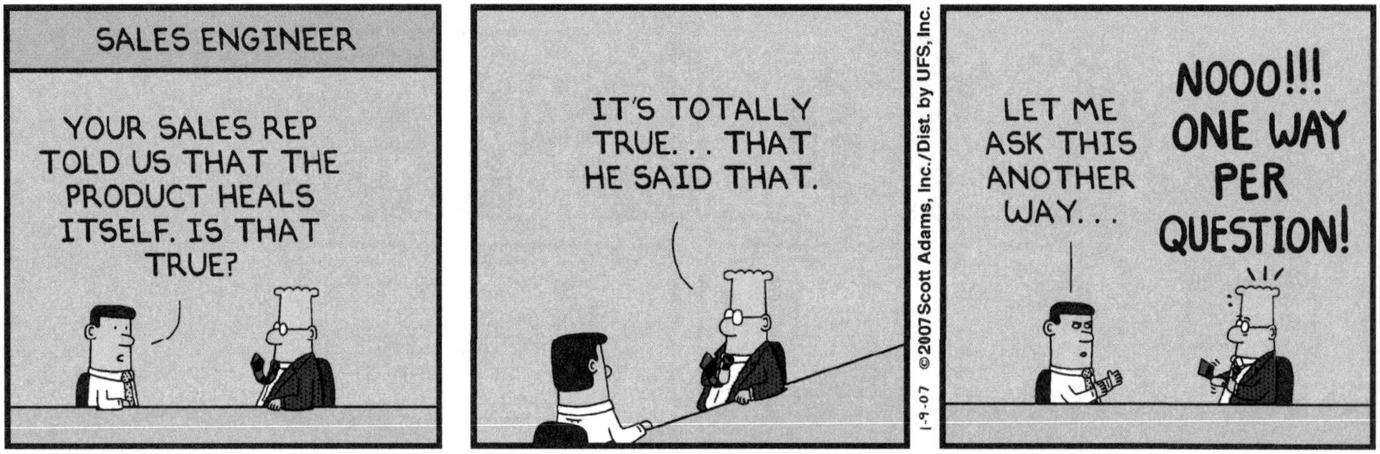
SALES ENGINEER
YOUR SALES REP TOLD US THAT THE PRODUCT HEALS ITSELF. IS THAT TRUE?
IT'S TOTALLY TRUE. . . THAT HE SAID THAT.
1-9-07 ©2007 Scott Adams, Inc./Dist. by UFS, Inc.
LET ME ASK THIS ANOTHER WAY. . .
NOOO!!! ONE WAY PER QUESTION!

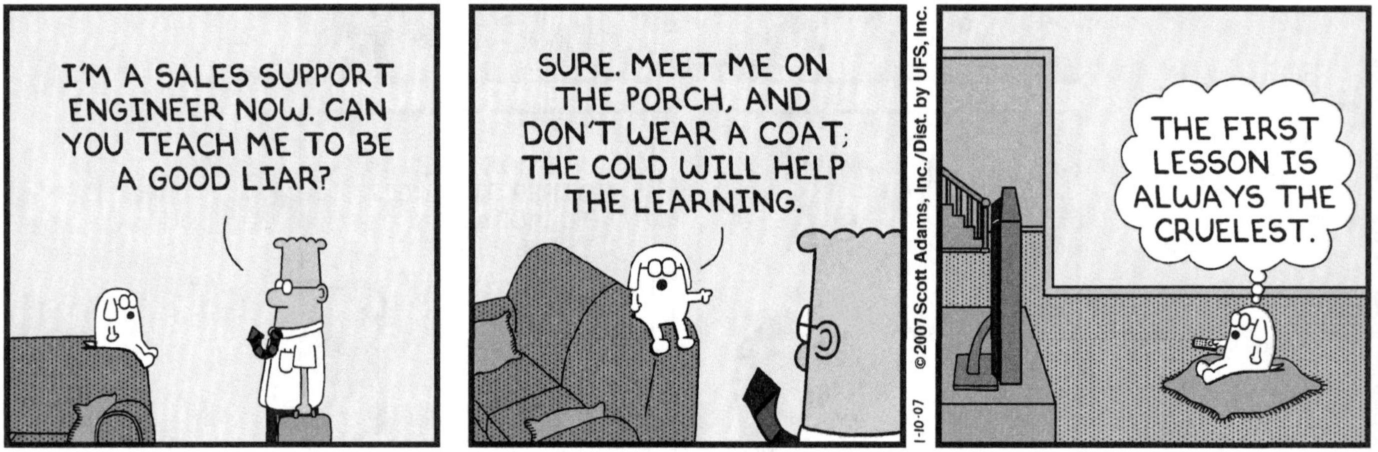
I'M A SALES SUPPORT ENGINEER NOW. CAN YOU TEACH ME TO BE A GOOD LIAR?
SURE. MEET ME ON THE PORCH, AND DON'T WEAR A COAT; THE COLD WILL HELP THE LEARNING.
1-10-07 ©2007 Scott Adams, Inc./Dist. by UFS, Inc.
THE FIRST LESSON IS ALWAYS THE CRUELEST.

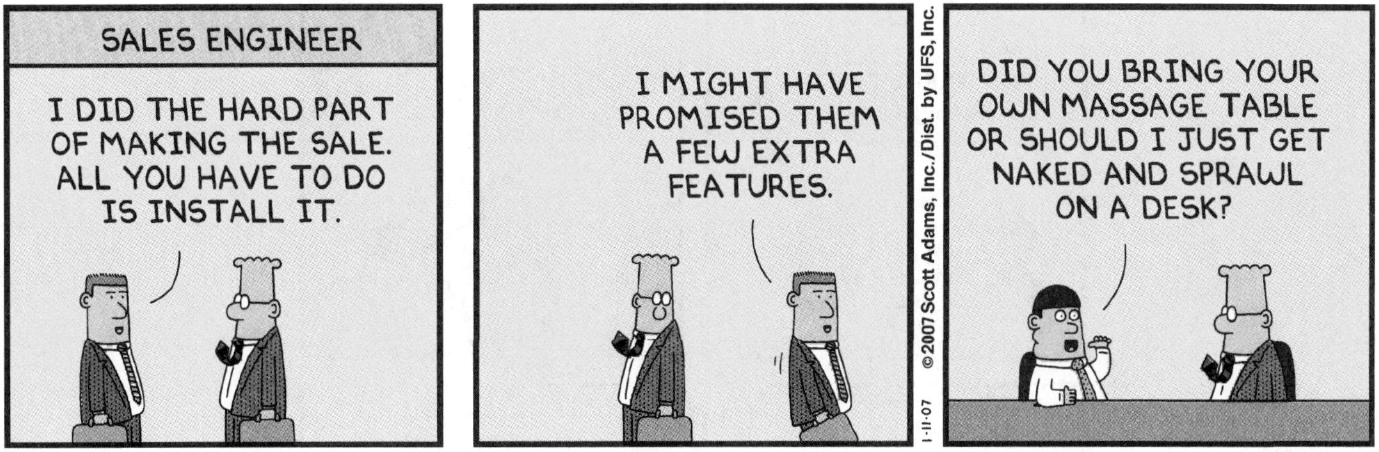
SALES ENGINEER
I DID THE HARD PART OF MAKING THE SALE. ALL YOU HAVE TO DO IS INSTALL IT.
I MIGHT HAVE PROMISED THEM A FEW EXTRA FEATURES.
DID YOU BRING YOUR OWN MASSAGE TABLE OR SHOULD I JUST GET NAKED AND SPRAWL ON A DESK?
1-11-07 ©2007 Scott Adams, Inc./Dist. by UFS, Inc.

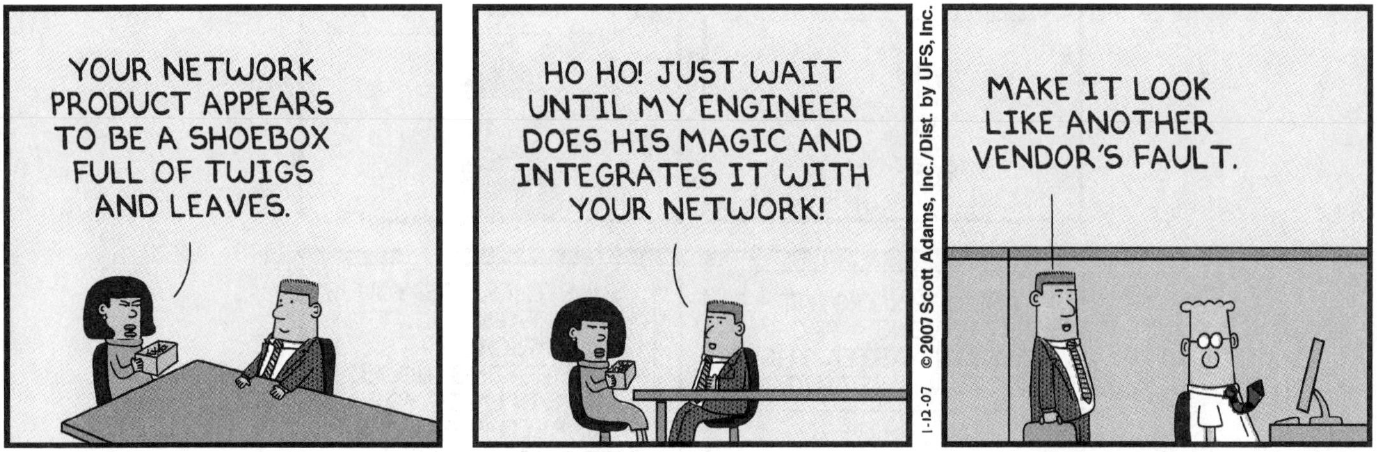
YOUR NETWORK PRODUCT APPEARS TO BE A SHOEBOX FULL OF TWIGS AND LEAVES.
HO HO! JUST WAIT UNTIL MY ENGINEER DOES HIS MAGIC AND INTEGRATES IT WITH YOUR NETWORK!
MAKE IT LOOK LIKE ANOTHER VENDOR'S FAULT.
1-12-07 ©2007 Scott Adams, Inc./Dist. by UFS, Inc.

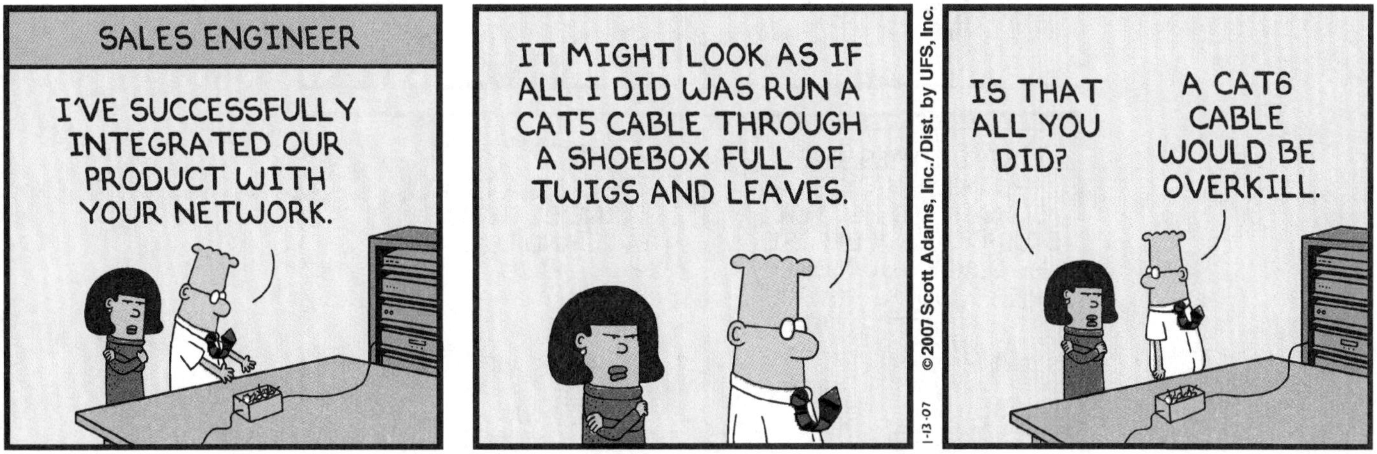
SALES ENGINEER
I'VE SUCCESSFULLY INTEGRATED OUR PRODUCT WITH YOUR NETWORK.
IT MIGHT LOOK AS IF ALL I DID WAS RUN A CAT5 CABLE THROUGH A SHOEBOX FULL OF TWIGS AND LEAVES.
IS THAT ALL YOU DID?
A CAT6 CABLE WOULD BE OVERKILL.
1-13-07 ©2007 Scott Adams, Inc./Dist. by UFS, Inc.

DID YOU SET UP MY PRE-MEETING FOR WEDNESDAY?
YES. IT'S ON THURSDAY.
YOU SCHEDULED MY PRE-MEETING FOR THE DAY AFTER THE MEETING?
THAT WAS THE ONLY DAY THAT EVERYONE COULD MAKE IT.
THERE'S NO POINT IN HAVING A PRE-MEETING AFTER THE ACTUAL MEETING.
SURE THERE IS. YOU CAN TALK ABOUT HOW MUCH BETTER THE MEETING WOULD HAVE BEEN IF YOU HAD BEEN PREPARED.
HERE COMES THE POINTY-HAIRED BOSS. YOU'D BETTER SCURRY AWAY BEFORE HE GIVES YOU MORE WORK.
THERE'S A FINE LINE BETWEEN EVIL AND UNDER-PAID.
© 2007 Scott Adams, Inc./Dist. by UFS, Inc.
1/14

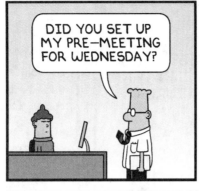

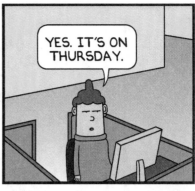

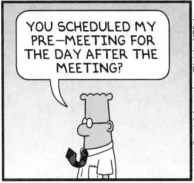

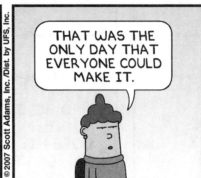

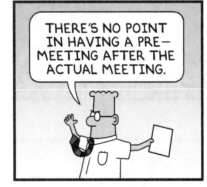

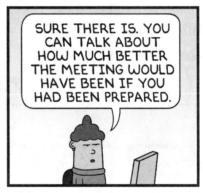

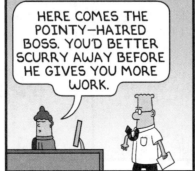

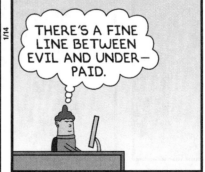

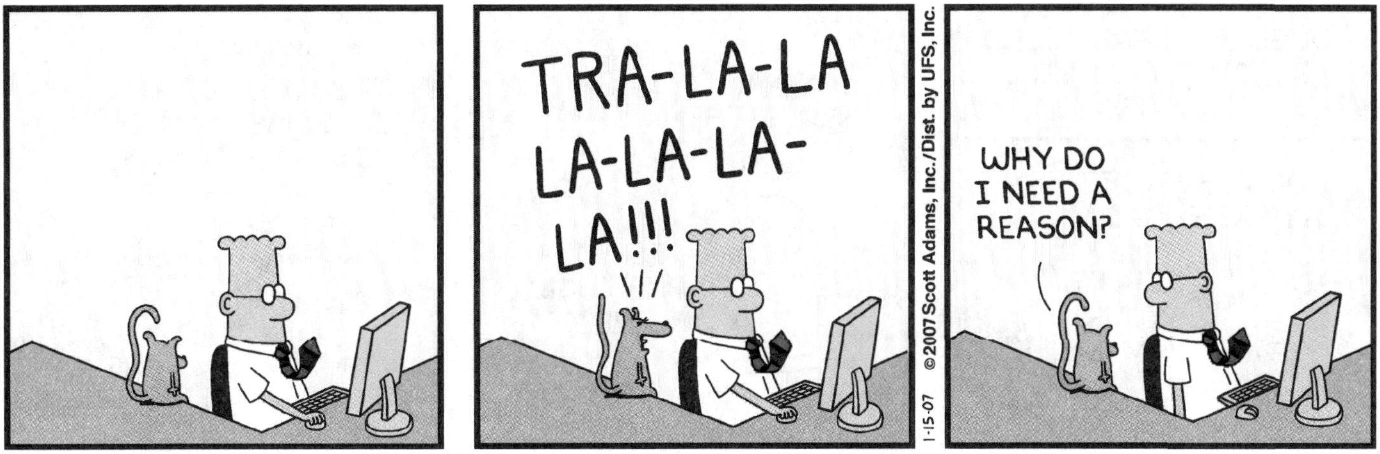
TRA-LA-LA LA-LA-LA-LA!!!
1-15-07 © 2007 Scott Adams, Inc./Dist. by UFS, Inc.
WHY DO I NEED A REASON?

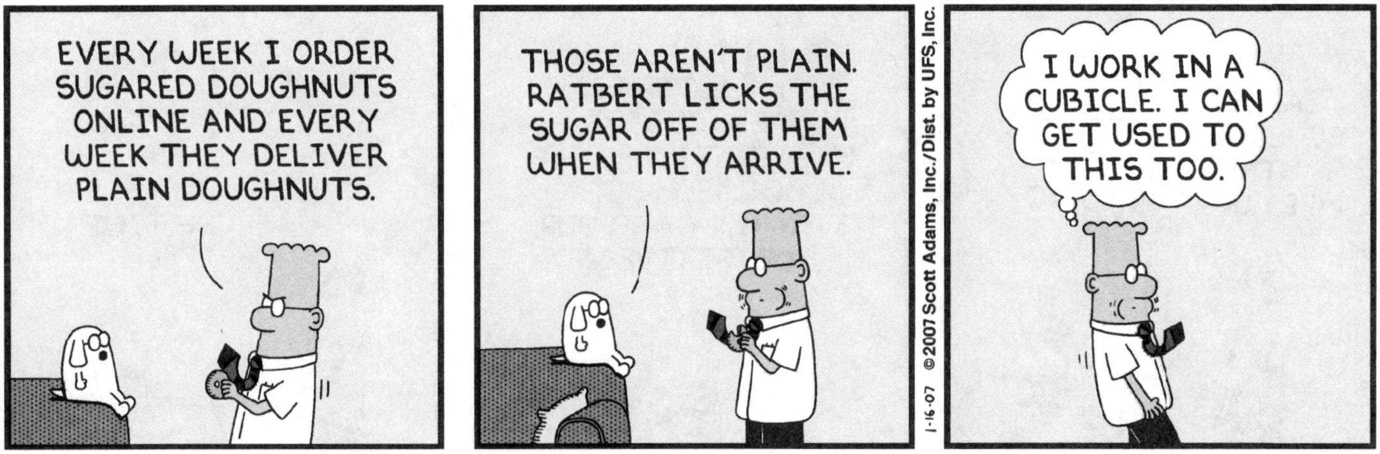
EVERY WEEK I ORDER SUGARED DOUGHNUTS ONLINE AND EVERY WEEK THEY DELIVER PLAIN DOUGHNUTS.
THOSE AREN'T PLAIN. RATBERT LICKS THE SUGAR OFF OF THEM WHEN THEY ARRIVE.
1-16-07 © 2007 Scott Adams, Inc./Dist. by UFS, Inc.
I WORK IN A CUBICLE. I CAN GET USED TO THIS TOO.

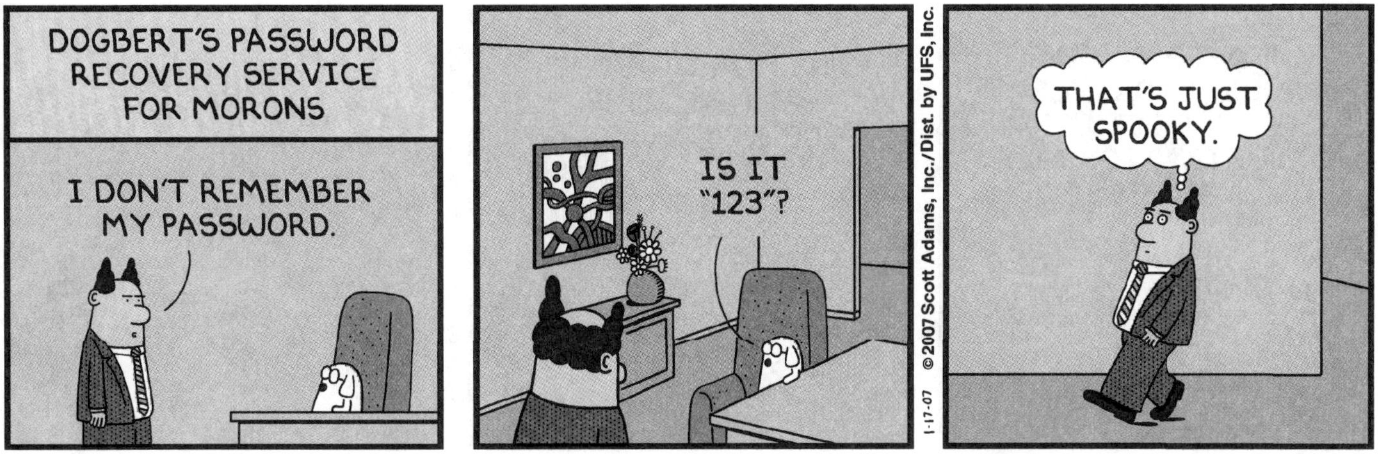
DOGBERT'S PASSWORD RECOVERY SERVICE FOR MORONS
I DON'T REMEMBER MY PASSWORD.
IS IT "123"?
1-17-07 © 2007 Scott Adams, Inc./Dist. by UFS, Inc.
THAT'S JUST SPOOKY.

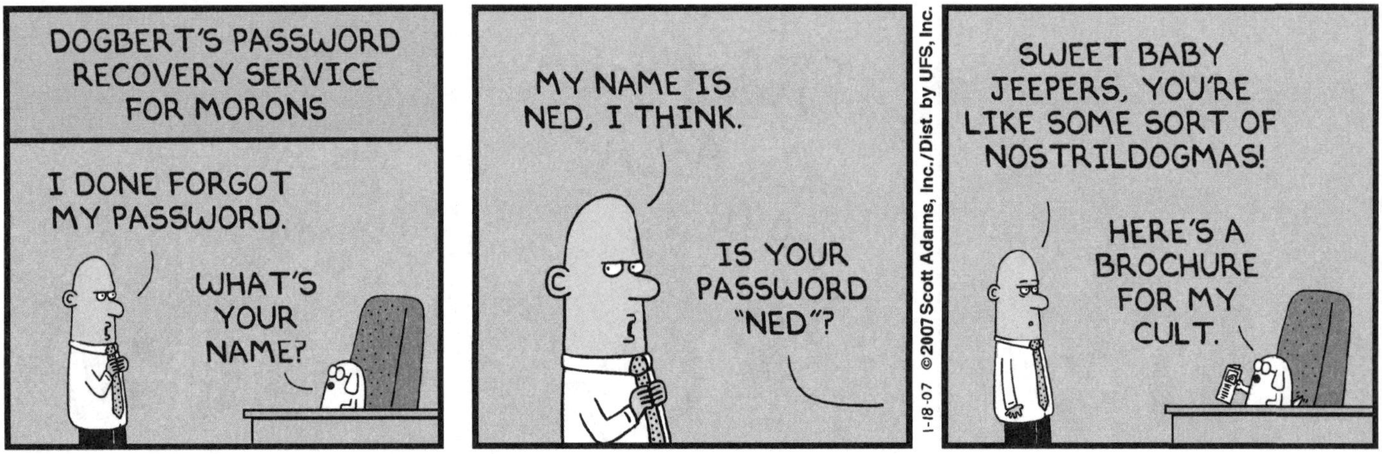
DOGBERT'S PASSWORD RECOVERY SERVICE FOR MORONS
I DONE FORGOT MY PASSWORD.
WHAT'S YOUR NAME?
MY NAME IS NED, I THINK.
IS YOUR PASSWORD "NED"?
SWEET BABY JEEPERS, YOU'RE LIKE SOME SORT OF NOSTRILDOGMAS!
HERE'S A BROCHURE FOR MY CULT.
1-18-07 ©2007 Scott Adams, Inc./Dist. by UFS, Inc.

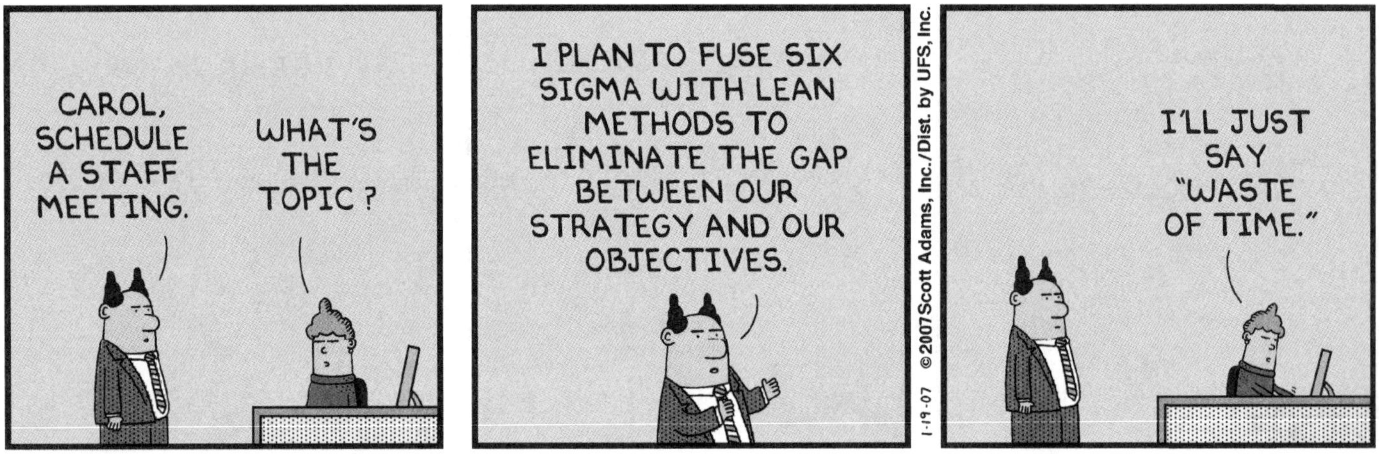
CAROL, SCHEDULE A STAFF MEETING.
WHAT'S THE TOPIC ?
I PLAN TO FUSE SIX SIGMA WITH LEAN METHODS TO ELIMINATE THE GAP BETWEEN OUR STRATEGY AND OUR OBJECTIVES.
I'LL JUST SAY "WASTE OF TIME."
1-19-07 ©2007 Scott Adams, Inc./Dist. by UFS, Inc.

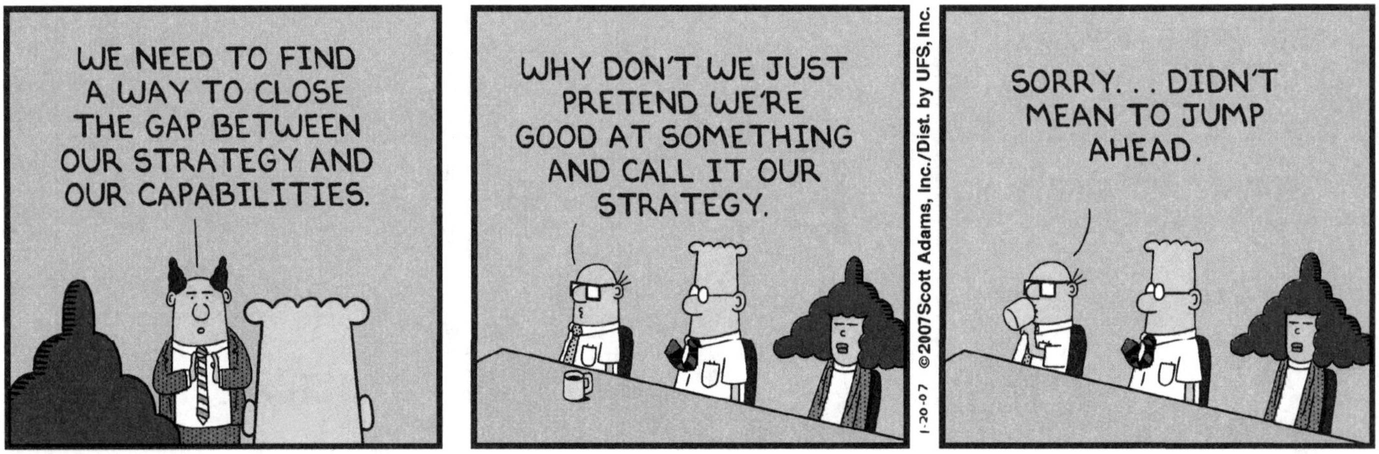
WE NEED TO FIND A WAY TO CLOSE THE GAP BETWEEN OUR STRATEGY AND OUR CAPABILITIES.
WHY DON'T WE JUST PRETEND WE'RE GOOD AT SOMETHING AND CALL IT OUR STRATEGY.
SORRY. . . DIDN'T MEAN TO JUMP AHEAD.
1-20-07 ©2007 Scott Adams, Inc./Dist. by UFS, Inc.

FROM NOW ON, ALL TRAVEL MUST BE BOOKED THROUGH THE CORPORATE TRAVEL WEB SITE.
OUR TRAVEL WEB SITE IS TERRIBLE.
IT ONLY LETS YOU BOOK THE CHEAPEST FLIGHT, AND THAT'S ALWAYS ON ELBONIAN AIRLINES.
DON'T BE SUCH A SNOB. WHAT'S WRONG WITH USING A DISCOUNT AIRLINE?
WELL, THEY LIST THEIR DESTINATION AIRPORTS AS "WHATEVER LOOKS SOFT."
THE MEALS IN FIRST CLASS ARE MADE OF ANYONE WHO DIES IN COACH.
THEIR ENTIRE SECURITY SCREENING PROCESS INVOLVES SHOUTING AT EACH PASSENGER "ARE YOU OSAMA BIN LADEN?!!!"
AND I ONCE SAW A BAGGAGE HANDLER WEARING MY DRESS.
WHINER.
© 2007 Scott Adams, Inc./Dist. by UFS, Inc.
1-21-07

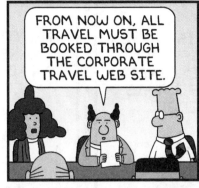

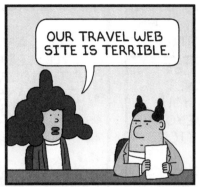

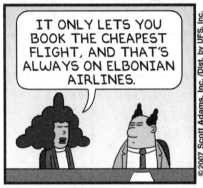

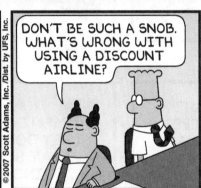

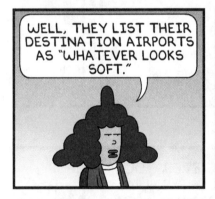

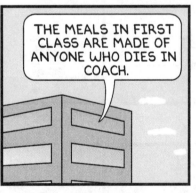

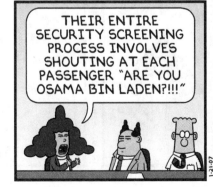

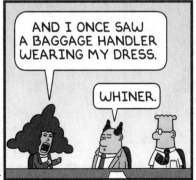

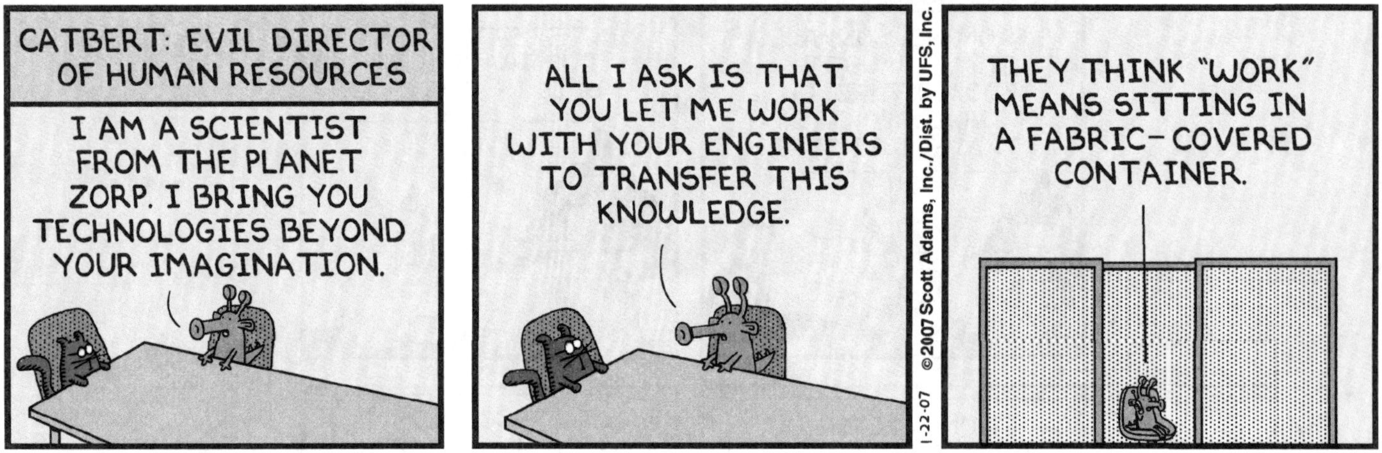
CATBERT: EVIL DIRECTOR OF HUMAN RESOURCES
I AM A SCIENTIST FROM THE PLANET ZORP. I BRING YOU TECHNOLOGIES BEYOND YOUR IMAGINATION.
ALL I ASK IS THAT YOU LET ME WORK WITH YOUR ENGINEERS TO TRANSFER THIS KNOWLEDGE.
1-22-07 ©2007 Scott Adams, Inc./Dist. by UFS, Inc.
THEY THINK "WORK" MEANS SITTING IN A FABRIC-COVERED CONTAINER.

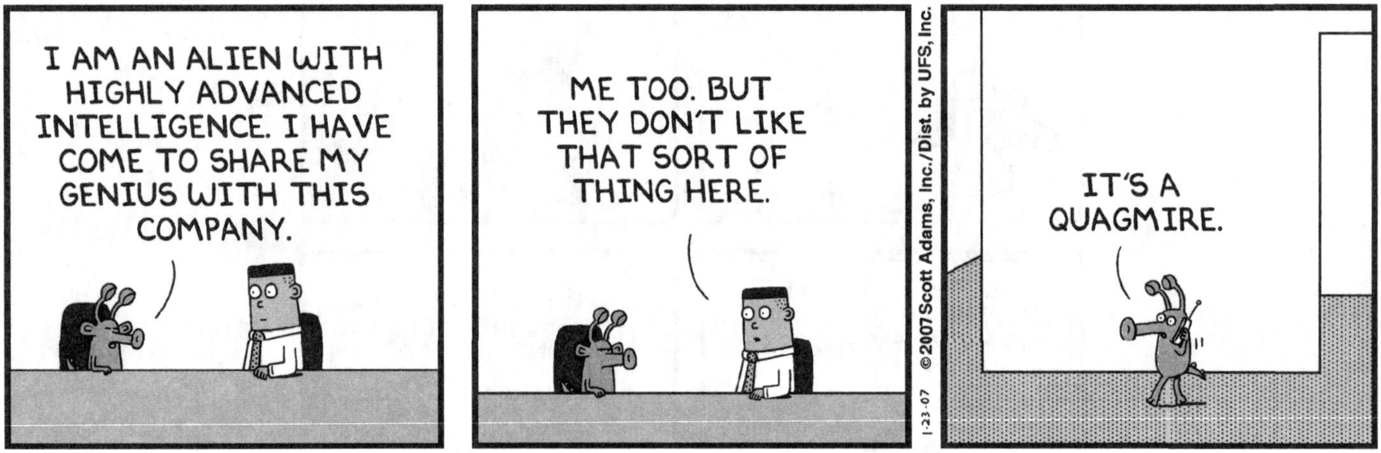
I AM AN ALIEN WITH HIGHLY ADVANCED INTELLIGENCE. I HAVE COME TO SHARE MY GENIUS WITH THIS COMPANY.
ME TOO. BUT THEY DON'T LIKE THAT SORT OF THING HERE.
1-23-07 ©2007 Scott Adams, Inc./Dist. by UFS, Inc.
IT'S A QUAGMIRE.

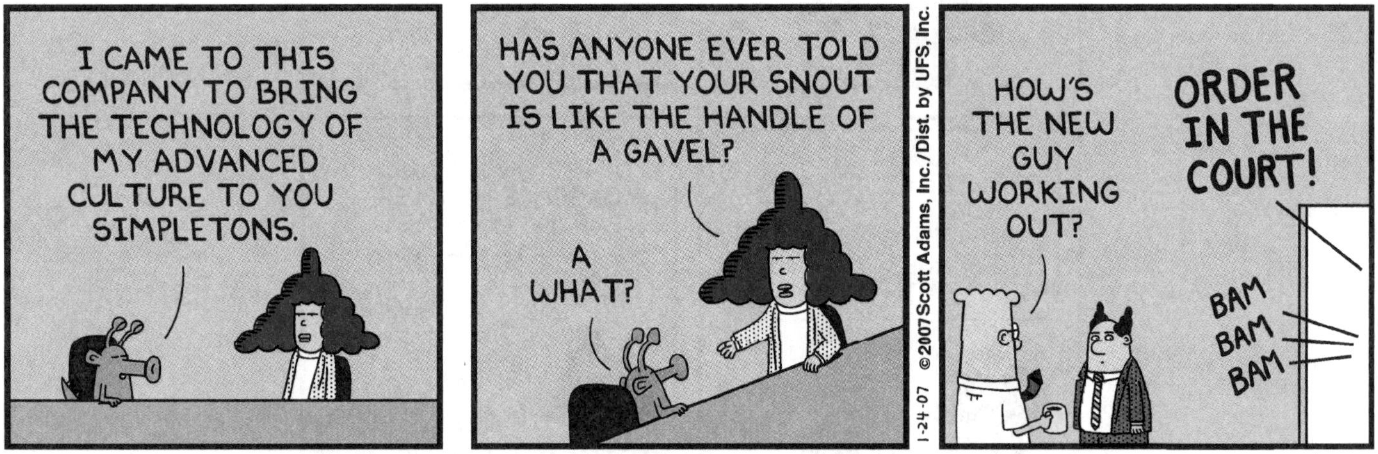
I CAME TO THIS COMPANY TO BRING THE TECHNOLOGY OF MY ADVANCED CULTURE TO YOU SIMPLETONS.
HAS ANYONE EVER TOLD YOU THAT YOUR SNOUT IS LIKE THE HANDLE OF A GAVEL?
A WHAT?
1-24-07 ©2007 Scott Adams, Inc./Dist. by UFS, Inc.
HOW'S THE NEW GUY WORKING OUT?
ORDER IN THE COURT!
BAM
BAM
BAM

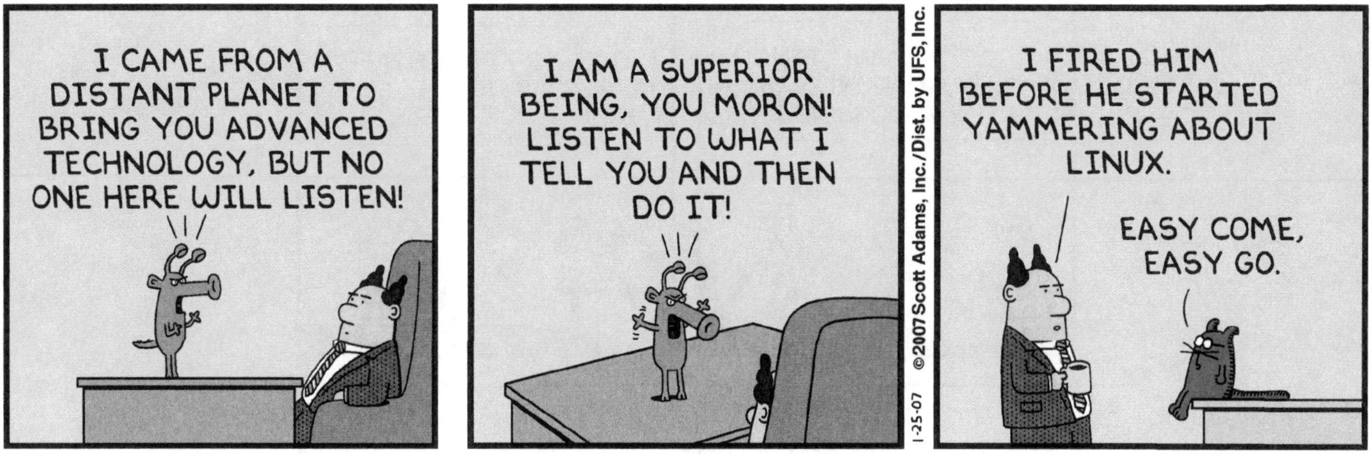
I CAME FROM A DISTANT PLANET TO BRING YOU ADVANCED TECHNOLOGY, BUT NO ONE HERE WILL LISTEN!
I AM A SUPERIOR BEING, YOU MORON! LISTEN TO WHAT I TELL YOU AND THEN DO IT!
1-25-07 ©2007 Scott Adams, Inc./Dist. by UFS, Inc.
I FIRED HIM BEFORE HE STARTED YAMMERING ABOUT LINUX.
EASY COME, EASY GO.

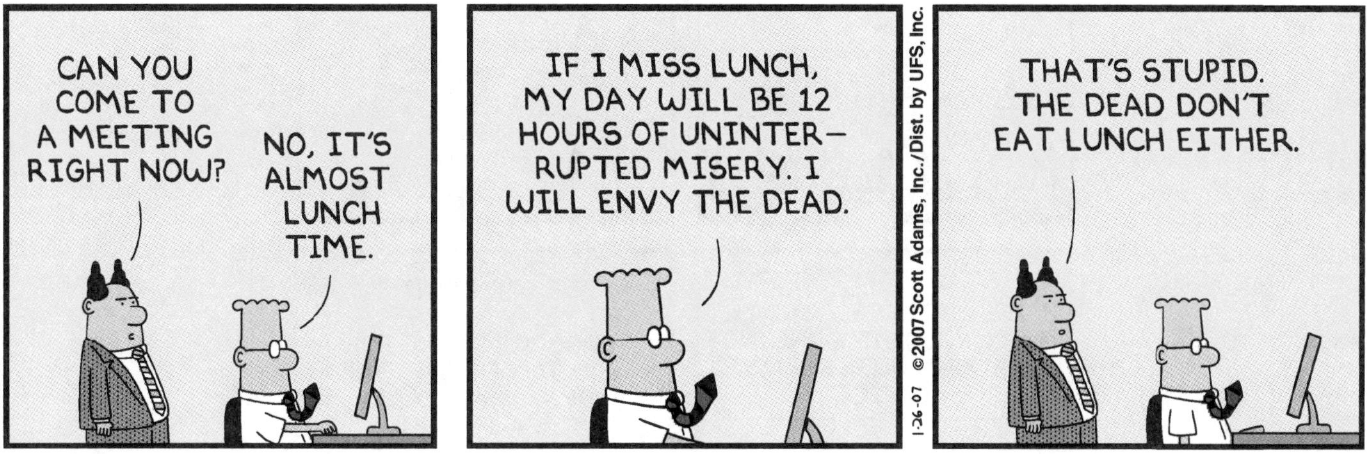
CAN YOU COME TO A MEETING RIGHT NOW?
NO, IT'S ALMOST LUNCH TIME.
IF I MISS LUNCH, MY DAY WILL BE 12 HOURS OF UNINTER–RUPTED MISERY. I WILL ENVY THE DEAD.
1-26-07 ©2007 Scott Adams, Inc./Dist. by UFS, Inc.
THAT'S STUPID. THE DEAD DON'T EAT LUNCH EITHER.

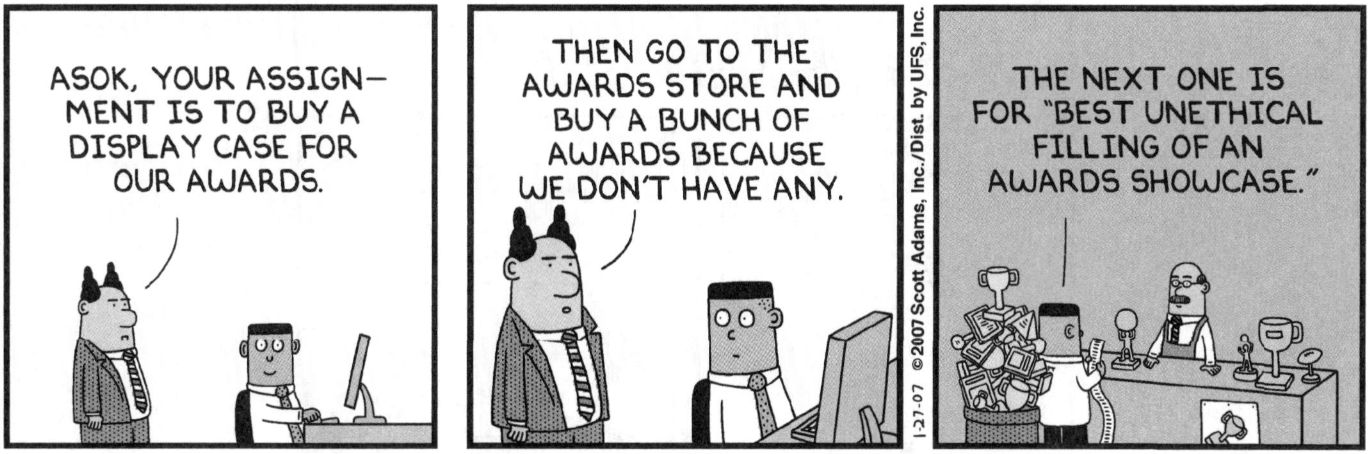
ASOK, YOUR ASSIGN–MENT IS TO BUY A DISPLAY CASE FOR OUR AWARDS.
THEN GO TO THE AWARDS STORE AND BUY A BUNCH OF AWARDS BECAUSE WE DON'T HAVE ANY.
1-27-07 ©2007 Scott Adams, Inc./Dist. by UFS, Inc.
THE NEXT ONE IS FOR "BEST UNETHICAL FILLING OF AN AWARDS SHOWCASE."

I ENJOYED MEETING YOUR STAFF. KEEP UP THE GOOD WORK.
THIS ISN'T MY STAFF. I REPORT TO THE GUY WHO REPORTS TO YOU.
REALLY? WHICH ONE OF YOU REPORTS TO ME?
WELL, THAT EXPLAINS WHY YOU KEEP HANGING AROUND OUTSIDE MY OFFICE.
I'VE BEEN GOING TO YOUR OFFICE FOR YEARS, WAITING FOR YOU TO GET OFF THE PHONE SO I COULD TALK TO YOU.
I'VE BEEN MAKING FAKE PHONE CALLS FOR YEARS, HOPING THE WEIRDO OUTSIDE MY OFFICE WOULD GO AWAY.
KEEP UP THE GOOD WORK.
© 2007 Scott Adams, Inc. /Dist. by UFS, Inc.
1-28-07

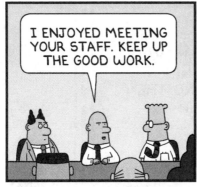

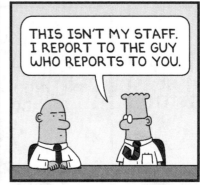

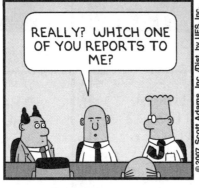

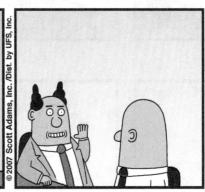

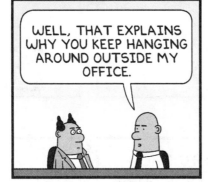

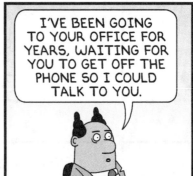

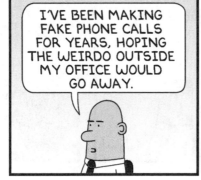

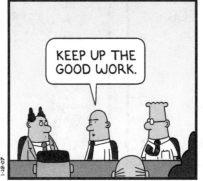

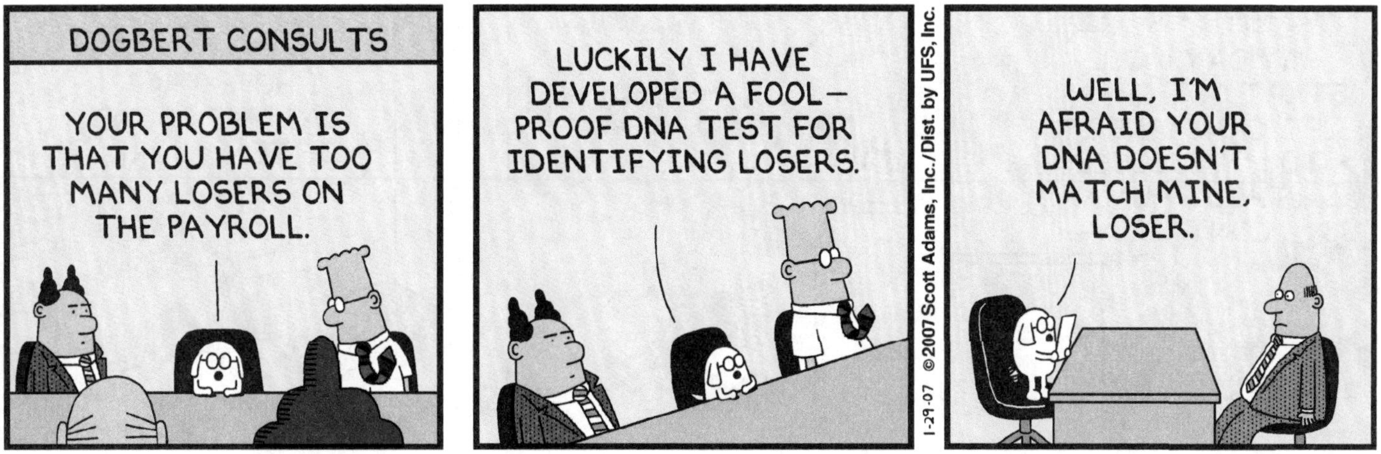
DOGBERT CONSULTS
YOUR PROBLEM IS THAT YOU HAVE TOO MANY LOSERS ON THE PAYROLL.
LUCKILY I HAVE DEVELOPED A FOOL-PROOF DNA TEST FOR IDENTIFYING LOSERS.
1-29-07 © 2007 Scott Adams, Inc./Dist. by UFS, Inc.
WELL, I'M AFRAID YOUR DNA DOESN'T MATCH MINE, LOSER.

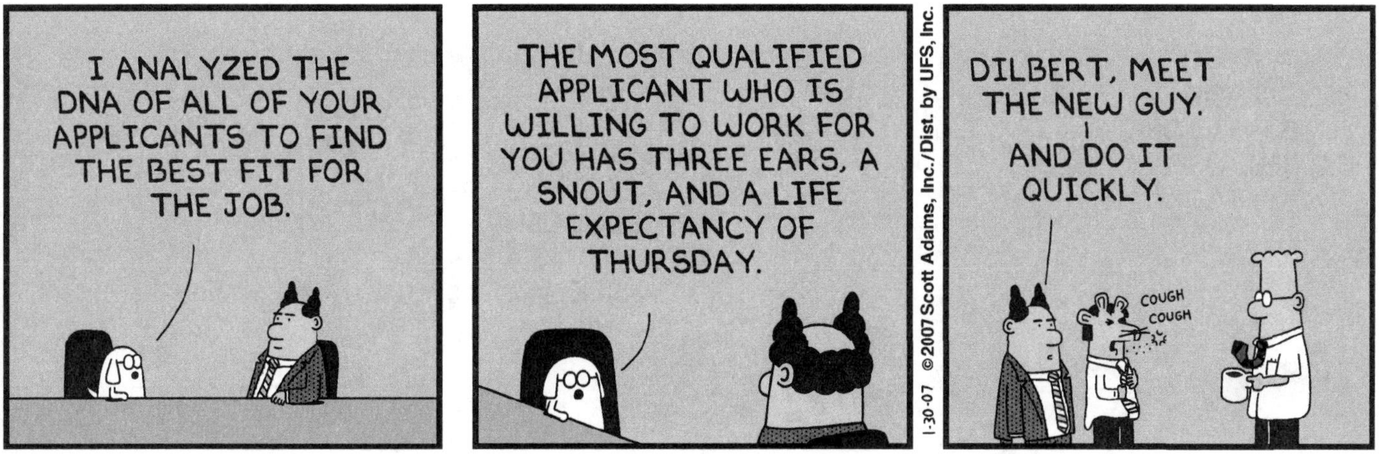
I ANALYZED THE DNA OF ALL OF YOUR APPLICANTS TO FIND THE BEST FIT FOR THE JOB.
THE MOST QUALIFIED APPLICANT WHO IS WILLING TO WORK FOR YOU HAS THREE EARS, A SNOUT, AND A LIFE EXPECTANCY OF THURSDAY.
1-30-07 © 2007 Scott Adams, Inc./Dist. by UFS, Inc.
DILBERT, MEET THE NEW GUY.
AND DO IT QUICKLY.
COUGH COUGH

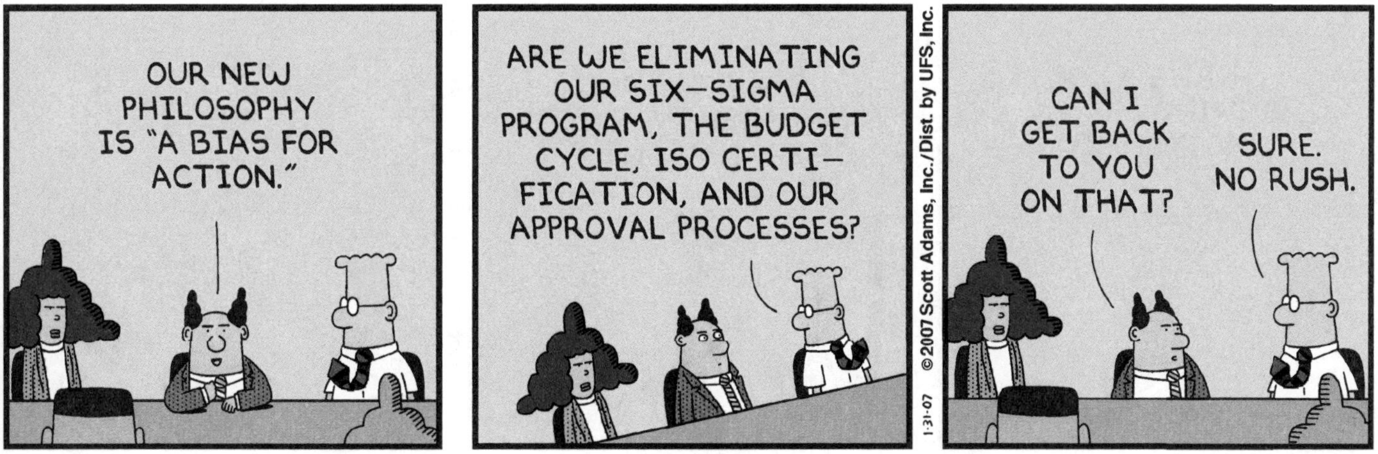
OUR NEW PHILOSOPHY IS "A BIAS FOR ACTION."
ARE WE ELIMINATING OUR SIX-SIGMA PROGRAM, THE BUDGET CYCLE, ISO CERTI-FICATION, AND OUR APPROVAL PROCESSES?
1-31-07 © 2007 Scott Adams, Inc./Dist. by UFS, Inc.
CAN I GET BACK TO YOU ON THAT?
SURE. NO RUSH.

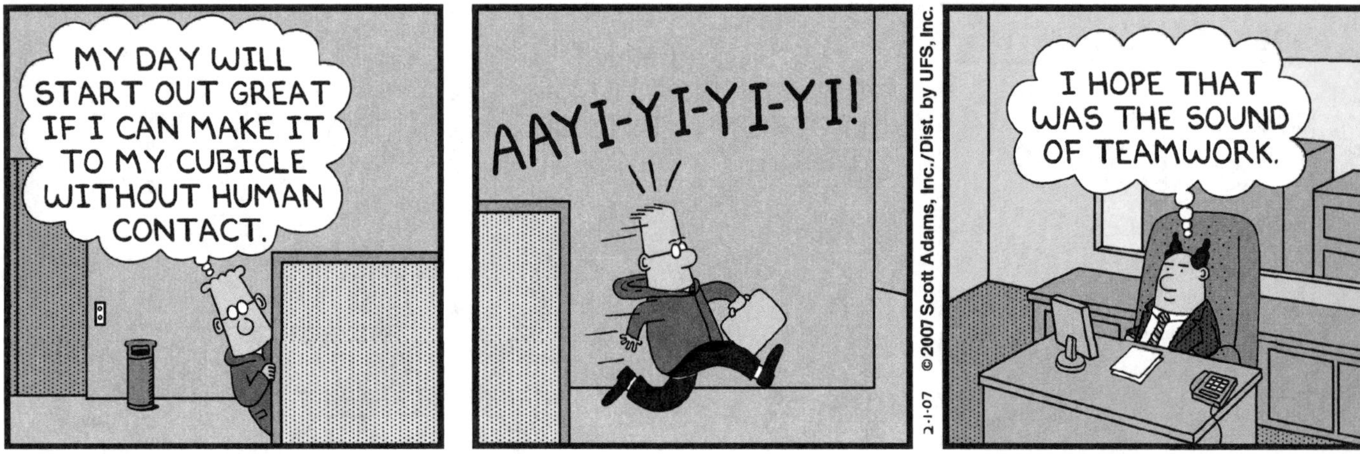
MY DAY WILL START OUT GREAT IF I CAN MAKE IT TO MY CUBICLE WITHOUT HUMAN CONTACT.
AAYI-YI-YI-YI!
2-1-07 ©2007 Scott Adams, Inc./Dist. by UFS, Inc.
I HOPE THAT WAS THE SOUND OF TEAMWORK.

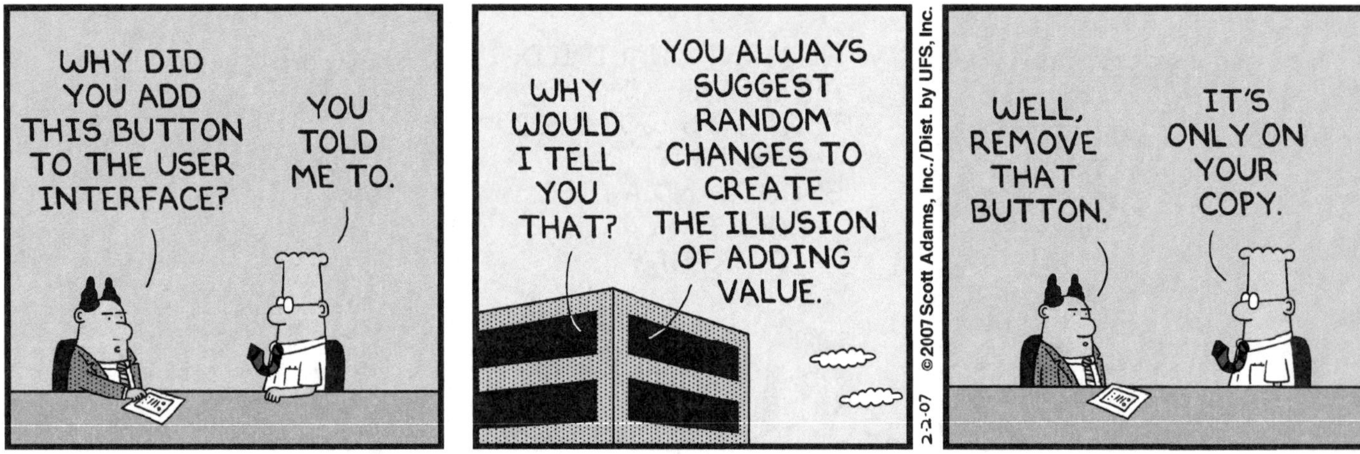
WHY DID YOU ADD THIS BUTTON TO THE USER INTERFACE?
YOU TOLD ME TO.
WHY WOULD I TELL YOU THAT?
YOU ALWAYS SUGGEST RANDOM CHANGES TO CREATE THE ILLUSION OF ADDING VALUE.
2-2-07 ©2007 Scott Adams, Inc./Dist. by UFS, Inc.
WELL, REMOVE THAT BUTTON.
IT'S ONLY ON YOUR COPY.

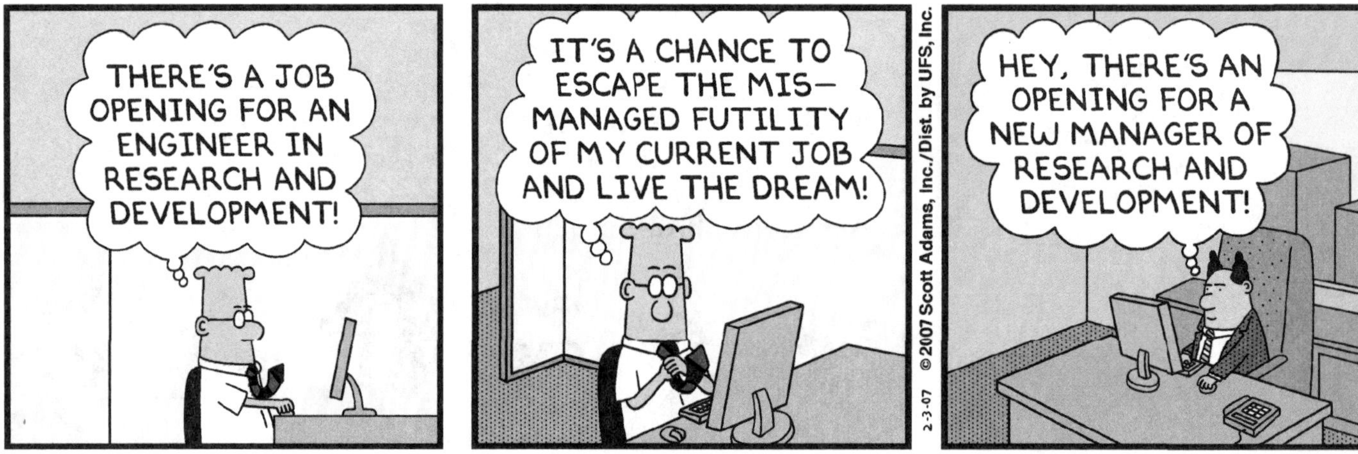
THERE'S A JOB OPENING FOR AN ENGINEER IN RESEARCH AND DEVELOPMENT!
IT'S A CHANCE TO ESCAPE THE MIS— MANAGED FUTILITY OF MY CURRENT JOB AND LIVE THE DREAM!
2-3-07 ©2007 Scott Adams, Inc./Dist. by UFS, Inc.
HEY, THERE'S AN OPENING FOR A NEW MANAGER OF RESEARCH AND DEVELOPMENT!

I'D LIKE TO KICK OFF THE PROJECT BY ASSIGNING BLAME FOR ITS EVENTUAL FAILURE.
SHOULDN'T WE DO THAT AFTER THE PROJECT IS OVER?
I SEE NO REASON TO WAIT.
©2007 Scott Adams, Inc./Dist. by UFS, Inc.
WELL... OKAY.
OUR BOSS WILL MAKE US USE THE WRONG VENDOR.
WALLY WON'T DO ANY WORK. ALICE WILL ALIENATE THE CLIENT, AND TED IS GENERALLY WORTHLESS.
IN SUMMARY, MY EXCELLENT WORK WILL BE RENDERED MOOT BY NINCOMPOOPS.
2-4-07
DO YOU EVEN WORK HERE?
NO, I WAS JUST IN THE NEIGHBOR-HOOD.

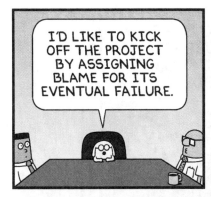

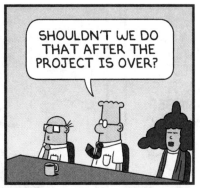

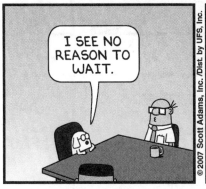

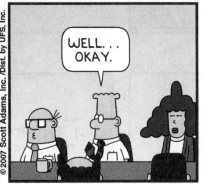

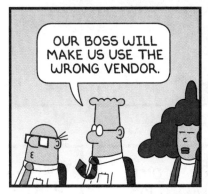

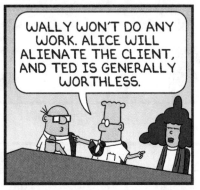

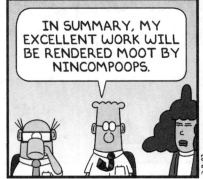

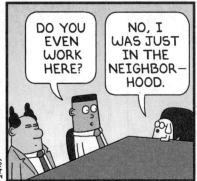

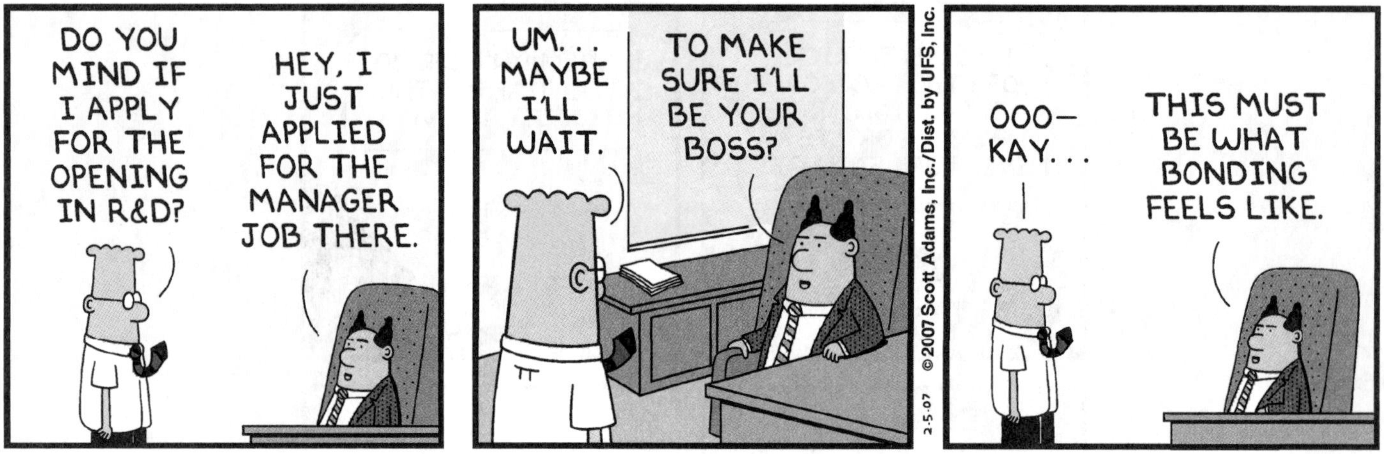
DO YOU MIND IF I APPLY FOR THE OPENING IN R&D?
HEY, I JUST APPLIED FOR THE MANAGER JOB THERE.
UM... MAYBE I'LL WAIT.
TO MAKE SURE I'LL BE YOUR BOSS?
© 2007 Scott Adams, Inc./Dist. by UFS, Inc.
2-5-07
OOO– KAY...
THIS MUST BE WHAT BONDING FEELS LIKE.

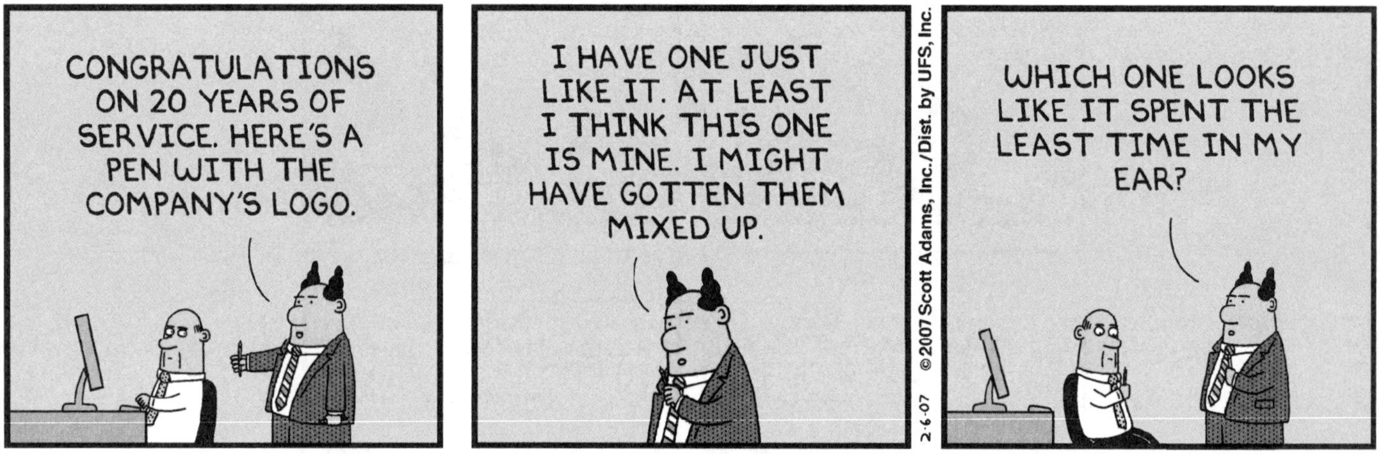
CONGRATULATIONS ON 20 YEARS OF SERVICE. HERE'S A PEN WITH THE COMPANY'S LOGO.
I HAVE ONE JUST LIKE IT. AT LEAST I THINK THIS ONE IS MINE. I MIGHT HAVE GOTTEN THEM MIXED UP.
© 2007 Scott Adams, Inc./Dist. by UFS, Inc.
2-6-07
WHICH ONE LOOKS LIKE IT SPENT THE LEAST TIME IN MY EAR?

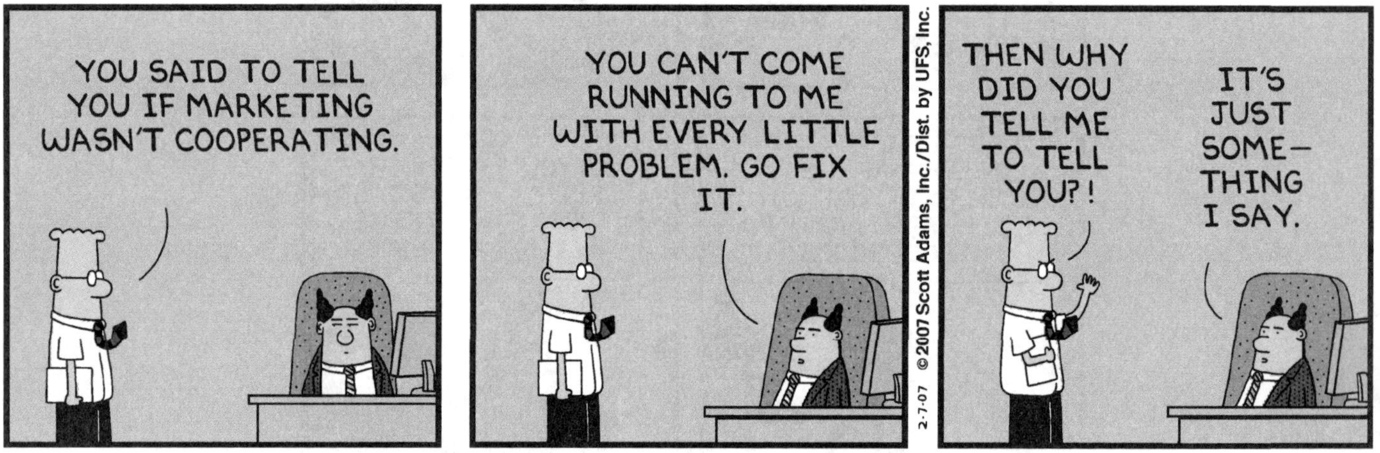
YOU SAID TO TELL YOU IF MARKETING WASN'T COOPERATING.
YOU CAN'T COME RUNNING TO ME WITH EVERY LITTLE PROBLEM. GO FIX IT.
© 2007 Scott Adams, Inc./Dist. by UFS, Inc.
2-7-07
THEN WHY DID YOU TELL ME TO TELL YOU?!
IT'S JUST SOME– THING I SAY.

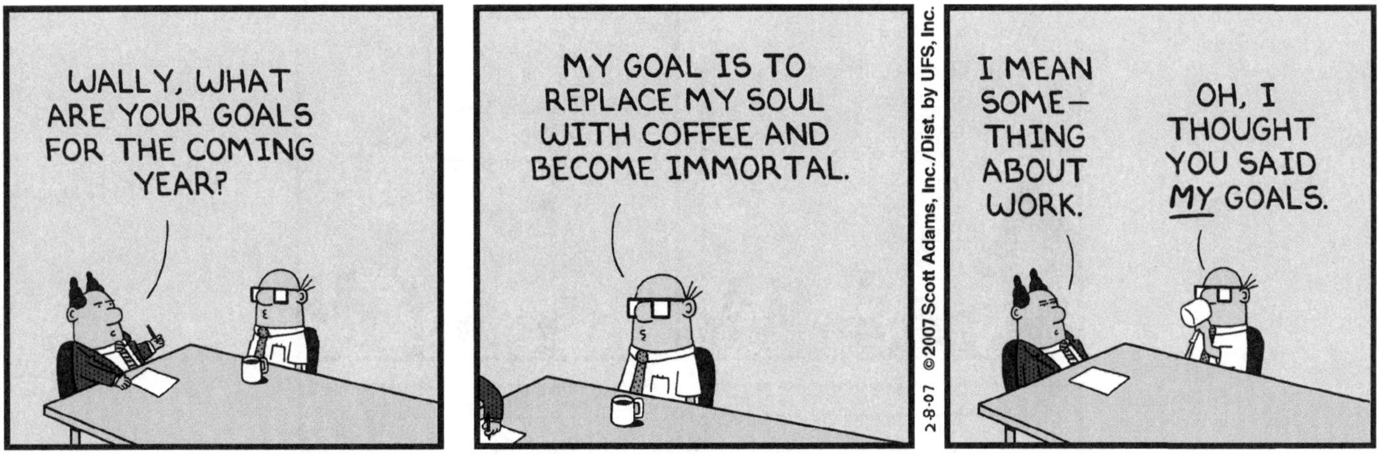
WALLY, WHAT ARE YOUR GOALS FOR THE COMING YEAR?
MY GOAL IS TO REPLACE MY SOUL WITH COFFEE AND BECOME IMMORTAL.
2-8-07 ©2007 Scott Adams, Inc./Dist. by UFS, Inc.
I MEAN SOME-THING ABOUT WORK.
OH, I THOUGHT YOU SAID MY GOALS.

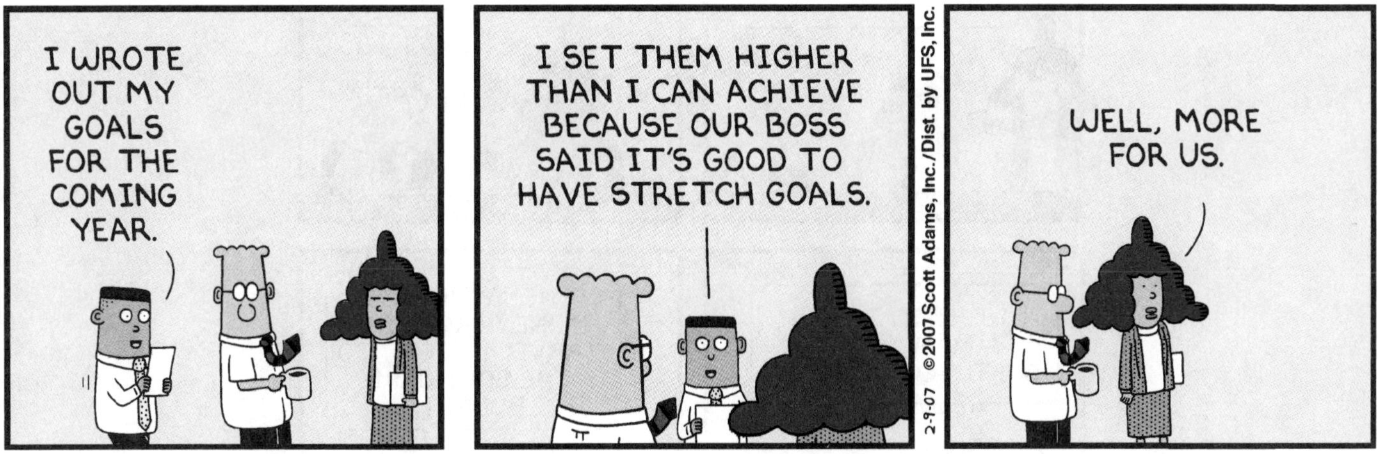
I WROTE OUT MY GOALS FOR THE COMING YEAR.
I SET THEM HIGHER THAN I CAN ACHIEVE BECAUSE OUR BOSS SAID IT'S GOOD TO HAVE STRETCH GOALS.
2-9-07 ©2007 Scott Adams, Inc./Dist. by UFS, Inc.
WELL, MORE FOR US.

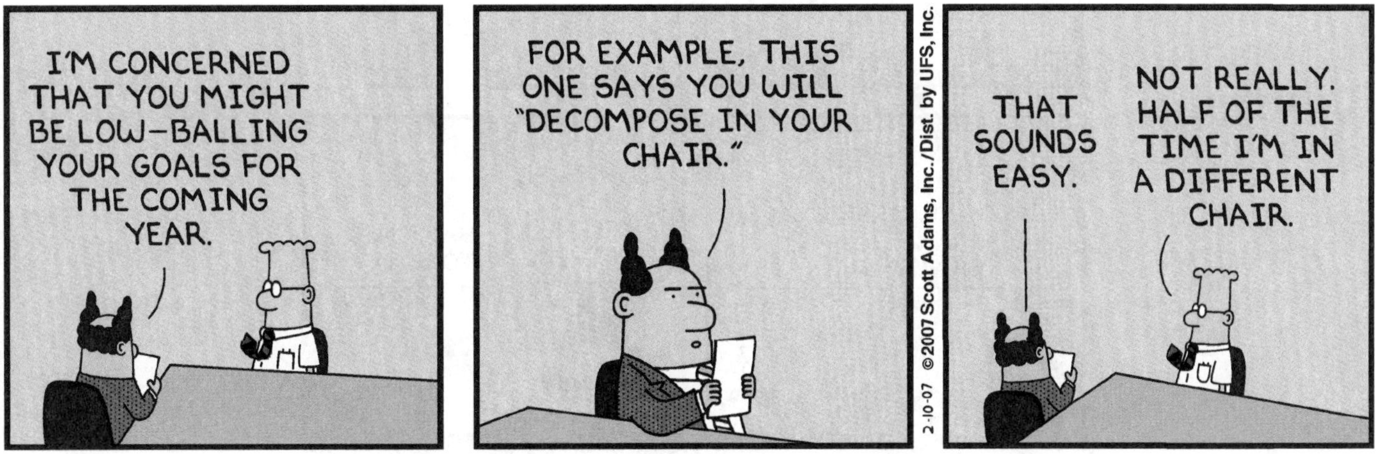
I'M CONCERNED THAT YOU MIGHT BE LOW-BALLING YOUR GOALS FOR THE COMING YEAR.
FOR EXAMPLE, THIS ONE SAYS YOU WILL "DECOMPOSE IN YOUR CHAIR."
2-10-07 ©2007 Scott Adams, Inc./Dist. by UFS, Inc.
THAT SOUNDS EASY.
NOT REALLY. HALF OF THE TIME I'M IN A DIFFERENT CHAIR.

OUR TRAVEL BUDGET IS SHOT.
WE'LL TAKE MONEY OUT OF THE TRAINING BUDGET.
WE NEED TRAINING TO SUPPORT OUR NEW PRODUCT.
WE'LL USE THE SOFTWARE BUDGET FOR TRAINING.
WE NEED TO DO A MANDATORY SOFTWARE UPGRADE.
FINE. MOVE SOME MONEY FROM THE TRAVEL BUDGET TO THE SOFTWARE BUDGET.
GEEZ, YOU PEOPLE DO NOTHING BUT COMPLAIN. MEANWHILE I'M MANAGING MY BRAINS OUT.
I WONDERED WHAT HAPPENED TO THEM.
HAPPENED TO WHAT?
©2007 Scott Adams, Inc. /Dist. by UFS, Inc.
2-11-07

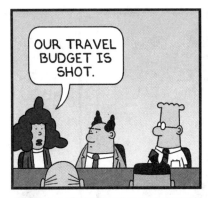

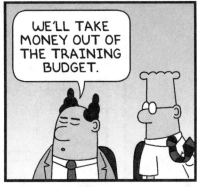

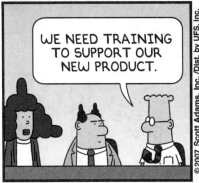

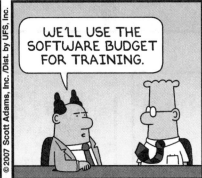

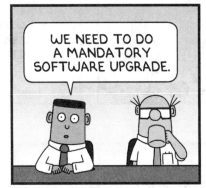

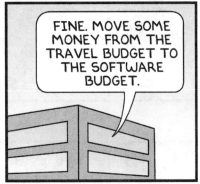

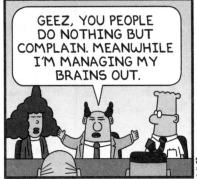

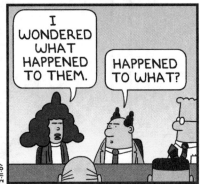

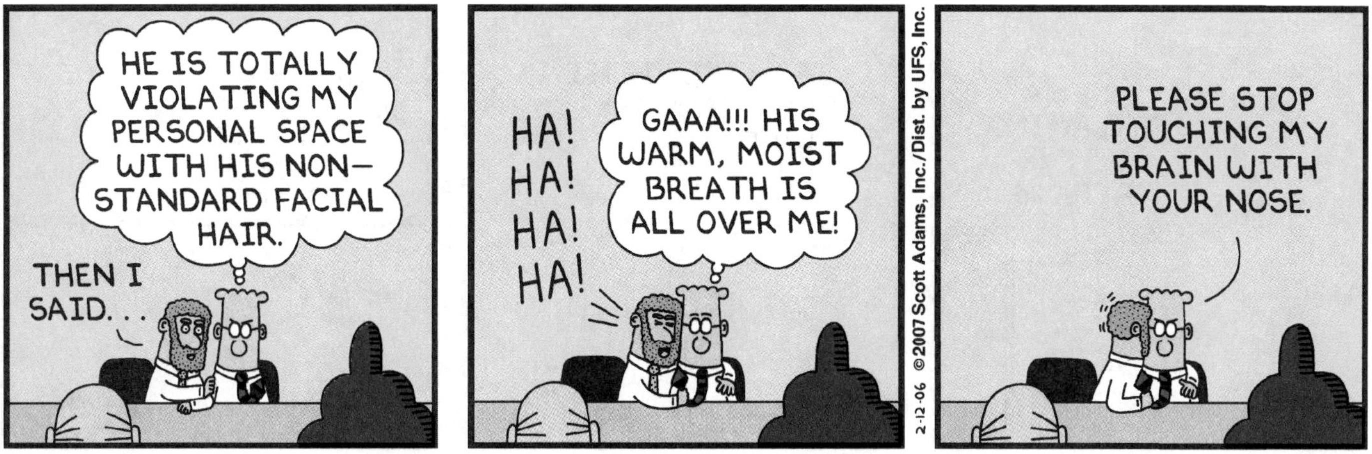
HE IS TOTALLY VIOLATING MY PERSONAL SPACE WITH HIS NON-STANDARD FACIAL HAIR.
THEN I SAID. . .
HA! HA! HA! HA!
GAAA!!! HIS WARM, MOIST BREATH IS ALL OVER ME!
2-12-06 © 2007 Scott Adams, Inc./Dist. by UFS, Inc.
PLEASE STOP TOUCHING MY BRAIN WITH YOUR NOSE.

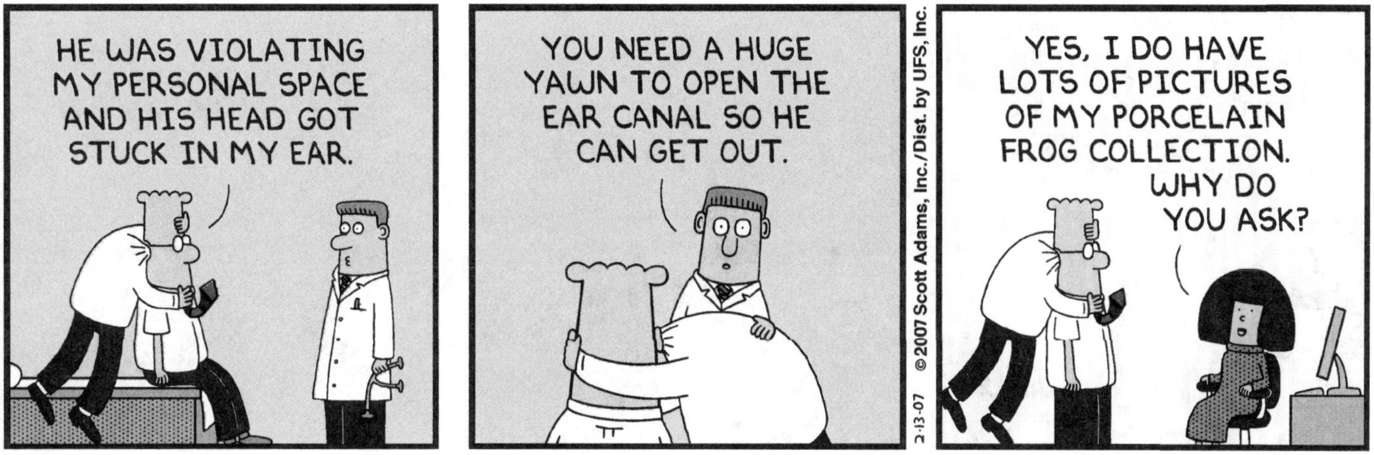
HE WAS VIOLATING MY PERSONAL SPACE AND HIS HEAD GOT STUCK IN MY EAR.
YOU NEED A HUGE YAWN TO OPEN THE EAR CANAL SO HE CAN GET OUT.
2-13-07 © 2007 Scott Adams, Inc./Dist. by UFS, Inc.
YES, I DO HAVE LOTS OF PICTURES OF MY PORCELAIN FROG COLLECTION.
WHY DO YOU ASK?

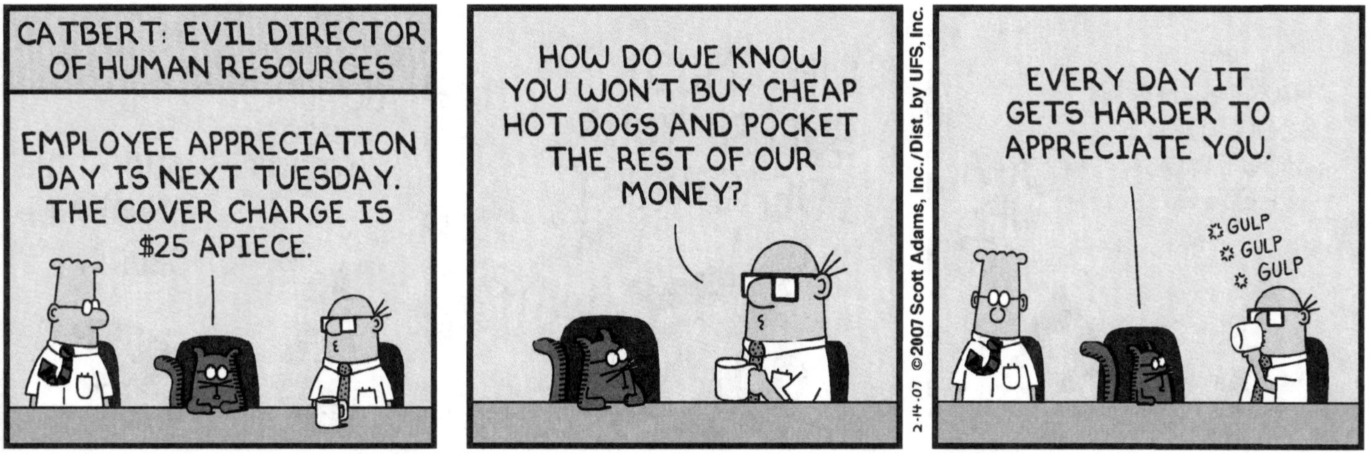
CATBERT: EVIL DIRECTOR OF HUMAN RESOURCES
EMPLOYEE APPRECIATION DAY IS NEXT TUESDAY. THE COVER CHARGE IS $25 APIECE.
HOW DO WE KNOW YOU WON'T BUY CHEAP HOT DOGS AND POCKET THE REST OF OUR MONEY?
2-14-07 © 2007 Scott Adams, Inc./Dist. by UFS, Inc.
EVERY DAY IT GETS HARDER TO APPRECIATE YOU.
GULP
GULP
GULP

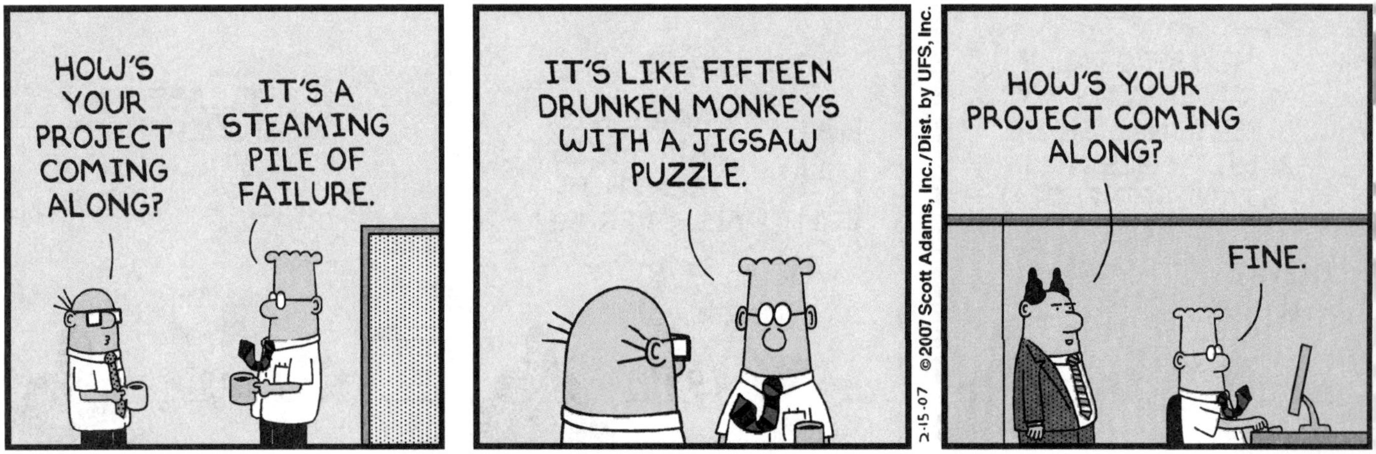
HOW'S YOUR PROJECT COMING ALONG?
IT'S A STEAMING PILE OF FAILURE.
IT'S LIKE FIFTEEN DRUNKEN MONKEYS WITH A JIGSAW PUZZLE.
2-15-07 ©2007 Scott Adams, Inc./Dist. by UFS, Inc.
HOW'S YOUR PROJECT COMING ALONG?
FINE.

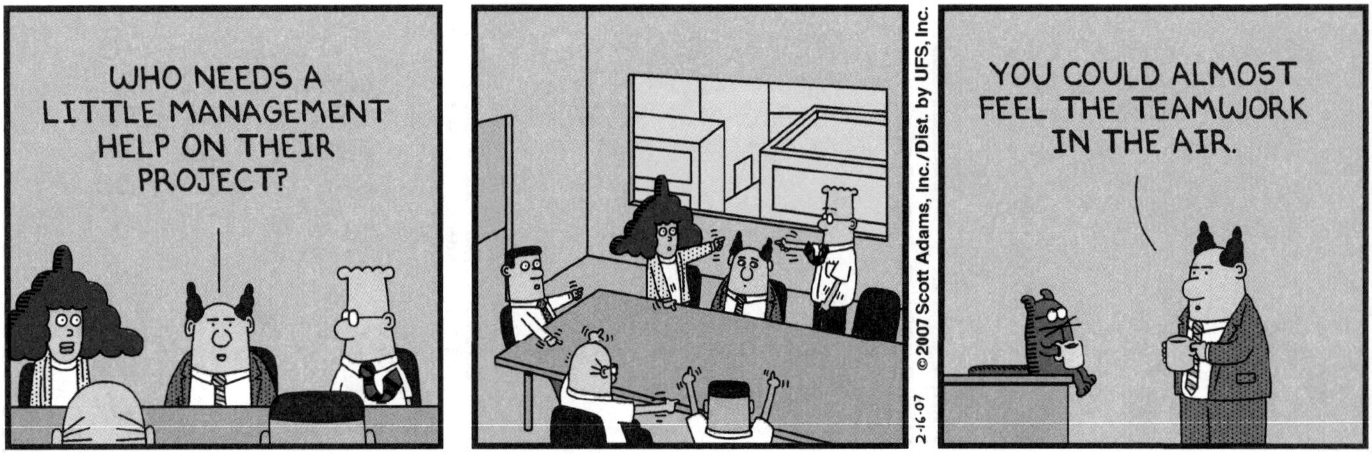
WHO NEEDS A LITTLE MANAGEMENT HELP ON THEIR PROJECT?
2-16-07 ©2007 Scott Adams, Inc./Dist. by UFS, Inc.
YOU COULD ALMOST FEEL THE TEAMWORK IN THE AIR.

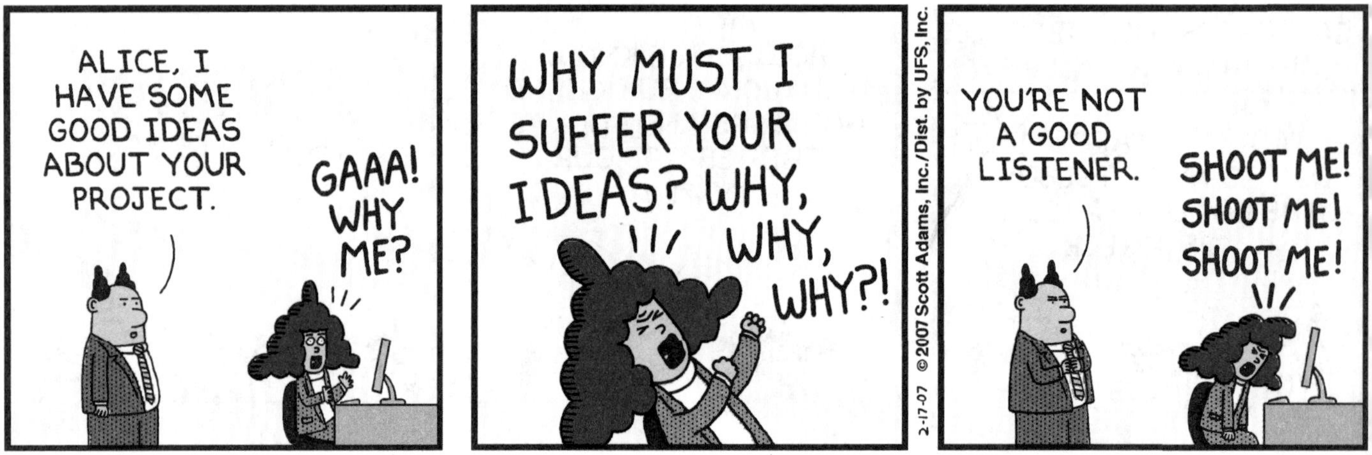
ALICE, I HAVE SOME GOOD IDEAS ABOUT YOUR PROJECT.
GAAA! WHY ME?
WHY MUST I SUFFER YOUR IDEAS? WHY, WHY, WHY?!
2-17-07 ©2007 Scott Adams, Inc./Dist. by UFS, Inc.
YOU'RE NOT A GOOD LISTENER.
SHOOT ME! SHOOT ME! SHOOT ME!

CATBERT: EVIL DIRECTOR OF HUMAN RESOURCES
THE NEW COMPANY HEALTH PLAN IS GOOGLE.
FROM NOW ON, EMPLOYEES MUST USE GOOGLE TO DIAGNOSE THEIR OWN ILLNESSES.
FOR EXAMPLE, THIS GUY HAS A GROWTH ON HIS NECK.
I DO?
A QUICK SEARCH ON MY BLACKBERRY TELLS ME IT'S. . .
WHAT IS IT?!!
OOH. WOW.
A PREGNANT TERMITE CRAWLED INTO YOUR MOUTH AND BUILT A HIVE IN YOUR ESOPHAGUS.
GAAA!!!
STOP BEING A BABY.
THE TREAT-MENT FOR THAT IS. . .
DO YOU HAVE AN ARC WELDER AND A BARREL OF KEROSENE?
©2007 Scott Adams, Inc. /Dist. by UFS, Inc.
2-18-07

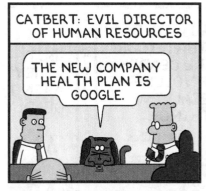

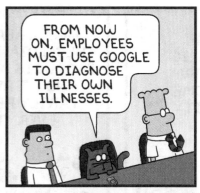

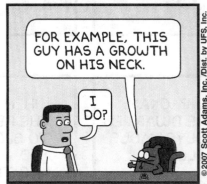

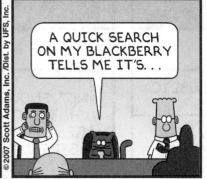

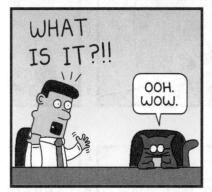

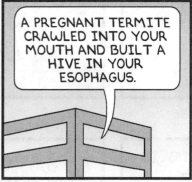

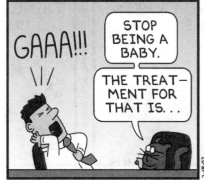

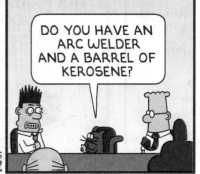

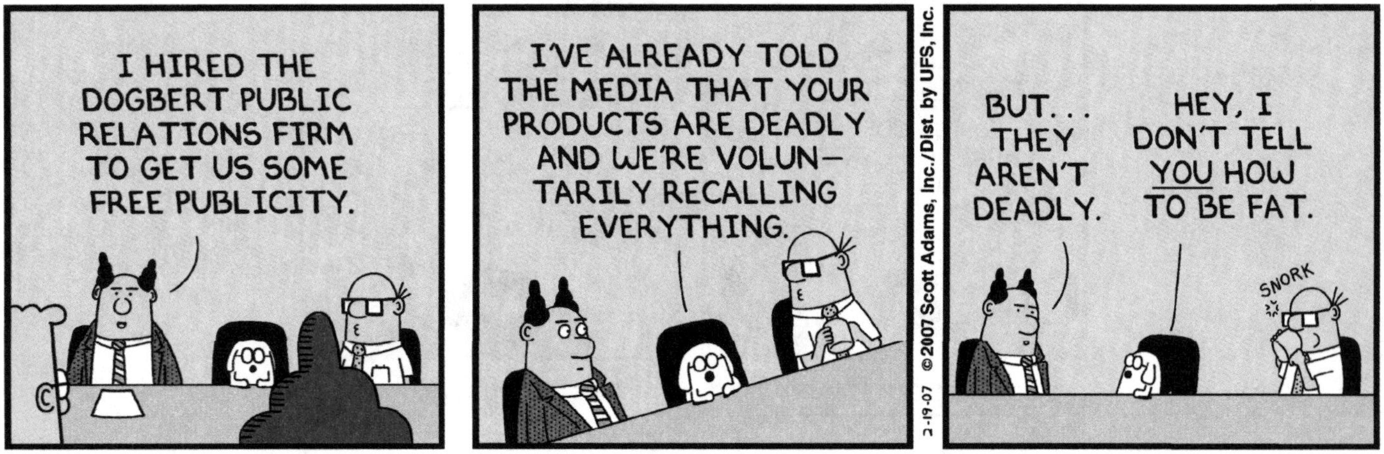
I HIRED THE DOGBERT PUBLIC RELATIONS FIRM TO GET US SOME FREE PUBLICITY.
I'VE ALREADY TOLD THE MEDIA THAT YOUR PRODUCTS ARE DEADLY AND WE'RE VOLUNTARILY RECALLING EVERYTHING.
BUT... THEY AREN'T DEADLY.
HEY, I DON'T TELL YOU HOW TO BE FAT.
SNORK
2-19-07 ©2007 Scott Adams, Inc./Dist. by UFS, Inc.

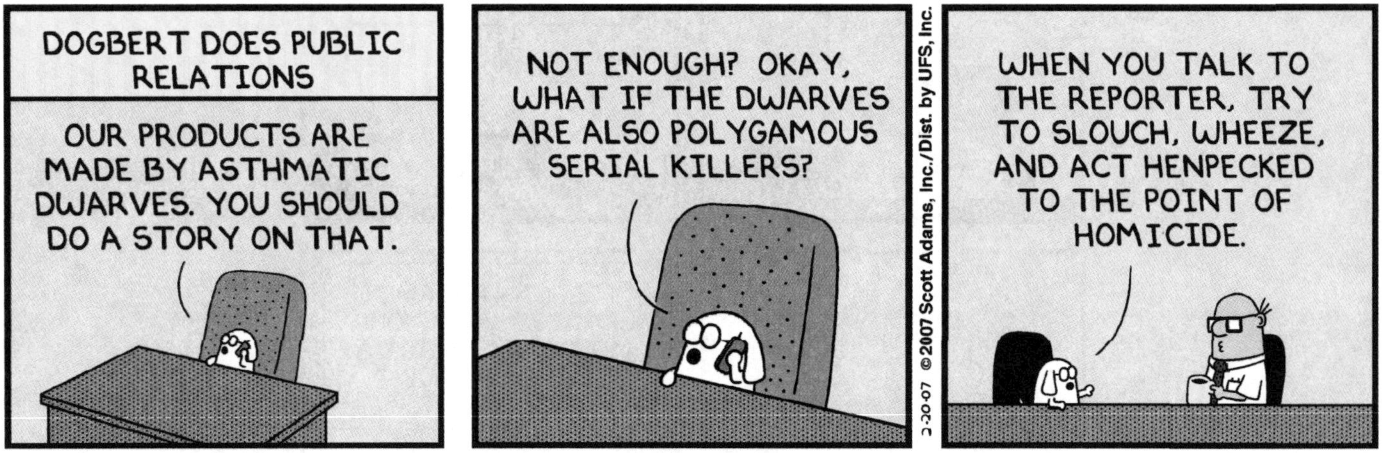
DOGBERT DOES PUBLIC RELATIONS
OUR PRODUCTS ARE MADE BY ASTHMATIC DWARVES. YOU SHOULD DO A STORY ON THAT.
NOT ENOUGH? OKAY, WHAT IF THE DWARVES ARE ALSO POLYGAMOUS SERIAL KILLERS?
WHEN YOU TALK TO THE REPORTER, TRY TO SLOUCH, WHEEZE, AND ACT HENPECKED TO THE POINT OF HOMICIDE.
2-20-07 ©2007 Scott Adams, Inc./Dist. by UFS, Inc.

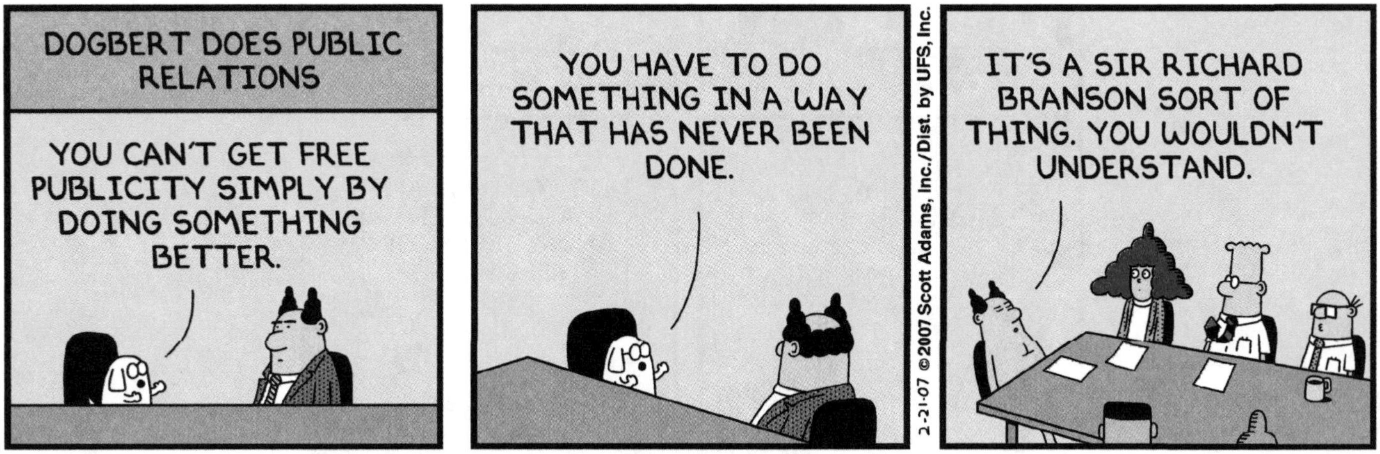
DOGBERT DOES PUBLIC RELATIONS
YOU CAN'T GET FREE PUBLICITY SIMPLY BY DOING SOMETHING BETTER.
YOU HAVE TO DO SOMETHING IN A WAY THAT HAS NEVER BEEN DONE.
IT'S A SIR RICHARD BRANSON SORT OF THING. YOU WOULDN'T UNDERSTAND.
2-21-07 ©2007 Scott Adams, Inc./Dist. by UFS, Inc.

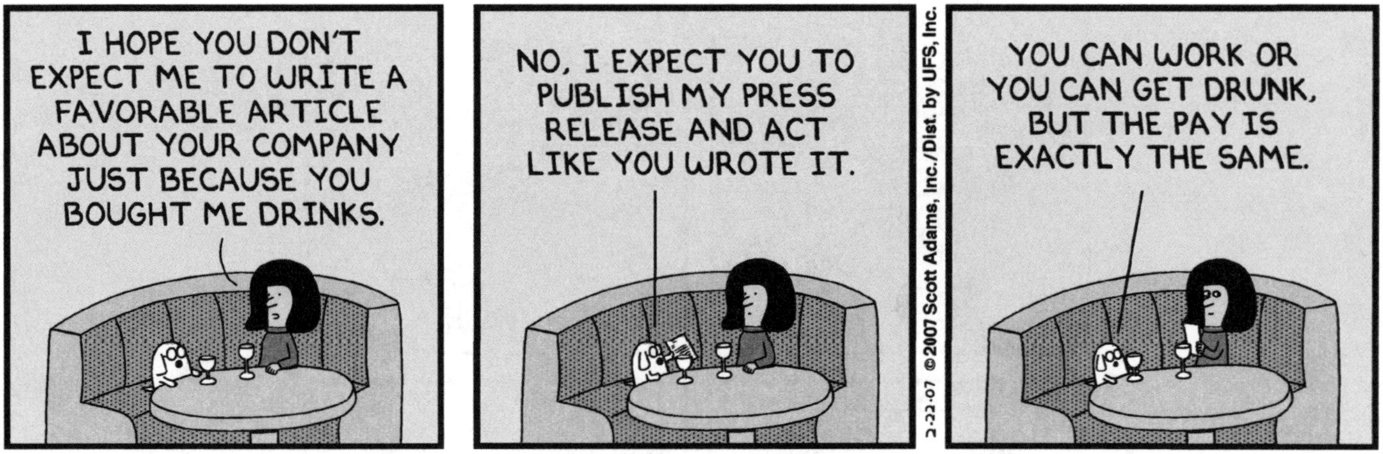
I HOPE YOU DON'T EXPECT ME TO WRITE A FAVORABLE ARTICLE ABOUT YOUR COMPANY JUST BECAUSE YOU BOUGHT ME DRINKS.
NO, I EXPECT YOU TO PUBLISH MY PRESS RELEASE AND ACT LIKE YOU WROTE IT.
2-22-07 © 2007 Scott Adams, Inc./Dist. by UFS, Inc.
YOU CAN WORK OR YOU CAN GET DRUNK, BUT THE PAY IS EXACTLY THE SAME.

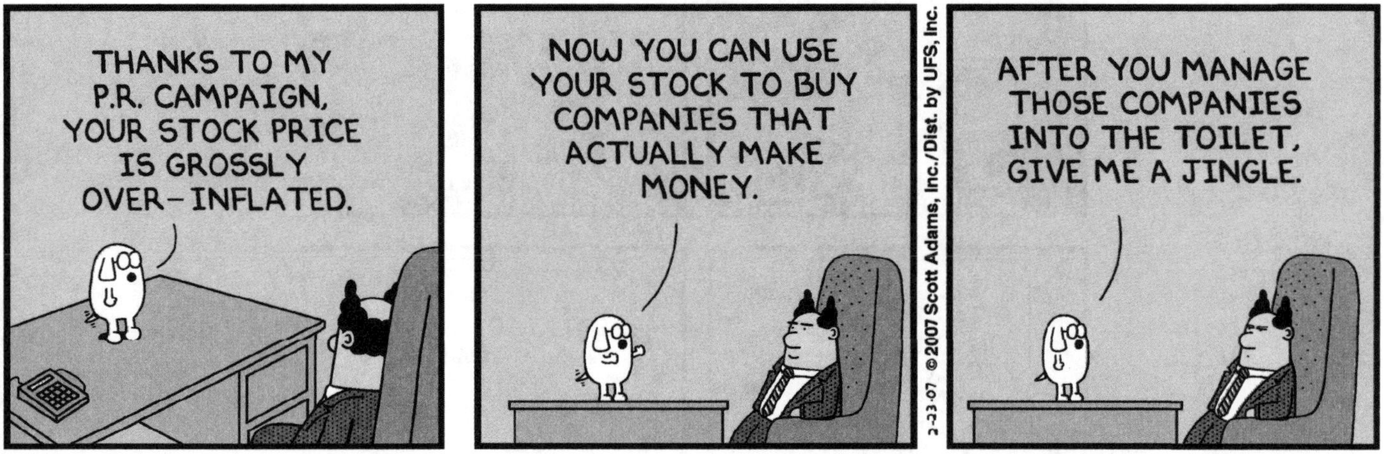
THANKS TO MY P.R. CAMPAIGN, YOUR STOCK PRICE IS GROSSLY OVER-INFLATED.
NOW YOU CAN USE YOUR STOCK TO BUY COMPANIES THAT ACTUALLY MAKE MONEY.
2-23-07 © 2007 Scott Adams, Inc./Dist. by UFS, Inc.
AFTER YOU MANAGE THOSE COMPANIES INTO THE TOILET, GIVE ME A JINGLE.

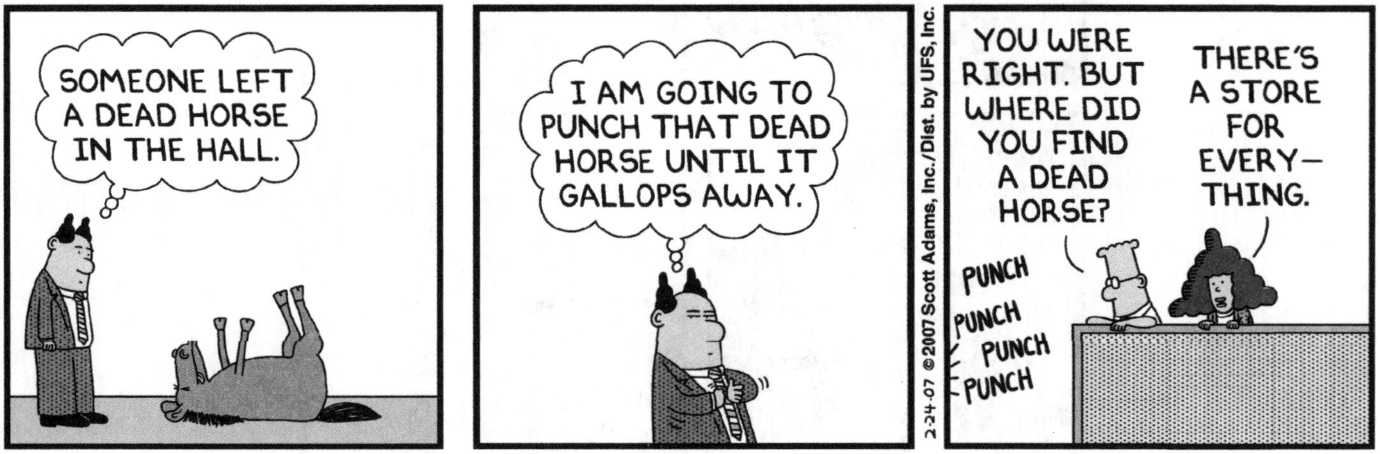
SOMEONE LEFT A DEAD HORSE IN THE HALL.
I AM GOING TO PUNCH THAT DEAD HORSE UNTIL IT GALLOPS AWAY.
2-24-07 © 2007 Scott Adams, Inc./Dist. by UFS, Inc.
YOU WERE RIGHT. BUT WHERE DID YOU FIND A DEAD HORSE?
THERE'S A STORE FOR EVERY-THING.
PUNCH
PUNCH
PUNCH
PUNCH

YOU'LL BE IN CHARGE OF THIS PROJECT.
WHAT'S MY BUDGET?
I'LL NEED TO APPROVE ALL EXPENSES.
WHO WILL REPORT TO ME?
YOUR TEAM WILL REPORT TO ME AND I'LL TELL THEM WHAT TO DO.
I'LL START ON THE PROJECT PLAN.
UM. . .
SKIP THAT PART. I ALREADY HAVE A PLAN IN MY HEAD.
HYPOTHETICALLY, WHO WOULD TAKE THE BLAME IF THIS PROJECT FAILED?
WELL, YOU'RE IN CHARGE. . .
© 2007 Scott Adams, Inc./Dist. by UFS, Inc.
2-25-07

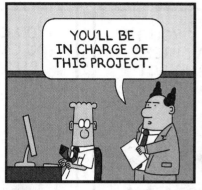

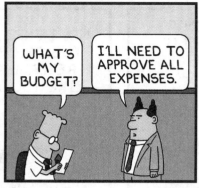

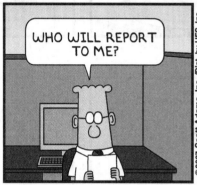

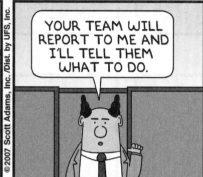

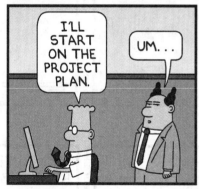

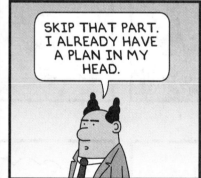

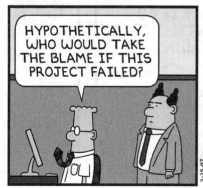

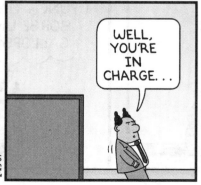

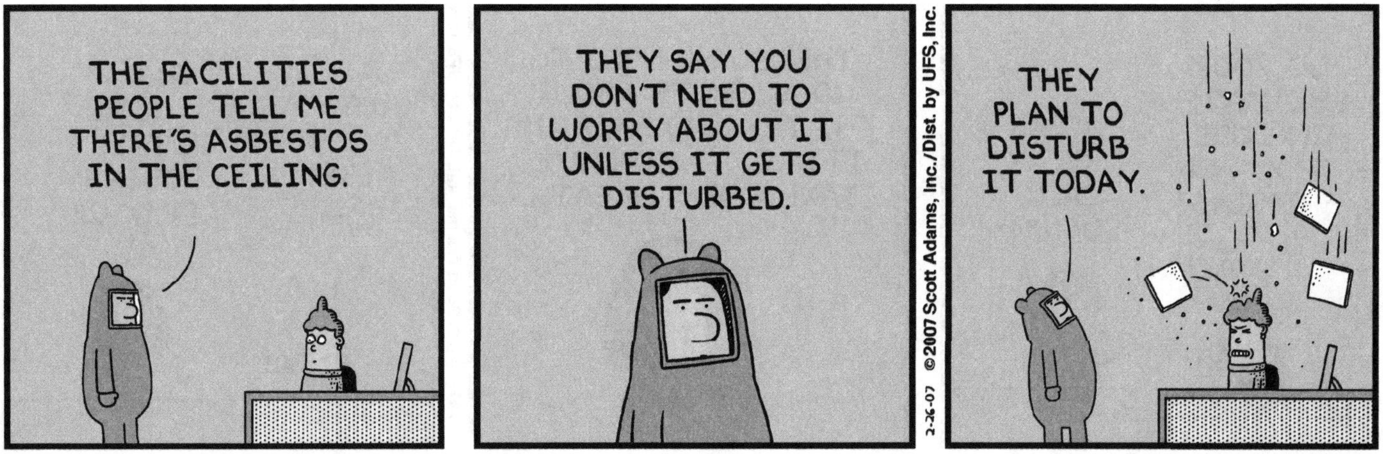
THE FACILITIES PEOPLE TELL ME THERE'S ASBESTOS IN THE CEILING.
THEY SAY YOU DON'T NEED TO WORRY ABOUT IT UNLESS IT GETS DISTURBED.
2-26-07 ©2007 Scott Adams, Inc./Dist. by UFS, Inc.
THEY PLAN TO DISTURB IT TODAY.

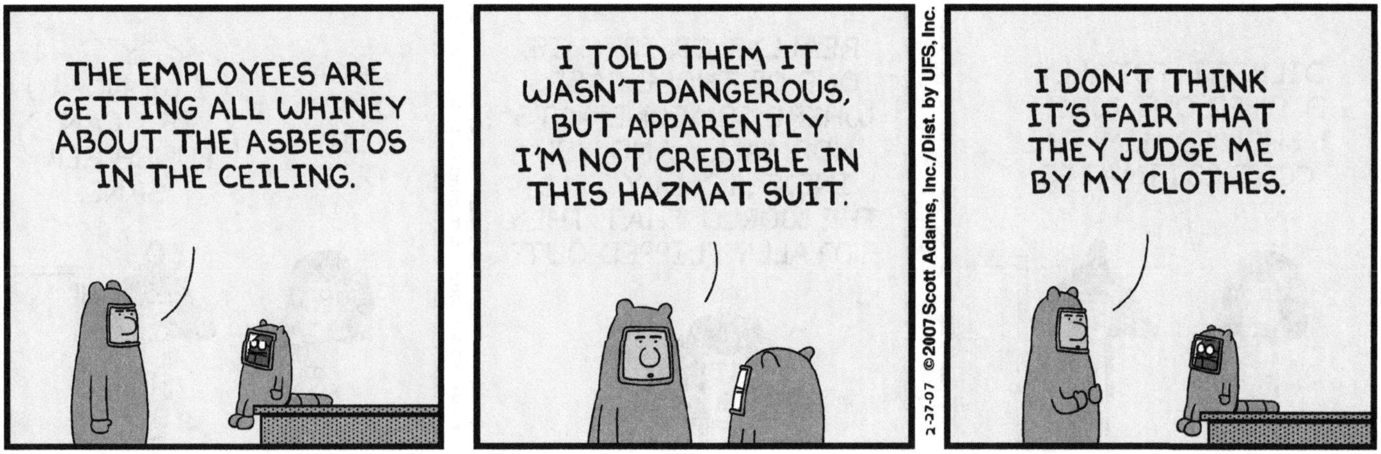
THE EMPLOYEES ARE GETTING ALL WHINEY ABOUT THE ASBESTOS IN THE CEILING.
I TOLD THEM IT WASN'T DANGEROUS, BUT APPARENTLY I'M NOT CREDIBLE IN THIS HAZMAT SUIT.
2-27-07 ©2007 Scott Adams, Inc./Dist. by UFS, Inc.
I DON'T THINK IT'S FAIR THAT THEY JUDGE ME BY MY CLOTHES.

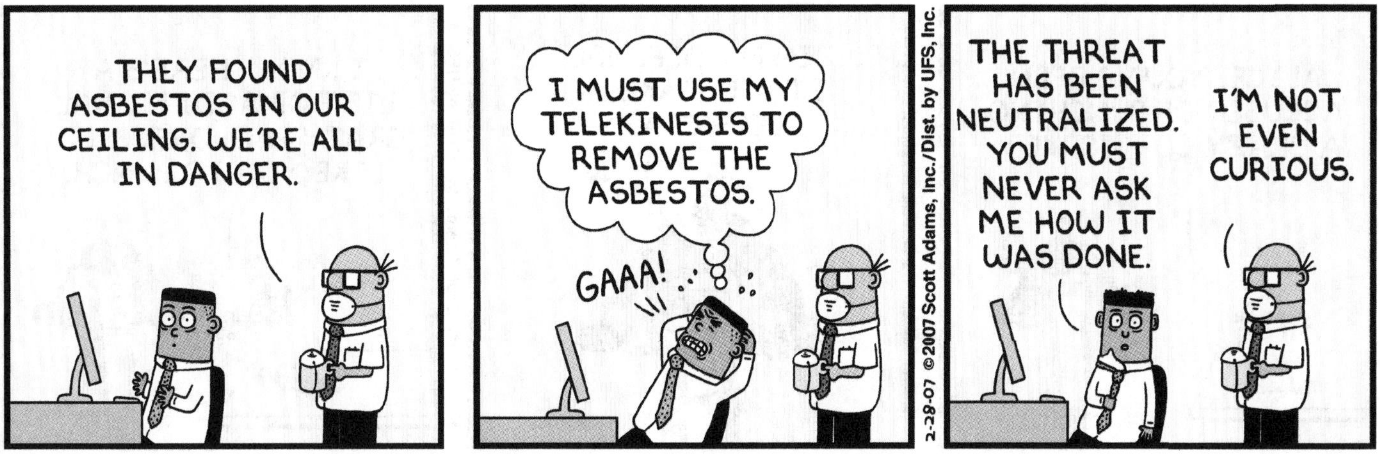
THEY FOUND ASBESTOS IN OUR CEILING. WE'RE ALL IN DANGER.
I MUST USE MY TELEKINESIS TO REMOVE THE ASBESTOS.
GAAA!
2-28-07 ©2007 Scott Adams, Inc./Dist. by UFS, Inc.
THE THREAT HAS BEEN NEUTRALIZED. YOU MUST NEVER ASK ME HOW IT WAS DONE.
I'M NOT EVEN CURIOUS.

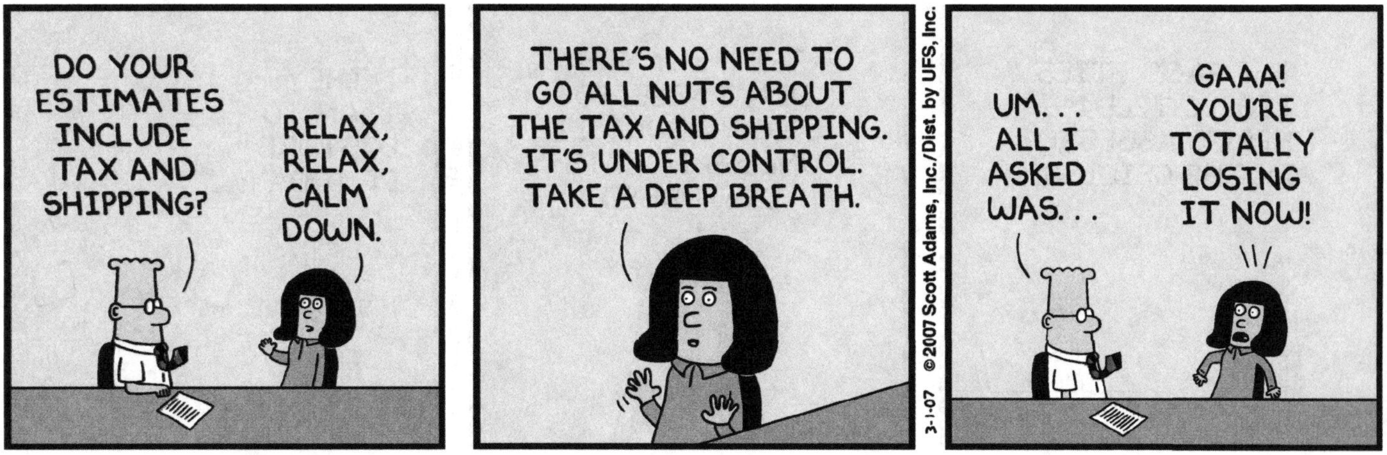
DO YOUR ESTIMATES INCLUDE TAX AND SHIPPING?
RELAX, RELAX, CALM DOWN.
THERE'S NO NEED TO GO ALL NUTS ABOUT THE TAX AND SHIPPING. IT'S UNDER CONTROL. TAKE A DEEP BREATH.
3-1-07 ©2007 Scott Adams, Inc./Dist. by UFS, Inc.
UM... ALL I ASKED WAS...
GAAA! YOU'RE TOTALLY LOSING IT NOW!

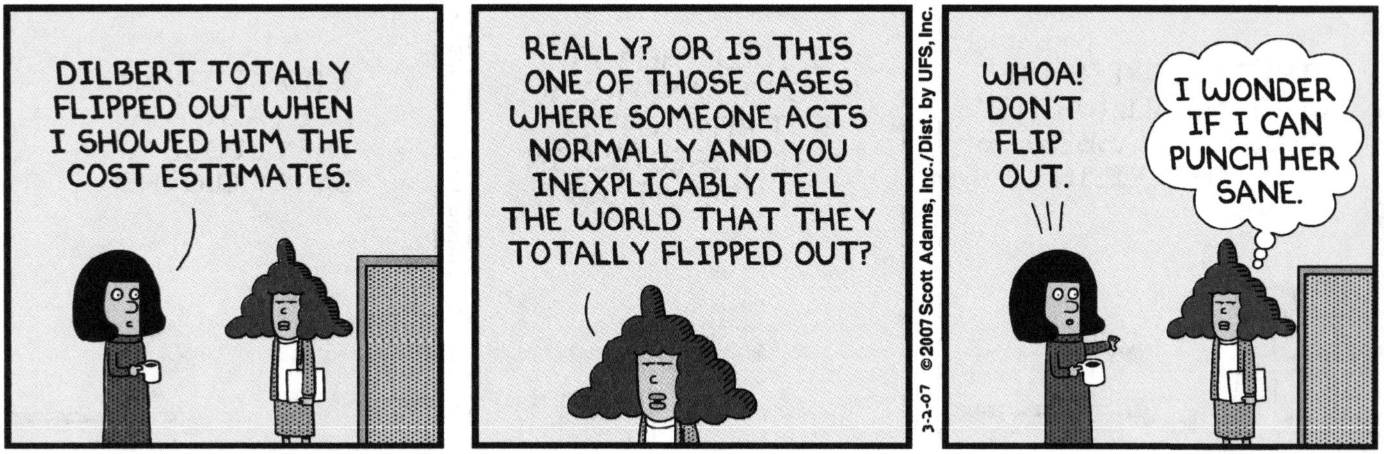
DILBERT TOTALLY FLIPPED OUT WHEN I SHOWED HIM THE COST ESTIMATES.
REALLY? OR IS THIS ONE OF THOSE CASES WHERE SOMEONE ACTS NORMALLY AND YOU INEXPLICABLY TELL THE WORLD THAT THEY TOTALLY FLIPPED OUT?
3-2-07 ©2007 Scott Adams, Inc./Dist. by UFS, Inc.
WHOA! DON'T FLIP OUT.
I WONDER IF I CAN PUNCH HER SANE.

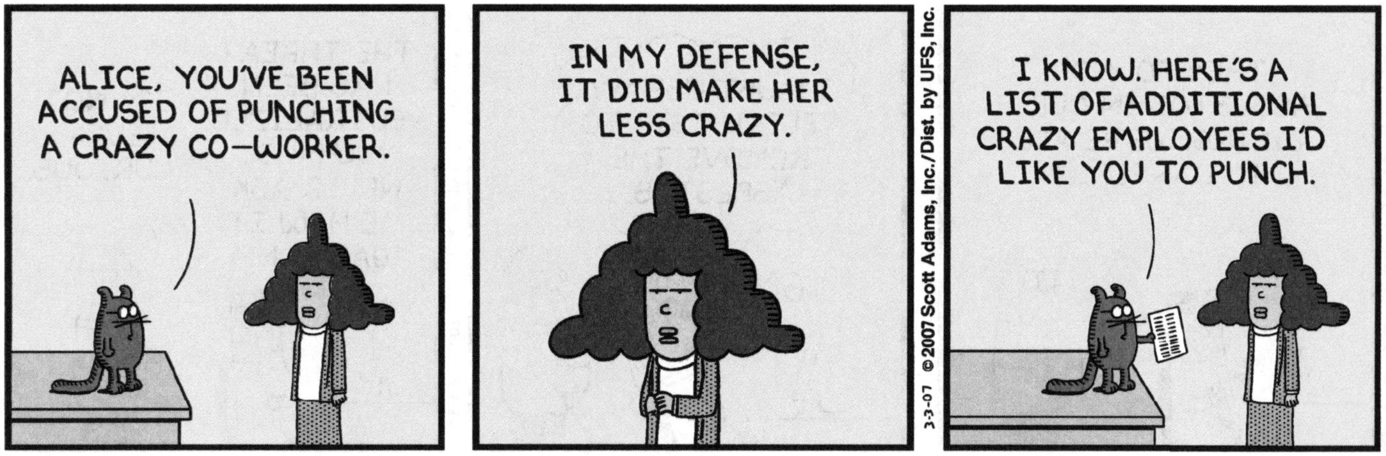
ALICE, YOU'VE BEEN ACCUSED OF PUNCHING A CRAZY CO-WORKER.
IN MY DEFENSE, IT DID MAKE HER LESS CRAZY.
3-3-07 ©2007 Scott Adams, Inc./Dist. by UFS, Inc.
I KNOW. HERE'S A LIST OF ADDITIONAL CRAZY EMPLOYEES I'D LIKE YOU TO PUNCH.

MAY I SEE THE VACATION SCHEDULE?
WHY DO YOU WANT IT?
NO REASON.
WELL, TED, I HOPE YOU'RE ENJOYING YOUR VACATION.
© 2007 Scott Adams, Inc./Dist. by UFS, Inc.
WALLY, DO YOU HAVE THE COST ESTI- MATES?
I'M WAITING FOR TED'S INPUT. HE'S ON VACA- TION.
HOW ABOUT THE REVISED TIME- LINE?
I'M WAITING FOR TED.
DO YOU NEED ANY OFFICE SUPPLIES? I'M GOING TO THE STORE.
MAYBE SOME PENS.
LIMITED SELECTION BUT EXCELLENT PRICES.
TED
3-4-07
THANKS.
SO, I UNDER- STAND YOU HAVE A VACA- TION NEXT WEEK.

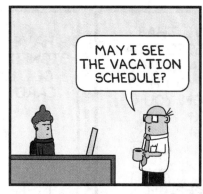

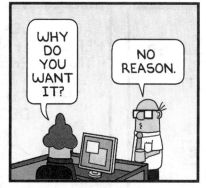

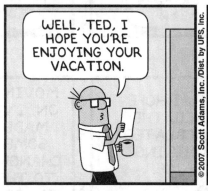

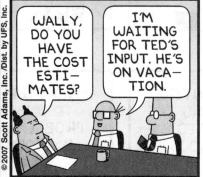

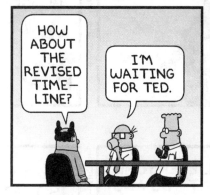

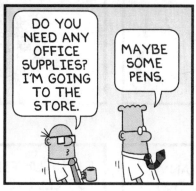

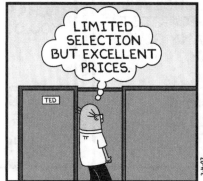

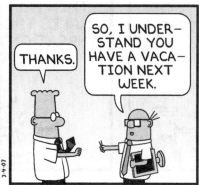

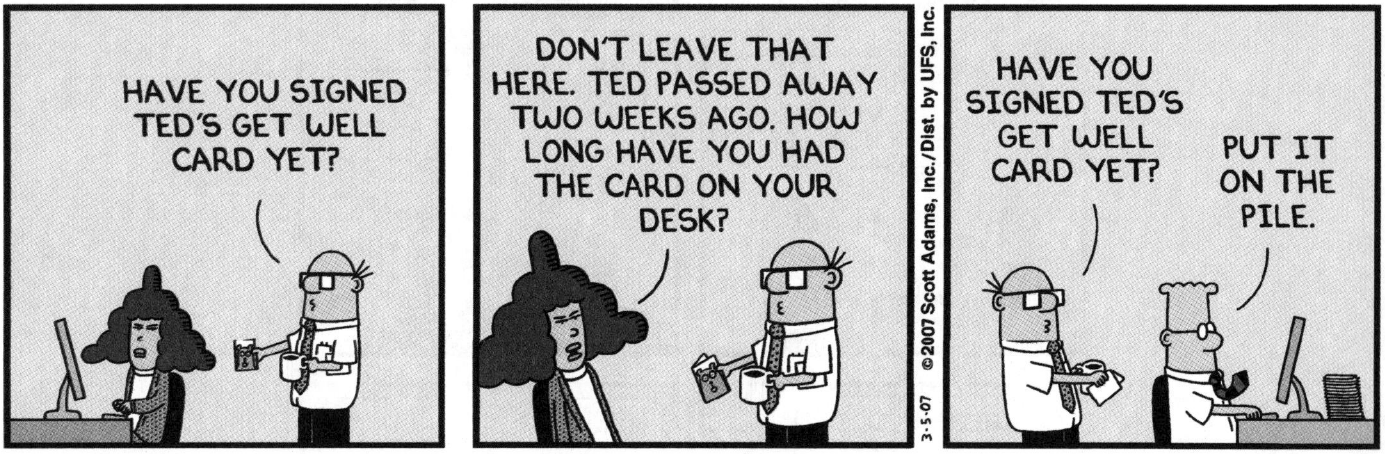
HAVE YOU SIGNED TED'S GET WELL CARD YET?
DON'T LEAVE THAT HERE. TED PASSED AWAY TWO WEEKS AGO. HOW LONG HAVE YOU HAD THE CARD ON YOUR DESK?
HAVE YOU SIGNED TED'S GET WELL CARD YET?
PUT IT ON THE PILE.
3-5-07 ©2007 Scott Adams, Inc./Dist. by UFS, Inc.

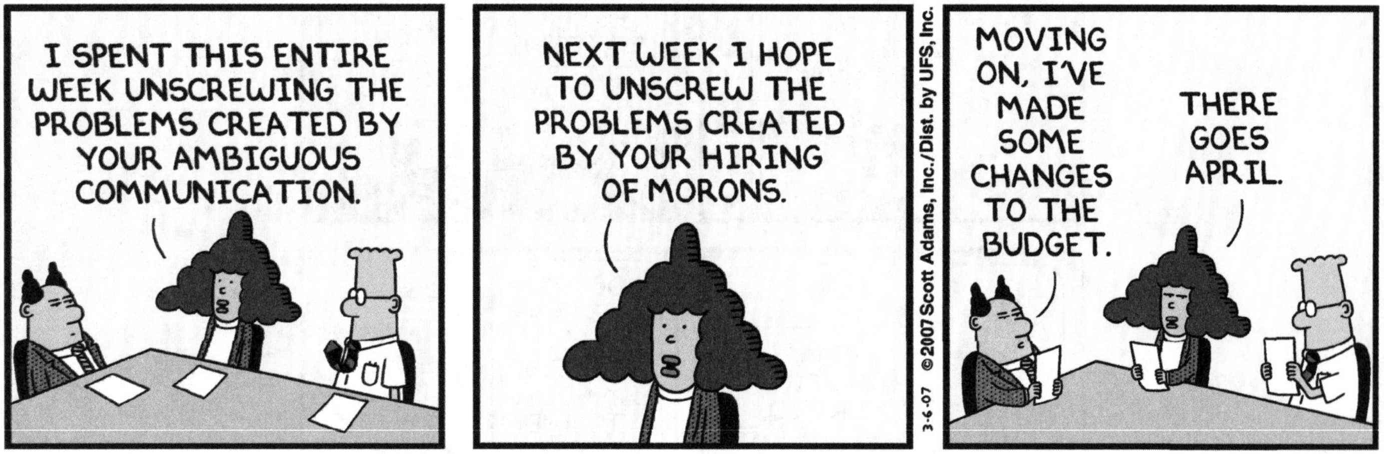
I SPENT THIS ENTIRE WEEK UNSCREWING THE PROBLEMS CREATED BY YOUR AMBIGUOUS COMMUNICATION.
NEXT WEEK I HOPE TO UNSCREW THE PROBLEMS CREATED BY YOUR HIRING OF MORONS.
MOVING ON, I'VE MADE SOME CHANGES TO THE BUDGET.
THERE GOES APRIL.
3-6-07 ©2007 Scott Adams, Inc./Dist. by UFS, Inc.

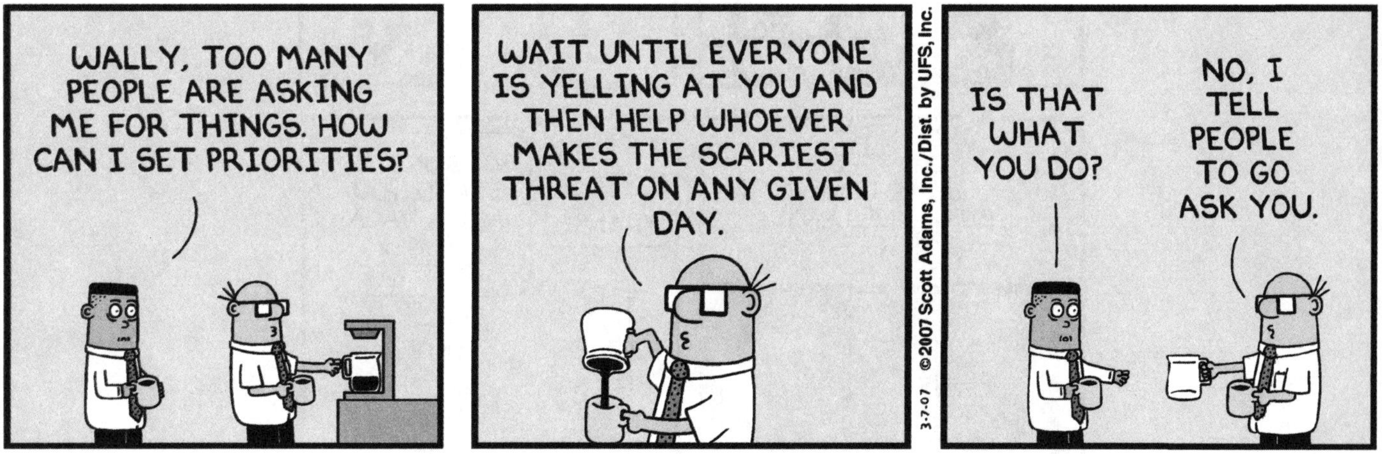
WALLY, TOO MANY PEOPLE ARE ASKING ME FOR THINGS. HOW CAN I SET PRIORITIES?
WAIT UNTIL EVERYONE IS YELLING AT YOU AND THEN HELP WHOEVER MAKES THE SCARIEST THREAT ON ANY GIVEN DAY.
IS THAT WHAT YOU DO?
NO, I TELL PEOPLE TO GO ASK YOU.
3-7-07 ©2007 Scott Adams, Inc./Dist. by UFS, Inc.

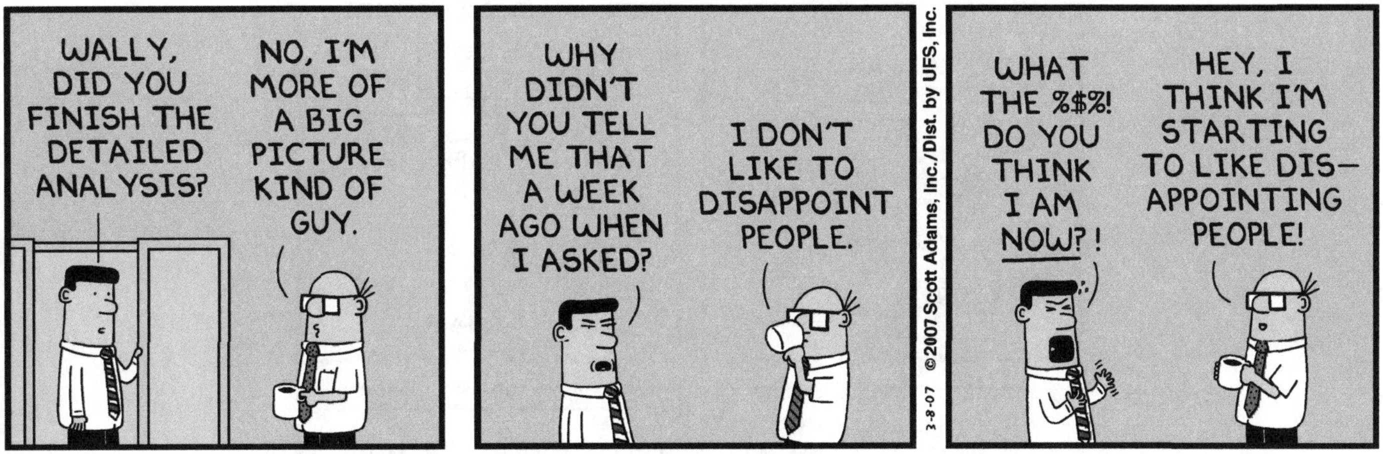
WALLY, DID YOU FINISH THE DETAILED ANALYSIS?
NO, I'M MORE OF A BIG PICTURE KIND OF GUY.
WHY DIDN'T YOU TELL ME THAT A WEEK AGO WHEN I ASKED?
I DON'T LIKE TO DISAPPOINT PEOPLE.
3-8-07 © 2007 Scott Adams, Inc./Dist. by UFS, Inc.
WHAT THE %$%! DO YOU THINK I AM NOW?!
HEY, I THINK I'M STARTING TO LIKE DIS-APPOINTING PEOPLE!

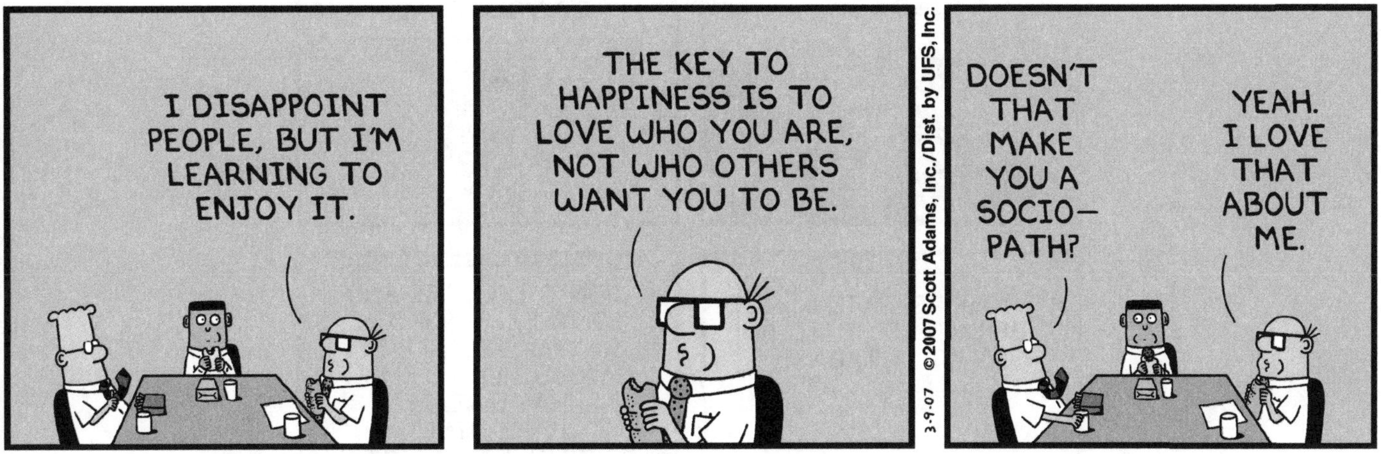
I DISAPPOINT PEOPLE, BUT I'M LEARNING TO ENJOY IT.
THE KEY TO HAPPINESS IS TO LOVE WHO YOU ARE, NOT WHO OTHERS WANT YOU TO BE.
3-9-07 © 2007 Scott Adams, Inc./Dist. by UFS, Inc.
DOESN'T THAT MAKE YOU A SOCIO-PATH?
YEAH. I LOVE THAT ABOUT ME.

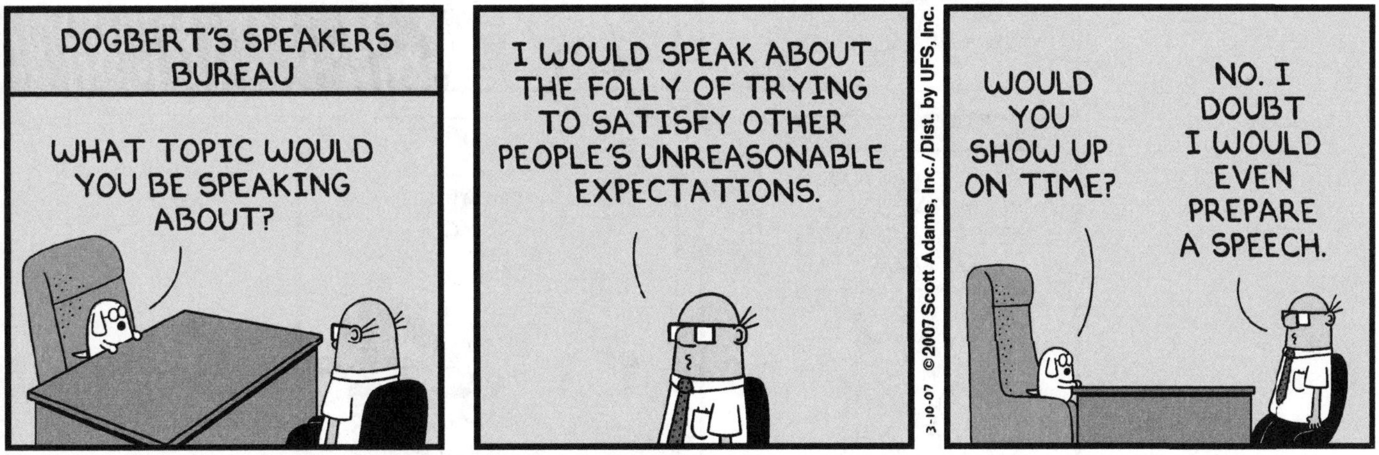
DOGBERT'S SPEAKERS BUREAU
WHAT TOPIC WOULD YOU BE SPEAKING ABOUT?
I WOULD SPEAK ABOUT THE FOLLY OF TRYING TO SATISFY OTHER PEOPLE'S UNREASONABLE EXPECTATIONS.
3-10-07 © 2007 Scott Adams, Inc./Dist. by UFS, Inc.
WOULD YOU SHOW UP ON TIME?
NO. I DOUBT I WOULD EVEN PREPARE A SPEECH.

EVERY COMPANY NEEDS GOALS.

GOALS

WE HAVE DIVISION GOALS, DEPARTMENT GOALS, DISTRICT GOALS, PERSONAL GOALS AND AFFILIATE GOALS.

YOU WILL ALL ATTEND A FOUR-HOUR TRAINING SESSION ON HOW TO WRITE GOALS.

© 2007 Scott Adams, Inc. /Dist. by UFS, Inc.

EVERY WEEK YOU WILL REPORT ON HOW YOU ARE DOING COMPARED TO YOUR GOALS.

THOSE REPORTS WILL BE ENTERED INTO A GIANT DATABASE.

WON'T THE SIZE AND COMPLEXITY OF THE DATABASE MAKE IT IMPOSSIBLE TO KNOW WHAT'S REALLY HAPPENING?

YES. THAT'S WHY YOUR RAISES WILL BE BASED ON WHAT YOU LOOK LIKE.

3-11-07

BUMMER FOR YOU.

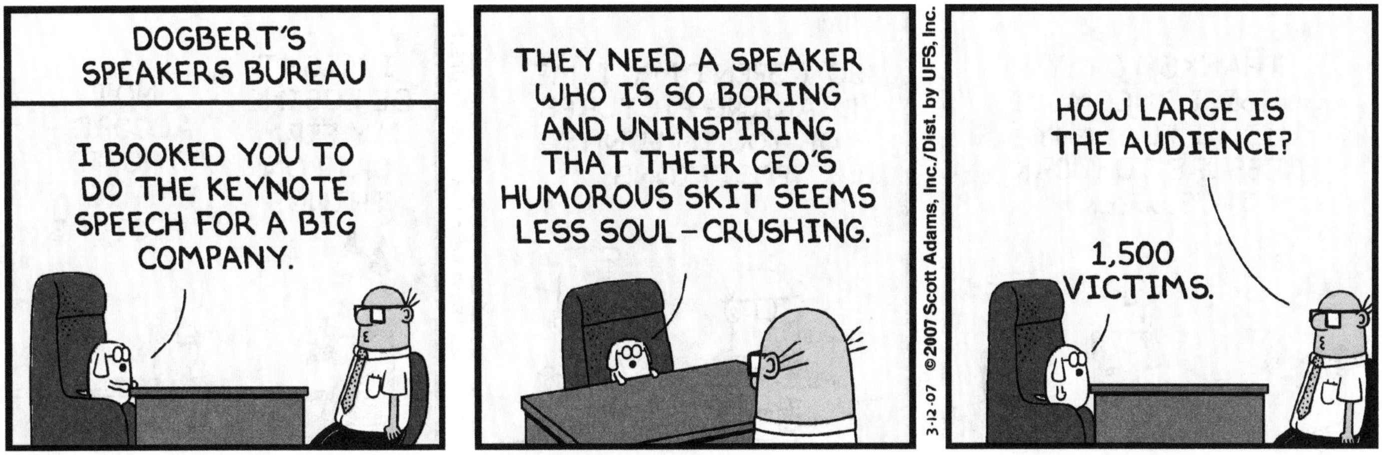
DOGBERT'S SPEAKERS BUREAU
I BOOKED YOU TO DO THE KEYNOTE SPEECH FOR A BIG COMPANY.
THEY NEED A SPEAKER WHO IS SO BORING AND UNINSPIRING THAT THEIR CEO'S HUMOROUS SKIT SEEMS LESS SOUL-CRUSHING.
HOW LARGE IS THE AUDIENCE?
1,500 VICTIMS.
3-12-07 ©2007 Scott Adams, Inc./Dist. by UFS, Inc.

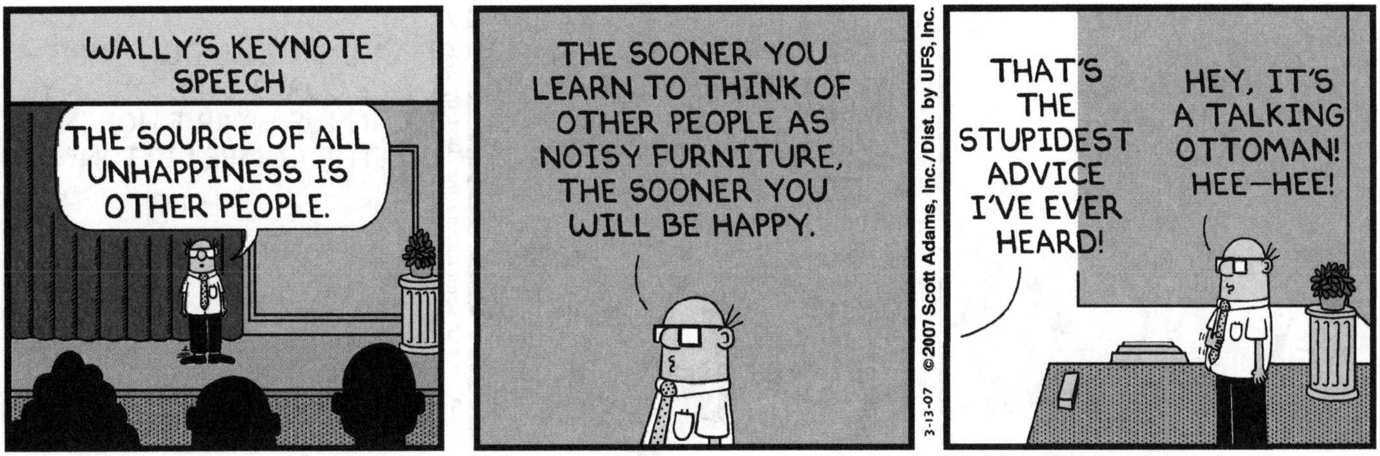
WALLY'S KEYNOTE SPEECH
THE SOURCE OF ALL UNHAPPINESS IS OTHER PEOPLE.
THE SOONER YOU LEARN TO THINK OF OTHER PEOPLE AS NOISY FURNITURE, THE SOONER YOU WILL BE HAPPY.
THAT'S THE STUPIDEST ADVICE I'VE EVER HEARD!
HEY, IT'S A TALKING OTTOMAN! HEE-HEE!
3-13-07 ©2007 Scott Adams, Inc./Dist. by UFS, Inc.

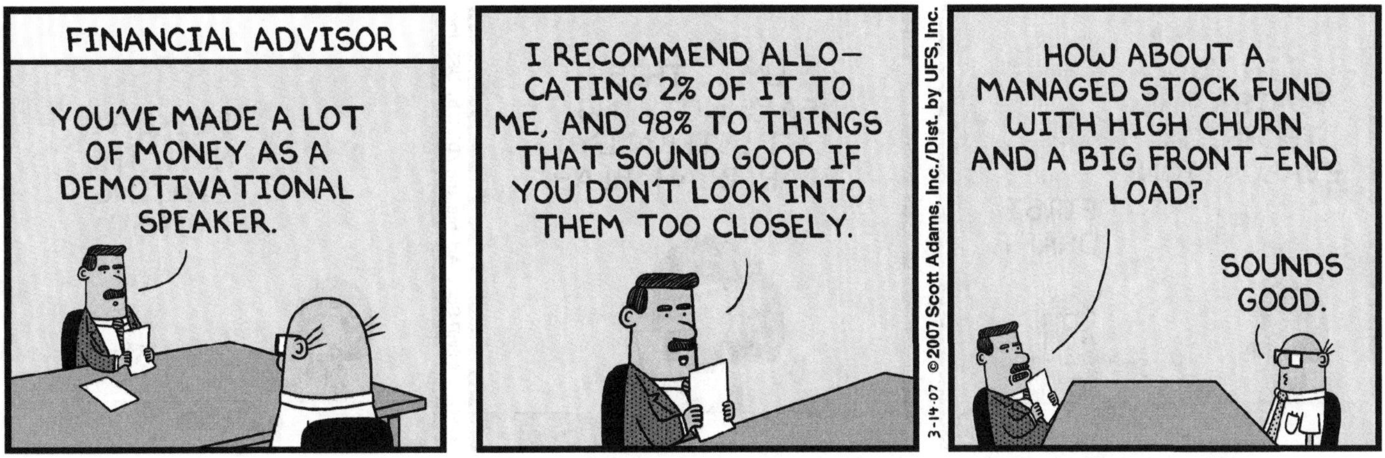
FINANCIAL ADVISOR
YOU'VE MADE A LOT OF MONEY AS A DEMOTIVATIONAL SPEAKER.
I RECOMMEND ALLOCATING 2% OF IT TO ME, AND 98% TO THINGS THAT SOUND GOOD IF YOU DON'T LOOK INTO THEM TOO CLOSELY.
HOW ABOUT A MANAGED STOCK FUND WITH HIGH CHURN AND A BIG FRONT-END LOAD?
SOUNDS GOOD.
3-14-07 ©2007 Scott Adams, Inc./Dist. by UFS, Inc.

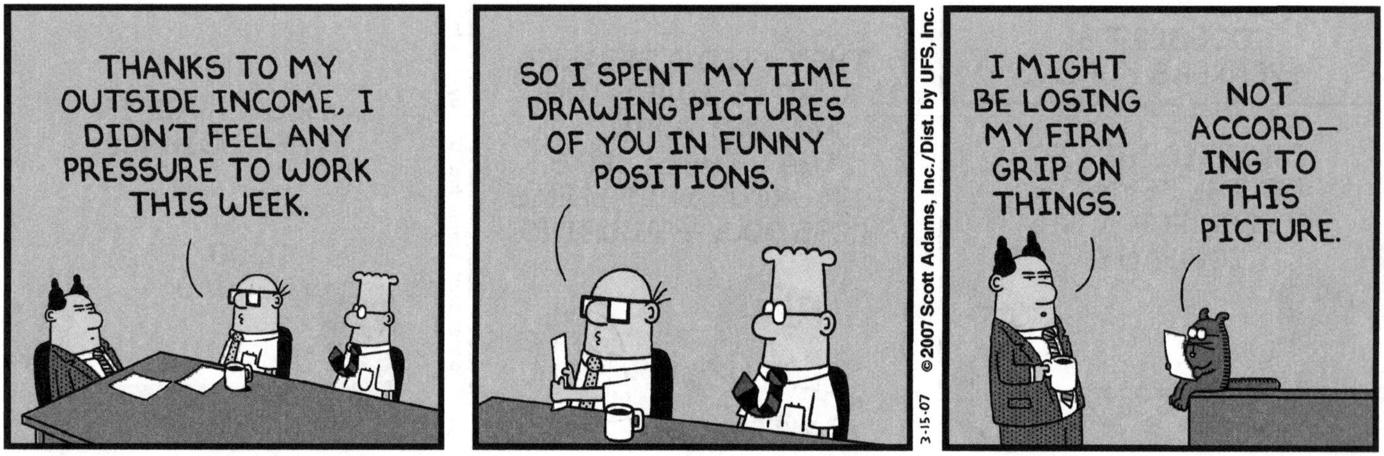
THANKS TO MY OUTSIDE INCOME, I DIDN'T FEEL ANY PRESSURE TO WORK THIS WEEK.
SO I SPENT MY TIME DRAWING PICTURES OF YOU IN FUNNY POSITIONS.
3-15-07 ©2007 Scott Adams, Inc./Dist. by UFS, Inc.
I MIGHT BE LOSING MY FIRM GRIP ON THINGS.
NOT ACCORD-ING TO THIS PICTURE.

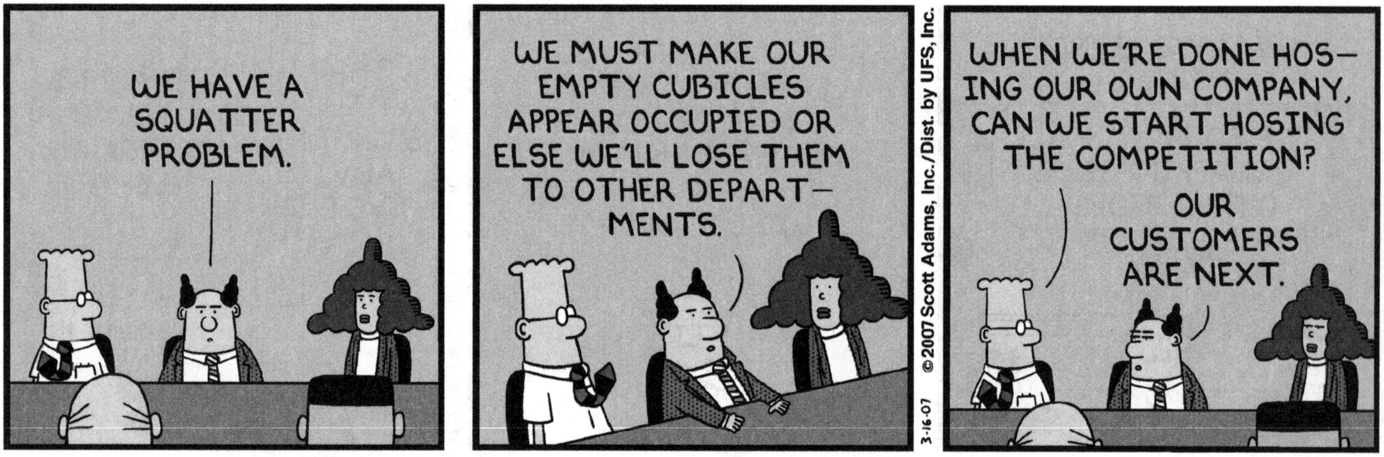
WE HAVE A SQUATTER PROBLEM.
WE MUST MAKE OUR EMPTY CUBICLES APPEAR OCCUPIED OR ELSE WE'LL LOSE THEM TO OTHER DEPART-MENTS.
3-16-07 ©2007 Scott Adams, Inc./Dist. by UFS, Inc.
WHEN WE'RE DONE HOS-ING OUR OWN COMPANY, CAN WE START HOSING THE COMPETITION?
OUR CUSTOMERS ARE NEXT.

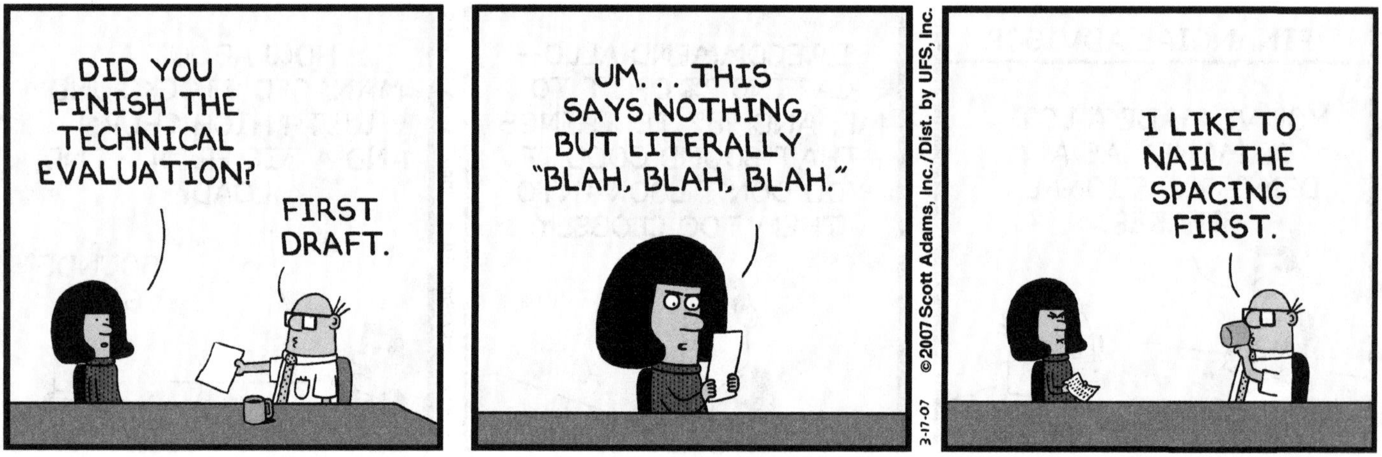
DID YOU FINISH THE TECHNICAL EVALUATION?
FIRST DRAFT.
UM. . . THIS SAYS NOTHING BUT LITERALLY "BLAH, BLAH, BLAH."
3-17-07 ©2007 Scott Adams, Inc./Dist. by UFS, Inc.
I LIKE TO NAIL THE SPACING FIRST.

SOME BATTERIES IN THE LAB LEAKED.
I CLEANED IT UP, BUT THERE WAS NO PLACE TO PUT ALL OF THE HAZARDOUS WASTE.
I COULDN'T PUT IT IN THE REGULAR TRASH OR THE RECYCLING BIN.
IT'S NOT LEGAL TO POUR IT DOWN THE DRAIN OR FLUSH IT.
SO I PUT IT BETWEEN TWO PIECES OF BREAD AND LEFT IT IN THE BREAK ROOM REFRIGERATOR.
GAAA!!!
NOT REALLY. I JUST WANTED TO FIND OUT WHO'S BEEN EATING MY LUNCH.
YOU MEAN I'M NOT GOING TO DIE?
NOT INSTANTLY.
©2007 Scott Adams, Inc./Dist. by UFS, Inc.
3-18-07

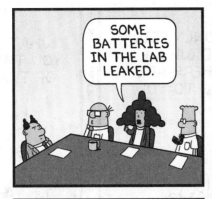

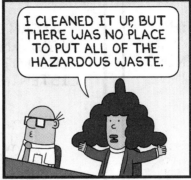

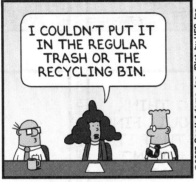

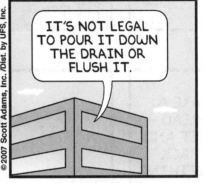

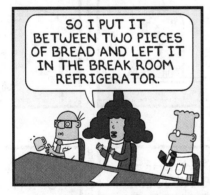

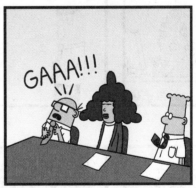

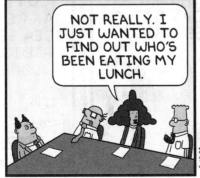

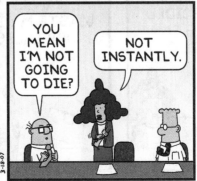

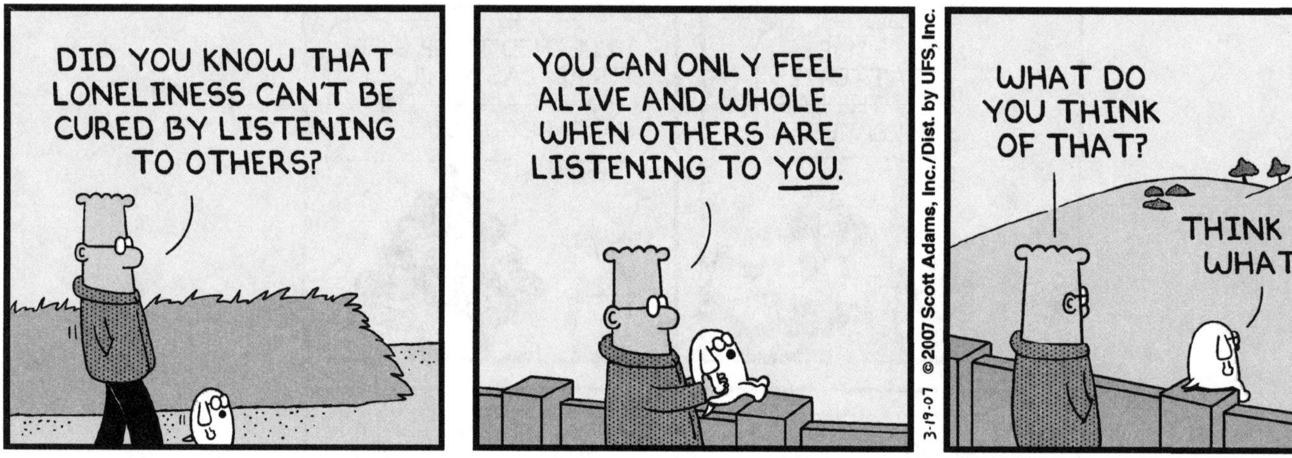
DID YOU KNOW THAT LONELINESS CAN'T BE CURED BY LISTENING TO OTHERS?
YOU CAN ONLY FEEL ALIVE AND WHOLE WHEN OTHERS ARE LISTENING TO YOU.
3-19-07 ©2007 Scott Adams, Inc./Dist. by UFS, Inc.
WHAT DO YOU THINK OF THAT?
THINK OF WHAT?

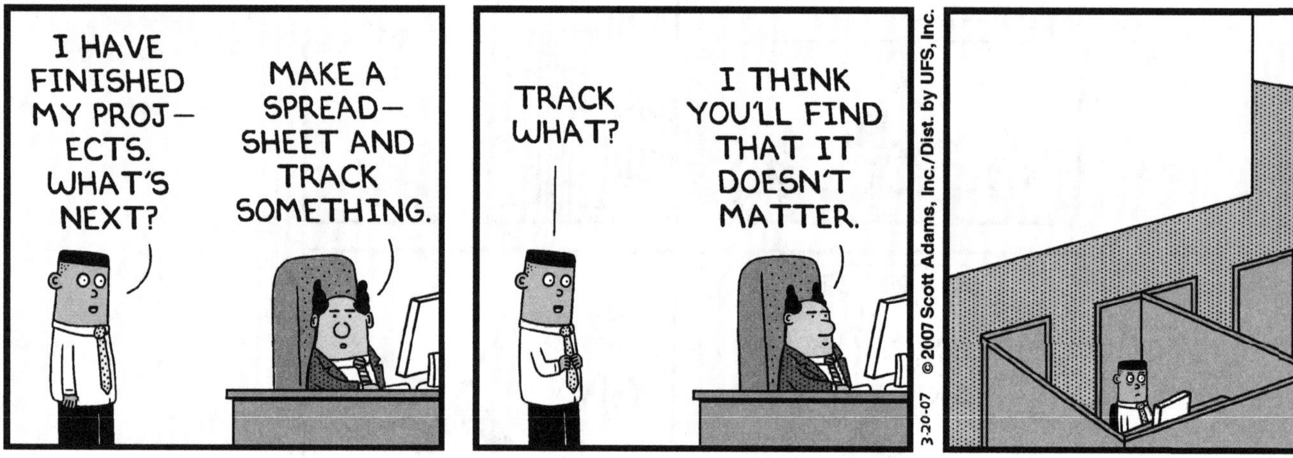
I HAVE FINISHED MY PROJ-ECTS. WHAT'S NEXT?
MAKE A SPREAD-SHEET AND TRACK SOMETHING.
TRACK WHAT?
I THINK YOU'LL FIND THAT IT DOESN'T MATTER.
3-20-07 ©2007 Scott Adams, Inc./Dist. by UFS, Inc.

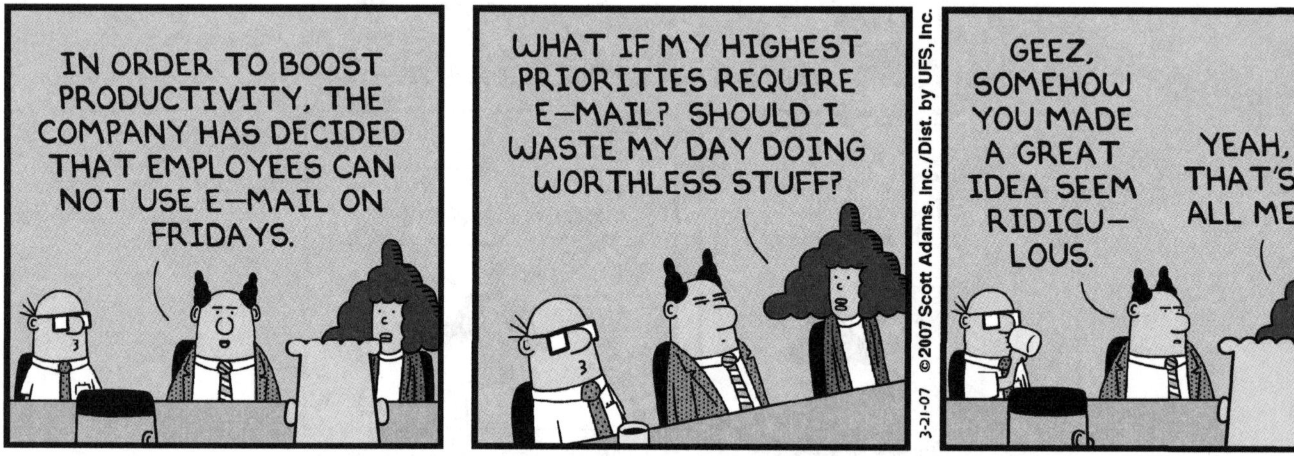
IN ORDER TO BOOST PRODUCTIVITY, THE COMPANY HAS DECIDED THAT EMPLOYEES CAN NOT USE E-MAIL ON FRIDAYS.
WHAT IF MY HIGHEST PRIORITIES REQUIRE E-MAIL? SHOULD I WASTE MY DAY DOING WORTHLESS STUFF?
3-21-07 ©2007 Scott Adams, Inc./Dist. by UFS, Inc.
GEEZ, SOMEHOW YOU MADE A GREAT IDEA SEEM RIDICU-LOUS.
YEAH, THAT'S ALL ME.

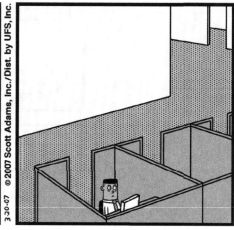

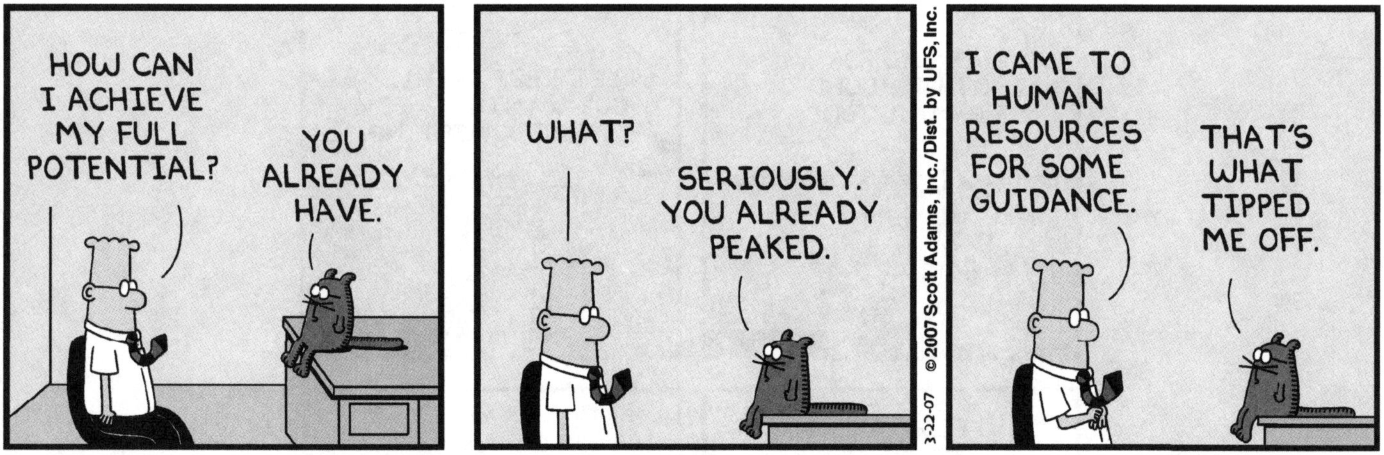
HOW CAN I ACHIEVE MY FULL POTENTIAL?
YOU ALREADY HAVE.
WHAT?
SERIOUSLY. YOU ALREADY PEAKED.
3-22-07 © 2007 Scott Adams, Inc./Dist. by UFS, Inc.
I CAME TO HUMAN RESOURCES FOR SOME GUIDANCE.
THAT'S WHAT TIPPED ME OFF.

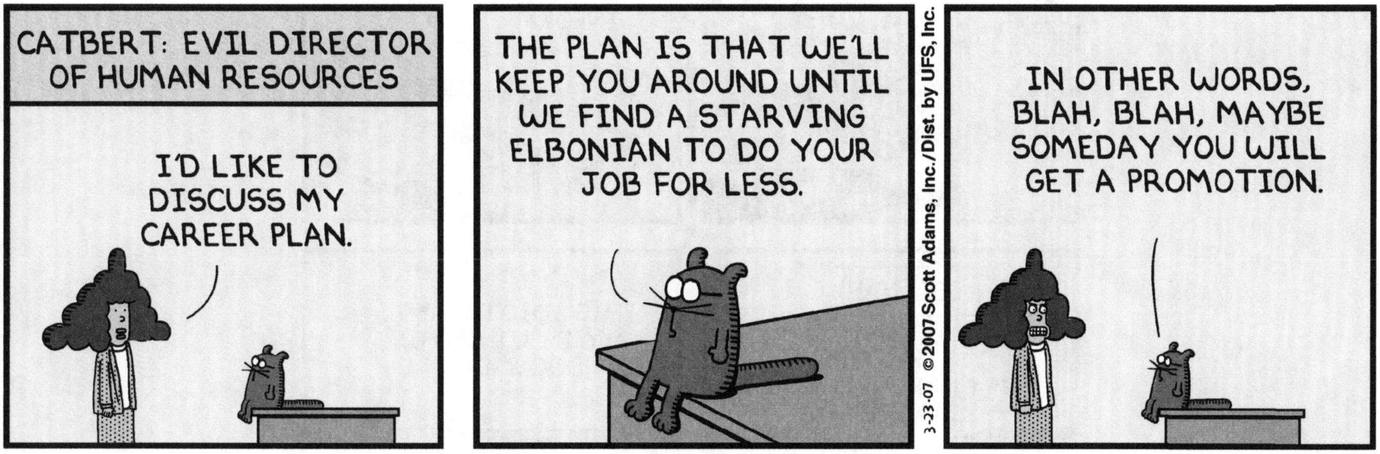
CATBERT: EVIL DIRECTOR OF HUMAN RESOURCES
I'D LIKE TO DISCUSS MY CAREER PLAN.
THE PLAN IS THAT WE'LL KEEP YOU AROUND UNTIL WE FIND A STARVING ELBONIAN TO DO YOUR JOB FOR LESS.
3-23-07 © 2007 Scott Adams, Inc./Dist. by UFS, Inc.
IN OTHER WORDS, BLAH, BLAH, MAYBE SOMEDAY YOU WILL GET A PROMOTION.

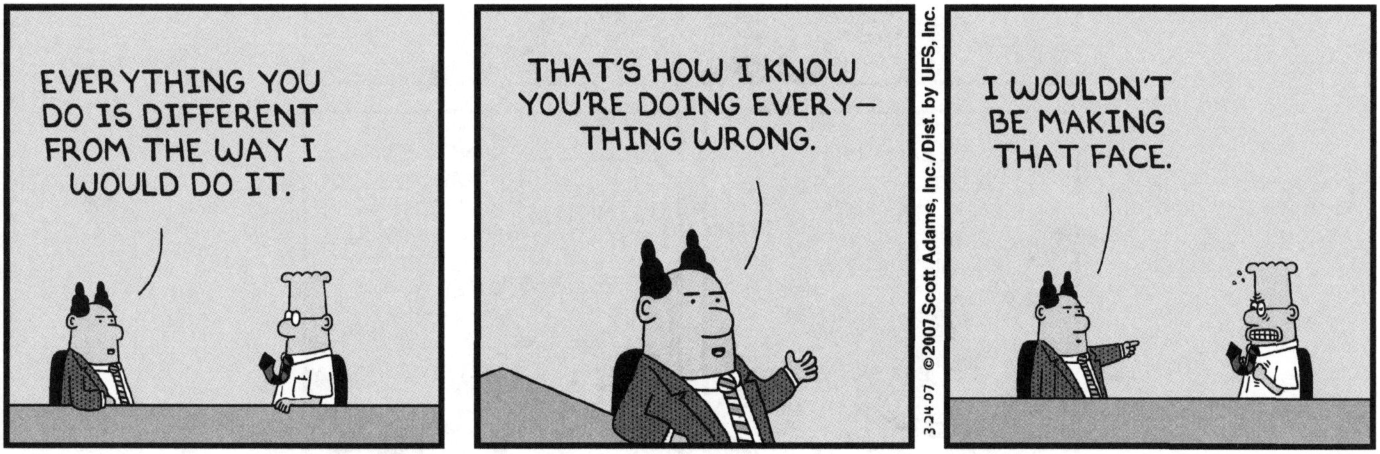
EVERYTHING YOU DO IS DIFFERENT FROM THE WAY I WOULD DO IT.
THAT'S HOW I KNOW YOU'RE DOING EVERY-THING WRONG.
3-24-07 © 2007 Scott Adams, Inc./Dist. by UFS, Inc.
I WOULDN'T BE MAKING THAT FACE.

AND NOW FOR ANOTHER ROUND OF E-MAIL JUDO.
LET'S SEE. . . THIS GUY WANTS ME TO ATTEND A MEETING.
EEE—YAH!
I'LL TELL HIM I'M BOOKED.
THIS GUY WANTS SOME INFORMATION.
EEE—YAH!
I'LLTELL HIM MY HARD DRIVE CRASHED.
THIS IDIOT WANTS MY INPUT ON HIS DOCUMENT.
EEE—YAH!
I'LL TELL HIM THE ATTACHMENT WON'T OPEN.
WHO'S WINNING TODAY?
NOT THE PEOPLE WHO SENT ME E—MAIL
EEE—YAH!.
©2007 Scott Adams, Inc./Dist. by UFS, Inc.
3-25-07

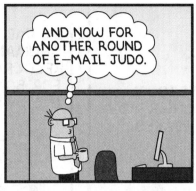

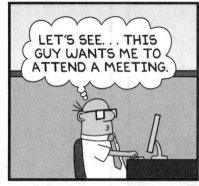

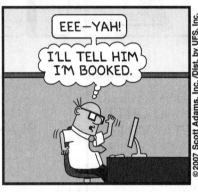

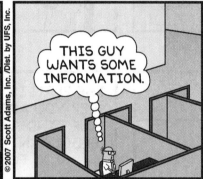

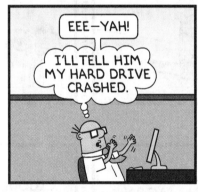

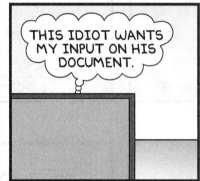

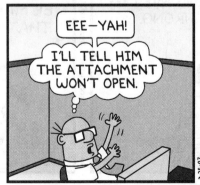

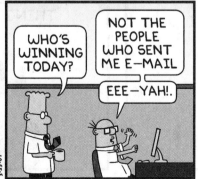